GEORGE WASHINGTON

WASHINGTON AT AGE OF SIXTY-ONE

Portrait by Edward Savage, painted in 1793. Reproduced from the Original in the Art Institute. of Chicago.

George Washington

The Image and the Man

By

W. E. Woodward

LIVERIGHT

NEW YORK

LIVERIGHT PAPERBOUND EDITION 1972

1.987654321

* * *

ISBN: 0-87140-806-6 (Black and Gold)

ISBN: 0-87140-074-X (Paper)

LC Number: 70-184103

Printed in the United States of America

PREFACE

When I write a biography I keep clearly in mind, from the beginning to the end of the work, that I am telling the life story of a human being. I think that attitude toward the subject is essential, otherwise the book will have no freshness, no vividness, and will be as lifeless as a marble statue.

I try to bring the people of the past to life, in a certain definite sense; and to do that I imagine that I am simply a newspaper reporter, standing by and looking on. I have seen George Washington as a boy in Virginia, as the leader of an expedition into the wilderness, as a general in the American Revolution, as the first of our presidents—and in many other circumstances that called for courage and common sense.

I was inspired to write "George Washington, the Image and the Man" by the perusal of the books that had been written about him. In many of them he was depicted as a godlike character who never made a mistake in his life and who was always moved by infinite wisdom, foresight and courage, and who possessed all of the admirable human traits, day in and day out.

As a work of fiction that was all very well, but I could not bring myself to believe that such a person ever really lived. Besides, such mythical presentations of Washington's character and achievements could only be discouraging to young people, for it would seem—naturally enough—that there was no use in following in his footsteps, or in trying to adapt his admirable qualities, for it would be impossible to emulate him successfully.

For the reasons set forth above I decided to write a biography of the Father of Our Country in which I would treat him as a human being—one of exceptional ability, of course, but not without faults or failings. That is the spirit which runs

Preface

through this book. It is the true story of George Washington's life, presented to the reader as a factual narrative.

I must say that as my work on the book progressed my admiration for Washington grew, and today he is one of my cherished heroes. I can only wish that there were men like him in every generation.

W. E. Woodward

December 1945.

CONTENTS

ILLUSTRATIONS

GEORGE WASHINGTON

GEORGE WASHINGTON

CHAPTER I

THE GENTEEL WASHINGTONS

§ 1

GEORGE WASHINGTON came of a family that must be called undistinguished, unless a persistent mediocrity, enduring many generations, is in itself a distinction. With the exception of the illustrious George there is no record of a Washington who ever attained anything more than a quickly fading celebrity. The name is unknown in science, in literature, in art, in commerce, in large-scale industry.

The Sulgrave Washingtons were parochial English squires. They had a coat of arms and a family tree on which a Sir or a Colonel bloomed now and then. Their family motto was *Exitus Acta Probat*, which may be translated, "The end justifies the means." Jesuitical, to be sure, but not important, for no doubt it influenced the conduct of the Washingtons about as little as mottoes usually influence conduct.

They were sane and dull people, these Washingtons, and excessively normal. Men of this type, in all ages of history, have presented an opaque surface to the fresh thought of their time. They are conservative by instinct. But their vitality is tough and deeply rooted, and their stolidity is antiseptic. They are immune to the fructifying quality of genius.

Sulgrave is a tiny manor of Northamptonshire. The country thereabouts reminds one of southern Connecticut. A panorama of white meandering roads, gently swelling hills and ancient farms. In a yard of mouldering graves stands a still and pensive church with a square tower. The gardens are full of English roses and glossy green ivy clings to the walls.

At times the sky is flat and melancholy and a foggy mist is drawn among the trees like a torn grey veil.

Even on the clearest days it is a quiet, brooding land. To one of vivid fancy the landscape seems to be holding its breath; there are secrets in its rustic silence. It is not at all like the glittering sun-and-sea splendour of Devon.

§ 2

George Washington was three generations away from Sulgrave. He knew nothing about it, and not much about his English ancestry. On occasion he said that his forefathers had been men of Yorkshire or Lancashire, or so he thought. He was mistaken, but before his statement was known to be a mistake it had led the ancestor-seekers a long and arduous chase.

The Washingtons of Sulgrave were small gentry, which means that they were one degree above the yeoman farmer in the English social scale. They have been described as "men of property and standing," though, to be sure, their property was not large, and their standing, which seems to have shifted up and down with the varying fortunes of the Stuart Kings, was never one of eminence.

One of the Washingtons became a rich merchant in Leeds. Another, named Joseph, is said to have been a learned lawyer and author. He may have been a good lawyer, but he was not good enough to have made any definite impression on the legal history of his period. As to his authorship, time has mercifully drawn over his literary works the shroud of oblivion, and we are spared the pain of their perusal.

Sir William Washington married a half-sister of the Duke

of Buckingham, as some of George Washington's biographers point out with a little flourish of pride. To be married to a sister of the scandalous George Villiers was no doubt a career in itself, requiring hardihood and perseverance, but we are left in ignorance as to how Sir William acquitted himself in that position.

One of the Washingtons went to Germany at the time of Cromwell and founded a line of barons. George Washington Parke Custis reproduces, in his rambling book, a letter written in 1844 by one of these German Washingtons. This Teutonic kinsman explains how he is collaterally related to the Father of our Country, and signs himself: "Royal Bavarian Chamberlain, Lieutenant-General and aide-de-camp to his Majesty the King, Commander of the Order of Civil Merit of the Bavarian Crown, of the Greek Order of the Saviour, of the British Military Order of the Bath, Knight of the Royal French Order of the Legion of Honor, and Lord of Notzing."

We hear no more of the Lord of Notzing, but around 1924 there appeared in a New York newspaper an interview with the current Baron von Washington in which he declared that he refused to take part in the World War as soon as America entered it, as he had a sentimental feeling which prevented him from slapping our smiling land in the face.

There was another Washington—this one was called Sir Henry—who took up the royalist cause in the English Civil War and fought valiantly against Cromwell. And there was still another Washington who died for King Charles.

None of this has any value. It throws no light on George Washington's character; it proves nothing, and serves only to satisfy curiosity. If it proved anything at all it would prove that the Washingtons were habitually opposed to democracy and progress, but it does not prove even that. The study of heredity is of small worth in appraising human values, because its conclusions are so often contradicted by facts.

§ 3

The Washingtons were inland people, living in the middle of England, but a curious dim strain of seafaring runs through their lives. Now and then we see one or another of them in a sea-mist, surrounded by legends of ocean adventure and the sailing of ships. But these pictures are too fragmentary and too dim; we do not know how much of the seagoing is fact and how much is fancy.

But we do know that when John Washington came to Virginia in 1657 he assisted, as second man, in sailing the vessel. He came as a gentleman-adventurer, and probably worked for his passage, acting as a mate of the ship.

This John Washington, who was the great-grandfather of George, was himself the son of Rev. Lawrence Washington, the rector of Purleigh. The reverend clergyman was a royalist who fell into misery when Cromwell's Parliament got the upper hand. There is a variance of opinion as to his character. Some say that he was a scholarly gentleman of high motives, dignity and wit; others contend that he was a village drunkard with only a rudimentary sense of duty, and of frowsy habits. Parliament appears to have held the latter opinion, for it discharged him from the living at Purleigh on the ground

> . . . that he is a common frequenter of Ale-houses, not only himself sitting dayly tippling there, but also encouraging others in that beastly vice, and hath been oft drunk, and hath said, *That the Parliament have more Papists belonging to them in their Armies than the King had about him or in his Army, and that the Parliament's Armie did more hurt than the Cavaliers.* . . .

It was an age of moist morals; but on the other hand, the living at Purleigh was lucrative, and very likely Cromwell's Parliament was anxious to get the reverend Lawrence out of it on any flimsy excuse. The truth is, I fancy, that he was

merely an outspoken royalist, and that the drinking part of
the charge was added to make it sound more convincing.
Under these circumstances it seems fair to give him the benefit
of the doubt, and let him live in our history as a kindly decent
parson with a slightly humid disposition.

John, the son of the rector, was forced to leave home by the
pinch of poverty. In his twenty-sixth year he appeared in the
rude colony of Virginia with the intention of growing up with
the country. He had everything to gain and nothing to lose.

He did very well. We hear of him next as a member of the
House of Burgesses, the local colonial legislature. He became
a dignitary in a small way. He took up land; he took a second
wife; he took up arms; he was made a colonel of militia.

As a soldier he was without distinction, and on one occasion
he got himself in a mess which brought down upon him the
vituperation of the "brittle and peevish" Berkeley, who was
then the royal governor of the province.

This trouble occurred in 1675 at the time of an Indian war.
Colonel John Washington, in co-operation with some Maryland
militia, had driven a party of Indians into a blockhouse. Five
of the Indians, trusting in the white man's military code, came
out for a parley under a flag of truce. Their judgment was
bad. They learned that military honour did not apply to dealings with Indians, for they were all five put to death.

Hearing of the occurrence, the brittle Berkeley went all to
pieces, and criticized John Washington in a tone of wrath.
"If they [meaning the Indian envoys] had killed my grandfather and grandmother," exclaimed the irate governor, "my
father and mother and all my friends, yet if they had come to
treat of peace they ought to have gone in peace."

As soon as it was possible to get in a word edgewise Colonel
John Washington explained that it was not he who had killed
the Indians; and that the Maryland commander had ordered
it done. This was quite true; it appears however, that John

Washington had made no protest. After some angry talk the matter was dropped.

Nevertheless, there must have been something about the incident and its resulting commotion that affected John Washington deeply, for we hear no more of him as a public character; and a year or so later he laid himself down and died—which he had no visible reason in the world for doing, as he was only forty-six.

Next appears Lawrence Washington, son of John—as dim a ghost as ever flitted through history. He was the grandfather of George, and I feel that I ought to say something about him, but his image is so pale and wispy that it falls to pieces at the least attempt at resuscitation. Lawrence has evidently decided to stay dead, so we shall leave him dead, and pass on. Before dying he made a will, leaving "a pulpit cloth and cushion" to the local parish church.

Then we come to Augustine, who was the son of this Lawrence, and who was born in 1694. We know a good deal about him, but the full tale of his life would make the dullest biography in all literature.

He was a bustling person, without imagination or intellectual urge. As a youth he was sent to school in England; as a man he "followed the sea" for awhile—which means that he went back and forth from Virginia to London with the ships, carrying Virginia produce, probably more as a supervisor of the cargo than as a sailing master. He inherited his father's land, and passed his life measuring and weighing, buying and selling, counting and computing. At one time he was manager and part owner of an iron mine and a smelting furnace near Fredericksburg. He married twice.

His second wife was the mother of George Washington. Her name was Mary Ball; and she was the daughter of Colonel Joseph Ball of Virginia. Augustine Washington became acquainted with her in England. She was there visiting her

English relatives, and he had gone to London on some Virginia business.

A contemporary of Mary Ball whose name has been lost in the desert of anonymity describes her at the age of sixteen as having hair "like unto flax," and cheeks "like May blossoms." Somebody else who knew her wrote that her eyes were light blue or grey in colour.

She was neither delicate nor literary. Her education was deficient. Whatever she may have been in early youth, she developed in her maturity a hard, querulous, managing manner.

Augustine Washington was a good procreator. Four children by Jane Butler—his first wife—and six by Mary Ball. The first of the Mary Ball progeny was born at Bridges' Creek, in Westmoreland County, at ten o'clock in the morning of Feb. 11, 1732—a date which has now become Feb. 22nd, through a change in the calendar.

The house in which George Washington came into being was burned down long ago, but the faithful Lossing obtained a hearsay description of it which is probably accurate enough. It was, he says, "of the better class of plain Virginia farm houses. It had four rooms, with an enormous chimney at each end, on the outside." Its roof was of the long, sloping kind, and there was an attic under the bare shingles. A porch in front, it sat low on the ground, was built of wood—probably unpainted—and was not an impressive structure.

Not far away is the Potomac, with its glint of blue water. A land of salty marshes and tangled forests, checkered here and there with primitive clearings over which slow slaves moved indolently about their tasks. On this February morning there is a stir about the dull little house; black servants and old women go in and out; a horse or two is tied to the hitching-post; grey wood-smoke rises from the chimneys into the soft Southern air; and there is the wail of a new-born babe.

Something tremendous had happened to the Washington family, but they were not then aware of it. No longer were they to pin their renown to a penny-squeezing merchant **at** Leeds; nor to a musty lawyer writing briefs in Gray's Inn; nor to a smooth and buttery Sir who gets himself married to the half-sister of a bastard duke; nor to somebody who fatuously died for Charles I; nor to an addled colonel of militia.

That mewing infant will so illumine the name of Washington that it will shine to the far corners of the earth. He is destined to rise to an astral plane of celebrity so high that even his faults will dazzle us and become, by reflection, our virtues.

§ 4

We possess certain definite facts concerning the childhood of Washington, but they are so few in number that all of them might be compressed into one short paragraph. As to their import, they are trivial and inconsequential.

There is no letter in existence (so far as I know) from Mary Washington to any of her friends in which she describes little George; no record of pretty incidents and baby talk, such as mothers love to write. But in explanation we must not overlook the fact that Mary Washington was almost illiterate, although she had been to London. Her letters were few in number and lean in fancy. She had no knack of expression— and no time to spare, as she was busy having children and looking after them.

We do not know who George's playmates were; presumably they were his brothers and his sisters. We know nothing about his childish likes and aversions, what he ate, what he wore, or how he spent his time.

The Cannot-Tell-a-Lie incident of the cherry tree and the hatchet is a brazen piece of fiction made up by a minister named the Rev. Mason L. Weems, who wrote a life of our country's father which is stuffed with this and similar fables.

We know very little more of Washington's early childhood

than we do of Shakespeare's—and with much less excuse, as Washington belongs to the modern world.

There is something singular about this reticence. At the age of forty-five George Washington had become world-famous. Many people then living must have known him as a small child. Is it not strange that, with all the incentive of celebrity, they did not tell the world something about his childish exploits? And it is equally strange that he says so little about himself in the way of early reminiscence.

We may nevertheless read his life backward and deduce, with a reasonable degree of certainty, that he was a proud and touchy boy. Proud, surely, for he walked in pride all his life. His touchiness was a hard self-assertion. During his whole life long he was jealous of his own rights and privileges, and very tenacious in maintaining them in matters affecting property. One may readily conceive how such a character might have been developed and sharpened in an unluxurious and crowded household.

My own impression is—and it must be taken merely as an impression—that George, as a child, was somewhat neglected. In this primitive society, in a home filled with children and slatternly servants, neglect was perhaps unavoidable. Besides, the whole current of Virginia social life, adopted bodily from England, favoured the eldest son. The law of primogeniture was in force, and continued in force until Thomas Jefferson got it abolished, thirty-odd years later. Under it the eldest son received the major part of the family inheritance; the younger children got only the scraps and leavings.

Lawrence Washington was Augustine's eldest son. He was the first child by Jane Butler, and was fourteen years older than his half-brother George. It was Lawrence who was sent to the Appleby school in England, where he learned English manners and a little Latin, and it was he who was expected to succeed his father.

In Lawrence's career there was the roll of drums and the

flash of fire, for he had served in England's distant wars. We shall see as we go along that his career was probably adopted by George Washington as a life-pattern. There is no doubt that he lived in George's day-dream as a shining hero.

People said when they saw the two brothers together that Lawrence was "a Washington" and George was "a Ball." They meant, of course, that George looked like the men of his mother's family, while his half-brother resembled the Washingtons.

The second son, Augustine (called "Austin") was also a child of Jane Butler. Both Lawrence and "Austin" were much older than George. Before he had reached the age of ten they had gone away, married and had homes of their own.

But the five small children of Mary Ball Washington grew up together in the cluttered farm house across the Rappahannock from Fredericksburg. In this house, which no longer exists, the Augustine Washington family lived during the greater part of George's childhood. There was George; and Elizabeth, who was born in 1733, and who was the only sister who lived through childhood; Samuel, who came in 1734, John Augustine (called "Jack"), who was born two years later; and Charles, the youngest son, born in 1738.

There is a strange remoteness about these secondary Washingtons. The great George does not drag them into history by the hand. They are distant figures, with blurred faces, lost in the crowd of spectators.

Yet George's relations with them all were pleasant enough. They visited him and he visited them, and for "Jack" and Betty he appeared to have a deep affection.

They did not take any part in public life, but some of their careers were faintly interesting. That of Samuel, for one. He was a gentle, affectionate ne'er-do-well who married no less than five times, and was frequently pulled out of debt by George's fraternal beneficence. He spent his life, it seems, in uxorious duties, and had no time for money-making. Many of his descendants are living to-day.

Augustine, the second of the Jane Butler children, was a man of substance and lived in fine style, though he never attained any celebrity.

Elizabeth (or "Betty") married Col. Fielding Lewis of Fredericksburg, and brought into the world a swarm of sons. Mrs. Lewis resembled her distinguished brother so closely that, it was said, she would have been mistaken for General Washington if she had worn a long military cloak and a three-cornered hat.

She is not mentioned among the famous beauties of the day.

"Jack" managed George's plantation affairs while the French and Indian war was going on; and his management was evidently not very good, for brother George found things in a run-down condition when he returned from the campaigns in the quality of colonel, brimming over with renown. Jack's son Bushrod became a justice of the Supreme Court of the United States, and he inherited Mount Vernon. It was he who tore out the pages of Washington's diaries and records by the handfuls and gave them away as souvenirs to casual visitors.

CHAPTER II

THE SENSE OF NUMBERS

§ 1

Though the home of Augustine Washington's family was primitive, crowded and inconvenient, we should not think of it as squalid. There was no baronial splendour about it, and it could not be compared with Nomini Hall, the imposing mansion of the Carters in Westmoreland, or with that of the Byrds at Westover, or with the stately home of the Lees at Stratford; yet the Washingtons were gentle people, full of pride and traditions.

Colonial Virginia already possessed a well-defined aristocracy, but there was hardly anything that could be properly called a middle class. In descending from the aristocratic heights one fell down a precipice, without stairs or elevator, to land among an indiscriminate welter of slaves, indented servants, backwoodsmen and coast-town mechanics.

The aristocratic class was the governing class; and the limited mental outlook of the Washingtons did not prevent them from belonging to it. With a few exceptions the intellectual trajectory of the entire ruling class was short and flat. Their attention was fixed on land and slaves, on tobacco and timber. They had no fancies, no intellectual flights, no abstractions. There was not a poet nor a philosopher among them.

The Washingtons fitted in this society with the close fit of hand and glove. They were men of high courage, of gentle manners and habits. Moreover, they had a self-conscious sense of class, and a passionate desire for land.

Manual labour in Virginia was already treated with contumely—a common phenomenon in all social systems based on slavery. Before the Revolution the higher and lower classes were drifting further apart, instead of closer together, and the air was full of class antagonisms. There was a general feeling among the lower classes that some indispensable definitions had been omitted from the lexicon of human rights. This condition of affairs had several concurrent causes, chief of which was perhaps the monopolisation of the land by the oligarchy that ruled the colony. Another underlying cause of discontent was the close-corporation conception of things in general which the governing aristocracy had built up among themselves. It had become extremely difficult for any man outside of their circle, whatever his attainments might be, to achieve any kind of success. Nevertheless, some did; Patrick Henry for one.

These distinctions are highly important in a historical sense. By keeping them in mind we shall understand more clearly the rise of George Washington and the basic causes of the American Revolution.

Augustine Washington owned six plantations. To form a mental picture of them the first thing to do is to forget the meaning of the word "plantation" as we use it to-day. His plantations did not consist of smooth wind-rippled fields, rich pastures and velvety lawns. They were huge primitive clearings, pockmarked with holes and spotted with stumps. Wretched roads of ruts and mud led to them. The plantation houses were crazy structures of undressed boards. Gangs of indifferent slaves wandered about these clearings, and did as little work as they could.

Like nearly everybody else, Augustine Washington was land poor. Like nearly everybody else, he lacked ready money. But his family did not lack food, nor horses to ride, nor servants to wait on them, nor clothes—such as they were. He managed indeed to drink enough wine and eat enough rich food to give himself a fine case of gout, which eventually caused his death,

Their roughness of life was inevitable in a pioneer land; they considered it only temporary; and, although their existence was almost as hard as that of the poorer farmers and backwoodsmen, they were immeasureably above these lower elements of the colony in social standing, as well as in habit and tradition.

§ 2

Nowadays men are morose with living in a world that has grown too large for them. Morose and bitter, or defiant and gay. One need not be a clairvoyant to detect a sense of foreboding beneath the exultation over what is called modern progress. We are the victims of our own inventions; we see civilization strangely shattering before the driving power that we hoped would save it.

Daily we are deluged by a flood of half-comprehended ideas, by showers of intricate and plausible falsehoods. Distant events and unseen men cut us to the heart. Our fate, as individuals, is no longer in our own hands; it comes from remote sources that are both dim and unintelligible. Our careers are twisted out of shape by mystifying economic laws which we have had no part in making, and which possess all the inhuman attributes of invisible gods. There is a feeling of a sinister sleight-of-hand at work in the affairs of men.

The world into which young Washington came was very different. It was by no means too large. Henry Adams, with his instinct for compact phrases, calls it a "small and cheerful world"—but both its smallness and cheerfulness were relative. People were dissatisfied, as they have always been; but then they thought they were able to lay their hands on the things that made them unhappy. Life was almost devoid of theory. If they were without poetry, they were also without hopeless dilemmas. They were a practical people, the colonial Americans. They lived under conditions that made practicality a cardinal virtue.

Now in this small and cheerful world we see the small Washington getting a small amount of education.

There was no regular school near Augustine Washington's home, or so it seems, and George at the age of six or seven was turned over to a Mr. Hobby, sexton of a nearby church, to receive whatever sluggish pothook instruction the sexton could give.

Mr. Hobby's business was not to teach people, but to bury them; and he was without renown in the field of book-learning. No matter. In a primitive society queer shifts are made. A man may be at one and the same time a horse-shoer and a dentist.

To the sexton-teacher George goes, his horn-book in his hand, wearing buckles on his shoes and a little coat of the color of plum.

In this churchyard school he learned the alphabet and how to make crude, curly letters. No doubt he heard the rambling story of many a departed soul and spelled the mossy headstone names while the sexton mused on the fate of some poor country Yorick.

But there was no moody Hamlet in this boy. To him a dead man was a dead man; a house was a house; and a spade was a spade. He was firmly planted in the everyday practicality that makes nations and then ruins them. The imagination that breeds vice was not in him; nor was the imagination that breeds fear.

Pretty soon the sexton was dried up; he had taught all he knew; there was no more water in that well. George had acquired a sort of vague capacity to read, a little arithmetic, and the foundation of the fantastic system of spelling that bedevilled him to the end of his days. He was never able to get the i's and the e's right in such words as *ceiling;* he always wrote *blew* when he meant the color blue; lie was *lye;* and oil was *oyl* in his orthography.

Down in Westmoreland county, near the old home of the

Washingtons, a Mr. Williams presided at a more generous fount of knowledge. There George was sent, and as the school was thirty miles or so from his father's home he lived with his half-brother Augustine—the one nicknamed "Austin"—who had grown up and had a home of his own in Westmoreland.

The colourless Mr. Williams, who exists to us only as a name, appears to have specialized in mathematics. It was he who taught George the round bold handwriting that makes Washington's letters so legible.

In the science of numbers he had an apt pupil in little George, who loved arithmetic as many another boy has loved Shelley. At his tongue's end were all the weights and measures —avoirdupois, pints and gallons, cords of wood, peck of peas, long division, subtraction. I doubt if we can find in history any other character of the first importance who had a passion for counting equal to that of George Washington. During his whole life he kept his eye on the *number* of things. Every penny he owned and every foot of land was set down, over and over again, in the most orderly and meticulous manner.

The enumeration of things seemed to afford an outlet for a sort of mental voluptuousness. At one time when he was managing five plantations and several hundred slaves he calculated laboriously the number of seed in a pound Troy weight of red clover, and found that a pound contained 71,000 seed. Then he calculated the seed in a pound of timothy, and learned that there were 298,000. Large numbers these, but he got into astronomical dimensions when he set out to calculate the number of seed in a pound of New River grass, and discovered the total to be 844,800.

There is also, in his handwriting, a memorandum giving the number of windows in each of the houses on the Mount Vernon estate, and the "no. of Paynes" in each window.

He was never too busy to spare the time to do this counting and measuring. In 1786 he measured the exact altitude of the piazza at Mount Vernon above the high-water mark of the river, and found it to be 124 feet 10½ inches.

These are the gestures of a man who loves material possessions with a passionate intensity. His counting was limited to the enumeration of the things he possessed, or which might bear some tangible relation to his possessions. In his various enumerations, treasured in the archives, there is no list of authors, nor of historical events, nor of works of art.

I cannot find that he ever wrote out his ideas in logical sequence for his own guidance as Lincoln did, and as Jefferson did.

He was not an idea-man but a thing-man.

§ 3

In a back eddy of the stream of time there floated for more than a hundred years, hidden from the eyes of men, a relic of that period. In Virginia, a century after his schooldays were ended, there was found a curious little book that had been owned and used by George Washington as a boy. Its title is "The Young Man's Companion"; it was published in London; its author was W. Mather; and to-day the precious tome has a high market value.

To George "The Young Man's Companion" was a companion indeed. His name, in his own handwriting, is on the flyleaf, and its pages are well-thumbed. The book tells how to measure lumber and land, how to be a gentleman, how to set out useful trees, how to write letters to people of quality, how to make ink with scant materials, how to calculate interest, how to draw up legal papers. It tells all this, and more. It is crammed full of facts divested of their underlying ideas. Everything in it answers *How* and nothing in it answers *Why*.

There are evidences that he laboured over it and learned it well. Many of its maxims were copied out by him, and these copies are still in existence.

His education was severely limited in its quality as well as in its scope. The efforts which have been made at various times to depict him as a highly educated man—self-educated, of course—are, all of them, contributions to the slobbery mass of flubdub in which he has been submerged so long that it has hardened around him and can be chiselled off in chunks.

It is true that compared with the common people of his day he was well-educated, for, as a rule, they could hardly read and write. But he was not educated up to the average level of people of his own aristocratic class. Literary and classical allusions seldom appear in his writings, although it was the custom of his time to sprinkle the written word liberally with the fragrance of Greece and Rome. He knew no French. It fell to his lot to have a great deal to do with the French, as enemies and as friends; but he seems to have had no curiosity whatever about their language. Now and then, on rare occasions, he uses in his writings a French word or phrase, which is almost always spelled wrong.

How familiar this seems to any one who knows modern "captains of industry." Economy of effort is a basic trait of their character, as it was of Washington's. The typical financial magnate never goes to the trouble of learning a foreign language, no matter how much business he does with the people who speak it. He does not learn it because it is not necessary and he is devoid of intellectual curiosity. He knows that he can always employ interpreters.

In his youth Washington read some numbers of the *Spectator*—he made a memorandum to that effect—but he had small taste for books. People who do not acquire the reading habit early in life never acquire it.

His attainments in the science of numbers were arithmetical rather than mathematical. He appeared, however, to understand simple algebraic equations, which he called "the rule of three."

Among the nine hundred volumes of his library at the time

of his death there was but little poetry, and not much of what is known as "polite" literature.

He was a man of hands; not without brains, but with hand and brain moving together. He did not amuse himself with thought. He used thought only as a mode of action. He moved through this world like a thinking hand.

Without a glance at his library, intuition tells us that we shall find there many practical treatises, well-named "hand-books." Turning to the list we find—among many similar works:

The Farmer's Assistant, an essay on the diseases of horses.

Anderson on Agriculture, in four volumes.

Price's *Carpenter*, a book on the craftsmanship of wood-work.

The Complete Farmer.

Boswell on Meadows.

Gibson's *Diseases of Horses.*

There is an aroma of leather harness and dried hay about this literature. In fancy one sees him refreshing himself at these springs of learning, then walking sedately through the stables, running his hands over the horses' fetlocks and fondling their wiry manes; then passing into the cool dusk of the barn and watching the pigeons fly through its great door, while he silently calculates the amount of fodder stored there.

His choice of books reflected his practical, unimaginative character. These treatises have to do with agriculture because men got rich in that day through land, and the cultivation of land. If he lived in this present age his library would probably contain many books on money and investment, besides, of course, such sterling works as *The Gasoline Engine in Sickness and Health.*

He read some of these practical books very thoroughly. Duhamel's *Practical Treatise of Husbandry*, in an English translation, came into his hands in 1760, and he was so interested in it that he made a laborious abstract of the entire book.

It is customary to attribute his errors in diction and spelling to the confused grammar and orthography of the time. It is quite commonly supposed, I believe, that nobody could really spell or write grammatically until well along in the nineteenth century. This supposition is erroneous. Educated people knew how to spell at that time, and they were more familiar with grammar than educated people are to-day. Alexander Hamilton could spell; and so could Jefferson, and John Dickinson and Benjamin Franklin, and everybody else who had a good education.

§ 4

In 1743, Augustine Washington, who had bustled about Virginia for forty-nine years with his pockets full of memoranda and his head full of arrangements, suddenly found that he had to die, and all his bustling stopped.

George was a younger son, and his father, in his will, provided a younger son's portion for him. On reaching the age of twenty-one he was to have the Cherry Tree Farm on the Rappahannock. This was the farm on which his parents had lived. It consisted of two hundred and eighty acres. In addition, he was to have a share of the land of Deep Run, three cheap town lots in Fredericksburg and ten negro slaves.

This legacy was small—but small as it was, he never received any of it until his mother's death, forty-six years later. During his mother's lifetime he never claimed the property. She continued to live on the farm and use it as her own. When it came to him eventually he had lost his youth and his peace of mind; he had grown rich, famous and irritable. This stale egg of fortune, when he got it, was of very little consequence to him.

It is natural to expect that a youth of such keen pride and self-reliance would soon be doing something for himself. Setting out to choose a career he followed his own inclination.

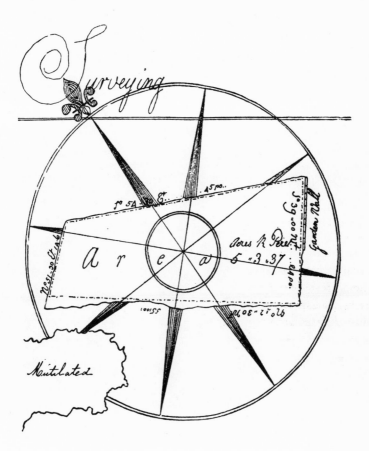

Plan of Turnip Field made by George Washington at the age of fifteen

He liked to measure and count, but most of all he liked to measure land. If he had any inward struggle between choosing the profession of surveying or becoming one of the colony's brilliant bookkeepers, surveying must have won easily, for the surveying of land was then one of the few varieties of work high in gentlemanly esteem. It was in reality an important job in a country where titles and boundaries elbowed each other in chaotic confusion.

He liked to show off his talents. When he was living with his half-brother Lawrence at Mount Vernon—he was then a boy of thirteen or fourteen—he would, on occasion, survey the turnip field or the pine barren while his brother's guests looked on. It makes an interesting picture. Late in the afternoon, after dinner, which was at three o'clock. The ladies and gentlemen stand in groups on the edge of the field while young George, with a negro to help him, peers through his surveying instrument, motions authoritatively right and left, and jots down memoranda. The guests are somewhat bored, they had rather be playing at cards, but there is a patronising spirit among them; they think George is wonderful, and say so. Afterwards he appears among them at the card tables with the turnip field finely plotted and drawn to scale on a piece of paper.

Youth has no originality; it repeats itself. He was doing what the modern boy does when he takes you upstairs to show you proudly the thingamajigs of his home-made radio set.

George went to live with his brother Lawrence in 1746. We do not know exactly why he left his mother's home, but we are at liberty to guess. Perhaps his mother found it difficult to provide for all her children. It may have been that George needed an elder brother's guidance.

His school-days were over. He does not appear to have gone beyond the elementary grades, though some of the higher branches were taught at the school of the Rev. Mr. Marye, which he attended for a brief spell.

CHAPTER III

LOVE AND THE FAIRFAXES

§ 1

AMONG the Virginia Washingtons Lawrence spoke as a cymbal speaks among the flutes. There was nothing of the country bumpkin about him. He knew England; he knew the ways of fashion; he had lived through the desperate adventures of war; he had married a lovely lady of high family; he was different from any person whom George had ever met.

Lawrence was probably a free-thinker. We do not know this for a certainty; we have no direct evidence, but he is on record in his own words as an advocate of religious liberty (said to have been the first agitator for religious freedom in Virginia) at a time when such a course meant trouble and controversy.

The Established Church—that is, the Church of England established in Virginia—had a political function. The vestry of each parish was the seat of local legislation; a vestryman had a place in the scheme of things somewhat like that occupied to-day by an alderman. Lawrence was a member of the church; everybody who expected to take any part in local politics had to be. Under the circumstances his talk of religious freedom was revolutionary in a very definite sense.

Lawrence had served as an officer in the expedition which had been sent to take Cartagena in South America during the tragic and grotesque "War of Jenkins' Ear." I shall say a little about this fiasco, which George heard at first-hand from his brother.

The war originated in a flare-up of a long simmering dispute which England and Spain had carried on for a generation over certain maritime rights in the West Indies. It was an international quarrel in which the original cause of disagreement had disappeared behind a maze of minor and secondary irritations. The whole affair had become gibbering and senile. Both England and Spain were looking it over with the idea of giving it a decent burial, when a merchant captain named Jenkins sailed into an English port with his own left ear in his pocket and a tale of woe on his tongue.

He said that a Spanish revenue cutter had boarded him off Havana. The Spaniards searched his vessel, tied him to a mast, and one of them sliced off his ear with a sword. Then they threw his ear in his face, and told him to take it home to his king. In reply Jenkins said simply, "I commend my soul to God and my cause to my country"—a statement which certainly indicates considerable presence of mind under the circumstances.

Having thus put Soul and Cause in their proper pigeonholes, Jenkins did sail home, and the shrivelled ear was exhibited around London. A wave of moral fury ran over England and spread to her colonial children across the Atlantic. There was talk of Down with Popery, English Courage, hated Minions of the Inquisition, et cetera.

(After the war it was discovered that Jenkins had lost his ear in another way, and that his tale was a lie from start to finish.)

An expedition to capture Cartegena was planned, and the North American colonies were asked by the British government to furnish three thousand men, who were to co-operate with the royal forces. The American volunteers, filled with indignation against Spain and all her deviltries, were greatly in excess of three thousand, and many men had to be left behind.

It is a pity that where the heart is so full the mind is so empty. When the colonials reached the rendezvous at Jamaica they learned that the British War Office had not made any

provision for feeding, clothing or paying them, although
the British troops were well fed, paid and clothed. So there
they were, scrambling for desultory leavings of food, penni-
less and forlorn, in their thick woolen clothes under a blistering sun.

In the conception and management of this military effort
an enormous amount of pure asininity was compressed into
a short time and a limited space. In the first place there was
no reason for the expedition at all. Cartegena was merely a
fly-blown huddle of Spanish huts on the edge of a bay filled
with sharks. It had no strategic value and was not worth
having.

The English assault was gallantly made. Swamps, fever,
rotten food, night attacks when the cannon spat yellow flame
and detachments got lost in the darkness. The English and
the colonials were so badly beaten that even the Spanish had
compassion for them, and allowed them to depart unmolested.[1]
Of the thirty-seven hundred colonial troops engaged only
eleven hundred came back.

Young George was about ten years old when Lawrence came
home from the war and visited his parents. We can imagine
his homecoming. The tanned and erect stripling of an officer
in his uniform; the Washingtons and the neighbours listening
in silence as he tells of the Spaniards and the whistling bullets,
of the desperate ventures, of the dying men, of the smoky can-
nonades; and George listening with eager ears.

In his early manhood George wrote that he was "strongly
bent to arms." Is it not likely that he dreamed of following
in his brother's footsteps?

Lawrence had returned from Cartegena with the seeds of
the tuberculosis which was eventually to cause his death. He
was never to be well again, but he did not know it then. In
a year or so after his return he married Ann Fairfax, daughter

---

[1] Tobias Smollett was on this expedition, and there is a splendid and
accurate account of it in *Roderick Random*.

of William Fairfax of "Belvoir," and brought her to his home, which he re-named Mount Vernon in honour of Admiral Vernon.

In his brother's home young George Washington bloomed. The life at Mount Vernon was spirited and full of tone. There he met the fine people of the colony—the Lees, the Masons, the Carys, the Fairfaxes, the Fauntleroys—met them and was one of them. He showed off his surveying talent; rode breakneck after the foxhounds; flirted awkwardly with the girls in the pompous, chivalrous way of colonial high life; assisted his brother around the plantation; and on Sundays listened meekly to the sermons in the little stained-glass church.

And he had the good luck to become acquainted with Lord Thomas Fairfax.

§ 2

In the queer mess of human destiny the determining factor is Luck. For every important place in life there are many men of fairly equal capacities. Among them Luck decides who shall accomplish the great work, who shall be crowned with laurel, and who shall fall back into obscurity and silence.

Ability counts in human affairs, but Luck counts, too—and as one approaches the summit in any sphere of effort Luck counts more and more. The proverbial saying that there is plenty of room at the top is the reverse of the truth. There is never any room at the top, though there is plenty at the bottom. Men who reach the top arrive there through a linked-up series of fortuitous circumstances in which capacity and chance are combined.

The turning points of lives are not the great moments. The real crises are often concealed in occurrences so trivial in appearance that they pass unobserved.

One of the important turning points of George Washington's life was his meeting with Lord Fairfax. It is entirely probable

that he did not realise its importance—at any rate, he never
said anything to lead us to believe that he did—but we can
see it clearly now, in historical perspective.

This nobleman, who was a bachelor and past the age of
fifty when he met young Washington, possessed in Virginia
an almost incredible estate of five million four hundred thousand acres. He owned more land than there is in the state
of New Jersey. It was all in a single tract, in the Northern
Neck of Virginia; twenty-one counties have been made of it.

The origin of these Fairfax holdings is interesting. When
Charles II was a fugitive without a kingdom he was supported
by Louis XIV, and kept a sort of shabby court at Saint
Germain-en-Laye. His entourage specialised in dissoluteness
and scandal as industriously as other men specialise in chem-
istry or stamp-collecting. His courtiers were hard up, and
Charles had nothing to give them. One day, in place of a
more tangible largess, he distributed Virginia land grants
among them with the lavishness of a man who is giving away
something that he does not own. It is hardly necessary to
say that he had no authority in Virginia, or anywhere else.

A certain Lord John Culpeper managed to get hold of the
grants made to his fellow-courtiers. When Charles came again
to his throne Culpeper persuaded the monarch to give his
kingly validity to the whole proceeding. Lord Fairfax was
the grandson and heir of Lord Culpeper; the consolidated
estate came to him in natural descent.

No one had ever paid anything for this huge domain; no one
had ever done any work to acquire it. Any forlorn negro in
Virginia had as much moral right to this land as Lord Fairfax
ever had.

He had no moral right—but, nevertheless his legal right was
strong. It was fortified by fierce-looking documents carrying
heavy seals. He could keep people from settling on the land;
he could sell it wholesale or retail; he could build houses on it
or tear down the houses of people who had built on it without

his permission. During the Revolution (in 1777) it was con-
fiscated by the state of Virginia on the ground that Lord Fairfax was a British subject. But, two years later, a velvet-
footed act of restoration slipped quietly through the Virginia
assembly. At least, so it appears, for the act reads two different ways and is dripping with guile.

Thereupon, lawsuits began between the people of Virginia
and the heirs of Lord Fairfax. The state finally succeeded in
getting rid of the Fairfax nuisance, in spite of the learned and
reputable John Marshall, afterwards Chief Justice of the
Supreme Court of the United States, who appeared as attorney
for the Fairfax heirs and attempted, by every possible legal
device, to keep them in possession.

In 1746 Lord Fairfax came to Virginia to live on his estate.
He was a cousin of the William Fairfax who owned Belvoir,
the plantation next to Mount Vernon, and whose daughter had
married Lawrence Washington. Woodrow Wilson says in
his lofty romantic style, that Lord Fairfax was "a man strayed
out of the world of fashion . . . a man of taste and culture,
he had written with Addison and Steele for the *Spectator.*"

Yes . . . culture . . . Addison . . . Steele . . . clubs . . .
fine old gentleman . . . another Pendennis.

He was actually a cynical, bitter old man with a hook-nose
and a smell of Madeira wine. Only cynical, embittered men
leave London at the age of fifty to live in a wilderness.

§ 3

Now we have the great lord, worn sharp and thin by the
acid of experience, and the lanky, large-boned, big-knuckled
youth who was George Washington, and who was not worn
by experience nor anything else.

He became a youthful favourite of Lord Fairfax, but who
knows why? He could ride splendidly and shoot well. Lord
Fairfax liked that. Fox-hunting occupied his time, and that

of his neighbours, to an extent that is almost unbelievable. There were no theatres, no fashionable assemblies, no daily papers—and but few of any kind—no elegant shops, and nothing to do but play cards and hunt game.

Some one writes from Belvoir to Mount Vernon: "His Lordship proposed drawing Mudd Hole to-morrow, first kill-ing a Fox; and then to turn down a Bagged Fox before your door for ye diversion of ye Ladys. . . . We took the Fox yesterday without Hurt."

Young George Washington was dependable, forthright, and honest. No doubt Lord Fairfax liked that, too, for he had come from a land of sinuous lickspittles where *Mr. Snake* would, before long, flourish in the *School for Scandal.* And, moreover, young Washington said very little. He did not ask the keen and searching questions which make wealthy elderly gentlemen uneasy and wonder what the world is coming to.

At that time Washington was only sixteen, but he looked much older. He wore a number thirteen shoe and Lafayette said that his hands were the largest "I have ever seen on a human being." He was about six feet tall, with grey-blue eyes and reddish brown hair.

The noble Fairfax thought the time was ripe to have his land surveyed and his titles put in order. It was high time, indeed. Farmers were coming down from Pennsylvania and settling in the Fairfax wilderness, without rhyme or reason, as bold as you please, just as if the land were not already owned by somebody else.

He gave the job of surveying the lands behind the Blue Ridge—in the Shenandoah Valley—to his relative, young George William Fairfax (son of the William of Belvoir), who was assisted by George Washington and an experienced sur-veyor named Mr. Genn. This is, I think, the first opportunity that George had ever had of making any money. The pay he received was large—at least so it seems to me—for he says in a letter about the job that "A Dubbleloon is my constant gain every Day that the weather will permit my going out and sometimes Six Pistoles." At that time a doubloon was the equivalent of about $7.20; and a pistole was worth $3.60; approximately.

The surveyors left on March 11, 1748, and reached Mount Vernon again on April 13th. It was a busy month for George Washington, and apparently a happy one. On March 23rd he wrote in his diary:

> Rain'd till about two oClock and Clear'd when we were agreeaby surpris'd at y. sight of thirty odd Indians coming from War with only one Scalp. We had some Liquor with us of which we gave them Part it elevating there Spirits put them in y. Humour of Dauncing of whom we had a War Daunce there manner of Dauncing is as follows Viz They clear a Large Circle and make a Great Fire in y. middle then seats themselves around it y. Speaker makes a grand speech telling them in what Manner they are to Daunce after he has finished y. best Dauncer jumps up as one awaked out of a Sleep and runs and Jumps about y. Ring in a most comicol Manner he is followed by y. Rest then be̦̦gins there Musicians to play ye Musick is a Pot half (full) of water with a Deerskin Stretched over it as tight as it can and a goard with some Shott in it to Rattle and a Piece of an horses Tail tied to it to make it look fine y. one keeps Rattling and y. other Drumming all y. (time) while y. others is Dauncing.

He was "agreeaby surpris'd." Not much fear of thirty Indian warriors carrying a bloody scalp. He has, apparently, neither fear nor curiosity. He does not give the name of their tribe; perhaps was not sufficiently curious to inquire. He has no thought for the symbolism of their dance, nor for the weird poetry of grotesque painted bodies gyrating around a fire under the solemn firelit trees. It is a vaudeville show. All he wants to do is to give them enough liquor to start them cutting capers.

This is the leathery insensitiveness of a hard-eyed country youth at a circus. As such boys grow into men the world shapes itself more and more into an arena for the exercise of their authority and pleasure. They are at the other end of the human scale from the thinker, the poet and the dreamer. They are the men who rule the world but do not make it. Finding the world already and unaccountably made by some one else, they take possession of it.

Young George did not mind hardships; he accepted things as he found them. During this trip he wrote:

> . . . I have not sleep'd above three Nights or four in a bed, but after Walking a good deal all the Day lay down before the fire upon a Little Hay Straw Fodder or bearskin whichever is to be had with Man Wife and Children like a Parcel of Dogs and Catts and happy he that gets the Birth nearest the fire. . . .

§ 4

Early in life Washington began to fumble with love. It was really fumbling, for he was never at ease in the technique of love and love-making. Like the art of swimming, the art of love is one of the simplest arts within human range, if one understands it. On the other hand, when it is not understood the course of love runs through a foot-tripping labyrinth in which strange, insuperable obstacles appear. Washington, I think, always found it something of a mystery.

In the presence of women he would often lose his simple forthright manner and turn himself into a pompous and mouthy sentimentalist—or else remain spell-bound and silent.

My impression is that he idealised women; and most women, in their hearts, detest idealisation. With good reason, too, for it puts them in a very uncomfortable position. To live every day on a plane of lofty and rather ethereal ideals is a discouraging outlook for a woman of spirit and sense, especially when the ideals have been invented by a man.

The idealisation of women is one of the well-known traits of highly masculine men. They do not understand feminine thought and feeling. To them women are strange beings of a superior order. Washington was intensely masculine.

In 1748, about the time of the Fairfax surveying expedition, he wrote to somebody whom he calls "Dear Robin" about an amatory experience of his own. The affair is hazily anonymous, unfortunately. A draft of the letter is in the notebook which he used to record his survey of the Fairfax estate. As it is quite lengthy, and deals with other matters, I shall quote only a pertinent extract.

> My place of Residence is at present at His Lordships[2] where I might was my heart disengaged pass my time very pleasantly as theres a very agreeable Young Lady Lives in the same house (Colo George Fairfax's Wife's Sister) but as thats only adding Fuel to fire it makes me the more uneasy for by often and unavoidably being in Company with her revives my former Passion for your Low Land Beauty whereas was I to live more retired from young Women I might in some measure eliviate my sorrows by burying that chast and troublesome Passion in the grave of oblivion or etarnall forgetfulness for as I am very well assured thats the only antidote or remedy that I shall be relieved by or only recess that can administer any cure or help to me as I am well convinced was I ever to attempt any thing I should only get a denial which would be only adding grief to uneasiness.

This "Low Land Beauty" has become as famous among the biographers of Washington as the Man in the Iron Mask is among French historians. She has been identified at hap-

[2] He means Lord Thomas Fairfax.

hazard with half a dozen young women of Westmoreland—
among them Mary Bland, Lucy Grymes and Betsy Fauntleroy.

The most convincing conjecture is that the Lowland beauty
was Miss Lucy Grymes, who afterwards married Henry Lee,
and became the grandmother of Gen. Robert E. Lee.

Whoever she may have been, it is evident that she had left
our hero in a state of despair. There is an air of impending
deliquescence in his utterance. He is about to melt away. He
is through with women—at sixteen. All is vanity; all is ashes,

> Whereas was I to live more retired from young Women
> I might in some measure eliviate my sorrows by burying
> that chast and troublesome Passion in the grave of obli-
> vion or etarnall forgetfulness.

What mooning and moping! But such maladies soon run
their course. The remedy for woman is woman. Strange ailment, strange remedy.

In the same note-book that records his desolation we find,
a few pages further on, this cryptic entry:

> 'Twas Perfect Love before ⎫
> But Now I do adore   ⎬ s. Young M. A. his Wife
>   ⎭

It would appear from this sentimental note that he was
adoring somebody's wife. Young M. A.'s wife.

Then we come to an acrostic in George's handwriting. Here
it is:

> From your bright sparkling Eyes I was undone;
> Rays, you have; more transperent than the Sun,
> Amidst its glory in the rising Day
> None can you equal in your bright array;
> Constant in your calm and unspotted Mind;
> Equal to all, but will to none Prove kind,
> So knowing, seldom one so Young, you'l Find.

Ah! woe's me, that I should Love and conceal
Long have I wish'd, but never dare reveal,
Even though severely Loves Pains I feel;
Xerxes that great, was't free from Cupids Dart,
And all the greatest Heroes, felt the smart.

You will observe that the acrostic spells "Frances Alexa—" obviously Frances Alexander. She has not been identified. The Alexanders were numerous in colonial Virginia. The next page of the note-book has been torn out, so the last lines of the acrostic are missing.

It would be as absurd to lay much stress on these fragments as it would be to reconstruct an unknown prehistoric animal from a single bone. All that they can prove is that he was thinking of love, and that he was a young man of some little experience in such matters.

Although we know very little with certainty as to Washington's relations with women, there are some facts which we know very well. One of them is that he was never obsessed by them. He never had an overwhelming love affair. In his history there is neither a Josephine nor a Beatrice. He never took his opinions from any woman, and never went out of his way to fashion his life to fit any woman's conception.

However, there was one who stood large in his young life. . . .

I have mentioned a George William Fairfax who accompanied Washington on the surveying trip. He was the son of William Fairfax of Belvoir, and Lawrence Washington had married his sister. On the survey he was as lovelorn as Washington, but the result was more happy, for on his return he married Miss Sally Cary, the eldest daughter of Colonel Wilson Cary.

Washington spent most of the winter of 1749 at Belvoir, as a guest of young Fairfax and his wife. Persons in the vicinity who were skilled in predicting and recording emotional disturbances mentioned the occurrence at that time of numerous perturbations at Belvoir. These seismic emotions were slight, hardly worth setting down in the larger annals, but sufficiently exciting nevertheless to warrant local attention.

Naïve folk declared that young Washington was in love with Mary Cary. This young lady is mentioned in the letter to "Dear Robin"—quoted above—as staying at Lord Fairfax's house.

Alas! It was, not to Miss Mary that he had given his affection, but to her married sister, Mrs. Sally Fairfax, his friend's wife. It was then all in germination, awaiting the flow of days and too nebulous to be placed in a definite category. But we shall hear of it later, with the passing of years.

It was in this period that he had another experience with girls which was dramatic enough, but not at all sentimental. One day he was taking a swim in the Rappahannock and two girls of low degree ran off with his clothes.

Only fancy! The Father of our Country standing by the river's brink in the golden sunset clad only in humourless dignity—for, although he had plenty of dignity he never had any humour—clothed in dignity, and wondering how to get home.

Eventually he got home somehow, and had the girls arrested. One of them was convicted of theft and was punished with fifteen lashes on her bare back.

§ 5

If he was precocious in love, he was also precocious in land, and of the two passions, the desire for land was the stronger.

In 1748 this boy of sixteen acquired his "Bullskin Plantation"—so named because of its proximity to Bullskin Creek. The place consisted of five hundred and fifty acres of wild land in Frederick county. He paid for it by doing work as a surveyor.

In 1750 he bought four hundred and fifty-six acres of one

McCracken; a cultivated farm probably, as he paid one hundred and twelve pounds for it, which would have been a very high price for uncleared land.

Two years later he bought five hundred and fifty-two acres more, paying a hundred and fifteen pounds. Before he was twenty-one years of age he was the owner of 1558 acres, all of which he had obtained by his own efforts.

The money for these purchases was earned by him as a surveyor. In 1748 he was recommended by Lord Fairfax for the post of official surveyor of Culpeper county, and was appointed after he had gone down to Williamsburg to take a sort of post-graduate course in the art and mystery of measurement. The county records of Virginia contain hundreds of his surveys, all drawn and annotated in his neat, clear manner.

One begins to see that the foundation of his character was a sense of material values.

The difference between the intellectual life and the material life is profound. It is the difference between the head and the hands.

The thinker gets himself entangled in a net of irrealisable negations, for all thinking—if carried far enough—lies down and dies, like a discouraged mathematician, in a prickly bed of surds and negatives.

But the material life is not negative; it is affirmative. It deals only with realisable affirmations.

CHAPTER IV

THE WORLD GROWS MORE COMPLICATED

§ 1

In the year 1751 the fact became perfectly obvious, even to those unlearned in medical lore, that Lawrence Washington would die unless something were done, and done soon.

At that time, and for many years afterwards, there was a general impression that tuberculosis was connected, in its origin and development, with cold weather. This error being assumed, the conclusion naturally was that the way to get rid of it was to go to a hot place and live there.

One of the favourite hot places of the day was the island of Barbados, a flowery little British island that broils gently in the tropical sun of the West Indies. It is about twenty-two hundred miles from Virginia and is almost in sight of the coast of South America.

In September of that year Lawrence Washington left for Barbados, and brother George went with him as nurse and companion. George kept a diary of the voyage, and here are some of the matters recorded:

Catched a Dolphin at 8 P. M., a Shark at 11 and one of his pilot fish. . . .

A large Sea and some Squals of Rain and fresh Breeze 'till 2 am the wind died away. . . .

The Seamen seemed disheartened confessing they had never seen such weather before. It was universally surmis'd their had been a violent hurricane not far distant. A prodigy in ye West appear'd towards ye suns setting abt. 6. P. M., remarkable for its extraordinary redness.

44

It is a pity that he did not describe the prodigy—whatever it was—more fully. It may have been merely a tropical sunset.

> This Morning arose with agreeably assurances of a certain and steady trade Wind which after near five Weeks buffiting and being toss'd by a fickle and Merciless ocean was glad'ening knews. . . .

They reached Barbados on Nov. 3rd, having been at sea since Sept. 28th. This voyage was the only one ever made outside the limits of the United States by George Washington. The journal contains a description of the island that is richly characteristic of Washington's manner of observation.

> There is several regular Risings in this Island one above another so that scarcely any part is deprived of a beautiful Prospect both of sea and Land what is contrary to the observation on other countrys is that each Rising is better than the other below. . . . Canes is from 40 to 70 pon of sugar each pon valued at 20/ out of which a third is deducted for expences unless Rum sells for 2/ and upwards pr. Gallon then it is though the Sugar is near clean.

He dined at the fort, and went to a play. Of the fort he says, "its pretty strongly fortified and mounts about 36 Guns within the fortifu. but 2 facine Batterys mg. 51."

The brothers were pleasantly received and agreeably entertained; except in one case, where the entertainment was a trifle queer, to say the least. A Major Clarke invited them to breakfast and dinner, but they were reluctant to go, as the Clarke family had smallpox.

It seems incredible that any one with smallpox in his house should give a dinner party, but this extraordinary Clarke person did that very thing. George and Lawrence faced smallpox with the punctilious courage of Virginia gentlemen. In a fortnight George was down with the disease.

He was up and about in three weeks, but there was an end to comeliness. For the rest of his life he was to show a face disfigured by pockmarks.

The hot climate did Lawrence no good. Some one suggested Bermuda, and he went there, while George returned home with the idea of taking Lawrence's wife to her husband. Before this could be done Lawrence came home dying, and did die at Mount Vernon on July 26th, 1752.

Lawrence left the Mount Vernon estate to his infant daughter, with George as his executor and manager. In case of his daughter's death, his will provided that George should inherit the property, though Mrs. Lawrence Washington was to receive annually a part of its income.

A strange twist of Fate had put him in his brother's place; in the place of the admirable Lawrence, whom George had glorified in the way that strong, slow-thinking, courageous men glorify delicate, quick-thinking, courageous men. He possessed the reversion of his brother's estate, and he stood in a parental relation toward his brother's child.

And he had his brother's military office.

When Lawrence took to his bed in his last days, he resigned his position as one of the adjutant-generals of the colony. George was appointed in his stead. There were four adjutant-generals, and it was an amateurish, ornamental sort of office. These officials were expected to overlook the militia of their districts and see that they were up to the mark. The salary was £150 a year, which was excellent pay for those days.

In a short time Lawrence's little daughter died, and George found himself the owner of Mount Vernon, with its manor house, its twenty-five hundred acres and its flock of slaves. In a few years he paid Lawrence's widow a lump sum in lieu of the annuity, and she released him from further payments.

Later, we shall see George marrying a lady of fortune, as

his brother had done, and becoming the stepfather of another little girl.

§ 2

Now there is no longer a simple story before us. We cannot go in a straight line any more. Powerful and remote personalities and events big with destiny are crowding in on this Virginia tobacco farmer. Our road has become circuitous and roundabout. The world in which Washington lives has suddenly grown very large, and very subtle—but he does not know it. If he would only look up from his fruit-tree planting he would see that the horizon has been pushed back three thousand miles. But he does not look up, and never did during his whole life. His capacity was for doing whatever lay before him to do. He never saw the larger horizons, and did not think much about them.

He is about to play a part on the world's chess board, first as a pawn; then as the next larger piece; then the next larger; and the next larger; until eventually the game will centre about him and everybody on earth will be staring at him.

Now we must take a glance about the world and see how the ancient rivalry of England and France for the possession of the American continent brought George Washington into public attention.

§ 3

On the map of North America as it was in 1753 the red splash of England's empire looked pretty thin. Thirteen English colonies in a row. On one side was the Atlantic, and on the three other sides lay the extensive but rather morose possessions of France and Spain.

At the top of the map was the haggard wolf-preserve of Canada, which was wholly French; or, to be more accurate, it was Indian with a dash of French.

In the other direction, south of Georgia, the proud Spaniard held the land of Florida, which contained at that time nothing much except pride and alligators.

To the westward, beyond the Appalachians, the French possessions had the generous dimensions of an imperial dream. There had been a time when white hands and lordly gestures fluttering over charts at Versailles and Fontainebleau had traced an American empire on paper.

Then the white hands had become bored, and the maps were laid away and forgotten for a hundred years.

But the dream had thrilled and amused. It had been a plaything for a little while; and before the white hands had turned to something else commands had been given. France was an absolute monarchy. People were supposed to do what they were told to do; they awaited the word of command, and when ordered they obeyed. Men with French speech on their lips floated in canoes down the Ohio and the Mississippi. They crossed the distant prairies and stared in wonder at the western wall of mountains. Priests came, too. Priests with a thirst for martyrdom in their eyes; priests who died, happy in oblivion, amid unwritten orgies of Indian torture.

When the white hands fluttered over the maps again France in the New World was not merely Canada; it was all the Middle West, the Great Lakes, and the valleys of the Mississippi, the Missouri and the Ohio. It began vaguely at the Appalachians and ended vaguely at the Rockies.

The French were stronger on claims than they were on colonisation. The white population of their enormous territory, including the long-settled province of Quebec, was less than that of the colony of Connecticut. In the English North American colonies, there were about one million three hundred thousand people in 1750, while the French had only an estimated eighty thousand.

From Lake Erie to the Mississippi—and beyond—were the tiny trading posts of His Most Christian Majesty, the King

of France. Half-commercial, half-military, they were inhabited by sharp-eyed fur traders, a few priests and a few
idle soldiers, all under the command of bored *chevaliers* who
existed in the misery of Indian wives and bad whisky.

You can imagine, then, the great middle West as a lonely
and sombre forest—broken here and there by the billowy sweep
of prairies. Turgid yellow rivers rolled through the heart
of these immemórial woods. The inhabitants of the region
were mostly Indians, and there were not many even of them,
for the Indian population of the continent has always been
absurdly small. Thousands of square miles without a single
inhabitant.

Further north, along the St. Lawrence, there was a kind
of make-shift civilisation. Now and then, amid the perfumes
and charades of the Faubourg St. Germain, some French
statesman would have a pang over Canada, and he would
give orders to send there forthwith a shipload of indigent and
bovine peasants. They were sent forcibly, of course, and upon
arrival were turned loose with a paternal supply of provisions
and told to make the best of it.

Besides the differences of language and religion, the French
and English colonists were essentially different types in character. The French-Canadian—of the common people—was a
dull, plodding fellow, gregarious, living close to his kind about
a church or fort, and accustomed to take orders from an
official or a priest. He was often, probably in most cases,
married to an Indian squaw. His manifest tendency was not
to assert himself, but to sink back into a sort of primitive
inarticulateness. He had but little enterprise and little resentment; his inclination was to stay wherever he was put.
In short, the inert body of French colonial civilisation had
to be held up by main strength, by the long arm of Paris,
or it would have expired from mere listlessness.

The English-American colonial peasant or backwoodsman

had, on the other hand, a temperament in which an excessive individuality was mingled with a spirit of defiance.

The early English settlers had brought their women with them; they had come to stay; and the American colonies had grown in population more rapidly, by natural increase, than any other civilised race has ever grown either before or since.

Families of ten children were common. Procreation was a public necessity as well as an amorous function. An announced belief in birth control would have instantly branded the announcer as something lower than a horse thief. Great families of strapping boys and husky wenches, quickly outgrowing their clothes and passing them on to new and lesser waves of progeny. Desultory reading, writing and ciphering. Huge appetites. Red apples. Hard cider. Tame wolves. Foot-races and athletic games. Religious conversion. Beartraps. The hottest peach brandy in the world. Hymns bawled. Country frolics. Bastards. Shotguns. The air was full of quarrelling and laughing, of praying and fighting, of loving and drinking.

It was an era of coarse food and coarse opinions.

§ 4

The Ohio Valley, and indeed the whole of the Mississippi basin, was claimed by the English. Their claim was founded on the touch-and-go visits made by Cabot, the English explorer, to the Atlantic coast in the sixteenth century; and on the original charters granted to the colonists by the English kings. In Virginia's charter, for example, granted by James I, the territory of the colony is described, in the sweeping generosity of pen and ink, as reaching in a broad belt from the Atlantic to the Pacific Ocean, or the "South Sea" as it was called with foggy geographic indecision.

The French based their claim to the territory on exploration and occupation—such as it was. Frenchmen had been over the land west of the mountains, down its rivers, and through its forests, fifty years before an Englishman had ever set foot on it.

In the middle decades of the eighteenth century the governing minds of England began to realise that the most fertile part of the American continent was in the hands of the French. They began to fear that the great American power was to be France and not England. Melancholy maps were passed around at Whitehall, and dust was blown off one ancient document after another.

The question might have remained in a state of indetermination for another generation if the land hunger of the American colonists had not brought it to an issue. This was not a land hunger of the common people, but of the ruling classes.

The reason is that, in the colonies of the eighteenth century, land implied power—as finance does to-day. The greed for land was the central phenomenon of that epoch, as the greed for money is of this present epoch.

In 1747 Governor Dinwiddie of Virginia, with nineteen other gentlemen, organised a speculative land concern, called the Ohio Company. The governor became a stockholder of the enterprise in his private capacity. Then—that done—he turned around and took up his official pen and gave his own company five hundred thousand acres of land in the Ohio Valley. The land was not his to give, as it was located in territory claimed by the French. But he counted on the military support of the British government, and he had obtained the government's approval of his enterprise.

Among the stockholders of the Ohio Company were Augustine and Lawrence Washington.

The French were alert and forehanded. They heard of the company, and of settlers coming into French territory. They began to build a chain of forts from Lake Erie to the Ohio, and down the river all the way to French New Orleans.

The attitude of the English government in handling this

dispute was one of haughty amazement. They were surprised and astounded. They could not imagine why interlopers like the French could for a moment . . . etc. and etc. Their policy was, according to circumstances, to consider the French as either non-existent or to hold their claims as of no value whatever. In maintaining this frame of mind they were trying to prevent argument. If the rival contentions had been brought into a conference for adjudication the English would have been beaten hands down, for the French claim was perfectly sound according to the international standards of that day— and of this day, too. Therefore, the English maintained that there was nothing to discuss. It must be said for their argument that it had the merit of brevity.

§ 5

In the autumn of 1753 the land-speculating Governor Dinwiddie resolved to send to the French commander in the disputed territory a written demand that he evacuate the region immediately.

His message read, in part, that "the lands upon the River Ohio in the Western Parts of the Colony of Virginia are so notoriously known to be the Property of the Crown of Great Britain, that it is a matter of equal Concern and Surprize to me to hear that a Body of French Forces are erecting Fortresses and making Settlements upon that River within his Majesty's Dominions."

The governor selected Major George Washington—then a major by virtue of being one of the colony's adjutant-generals—to carry this letter to the French commander and receive his reply.

CHAPTER V

RAW PRIDE OF YOUTH

§ 1

In the historical panorama of the eighteenth century Washington's letter-carrying mission to the French commander has the dimensions of a fly-speck; but here we must discuss it momentously, for it was a momentous affair to him.

Several months before his selection for this duty another Virginian had been entrusted with a smiliar message, but he failed to reach the French headquarters. The wilderness had baffled him and its slinking savages had tripped his feet. Returning the letter undelivered and somewhat soiled, he made his excuses to the governor and sank without a bubble into the sea of historical obscurity.

Now, with this fiasco fluttering at its heels, the job puts on airs. It ceases to be a messenger boy's errand. There is a Message-to-Garcia atmosphere about it. It is heavy with unborn heroism.

Washington might have declined to undertake the mission without causing any adverse comment. He was under no obligation to deliver a letter to a Frenchman in a wilderness three hundred miles away when there were many men in Virginia who had already been through the Ohio country and knew it—men who were acquainted with the Indians and the French.

Besides, the management of the estate which he had inherited occupied his entire time; he was very busy with his acres and his slaves.

His instant willingness to go on this journey is interesting, in the face of such good reasons for not going. Let us linger here for a moment and feel around in the darkness for some tangible motive. When we know a man very well, but do not know his reason for any particular action, we are usually able to deduce his motive by setting up his action against the background of his life.

In this case, as in many other similar circumstances, Washington's principal impulse seems to have been one of vanity. I know that it may be amazing to many people to think of the Father of our Country as having vanity, but I cannot help it. He was vain, and his vanity was a creative force, as it often is when it is a quality of strong characters. Vanity as an impulse has without a doubt been of far more benefit to civilisation than modesty has ever been.

Another man had attempted to deliver the letter and had not succeeded. There was a feeling of emulation; a mark of achievement was set. Washington knew that on his return he was sure to be talked about and admired. Consider a bony and awkward young man, whose hands and feet are too large, and who has a passionate admiration for the ladies, but without much success in that field. He lacks the nimble wit—and, indeed, the knowledge of woman—to shine in a drawing-room, but he shines among men; and he knows very well that masculine glory is reflected back among the women. Fortunately, too—otherwise many a great man would be without a wife.

He was not vain in a light and frivolous sense; consequently his vanity, covered as it was by a manner of cold simplicity, usually escaped the observation of those who had only a feeble capacity for penetration. It was like a river flowing underground and appearing suddenly now and then on the surface.

It made him try to be different from other men in unexpected ways, but always within the conventional pattern. He did not want to be different in fundamental character. What he wanted was to be different by being on a higher level. In this we discern the valuable quality of self-esteem, though his self-esteem frequently ran over into vanity; and his ideals were sometimes snobbish.

If he had been a man of ideas, as Jefferson was, his self-esteem would have expressed itself in intellectual altitudes, as Jefferson's did.

Washington was a man of money and action, and his vanity came to light in activities connected with money and action. When he was appointed Commander-in-Chief of the Continental army at the beginning of the Revolution he declined, with thanks, to accept the pay for the position, which was five hundred dollars a month—and he served without pay throughout the war. This action set him apart at once from all the other officers, who had to take their pay, as they needed it to live. It was a patriotic action, of course, but it was also a snobbish action, because it made an immediate distinction on the basis of property. Washington was the wealthiest man in the army. It was not a heavy sacrifice for him to give up five hundred dollars a month. Nor was his renunciation of much value to Revolutionary finances, as his salary was only a drop in the bucket compared to the enormous cost of the war. If he had cared to make a real money contribution to the American cause he could have given a great deal more without seriously damaging his own financial resources.

If vanity was his chief motive, as I think it was, in undertaking this letter-carrying mission to the French commander, I am equally sure that a strong secondary motive was his love of physical adventure. He was a huntsman by inclination as well as by habit. No doubt the journey to the Ohio appealed to him as an adventure. Another reason was certainly his instinct to do whatever was to be done, and to do it promptly. He was the original *"Do It Now"* man.

§ 2

He was brisk in action, for he started the same day he received the appointment, which was the last day of October in 1753. As French interpreter he engaged Captain Jacob Van

Braam, a Dutch soldier of fortune who had served with Lawrence Washington in the Spanish War. He appears to have been a hanger-on at Mount Vernon, where he taught George Washington the use of the broadsword and military tactics.

Christopher Gist, a famous backwoodsman of the time, was employed as a guide. In addition to these two there were four or five servants—Indian traders and the like—who could speak the Indian languages. They were all on horseback.

The first leg of the journey was to Logstown, an Indian village which was situated on the north bank of the Ohio, about seventeen miles beyond the site of the city of Pittsburgh. Logstown was the headquarters of Tanacharisson, an Indian chief who is better known in history as the Half-King.

The Half-King's curious title came from the fact that the Senecas, among whom he was the head man, were only semi-independent. The tribe was a vassal of the Iroquois.

Washington and his people remained at Logstown for several days, in a cloud of guttural Indian speech and council fire smoke. To persuade the Indians to hate the French and fight them was a part of his mission.

In his effort to obtain the friendship of these Indians Washington made sonorous speeches, with an interpreter at his elbow; and the Indians made sonorous speeches in reply. None of this talk had any depth; none of it touched on the real situation of the Indians. Both the English and the French wanted their land. They were, in fact, a doomed race; but the talk on both sides was highflown and romantic. In the end the Indians agreed to despise the French.

Then, this accomplished, the Half-King and several other Indians accompanied the expedition to the French general's fort, with the idea of breaking off relations with the French. This place—called Fort Le Bœuf—was twelve miles south of Lake Erie. It stood where Waterford, Pennsylvania, now stands.

The French received the mission with courtesy, good food and a variety of liquors. "They told me," Washington said, "That it was their absolute Design to take Possession of the Ohio, and by God, they would do it; For that altho they were sensible the English could raise two Men for their one; yet they knew their Motions were too slow and dilatory to prevent any Undertakings of theirs. They pretend to have an undoubted Right to the River, from a Discovery made by one La Salle 60 Years ago."

The French commander wrote a letter to the same effect to Governor Dinwiddie.

Then they started back; but the Half-King, after talking with the French, seemed to be much less enthusiastic over the prospects of the English, and the Indians gradually slipped away. It began to snow, and Washington came to the conclusion that the horses could not get through the snowdrifts which were piling up on the mountains.

So the horses were left behind to be brought in later by Van Braam. The situation was highly critical and dangerous, though this does not appear in Washington's account. His matter-of-fact coolness in the presence of danger is illuminating. We shall see it appear again and again throughout his life.

Washington, with Gist as his sole companion, started back to Virginia through the snow, on foot. Once they fell in a river and were almost frozen. On another occasion an Indian suddenly stepped out from behind a tree and fired point-blank at them at a distance of fifteen paces; but they reached home without serious mishap.

Governor Dinwiddie was pleased with Washington. He wanted an account of the trip written, that it might be printed for the enlightenment of the Council. Then he added that the manuscript had to be ready next day. Washington was aghast, but he set to work; and now, for a moment, we must watch the contortions of our hero in the toils of literature. He worked at the manuscript all night. In your fancy you may see him, a large, big-boned young man, sitting in a silent room before a little table decked with guttering candles. There is the inkpot and the paper and the goose-quill pen and the sand-shaker (looking like a salt-cellar) with the sand to be used in blotting the wet ink. At this equipment he looks in awe, as verbs and adjectives come creeping on all-fours through his mind.

When the work was finished he wrote a modest preface apologising for what he called its "numberless imperfections."

§ 3

Excitement now. Red-faced indignation. Hot talk by the stockholders of the Ohio Company. The most indignant people in the world, and the gloomiest, are disappointed land specu-lators. Was it possible that, after all, the French were to be allowed to destroy at one fell blow the hopes of millions yet unborn? Could it be possible that the grant of five hundred thousand acres would turn out to be mere worthless paper? Would honest men stand idly by and see their homes burned their women ravished, their children begging bread, while Frenchism and Popery were established in England's fairest colonies? Great excitement in the Ohio Company, but not much among the common people.

Governor Dinwiddie tried to get an appropriation from the Burgesses to equip a formidable military force to be used to expel the French, but the money-tight legislators voted it down.

There were other ways and means. The governor inspired the Ohio Company to begin the building of a fort, out of its own resources, at the junction of the Allegheny and Monon-gahela rivers. This outpost, afterwards held by the French and called Fort Duquesne, and then by the English and called Fort Pitt, is now held by steel millionaires and is called Pitts-burgh.

Then the governor wrote to the neighbouring colonies on the subject of the great menace. The answers were not encouraging. The Pennsylvania Assembly replied that His Majesty's claim to the Ohio lands was doubtful in their opinion. New York held the same views. "It appears that the French have built a fort at a place called French Creek," wrote the New York Assembly, "at a considerable distance from the River Ohio, which may, but does not by any evidence or information appear to us to be, an invasion of any of his Majesty's colonies."

Nevertheless, Governor Dinwiddie raised a force of two or three hundred men, shiftless idlers most of them, and paid them eight pence a day out of some funds which were at his disposal. The command of this force was given to a Colonel Fry, who was described by Governor Dinwiddie as "a man of good sense and one of our best mathematicians." He was instructed to proceed to the Ohio Company's fort, assist in building it, and to occupy it as a garrison.

The second in command of this expedition was George Washington.

§ 4

By the end of April, 1754, the advance detachment, composed of about one hundred and fifty men and commanded by Washington, had reached Will's Creek—a settlement which is now Cumberland, Md. Colonel Fry was still in Virginia. News had come that the French, a thousand strong and with eighteen pieces of artillery, had advanced upon the Ohio Company's half-finished fort and had compelled its surrender.

Bad news, indeed. To decide what to do, Washington called a council of his scraggy officers. One of them, a Captain MacKaye, sat apart from the rest. He held a King's commission, and all the others were only provincial officers. Although the expedition was a Virginia affair, with nothing royal about it, MacKaye refused to take orders from anybody, and conducted his company as a separate institution.

There was really nothing to do that was sensible except to stay where they were and await reinforcements, or fortify their position, or go back home. Word had come, however, that the French force had been considerably overestimated, and that they had only five hundred men and nine cannon. Small comfort. What could a hundred and fifty men do against five hundred?

Washington decided to stay where he was, so he sent to Col. Fry for reinforcements. Col. Fry—"best of mathematicians"—was a soldier whose military genius consisted of an infinite capacity for taking pains. Back in Virginia he drilled his men, built roads, and enforced discipline. Before he got through taking pains he fell off his horse and killed himself, and Washington became the commander of the expedition.

There was an irresolute air about the entire project. Washington marched his men back and forth and plainly did not know what to do. The odds were too great for Washington to take the offensive. His course was one of indecision; he was like a small and pugnacious terrier walking up and down and barking before a yard full of large and equally pugnacious foes. He possessed an utterly stubborn courage. Again and again this quality appears in his actions. It was the tough-fibred fortitude that conquers new empires, because it makes a man hold his ground regardless of odds. But while he was being so brave ,he might have built a decently strong fort, which he neglected to do.

Hare-brained schemes came into his mind. He learned from the Indians that the French camped outside of their in complete fortification at the forks of the Ohio. He conceived a plan of approaching the place at night and getting inside of the fort. An exploit that would have given joy to even the daring soul of Lawrence. Cartagena and the flaming guns!

Glorious! But his force was so unequal to the task that he

gave it up. Twenty-two years later, on the day after Christmas, 1776, he carried out this hare-brained scheme by attacking the British at Trenton on a snowy night and seizing the town before they were awake.

Now the Indian appears in the picture as the white man's hope. Where's the Half-King, noble ally and copper-coloured brother? Swift Indian runners, full of meat and bread, are dispatched toward the horizon. Get the Half-King, and the other chiefs. Bring them to the camp. The ancient friendship. The perfidious French. Two hearts that beat as one—the Indian heart and the English heart.

It is obvious that the program of arrangements called for a good deal of fighting on the part of the Indians.

The tall chiefs came to the flimsy little fort which Washington had flung together at Great Meadows, a place about forty miles from the French position. The tall chiefs lifting the open palm of friendship, but thinking God knows what.

Washington's talk to the Indians was not without guile. Here is an extract from it:

> The English do not intend to hurt you, or any of your allies; this report we know must have been forged by the French, who are always treacherous, asserting the greatest falsehoods whenever they think they will turn out to their advantage; they speak well, promise fine things, but all from the lips only; whilst their heart is corrupt and full of the poison of the serpent.
>
> You have been their children and they have done everything for you, but they no sooner thought themselves strong enough than they returned to their natural pride and drove you off from your lands, declaring you had no right on the Ohio.
>
> The English, your real friends, are too generous to think of ever using the Six Nations, their faithful allies, in such a manner; after you had gone to the governors of

Virginia and Pennsylvania they (at your repeated request) sent an army to maintain your rights; to put you again in possession of your lands, and to take care of your wives and children, to dispossess the French, to maintain your rights and to secure the whole country for you; for these very ends are the English arms now employed.[1]

In short, the war was for the purpose of making the world safe for the Indians.

§ 5

Indian striplings came, breathless with news. The French were approaching, they said, and were encamped not far away. A small party, but they did not know how many. They could lead Washington and his men to the spot.

Washington hid his ammunition and left a small guard over it. "With the rest of my men set out in a heavy rain, and in a night as dark as pitch, along a path scarce broad enough for one man; we were sometimes fifteen or twenty minutes out of the path before we could come to it again, and we would often strike against each other in the darkness."

At sunrise the Virginians and Indians reached the French camp in the dripping woods and made an immediate attack without preliminaries. There were about thirty French; most of them were asleep. Ten of them were killed, among them M. de Jumonville, the commander; one was wounded, and twenty-one were made prisoners.

This exploit had a terrific reverberation. The French

[1] This speech was included in Washington's journal which was captured by the French. They sent it to Paris, where it was translated into French and printed in 1756. A printed copy which reached New York was translated back into English, and was published in 1757. Washington read it and he said that it was "certainly and strangely metamorphosed," and that the English was "very incorrect and nonsensical," but he did not disown the substance of the journal. The speech given above therefore contains his argument to the Indians, though not in his own words.

claimed that their party was out under a flag of truce, that they bore dispatches and that Washington would have learned as much if he had hailed them before he rushed their camp and opened fire.

I do not know whether this is so. The evidence is confused.

There was a great commotion in France. Washington acquired there the reputation of being a murderer, and a French poet told the tale of his atrocity in stale iambic verse.

The Jumonville fight occurred on May 28th. The French became a swarm of angry bees. By the third day of July they had driven Washington into his patchwork fort in the Great Meadows. The rain was falling in torrents, and the French were besieging the place with seven hundred men. Washington had received some reinforcements by this time, and there were about three hundred and fifty bedraggled troops under his command.

Fort Necessity, as his fort was called, combined in its location and construction almost every conceivable military error. It was located in a bottom, by the side of a creek, with higher ground all around it. During even a moderate rain the place, draining the water from the surrounding slopes, turned itself into a boggy puddle of mud. At all times the interior of the work could be seen from the nearby elevations.

After nine hours of siege Washington decided to surrender. Though the most generous critic cannot excuse him for building his fort in such a position, no one can term his capitulation as anything less than urgently necessary. It was impossible for a man to lie down or sit down in the fort unless he was willing to take his repose in several inches of water.

The French terms were liberal enough. The command was to be allowed to march back to Virginia with the honours of war, though deprived of arms; and Washington, on behalf of Virginia, agreed not to build another fort on the Ohio for the period of a year.

Here the learned Van Braam comes forward again—skilled

in the lexicons, knowing the French of Paris, Touraine and
Picardy. The paper is given to him to construe by the light
of a candle in a dripping tent. The air is damp, the table is
damp, the ground is damp, clothes are damp, spirits are damp,
everything is damp. The French paper of capitulation says
very plainly that Washington acknowledges himself to be the
assassin of M. de Jumonville, but Van Braam translates
"l'assassinat" as "causing the death of" Jumonville. Quite
a different meaning. Men kill other men in war, but do not
assassinate them. They assassinate them only in time of peace,
though the effect is the same, so far as the victim is concerned.

Paul Leicester Ford says that one of the Virginia officers
declined to sign the capitulation because the word *assassinat*
was in it. I have not been able to ascertain what officer this
was, or to come upon Mr. Ford's source of information, and
I repeat his statement here solely on his well-known trust-
worthiness as a historian.

One may readily see that if Mr. Ford's assertion is correct,
it puts Washington in a bad light. In that case, it would
appear that Washington knew that he was confessing to an
assassination, and only took his stand of ignorance when he
found out that the paper was to be the focus of a large row in
Virginia. The question was complicated by the absence of
Van Braam. He had been taken by the French as a hostage,
and never returned to Virginia.

At any rate, Washington's disclaimer was finally accepted
by the House of Burgesses. They gave him a vote of thanks,
and a sum equivalent to $3.60 apiece to his men. War was
cheap in colonial times.

§ 6

That is all very well, but listen to the Half-King. He seems
to have been a half-and-half man all around, for he smoked
the pipe of alliance with Washington and accepted his rum

and supplies, then, as soon as the fighting began he drew his warriors off. They sat in the background, like spectators at a football game, and watched the French and the English fight it out.

He was not much use in warfare, but he was good at criticism. This is his comment:

> The colonel [meaning Washington] was a good-natured man, but had no experience; he took upon him to command the Indians as his slaves, and would have them every day upon the scout and to attack the enemy by themselves, but would by no means take advice from the Indians. He lay in one place from one full moon to the other, without making any fortifications, except that little thing on the meadow, whereas, had he taken advice, and built such fortifications as I advised him, he might easily have beat off the French. But the French in the engagement acted like cowards, and the English like fools.

Notwithstanding this disastrous failure, Washington found himself a popular hero on this return to Virginia.

In a military career the way to popular esteem has nothing to do with success or failure. The technique of heroism belongs to the dramatic arts. The military hero appeals to the imagination, and not to the reason, for war itself is an unreasonable and fantastic occurrence.

Consider, if you please, the respective positions of George Washington and Captain Trent. This last-named gentleman was the commander of the Ohio Company's immature fort on the site of Pittsburgh. His force consisted of thirty-three men. Five hundred French soldiers, with nine pieces of artillery, descended upon this feeble garrison, and it surrendered. Captain Trent was absent at the time, as he had gone to meet Washington for the purpose of urging him to hurry up. If he had been at the fort his presence would not have made any difference. Even Napoleon would have surrendered under the circumstances.

Captain Trent went back to Virginia to meet the scorn of a furious governor. That was the last of him; he was out of luck.

But what about Washington? Was there anything worthy of praise in his conduct? Hardly. Trent had only thirty-three men, and he surrendered to an opposing force of five hundred. Washington had three hundred and fifty men and he surrendered to a force of seven hundred, besides signing (perhaps unwittingly) a confession of murder. He had plenty of time to build and stock a fort that would have held off twice seven hundred Frenchmen . . . and he neglected to do it.

Washington got a vote of thanks and became a hero. His conduct thrilled the dramatic sense. The throb and stir of a Drury Lane melodrama were about it, especially in the big last act. We see the curtain rising on a stage illumined by the pale grey light of a wet and rainy afternoon. Mud. A tent in rags. Dead men. A wounded man, lying flat on the ground, breathes heavily, and attempts to speak. There is the rattle of gunfire and now and then the deafening roar of a cannon . . . young Washington enters and stands for an instant in the glare of the spotlight. His face is haggard and worn. He is the symbol of Virginia; and of Virginian courage.

The people of Virginia, in a time when there were neither theatres nor movies, considered it a splendid performance. They felt that, at last, there was an administration which was giving them some little return for the taxes it had collected for years and years.

§ 7

Suppose Captain Trent had been fatuous enough to fight the French with his thirty-three men, surrendering finally with a musket in his hands, a dabble of blood on his face, and their thirty-three corpses lying around him. . . .

§ 8

After the affair of Fort Necessity brother Jack—or John Augustine—received a letter from brother George, in which the campaign was briefly described. In this epistle he wrote, "I have heard the bullets whistle; and, believe me, there is something charming in the sound."

In that day all roads led to London; and, after awhile, "I have heard the bullets whistle . . . something charming in the sound" reached the imperial city, and was printed with an amusing comment by Horace Walpole.

"He has not heard many," remarked the stolid George II— himself the hero of Dettingen—"or he would not think them very charming."

Washington's youthful boast went around London, and people had a good laugh. Some were amused more than others; and some were not amused at all. Cecil Calvert wrote back to Baltimore from London, "The defeat of Major George Washington by his unmilitary skill is the subject here."

Criticism and laughter. But even so. . . .

He was only twenty-two and he was being talked about in London and his name had been printed in the newspapers there. Many a man lives a long life without his name appearing in print in any way, good or bad, until it appears as a paid funeral notice.

During the next spring we hear of Washington at a dinner given to a number of gentlemen in honour of General Braddock, who had just arrived from England. Col. John L. Peyton, who was at the dinner, wrote that Washington's countenance was "mild and pleasant, promising both wit and judgment. He is of a comely and dignified demeanour, and at the same time displays much self-reliance and decision. He strikes me as being a young man of an extraordinary and exalted character, and—"

Now, consider this prophecy from the Cassandra-like pen of Colonel Peyton:

"—is destined, I am of opinion, to make no inconsiderable figure in our country."

Here we have a glimpse of the remarkable impression that he always made on men. In appearance he was distinctly impressive. He was six feet two inches tall, though he invariably described himself as "six feet in stature"—a curious error for him to have made. His handshake was like hard steel, and his cold grey-blue eyes looked straight at people, in silent appraisal. Whenever he entered a room where he was not known, every one wondered who he was and felt that Somebody Special had arrived.

CHAPTER VI

THE CONFIDENT GENERAL BRADDOCK

§ 1

THE inscrutable wisdom which rumbles like thunder through the heads of the mighty must have been the inspiration of the British ministry when it sent General Edward Braddock, early in 1755, to America as the commander of His Majesty's forces. His appointment cannot be explained otherwise. To any brand of wisdom that is not inscrutable he appears to have been about the worst selection that could have been made.

Braddock had been a soldier all his life; he was about sixty years of age. His experience had been so extensive that he was choked with it, and had no capacity for absorbing new impressions. All his opinions had hardened into prejudices which were impervious to any known solvent. In manner he was brutal and arbitrary; in fortune he was desperate; he had lost nearly everything he possessed in the gambling clubs of London.

Washington's defeat and the French occupation of the Ohio territory had stirred the British government to action. They had resolved on a general war with France—the skirmish at Fort Necessity was looked upon as merely an impromptu clash—and Braddock's landing at Alexandria with two half-regiments was the first move.

He had hardly arrived in America before the British government, with a neat sense of forehandedness, gave instructions to privateers to seize every French vessel they came across, although France and England were then at peace. War was not declared until 1756, but before the close of the year 1755 the British had taken three hundred merchant ships and seven thousand French seamen.

This wholesale capture of French merchant vessels did not cause as much excitement at Versailles as any one living in the twentieth century would think it should have caused. The reason is that the French court was agitated to its core by a mighty question which eclipsed all other subjects. Madame de Pompadour, the king's mistress, had demanded the privileges of the *tabouret*—that is, the right to sit down at Court functions, like the royal princesses. The Court was sharply divided. One party saw the ruin of France in sight if this unheard-of self-assertion were encouraged; the other party, liberal in tendency, believed it to be a step in the direction of progress.

Louis XV eventually agreed with the more radical thinkers, and did give her the privilege of the tabouret. Indeed, he went further; he made her the Superintendent of the Queen, a position in which her duty was to see that the Queen behaved like a queen.

Under these circumstances one can understand why the French government neglected the dispute with England for the time being.

But with that question settled, let us leave Madame de Pompadour with her velvet tabouret, and return to the cast-iron Braddock.

The Potomac River before Alexandria is crowded with ships, and the little town is ready to burst with excitement. The thunder of the guns, the great white sails and the flaring naval flag of England. The redcoats come down the ships' sides in tight-lipped martial melancholy—mistaken for sternness—and there are drills, reviews, salutes, and bayonet charges at imaginary foes. The might of Britain is irresistible, and General Braddock proves it to the village of Alexandria. Dances and dinners. The neighbouring gentle-folk meet the officers. Flowered silks rustle and fans from London and Firenze flutter through the long quadrilles.

Recruiting goes on. The regiments are to be brought up to full strength. Recruiting and drills. Five colonial governors

are invited to a conference with the general, and they eventually
arrive.

It is arranged that Braddock is to move against Fort
Duquesne, which is the name given to the captured Ohio Company's fort. A report comes that the French have completed
it, and its walls are twelve feet thick. Another report is that
the Indians are now all on the side of the French.

Braddock was to take Fort Duquesne. Governor Shirley,
of Massachusetts, was to capture the French post at Niagara;
and William Johnson—an extraordinary Irishman who had
lived for years in a queer primitive fashion on a large estate
above Albany, and who had a special knack for making friends
with Indians—was to raise a force for the capture of Crown
Point on Lake Champlain.

After capturing Fort Duquesne Braddock was to march
on to Niagara and join Governor Shirley. "Duquesne can
hardly detain me more than three or four days," he said, "and
then I can see nothing that can obstruct my march to Niagara."

§ 2

To this Alexandria camp came Colonel George Washington,
dining with the officers, dancing at the balls, and looking with
a wistful eye at the preparations.

He had left the service the year before because of an order
issued by the British War Office to the effect that provincial
officers, of whatever rank, should be subordinated to any
officer holding a King's commission. It was not clever of the
King's government to have done that—but the King's government was not clever in several other ways.

"You make mention," Washington wrote to a colonial official, "of my continuing in the service, and retaining my colonel's
commission. This idea has filled me with surprise; for, if you
think me capable of holding a commission that has neither
rank nor emolument annexed to it, you must entertain a very

contemptible opinion of my weakness, and believe me to be more empty than the commission itself. . . . Yet my inclinations are strongly bent to arms."

There can be no doubt that he wanted to take a part in these military operations, but his desire to preserve his dignity was even greater than his martial ardour.

Braddock's thinking was a sort of mental operation by which several antecedent prejudices were combined to form a new prejudice. He thought about colonial soldiers and had a boundless contempt for them. Nevertheless, some appreciation of Washington's soldierly qualities trickled through his airtight mind and he invited him to join the expedition. Braddock had no authority to give a commission higher than that of a captain, and Washington insisted on being a colonel or nothing. The matter was finally settled by Braddock making Washington his personal aide-de-camp. In this position he was outside the military hierarchy and was called Colonel by courtesy.

Washington joined the staff and Braddock settled down to a perpetual dinner-table dissertation on the defects, cowardice and lack of discipline of the American militia, Washington (being present company) alone excepted. The young man replied vigorously and so the discussion went on and on, in circles, day after day.

"Instead of blaming the individuals"—referring to contractors who failed to deliver supplies—"as he ought, he [General Braddock] charges all his disappointments to publick supineness, and looks upon the country, I believe, as void of honour and honesty. We have frequent disputes on this head, which are maintained with warmth on both sides, especially on his, who is incapable of arguing without, or giving up any point he asserts, let it be ever so incompatible with reason or common sense."

Thus Washington wrote to his friend William Fairfax.

§ 3

First and last, there was a good deal of writing to the Fairfax family. On May 14, 1755, he wrote to Mrs. Sally Fairfax from Fort Cumberland, where Braddock's column was
resting on its way to Fort Duquesne, that he has found out
why Mrs. Wardrope is a favorite with the general. The cause
of the fascination she exercises, he assures his correspondent,
is "nothing less than a present of delicious cake and potted
wood-cocks."

Mrs. Fairfax seems not to have replied to this letter, but in
June Washington takes his pen in hand again, and says to
Mrs. Sally:

> Dear Madam: When I had the happiness to see you
> last you expressed an inclination to be informed of my
> safe arrival in camp with the Charge that was intrusted
> to my care [he means the army's pay, which he con-
> veyed to Fort Cumberland], but at the same time desired
> it might be communicated in a letter to somebody of your
> acquaintance.

How stilted and formal these Virginia gentlefolk were in
their philandering! Wants to hear from him, but pretends
that she wants him to write, not to her, but to somebody of
her acquaintance. Of course, she was a married woman—and,
in that day, married women were not supposed to correspond
with young men.

> This I took as a gentle rebuke and a polite manner of
> forbidding my corresponding with you; and conceive this
> opinion is not illy founded when I reflect that I have
> hitherto found it impracticable to engage one moment
> of your attention.

A mere form of speech; he has known her very well for
seven years.

If I am right in this, I hope you will excuse the present presumption and lay the imputation to elateness at my successful arrival. If, on the contrary, these are fearful apprehensions only, how easy it is to remove my suspicions, enliven my spirits, and make me happier than the day is long by honouring me with a correspondence which you did once partly promise to do. . . .

Mrs. Sally Fairfax was a tall, handsome brunette, and is said to have been very attractive. There is some faint reason to believe that she encouraged Washington to read books, and that she talked to him on the subjects which are of interest to cultured people.

He acted occasionally in amateur plays in which she also appeared. Mrs. Fairfax was probably a woman of virtue, though the extremely slippery nature of this quality always gives it an air of uncertainty. I think that Washington had been in love with her from the time he first met her, but had never told her so. She was his friend's wife; and that alone, unless I am greatly in error as to his character, would have prevented him from revealing his affection in any definite manner.

In those days men only were supposed to possess individuality or to have desires. Men owned their wives; and to be very friendly with another man's wife was not only bad morals but also bad manners.

§ 4

Before Braddock had left England somebody in London had written to Lord Fairfax, describing Braddock as a general devoid of "both fear and common sense." By the time the expedition had reached Will's Creek—then renamed Fort Cumberland—the colonial officers with the column realised vividly that the common sense part of this observation was true. They were soon to learn that the fear part of it was equally accurate.

On the battlefields of Europe he had met the French, and he respected them as fighting men. But he knew that their force at Fort Duquesne was insignificant, and that they had to depend mainly on the Indians to do their fighting. For these Braddock's contempt was both ignorant and deep. He had been urgently advised by Washington and other colonials to allow his men to be taught the backwoods style of fighting, which was to scatter and take advantage of the shelter of rocks and trees; but he thought this beneath the dignity of a British soldier.

Braddock's superb confidence impressed the civilian population, though it caused misgivings among the colonial military officers. Benjamin Franklin tells, in his autobiography, of a subscription paper in circulation in Philadelphia at that time to raise money for fireworks which were to be used in celebrating the capture of Fort Duquesne. They asked the cautious Franklin to contribute, and "seemed surprised that I did not immediately comply with their proposal. 'Why the devil!' says one of them. 'You surely don't suppose that the fort will not be taken?'" To this Franklin replied that events i war are very uncertain. Thereupon the subscription wa dropped, and "The projectors thereby missed the mortificatio they would have undergone if the firework had been prepared.

Despite his metallic obstinacy, Braddock did accept one suggestion, which was from Washington, and was tragically unsound. It contributed greatly to his disaster, without a doubt. It came out of Washington's impetuous eagerness to be moving ahead. This was difficult to do on account of the wagon train, which wound itself over the hills like a long slithering snake; and on account of the large number of cattle which had been brought along for food.

On Washington's advice Braddock divided his force—it consisted of about 2200 men—and went ahead with half of them, while the remainder followed one or two days' behind.

With an undivided force, immensely superior in numbers
to anything the French could bring against him, he would have
been able, in all probability, to hold his ground, in spite of his
insistence on a mode of warfare wholly unsuitable to backwoods fighting.

The regular troops of the advance detachment were de-
pressed in spirit after they had left their comrades behind.
The silent forest closed around them. They felt themselves
sinking in it as a man sinks in deep green water. These
British troops were accustomed to war on the road-wrinkled
terrain of Europe. A skittish sense of panic grew in their
hearts. They thought they saw Indians behind every tree;
stories of men burned at the stake went around their camps.

The colonials were not at top-notch, either. All the military
flummery of Europe had been imposed on them, marching in
regular order, keeping step, and salutes to eighty-odd officers.

On July 9th, 1755, the first column had crossed the Mo-
nongahela, and was proceeding briskly toward Fort Duquesne,
which was about ten miles away. General Gage—then a Colonel
—whom we shall see twenty years later as Washington's adversary on the hills of Boston, was in command of the regiment
in front. With the column there was another British officer,
Horatio Gates, a red-faced captain, who was destined to rise
to eminence in the Continental army, and to become Washington's secret enemy.

The route lay through a beautiful country. Beautiful then,
but not so beautiful now, for the steel-manufacturing town
of Braddock is built on the spot. In winter the bare trees
stood on the hilltops against the cold sky like sharp visual
music, but on this July day there were no bare trees. Summer
poured from the hills in wind-rippled cascades of green. A
sea of primeval silence. . . .

§ 5

The stillness is broken like the shattering of glass . . . with such breath-catching suddenness that no one knows what has happened. From the green cascade of forest leaps a sheet of red fire. Among the hills there is the crackle of musketry. The marching ranks stagger for an instant like a man who has been struck across the eyes. . . .

From the blank face of the woods, and from the ravines that run down from the hills, rises a sound that resembles nothing else that comes from a human throat . . . a long piercing screech, thin in texture, pure raw sound, without consonants or vowels, like the blood cry of a fighting animal. The Indian war whoop.

The officers run along the ranks of pale-faced men . . . *Close up, steady now, battle order, platoon formation, load and fire!*

Battle order! Discipline! Who can doubt it? The steadiest troops of Europe are standing there in their scarlet coats. Standing there, huddled like rabbits in a pen.

They cannot obey their officers . . . cannot hear them . . . the fierce gunfire—and the screaming woods . . . and there are bloody men lying under foot. . . .

Riderless horses, wet red spots spreading on their flanks, come dashing back from the front with a clatter of hoofs and a thrash of stirrups.

Platoons load and fire! Fire at what? At the smiling green woods, still smiling, with the white smoke drifting lazily over the tree tops? Here and there among the leaves appears a painted Indian face or a white French one, but only for a flash, like people peeping from windows.

Down the road there is a swirl of men and plunging cattle . . . and horsemen riding rapidly. General Braddock is coming up . . . and at his side rides Colonel Washington, lean and gaunt, sitting on a pillow instead of a saddle. He has been ill for days, laid up with a fever, and brought along in a covered wagon.

A river of panic flows through the noise and smoke. . . .

But look at the Virginians! They have forgotten all they learned in the instruction camp at Alexandria. Every man of them has left the ranks and is sneaking behind a tree or a rock, or running bent-over along the ground, stalking something in the woods, like a weasel-hunter.

General Braddock rides among the Virginians, striking them with his sword, and shouting that they are a disgrace to the British service. He orders them to stand up in the open and fight like white men. They do not pay any attention to him; nobody pays any attention to him. He is everywhere in the confusion of the fight, shouting something or other. A man devoid of both fear and common sense.

Now Colonel Washington shines. He is also without fear, but not without common sense. Of that valuable commodity he and the Virginians appear to possess a monopoly on this occasion. Washington keeps the Virginians in hand. They hold back the enemy while the wreck of Braddock's army races to safety.

A target for a hundred rifles, Washington remains on horseback . . . but not on the same horse, nor on the saddle-pillow. That first horse has long ago been shot down, and the pillow is lost forever to men and museums. He is on his third horse, and there are four bullet holes in his coat. He is unwounded, though. Those whom the gods have kissed cannot die until their destined course is run.

The road is cluttered with pop-eyed fugitives who have thrown away their arms, with wounded horses, with fear-crazed cattle, with overturned wagons, with bleeding men, trampled upon while they were begging piteously to be taken along.

A British officer, writing of this rout, said, "the scene beggar'd description." Very likely it did; but description was not the only thing that was beggared. The opinion of Colonel George Washington as to the valour and steadiness of British troops was reduced to beggary, or worse. A few days after Braddock's defeat, in writing to his mother, he said, "The dastardly behaviour of those they call regulars exposed all others who were inclined to do their duty to almost certain death; and at last, in despite of all the efforts of the officers to the contrary, they ran as sheep pursued by dogs and it was impossible to rally them."

As for General Braddock, he was carried mortally wounded from the field and died two days later. Died of a gun-shot wound and a broken heart, either of which is extremely unpleasant. When both come together they are usually fatal.

§ 6

Across the sea, in the Houses of Parliament beside the flattish Thames, silk-coated secretaries arose and read, in pleasant voices and with delicate gestures, the reports of Braddock's battle in which the name of a Colonel or Mr. Washington appeared frequently and favourably.

Already those whom fame attracts were rising from the ground. On September 5th of that year, Joseph Ball, an uncle whom Washington had never seen, and who practised law in London, wrote:

> Good cousin: It is a sensible pleasure to me to hear that you have behaved yourself with such a martial spirit in all your engagements with the French. . . . We have heard of General Braddock's defeat. Everybody blames his rash conduct. . . . I desire you, as you may have opportunity, to give me a short account how you proceed. I am your mother's brother. I hope you will not deny my request. . . . Your loving Uncle.

CHAPTER VII

THE OBJECTIVE LIFE

§ 1

THE historian McMaster called Washington the most elusive character in history, and he is not alone in his opinion. Whatever other qualities our Country's Father may have possessed, there can be no doubt that historians and biographers consider him to have been well supplied with *elusiveness*.

McMaster said that he did not understand Washington's inner life. That is why he called him elusive. The inner life of a man is the stream of feelings and impulses that flows through his soul. It is a dim and chaotic mingling of doubts and desires, perceptions, intuitions, dreams and hopes. From this inner life come the motives that impel the personality; but before these impulses become visible in action they are moulded by the will and whittled down into presentable shape by the reason.

Everybody is supposed to have more or less inner life—at least, I believe that is the prevailing opinion—but men of rich experience in the world know that the total volume of inner life is unequally distributed. Writers, historians, philosophers and men of that tribe have more inner life than they really need. On the other hand, there are many people who could take on a large amount of inner life without being harmed at all.

McMaster thought that Washington's inner life had never been understood and probably never would be.

From him we get the impression of a great human figure, sitting in dusky isolation, like a heroic statue in an empty

plain. To reach it we must travel a road that has been worn
so deep by McMaster, and Irving, and Sparks, and Wilson,
and Lodge—and innumerable others—that we cannot see over
its sides. It is cluttered with the prayer tablets of the pilgrims
who have preceded us; and we are out of breath from climbing
over the hurdles of reverence and fancy. We approach on
tiptoe; we utter the sibilant whispers of awe.

No wonder Washington's character appears elusive. Anybody's would under the circumstances.

But suppose we get out of the road and, going straight
across the field, walk up to Washington as one man walks up
to another. Doing that, we shall find that he is not nearly
as elusive as he seemed to be.

The background of elusiveness has been painted in the
picture by biographers who have looked into Washington's
soul for the quivering inner life which they themselves possessed.
When they did not find it there they lost their bearings and ran
around in circles.

Washington's mind was the *business mind*. He was not a
business man, in the modern sense; he did not live in a business
age. But the problems which he understood, and knew how
to solve, were executive problems; and he approached them
in the great executive manner.

His type of personality is not uncommon in America. There
are many Washingtons among us to-day. I know six or seven
myself. Such men are usually found in executive positions in
large-scale industrial or financial enterprises.

It is not the highest type of mind. Far from it. But it
has a certain hard greatness of its own.

Washington was an intense realist.

The realist is often an individualist; the two qualities seem to
be linked together. Washington was both.

If you are a dreamer, as most people are, playing in secret
with butterfly fancies, you may find it difficult to understand

what true realism is, for even the most matter-of-fact conceptions of the imaginative life are glazed over and softened by
delicate mind-colours.

The mind of the realist revolves around men and things. He
likes to bend men to his will, and he likes to possess things,
but he has more pleasure in getting things than he does in
owning them. He likes to play with things as the dreamer
plays with ideas. In war he is on his highest plane of being,
for there he is able to use men in packs and hunt with them as
one hunts with dogs.

When there is no war the realist tries to create the similitude
of one. He contrives to have business wars; campaigns in
which salesmen are the soldiers, and in which the objective is
the defeat of business rivals. And in the intervals he engages
in war on animals, or on something else—on works of the
imagination which he happens to dislike—on people who hold
opinions differing from his own. Sometimes he organises
laudable wars against disease, or poverty, and then the realist
is at his best. He has a constructive as well as a destructive
side, and his two opposing impulses are intermingled and confused. But his wars are always physical wars. He does not
fight with ideas, but with material force of one kind or another.

Washington possessed the superb self-confidence that comes
only to men whose inner life is faint, for the inner life is full
of nameless doubts. In the desperate days at Valley Forge,
when the British held Philadelphia, and it seemed to most men
that the American cause was slowly dying of cold and hunger,
Washington wrote to John Parke Custis, "Lands are permanent—rising fast in value—and will be very dear when our
independency is established."

He had the great qualities of confidence, courage, perseverance, fortitude—and, even more, he had good luck, without
which these qualities would have been unavailing. We have
seen that, in a critical moment of his young life, he met Lord
Thomas Fairfax. We shall see soon that, in another critical

LIFE MASK OF WASHINGTON

Taken by the French sculptor Houdon in October, 1785. This is one of the most famous of Washington's portraitures. Observe how closely the features resemble the Washington shown in Savage's painting used as a frontispiece to this volume.

moment, he will meet and marry the wealthiest woman in Virginia.

And there is to come another crisis, later in life, when action merges gradually into ideas. The day of action will be over, and whatever is to be done must be done in the arena of thought. We shall see Washington standing in that arena, blinded by the glare, but it shall be his good luck to have at his side, and attached to his cause, a youth named Alexander Hamilton.

However, we are running far ahead of our story. Hamilton is not yet born. In a distant Caribbean Island which stands in a sapphire sea, and looks like something made of jade and ivory, there is a rich middle-aged Jew with a young wife. Through the close-drawn lattice windows she watches for the coming of a handsome ne'er-do-well Scotchman. Philandering sometimes has very tangible results. It did in this case, and the result was Alexander Hamilton. His mind had the lucidity of crystal. His ideas fell on the slow moving mind of Washington as sunlight falls on houses in Spain.

§ 2

In eighteenth century America people were ill at ease in writing letters; indeed, they were ill at ease in writing anything. Wives, in writing to their husbands, addressed them as "Dear Sir." The days of "Hello, old dear," were still far in the future. Slang had not yet soaked into the written word, though it gave a pungent quality to the speech of the people. It did not appear in literature until the middle of the nineteenth century, and its advent synchronises with the democratisation of ideas and the adoption of humour as a literary vehicle.

In taking up the pen, men put on a pompous air and opened the Latin dictionary. That is, they did if they laid claim to culture. If they were among the uncultured their letters

had the flat wooden style of a report of the United States
Weather Bureau.

The average colonial American did his letter writing in
heavy phrases; his intellectual joints creaked for the want of
oil. He was badly in need of humour, of lightness, of fancy.

Yet, even in that stiff age, Washington's letters to his
mother are so cold and formal that they stand in high relief
against the fabric of epistolary custom. They usually began
with "Honoured Madam." Some of his biographers have argued
that this form of salutation indicates extreme filial affection
combined with respect.

I cannot agree with them. It is perfectly natural, in any
state of society, for a man to address his mother as "Dear
Mother," or in place of that phrase, to use some other form
of endearment. When he fails to do so it seems to me that
he is either a pompous person or he dislikes his mother.

When Mary Washington heard of Braddock's disaster she
wrote a letter to her son, in which she begged him not to go
to the war again. This is his reply:

> Honoured Madam: If it is in my power to avoid going
> to the Ohio again, I shall; but if the command is pressed
> upon me, by the general *voice* of the country, and offered
> upon such terms as cannot be objected against, it would
> reflect dishonour upon me to refuse; and *that*, I am sure
> must or *ought* to give you greater uneasiness, than my
> going in an honourable command, for upon no other terms
> I will accept of it. At present I have no other proposals
> made to me, nor have I any advice of such an intention,
> except from private hands.

He seems to be addressing a public meeting—"general
voice"—"command is pressed upon me"—"reflect dishonour"—
"upon no other terms."

His letter is naturally supposed to be intimate and confidential—the letter from a son to his mother—but he does not

give the name of the person or persons who have told him that he might be appointed to the command.

Several lines above he hands his mother a reproof. He writes, "it would reflect dishonour upon me to refuse; and *that* must"—

Then he ponders a moment and decides to put in "or *ought* to give," and underscores the *ought*. She may not be uneasy, he thinks, about "dishonour," but he tells her that she ought to be. The haughty tone of this letter reveals quite as much, or more, than its plain, brutal statements. She is informed that she is to have nothing to do with his decision, and he fails to thank her for her solicitude.

It happened that, on the very day he wrote this letter, which was August 14, 1755, he was appointed commander of the Virginia forces, and he rode down to Williamsburg to confer with the governor. A large young colonel, sitting high on his horse, with a servant coming along behind on a nag of meaner breed. The roads are bad, and in places, the horses sink to their knees in mud. As he enters the taverns the loungers in the porch arise and stand in pawky silence.

Washington swam in this air of obeisance as a fish swims in the sea. It was his element; he liked it. He liked to be haughty and reserved; haughty and courteous. Supercilious and courteous at the same time. The bolder of the tavern loungers speak to him. They have not forgotten that he was, after all, only a surveyor a few years before. People have even been known to speak to General Pershing. They speak to Washington and inquire about the war. He replies crisply and briefly, with good nature, saying nothing whatever. Then the tavern loungers go home, and tell all he said—and more. . . . "I was talking to Colonel Washington this morning . . . and I advised . . . and he said . . . and I told him . . . and he told me. . . ."

His manner toward his mother was dictatorial, as the letter which I have printed above clearly shows. She relied on him

implicitly, it seems, not only for advice and financial management, but also in small matters which must have tried his
patience. While he was on Braddock's campaign she wrote
to him and asked him to send her some butter and a Dutch
servant. Fancy that! Butter and a Dutch servant from a
soldier in a wilderness. He replied in an "Honoured Madam"
letter that there were neither butter nor servants where he was.

To her brother Joseph, in London, she wrote in 1759 that
"There was no end to my troubles while George was in the
army, but he has now given it up."

§ 3

After Braddock's defeat Virginia was frightened. Her
Burgesses, among whom was a sprinkling of the Ohio Company's stockholders, voted forty thousand pounds for the
defence of the colony; and the governor (also a stockholder)
appointed George Washington, another stockholder, to the
chief command of the colony's troops. A regiment of a thousand men was to be raised immediately.

Pennsylvania was alarmed, too, and even more than Virginia,
for the wreckage of Braddock's army had come streaming
back through Philadelphia. The Pennsylvania Assembly voted
fifty thousand pounds.

The British government put Governor William Shirley, of
Massachusetts, in Braddock's place as commander of all the
troops in the colonies. The New England colonies and New
York raised a considerable army, in the miniature colonial
sense of size, for the capture of Crown Point and Niagara.

Both of these attempts petered out. Braddock's papers, containing a complete plan of the campaign, had fallen into the
hands of the French, and they were prepared to resist at
every point.

Governor Shirley found the French at Niagara so strongly
fortified, and so ferocious in their demeanour, that he gave up

the attack, and contented himself with building a silly little
fort at Oswego, which the French captured easily in the course
of the next year.

William Johnson had better luck.   An Irishman by birth,
he had become half Indian by inclination.   He was a muscular
backwoods sybarite, living in the splendour of tallow drippings
and a harem full of comely squaws in the wilderness beyond
Albany.   His little army sifted through the woods toward the
fortress of Crown Point on Lake Champlain.   He failed to take
Crown Point, but he met the French in a pitched battle and
gave them a beating.   In this engagement the raw, undisciplined farmers of New England behaved like veterans—a fact
which received much comment in London.

Johnson's battle was the only success of the year, and
William Johnson sat down to await the applause.   It came
soon, from the British government, in the shape of five thousand acres of land and the title of Baronet.

Now we have Sir William Johnson, and a new hero.   "For
a short time," Sloane says, "he was the hero of the nation in
both America and England."

I wonder what Washington thought of that.   He had not
been noticed officially by the British government for his work
—which had been truly heroic—in saving the remnant of
Braddock's army.   Proud and touchy as he was, he must have
felt this slight deeply.

There were others who thought that he had not been properly recognised—Governor Dinwiddie among them.   We find
his letters to British headquarters, recommending Washington
for a commission in the regular army, which Washington was
anxious to get.   He is, Dinwiddie wrote, "a very deserving
gentleman. . . . General Braddock had so high an esteem
for his merit, that he made him one of his aides-de-camp, and
if he had survived, I believe he would have provided handsomely
for him in the regulars."

Nice letter, but nothing came of it.

The controversy over precedence between the holders of royal commissions and provincial officers was one of the major annoyances of Washington's life at this period. While he was on the Virginia border, trying to defend the settlers in the Shenandoah valley against the Indians, there arrived at his camp a Captain Dagworthy, with thirty Maryland volunteers. The captain held a commission signed by the king, and he announced his intention of taking charge of things, by virtue of his rank.

Captain with no backwoods experience; colonel with a lot of it. Captain who would not recognise Destiny if he met her face to face; colonel who sat on Destiny's lap and felt in her pockets for knick-knacks.

Naturally Washington was annoyed. He wrote to the governor and threatened to resign if Dagworthy were put over him. The governor did not know what to do. He wanted Washington to remain in command of Virginia troops—but then, on the other hand, there was the royal authority. Still, Virginia had raised the troops . . . and Dagworthy had only thirty men . . . so what right had he . . . but, nevertheless, the government's order that British officers should rank provincials was explicit. . . .

There seemed to be nothing left for the governor to do but pick the petals of a daisy and let that decide. In the meantime Captain Dagworthy sat down and waited for nature to take its course. After awhile Dinwiddie conceived the bright idea of passing the controversy along to Governor Shirley, who was the Commander-in-chief. His plan was to write a letter to Shirley in Boston, but Washington had learned the value of the personal touch, so he wanted to present his own case in person.

The governor gave him permission to go, and he set out for Boston on Feb. 4, 1756, accompanied by two aides and two servants, all riding horseback.

The journey was a rather gorgeous affair. Washington travelled in the grand manner. He and his people were dressed in the most elegant fashion. He wore a buff-and-blue uniform. His stockings were of white silk with silver knee-buckles, and there were silver buckles on his shoes. To the white linen stock around his neck an affair of lace ruffles—the thing that women call a "jabot"—was pinned, so that it fell over his bosom like a flowing modern necktie. His hair, allowed to grow long, was drawn tightly back in a queue which was enclosed in a silk bag. On his shoulders a cloak—one side white and the other scarlet —and at his side a sword with a golden hilt. Over his enormous hands fell cuffs of lace.

All this sounds like a Fairy Prince on his travels, but we must not forget that his face was pockmarked. The air of a fighter which he carried most of his life could hardly have been concealed by fine clothes.

His aides were dressed in similar fashion, but not so fine; and the servants were decked out in white-and-scarlet livery.

After eleven days on the road he arrived in New York on February 15, 1756, and remained there about a week before going on to Boston. It was the first time that he had ever visited either New York or Boston.

New York was then a town of approximately ten thousand people, of whom about one-fifth were negro slaves. It extended from the Battery northward to where the City Hall now is— about a mile. All the shipping, the docks and wharves, were on the East River. The town faded out west of Broadway rather suddenly and ended in a long beach, which ran up to the line of Trinity church.

It was a lovely, quiet town, with a gleam of sky and water in all parts of it. The streets were lined with trees, which gave a pleasant shade. On warm summer nights the trees were alive with katydids. (After the Revolution, in 1790, all the trees

in the streets of New York were cut down by the municipal authorities on the ground that their shade was unhealthy.)

But there was always the nuisance of mud. There were dry
sidewalks, though the roadways were not paved. In wet
weather walking was almost impossible. Fine ladies went calling in sedan chairs, or in carriages.

People coming home late at night with their flickering
lanterns would often meet long lines of slaves, marching duskily,
with buckets on their heads. That was the sewage system in
its routine functions. The slaves took the sewage in pails to
the waterfronts and dumped it in the river.

In New York Washington lost eight shillings at cards and
spent six shillings at "Mrs. Baron's rout." But cards and
routs were a mere nothing when compared with the fascination
of the "Microcosm." He saw it twice. On one ocasion he
took six ladies with him, and five the next time. Altogether
he spent two pounds twelve shillings in the contemplation of
its wonders.

The Microcosm was a miniature Roman temple filled with
mechanism—"twelve hundred wheels and pinions." Mechanical figures sawed wood, played music, "beating exact time to
each tune," and fired guns. There was an illusion of a pond—
a metallic pond on which ducks swam, "reaching back with their
bills to pluck their wings."

In Boston there was no "Microcosm," but there were other
diversions. Gambling was one. He must have played for high
stakes there, for he lost six pounds.

Clothes occupied his attention, too. He spent £95.7s for
clothing and decoration—a huge amount, considering the
value of money.

In the matter of tips he was singularly inconsistent. Between
New York and Boston he put down "servants, ten shillings,"
which apparently means tips, and not very large ones. But
in Boston he gave a chambermaid £1.2s.6d. This was a large
gratuity—equivalent to about five dollars and a half.

He dined with Governor Shirley and won his dispute with the insignificant Dagworthy. Back to Virginia he rode with Shirley's ruling that, as long as there were no king's troops on the border, Washington's rank as colonel should be valid.

§ 5

It was not a soldier's job, but a night watchman's. The Indians preferred cattle-stealing to fighting. Now and then they would murder and scalp some remote cabin settler in order to keep on drawing rum and rations from the French.

The main theatre of war lay far north along the St. Lawrence and around Lake Champlain. There the fate of France in the New World was to be decided. There, in the capture of Quebec by Wolfe, her great adventure was to come to an end. Washington never met Wolfe, Murray, Lord Amherst, any of the great figures of this northern campaign.

But he was at it from the end of 1755 to the end of 1758. His mood was black and sour; he was irritable and disgusted. There were twenty or more small, halloo-ing skirmishes where men fought blindly in the woods, but Washington writes no more of "whistling bullets," nor of "charming sounds."

He does write, however. His penmanship is thoroughly exercised.

Most of his letters are to Governor Dinwiddie, and they are letters of complaint. He complains about the quality of his subordinate officers, about the food supplied to the men, about the lack of clothing and supplies, about the impossibility of maintaining discipline without an adequate military code to enforce it. He complains even about the weather.

He acquires the impression that Dinwiddie is a vacillating old fool, and he does not take much pains to conceal it.

"My orders," he writes, "are dark, doubtful, and uncertain; to-day approved, to-morrow condemned. Left to act and proceed at hazard, accountable for the consequences, and blamed without the benefit of defence."

A captain sent by Washington to take command of a distant tiny fort found the men dissatisfied and clamorous. Somewhat agitated, the young officer wrote to Washington at once of these conditions, and said he was surprised to find things in such shape.

Just take a glance at this sheet of ice, which Washington sent him in reply:

> Your suffering such clamours among the men argues great remissness in you. I imagined your being put there over them was partly with an intent to keep them quiet and passive, but this express, sent purely to humour them, would indicate that you were afraid to do your duty. Let me tell you, in your own words, that "I was very much surprised" at the contents of your letter, written in such a commanding style. And your demands were so express and peremptory, that the direction was the only thing which gave me the least room to suspect it could be written to any but John Roe, or some other of your menial servants. I am sorry to find your conduct so disagreeable to all the officers, as to ocasion two, who were appointed to your company, to resign.

Poor forlorn captain, away off there in his little fort, hoping for sympathy. But Washington himself did not hesitate at complaining, or at criticising his superiors.

Some of the people of Virginia did not like the way affairs were conducted among the troops on the border. Too much drinking and carousing, they said. Too much immorality, and so on. There was a newspaper controversy about it. Some one wrote an anonymous article in the Virginia *Gazette*, and signed it "Centinel X," in which Washington's management was denounced as a smear of inefficiency—but not in those words.

It is a curious article. Rather long. Begins with Roman history, of course. It seemed impossible to start any public screed without introducing Caligula and Cato the Censor in the first paragraph. But this writer does even better. He shows how laxity brought the Roman empire to ruin; and then he goes on to Persia and Babylon. They were brought to ruin, too, by laxity. Lust of power ruined the Persian satraps. He hints that Washington is a Persian satrap, but he does not mention Washington's name, nor anybody's name. Some of Washington's friends thought that Governor Dinwiddie had inspired the article.

Washington wanted to resign, but finally decided to remain. He wrote a reply to the article and sent it to a printer of the *Gazette* with ten shillings. If it was published the newspaper in which it appeared has been lost.

Not long afterwards he wrote to his captains that there were too many women hanging around the camps, and that thereafter they were to supply rations to only six women for every hundred men. The proportion seems a trifle small, but no doubt he decided to err on the safe side.

Throughout this long and undistinguished campaign Washington's temper was at the explosive point. In his letters there is a strain of criticism of official methods, and particularly of British official methods. Governor Dinwiddie was recalled to England in 1758, but months before he left a quarrel had developed between him and Washington. The young man had a low opinion of arm-chair generals.

He wrote to his friends of "the ease, sloth and fatal inactivity" of his superiors. In his opinion, he wrote, a full representation of the state of affairs should be made to the King. "Let him know how grossly his glory and interest, and the public money, have been prostituted. I wish I were sent immediately home [he means to England] as an aid to some other on this errand. I think, without vanity, I could set the conduct of this expedition in its true colours."

The governor was milder in disposition. On the eve of his departure he wrote to Washington, "My conduct to you from the beginning was always friendly, but you know I had great

reason to suspect you of ingratitude, which I am convinced
your own conscience and reflection must allow, I had reason to
be angry, but this endeavour to forget."

The governor was an antiquated person, and Washington
was a poor subordinate. He was too proud and domineering,
and too ready to criticise his superiors and go over their heads.
Besides, he was physically ill for a long time during this campaign; and that partly explains his bad temper.

His illness was mysterious, and is still a mystery. In
November of 1757 he wrote to a physician that he wanted him
to call "that I may have an opportunity of consulting you on
a disorder which I have lingered under for three Months past.
It is painful for me to write. Mr. Carlyle will say the rest."
The ailment, whatever it was, continued for several months,
and for a time it was thought that he would be unable to undertake the 1758 campaign, but by August of that year he was
in sound health again. It is strange that no record of the
nature of this sickness has come down to us. It was undoubtedly serious.

The war, so far as Washington was concerned, dribbled
away ingloriously in the autumn of 1758. Although Quebec
was not taken by Wolfe until 1759, and the treaty of peace
was not signed until 1763, the French were already beginning
to feel the tightening English grip. One by one they drew
in their outposts. The French empire in America was slowly
crumbling to pieces. Fort Duquesne, which had cost them so
much in effort and privation, was abandoned, secretly and
quietly; and Washington marched into an empty fort.

With that accomplished, Virginia was practically out of the
war. Washington made no effort to serve with the armies at
the north. It was eighteen years before he was again in
military service.

CHAPTER VIII

PEARLS AND PETTICOATS

§ 1

COLONEL DANIEL PARKE CUSTIS, a wealthy gentleman of Virginia, dawdled along as a bachelor until love had ceased to be a passion and had become a duty. Then he married a girl of eighteen, produced two children and died.

The memory of Colonel Custis deserves some recognition from our patriotic societies. He did a great deal for the Father of our Country, though what he did was done unwittingly. Nevertheless, he helped a lot, and we ought not to pass him in silence. He accumulated the largest fortune—or one of the largest—in Virginia, and obligingly departed this life. His widow, thus bereft at an early age, married George Washington and brought her fortune with her.

Washington, who had been one of the Best People all along, as we have seen, thereupon became one of the Very Best People.

Colonel Custis had been dead about a year when his widow—a small, dumpy young woman, with dark eyes and a sharpish nose—went on a visit to her friends the Chamberlaynes, near Williamsburg. This was in May, 1758.

She was a mild young widow, easy to control, and possessing the standard domestic virtues. The streak of romanticism which she had in common with all other women found its solace in the reading of novels about "female jilts" and daring lovers who abducted fabulously attractive young ladies and married them without their consent.

§ 2

Colonel Washington stopped for a bite to eat at Major Chamberlayne's—everybody was a major or a colonel—and he was in a hurry. That is, he was in as much of a hurry as Virginia courtesy permitted, for he was on his way to Williamsburg to see Governor Fauquier—who was Dinwiddie's successor—about the condition of the troops on the frontier, and he was eager to get back to his military post.

Major Chamberlayne, who had gone on his horse to the ferry to meet Washington, mentioned his guest . . . Mrs. Daniel Parke Custis . . . formerly Miss Martha Dandridge . . . agreeable lady . . . rich . . . slathers of money, slaves, land. . . .

And so, in pleasant converse, they reach the great, airy house, with its cool green blinds softening the hard whiteness of its walls. Under the verandah's tall columns there is a flutter of ladies. Tall leisurely columns and the tall Washington. Servants stand at the horses' heads, and stable boys are astir. Washington hands his riding gloves to his servant; the gravel of the driveway crunches under his feet.

"Mrs. Custis, may I present my friend Colonel Washington"—pause—"of whom you have doubtless heard."

Yes, Mrs. Custis had heard of Colonel Washington. Everybody had. And he had heard of Mrs. Custis, too. In Virginia she was quite as celebrated as George Washington, but in a different way. If he was the bravest man, she was certainly the wealthiest woman.

Only the brave deserve the rich.

It was swift work. The Colonel did not go on to Williamsburg that day. The governor and official business had to wait. During the long afternoon he and Mrs. Custis sat alone in a parlour of the Chamberlayne house. Love at first sight.

There had been other suitors for the hand of Martha Custis;

there usually are, for the hands of wealthy young widows. Stammering gentlemen, a little dazed by the bright face of gold, falling on their knees, kissing finger-tips, reciting memorised speeches and departing in mawkish confusion.

But Washington was as fearless in the face of gold as he was in the face of danger. The haze of oblivion lies over what he said that afternoon in the Chamberlayne parlour. We do not know what it was, but we know that it was effective.

Next morning he went on to consult the governor. In a few days he started back to the frontier, but stopped for a brief moment at the home of Mrs. Custis, on York River. Immediately thereafter their engagement was announced.

There is a persistent tradition that he had already been rejected by several wealthy ladies. On his trip to Boston in 1756 he is said to have proposed, during his brief sojourn in New York, to Miss Mary Philipse, a wealthy heiress, and to have been rejected by her. There is no first-hand evidence to support this legend. Nevertheless, it may be true; there is nothing inherently improbable about it.

Most of Washington's biographers write of the Mary Philipse episode as a historical fact, a position which is wholly unwarranted. Washington Irving, who was very careful in respect to actualities, could find no confirmation of the story and said that he doubted it.

In the case of Miss Betsy Fauntleroy, who rejected Washington's proposal, we are better supplied with evidence. In 1752, soon after his return from Barbados, he wrote a letter to William Fauntleroy, in which he made this reference to Miss Betsy: "I should have been down long before this. . . . I was taken with a violent Pleurise, but purpose as soon as I recover my strength, to wait on Miss Betsy in hopes of a revocation of the former cruel sentence, and see if I can meet with any alteration in my favor. I have enclosed a letter to her, which should be much obliged to you for the delivery of it."

§ 3

After George Washington's death his widow burned every letter that she had ever received from him, with the exception of three or four, a handful that escaped apparently by accident.

No one has ever explained the motive behind this letter-burning episode. Martha Washington knew at the time—indeed, the whole world knew—that George Washington was a star of the first magnitude in the field of history, and that every scrap of his writing would be treasured and printed. Did she feel **that** his letters to her were so sacred in their intimacy that **posterity** had no right to read them?

Possibly.

But there are other tenable hypotheses. She was anti-democratic and anti-public to an extreme degree. Considering her as surrounded by such limitations of perspective, one may readily conceive that her motive may have been simply one of aristocratic seclusion.

In destroying his letters she effectually effaced herself, for she lived only in his reflected light. But that may have been what she wanted. The highest form of pride is a disdainful humility.

From another point of view it is a reasonable inference that these letters did not show her and her husband in a satisfactory relation to each other. His letters—many of them—were probably dictatorial, for that was his ordinary manner in communicating with other members of his family.

However, these are merely conjectures. We do not know why she destroyed his letters. She never gave her reasons. The episode lies at the bottom of the ocean of silence that covers so much of Washington's private life.

One of the letters which eluded Martha's incendiary hand is dated June 15, 1758, and is written from the headquarters of the column on its way to Fort Duquesne. When this letter was written George and Martha had been engaged about a month. He wrote:

> My dear: We have begun our march for the Ohio. A courier is starting for Williamsburg, and I embrace the opportunity to send a few words to one whose life is now inseparable from mine. Since that happy hour when we made our pledges to each other, my thoughts have been continually going to you as another self. That an all powerful Providence may keep us both in safety is the prayer of your ever faithful and affectionate friend, Geo. Washington.

Good, friendly letter, but full of reserves. Not the cosy sort of writing that flows naturally from men in love when writing to the ladies who have accepted them. He embraces "the opportunity to send a few words," and he does send very few of them. One thinks that the brisk hurry of the campaign is the reason for his telegraphic style; yet on September 12th, he wrote a letter to Mrs. Sally Fairfax that is not a bit telegraphic in manner. It was written from the camp at Fort Cumberland, and runs in these words:

> Dear Madam: Yesterday I was honoured with your *short* but very agreeable favour of the first inst. How joyfully I catch at the happy occasion of renewing a correspondence which I feared was disrelished on your part, I leave to time, that never failing Expositor of all things, and to a monitor equally as faithful in my own Breast to Testifie. In silence I now express my joy. Silence, which in some cases—I wish the present—speaks more intelligibly than the sweetest Eloquence.
>
> If you allow that any honour can be derived from my opposition to our present System of management you destroy the merit of it entirely in me by attributing my anxiety to the animating prospect of possessing Mrs. Custis, when—I need not name it, guess yourself—should not my own Honour and My Country's welfare be the

excitement? 'Tis true I profess myself a votary to love. I acknowledge that a lady is in the case; and further, I confess that this Lady is known to you. Yes, Madam, as well as she is to one who is too sensible to her charms to deny the Power whose influence he feels and must ever submit to. I feel the force of her amiable beauties in the recollection of a thousand tender passages that I could wish to obliterate till I am bid to revive them; but experience, alas! sadly reminds me how impossible this is, and evinces an opinion, which I have long entertained, that there is a Destiny which has the sovereign control of our actions not to be resisted by the strongest efforts of Human Nature.

You have drawn me, my dear Madam, or rather I have drawn myself, into an honest confession of a Simple fact. Misconstrue not my meaning, 'tis obvious; doubt it not, nor expose it. The world has no business to know the object of my love, declared in this manner to—you, when I want to conceal it. One thing above all things, in this world I wish to know, and only one person of your acquaintance can solve me that or guess my meaning—but adieu to this till happier times, if ever I shall see them; the hours at present are melancholy dull—

Be assured that I am Dr. Madam with most unfeigned regard. Yr. most obedient, Most Obliged Hble. Servant, Geo. Washington.

This letter leaves no doubt, I think, that he was in love with Mrs. Fairfax. He catches "joyfully" at the "happy occasion" of writing to her; "in silence I now express my joy." He is a votary to love, and Mrs. Fairfax knows the object of his passion; "I confess that this Lady is known to you." Who can be known to any one better than one's own self?

Compare this outburst with the phrases in the letter to Martha. "We have begun our march for the Ohio . . . may Providence . . . our pledges to each other . . . faithful and affectionate friend."

Mrs. Fairfax replied promptly, but her letter has disappeared. A historical misfortune. She evidently pretended to misunderstand, and Washington wrote to her again on September 25th.

> Dear Madam: Do we still misunderstand the true meaning of each other's letters? I think it must appear so, tho' I would feign hope the contrary, as I cannot speak plainer without—but I'll say no more and leave you to guess the rest.
>
> [I omit most of this letter, as it is devoted mainly to a description of the military operations.]
>
> One thing more and then I have done. You asked if I am not tired at the length of your letter. No, Madam, I am not, nor never can be while the lines are an inch asunder to bring you in haste to the end of the paper. . . .

He says in this letter that he "cannot speak plainer without—" Yes, but without what? We may confidently supply the answer, which is that he cannot speak plainer without coming right out and telling her that he loves her. He does not want to do that, because she is his friend's wife and because he is engaged to another woman. But he wants her to know it, just the same.

§ 4

On January 6, 1759, George Washington married Martha Custis. In love with one woman and marrying another. Men had done this before, and will probably continue doing it; for with many people there are other considerations in contracting marriages than that of love; and, besides, in this case the woman he loved was already married to another man. Washington was twenty-seven years old, and Mrs. Custis was twenty-eight. The wedding was an imposing social event. Governor Fauquier was among the guests and the house buzzed from top to bottom with Virginia notables.

Every one felt that the young man had arrived. The snobs, who are the last to recognise any kind of merit, had given in. The standard of snobbery is high, we must admit, but even the snobbiest snob knew that there must be a great deal of merit in a young man who had been able to capture Virginia's largest unattached fortune.

Washington at the wedding, in his cold and steely blue, resembled a Gainsborough portrait. He wore a suit of blue cloth, the coat of which was lined with red silk and ornamented with silver trimmings. His waistcoat was made of embroidered white satin, his knee-buckles were of gold, and his hair was powdered.

Martha wore a white satin quilted petticoat, over which there was a heavily corded white silk overdress. She wore pearl ornaments; and her shoes had diamond buckles.

All the estate of Martha's late husband had been left to her by inheritance, with the exception of legacies to her young children—John Parke Custis and Martha (called "Patsy") Custis. The children's share amounted to about fifty thousand dollars apiece.

Under the laws of colonial Virginia a wife's property became her husband's through the act of marriage, so Washington found himself in possession of the major part of the Custis estate.

It was certainly needed, for at that time his own financial affairs were not in very good condition. He owned forty-nine slaves and about five thousand acres of land—cleared and uncleared—but things had become badly run down through his absence during the three years of campaigns. In 1757 he wrote to his London agent—he was then on the frontier—that he did not know whether he had any tobacco to ship or not, and added, "I am so little acquainted with the business relative to my private affairs that I can scarce give you any information concerning it."

Many people believed that he married Mrs. Custis solely

on account of her fortune. The fat John Adams was one. He was a friend and admirer of Washington—at times—but he was moody and changeable, as obese people frequently are. In one of his vitriolic moments he declared that George Washington would never have amounted to much if he had not married Mrs. Custis' money.

I do not think there is any sense in the statement that Washington's career was made by the Custis fortune. Obviously it helped him a great deal. It smoothed his way, made his road easier, and lifted him buoyantly over minor difficulties. But that is all. George Washington was a man of distinction before he married Mrs. Custis. He had already shown an extraordinary capacity for leadership; he was already on his way to a great career.

But did he marry for money?

The majority of his biographers, existing in mortal fear of the American public, have hinted timidly that although he loved Martha for herself alone, her fortune might have influenced him a tiny bit.

In trying to handle the subject in a manner which would be satisfactory to Truth as well as to the Daughters of the American Revolution historians have performed some feats of literary subtlety which should certainly be studied by those interested in the flexibility of words.

Consider this extract from a recent life of Washington by William Roscoe Thayer. He says that Thackeray declared that Washington married for money, then Mr. Thayer goes on:

> I do not believe this assertion, nor do I find evidence for it. Washington was always a very careful, far-seeing person, and no doubt had a clear idea of what constitutes desirable qualifications in marriage, but I believe he would have married a poor girl out of the work-house if he had really loved her.

If Mr. Thayer had not been a great historian he would have made a great lawyer. I agree with him; his statement carries conviction. Washington certainly had "a clear idea of what constitutes desirable qualifications in marriage." I, too, believe that "he would have married a poor girl out of the workhouse if he had really loved her."

But would he have loved a poor girl—possessing, as he did, a clear idea of what constitutes desirable qualifications?

The estate of the late Colonel Custis consisted of about seventy-five hundred acres of cleared land, and the same number of acres of timber, together with three hundred slaves, and cash and securities amounting to a sum equal to about one hundred thousand dollars. Part of this property belonged to Martha's children, and was to be held in trust for them until they became of age.

§ 5

Now they are married, happy, and settled down at Mount Vernon. Martha calls George her "Old Man"—a term still used in the South by wives in speaking of their husbands—and he calls her "Patsy." When she wants to persuade him to do anything she holds on to a button of his coat and looks up at his face with a smile. A tall, large-jointed man with a pock-marked face and icy cold blue eyes; and a plump little woman twisting his coat-buttons and pouting.

She is a gay little woman, but not frivolous. The gaiety of good health, good nature and a small mind.

The house is full of carpenters and masons, for Mount Vernon is being enlarged. There is an air of prosperity about the place. The gorgeous coach ordered from London finally arrives, its body green and its trimmings gilt.

§ 6

The famous Washington diary begins on January 1st, 1760, and continues—with some breaks, notably one of seven years during the Revolution—to the end of his life.

The first entry reads:

> Tuesday, 1. Visited my Plantations and received an Instance of Mr. French's great love of Money in disappointing me of some Pork, because the price had risen to 22/6 after he had engaged to let me have it at 20/.
>
> Called at Mr. Possey's [he means Posey's] in my way home and desired him to engage me 100 Bar'ls of Corn upon the best terms he could in Maryland.
>
> And found Mrs. Washington upon my arrival broke out with the Meazles.

Not a very good day. Human cupidity, measles, and a lack of corn. It seems strange that he should have to buy corn when he owned so much land and so many slaves, the two necessary ingredients of corn production. He had to buy pork, too, and that fact is equally interesting.

The explanation is, I think, that his plantations and their work had not yet been organised efficiently. Brother "Jack" supervised them during George's long absence on the frontier, but he probably allowed things to become shiftless and down at the heels.

Next day, "fearing a disappointment elsewhere in Pork," he takes Mr. French's supply on Mr. French's own terms; but he does not like Mr. French any more.

On the 3rd of January, he had his negroes fish in the Potomac with seines, "and got some fish, but was near being disappointed of my Boat by means of an Oyster Man, who had lain at my landing and plagued me a good deal by his disorderly behaviour."

Mrs. Washington's measles were getting better on the 5th and the lovely Mrs. Fairfax came over for a call. On the 6th the oyster man was ordered away.

> *Saturday 5th.* Mrs. Washington appeared to be something better. Mr. Green however came to see her at 11 o'clock and in an hour Mrs. Fairfax arrived. Mr. Green

prescribed the needful, and just as we were going to **Dinnr.**
Capt. Walter Stuart appeard with Doctr. Laurie. . . .

Sunday 6th. . . Mrs. Washington was a good deal better to-day; but the Oyster Man still continuing his Disorderly behaviour at my Landing I was obliged in the
most preemptory manner to order him and his compy,
away, which he did not Incline to obey till next morning.

He makes note, on the 12th, that "I was informed that Colo.
Cocke was disgusted at my House, and left because he see **an**
old Negroe there resembling his own Image."

The diary, or diaries—for there are many of them—are as
devoid of introspection as a furniture catalogue. He sets
down the state of the weather, then tells where he went and
what he did and who came to dinner.

But, even if we agree to let the diaries stand as vehicles of
skeletonised facts and turn to his letters, we find the same cold
impersonal spirit. His writings reveal nothing of the unfold-
ing of his own character—unless one knows how to read between the lines—nor does he show any vivid emotion over
memories, or at meeting people.

The diaries tell how and where he spent his time, and apparently very little time was spent in reading, or in intellectual
occupations. He read almost as little as the super-business-
men of to-day, and was as completely out of touch with the
profound thought of the time as they are. He possessed more
energy than thought, and his energy expressed itself in action.

His diaries show that the greater part of his leisure was
given to hunting, to card-playing, or to attendance at balls.

As to hunting—let us open the diary, and take at random
any month. The book falls open at January, 1770. The first
mention of hunting is on the 4th.

4. Went a hunting with Jno. Custis and Lund Washington. Started a Deer and then a Fox, but got neither.

Next day he had to look over his plantations, but he took his dogs with him.   Frequently he rode after foxes with a small field, sometimes alone, as the neighbouring gentry were few in number and occupied with other matters.

> 5. Rid to Muddy hole and Dock Run [two of his plantations].   Carrd. the Dogs with me, but found nothing. Mr. Warnr. Washington and Mr. Thruston come in the Evening.

More hunting on the 8th, 9th and 10th.

> 8. Went a huntg. with Mr. Alexander, J. P. Custis and Ld. W——n [he means Lund Washington].   Killd. a fox (a dog one) after 3 hours chase.   Mr. Alexr. went away and Wn. and Thruston came in ye aftern.

> 9. Went a ducking, but got nothing, the Creeks and Rivers being froze.   Mr. Robt. Adam dined here and returned.

> 10. Mr. W——n and Mr. Thruston set of home.   I went a hunting in the Neck and visited the Plantn. there. Found and killd a bitch fox, after treeing it 3 times and chasg. it abt. 3 Hrs.

No hunting for ten days.   Then, on the 20th, his companion is "Jacky" (John Parke) Custis, his stepson.   Young Custis was then about fifteen years old.

> 20. Went a hunting with Jacky Custis and catched a Bitch Fox after three hours chace—founded it on ye Ck. by J. Soals.

On the 23rd a strange thing occurred, so unusual that he set it down.

> 23. Went a hunting after breakfast and found a Fox at Muddy hole and killed her (it being a bitch), after a chace of better than two hours, and after treeing her

twice, the last of which times she fell dead out of the
Tree after being therein sevl. minutes apparently well.
Rid to the Mill afterwards. Mr. Semple and Mr. Robt.
Adam dind here.

Doubtless the poor little thing's heart burst from fright
and exhaustion. On the 27th he goes again.

27. Went a hunting, and after trailing a fox for a
good while the Dogs Raizd a Deer and run out of the
Neck with it, and did not (some of them at least) come
home till the next day.

Finally on the 30th, the sparkling, happy month closes with
the eighth hunt.

30. Went a hunting, and having found a Deer by
Piney Cover it run to the head of Accatinck before we
could stop the Dogs. Mr. Peake dined here.

The chase is a form of combativeness. It is the recreation
of steely, insensitive fighters. The lust for hunting reveals
lack of imagination, lack of sensitiveness. The great imaginative intellects are not found in the skulls of great hunters.
Any sensitive person who once sees a live fox torn to pieces
by dogs is not likely to go fox-hunting again.

Washington's combative instinct is interestingly revealed
in an order he sent to London soon after his marriage. He
wanted busts of Alexander the Great, Julius Cæsar, Marl-
borough, Prince Eugene, Charles XII of Sweden, Frederick
the Great of Prussia, soldiers' busts, all of them. In addition he wanted "statuettes of two wild beasts."

It took an interminable time to get anything from London,
and usually the orders were not properly filled. In this case
he was greatly dissatisfied, for in place of some of the warriors' busts, his London agents sent filigree poetic statues—
graces or nymphs or something—mere sentimental trash not
at all to his liking.

§ 7

In the year 1771 Washington began to make cryptic symbols in his diaries, evidently entries in cipher. These symbols appear on the margins opposite certain names or occurrences. They consist of single letters, numerals, dots and vertical lines. The clue to this secret record is unknown.

Mr. John C. Fitzpatrick, an official of the Library of Congress who prepared Washington's *Diaries* for publication, says in a letter to me:

> My personal opinion is that they [the symbols] are merely farm memoranda of some kind or another; but they must have been of relatively slight importance, as by comparison of these symbols with the diary entries for the days on which they are marked, nothing is noted which would give us the faintest clue for the reason of the markings. They could, of course, have been a record of card games but for the fact that oftentimes the entries are on days that Washington was not at Mount Vernon. It is a puzzle, but I take it to be so insignificant a one that there is no need of getting excited about it, especially as it can never be deciphered.

I am not the least bit excited about it, but I do not agree with Mr. Fitzpatrick that the symbols are probably records of insignificant events, or that they are farm memoranda. Washington was a most painstaking person in his voluminous writing about farm operations. As to card games, he gives invariably in his account books the amounts won or lost. There was no reason in the world for him to invent a cipher to record his ploughing and planting. I think the symbols, if they are ever solved, will reveal important information. As to what that information may be I cannot hazard a guess, but I am confident that men and women use symbols in their diaries only for the purpose of recording secrets of an important and highly personal nature.

§ 8

With the coming of the Custis fortune Washington had the means to indulge his lifelong desire for land. "In 1759 he bought of his friend Bryan Fairfax two hundred and seventy-five acres on Difficult Run, and about the same time from his neighbour, the celebrated George Mason of Gunston Hall, he acquired one hundred acres." I quote from Paul Leland Haworth's excellent book, *George Washington, Country Gentleman.*

There was a disagreeable episode in the purchase of eighteen hundred and six acres from a person named Clifton who had agreed to let Washington have the land for one thousand and fifty pounds, and then changed his mind. Clifton said his wife would not let him sell the land at that price. In the diary entry of March 2, 1760, we read: "Mr. Clifton came here to-day . . . and by his shuffling behaviour on the occasion convinced me of his being the trifling body represented."

On March 11th Washington learned that Clifton had sold the land to some one else for twelve hundred pounds. His diary says that this "convinced me that he was nothing less than a thorough pacd. Rascall, disregardful of any engagements of words or oaths not bound by Penalties."

Eventually, after much haggling, Washington got the land, but he had to pay twelve hundred and ten pounds for it.

Mr. Haworth says: "By 1771 he paid quit rents[1] upon an estate of five thousand five hundred and eighteen acres in Fairfax county; on two thousand four hundred and ninety-eight acres in Frederick county; on one thousand two hundred and fifty acres in King George; on two hundred and forty in Hampshire; on two hundred and seventy-five in Loudoun; on two thousand six hundred and eighty-two in Loudoun Fauquier —in all, twelve thousand four hundred and sixty-three acres.

[1] In a later chapter I shall explain the nature of quit rents.

The quit rent was two shillings and sixpence per hundred acres and amounted to £15.11.7."

This property was, of course, exclusive of the land held by him in trust for the minor heirs of the Custis estate.

The "celebrated George Mason of Gunston Hall" from whom land was purchased was a close friend and political mentor of Washington in these early years.

Mason was one of the wealthy men of Virginia, and he seems to have had clear modern ideas of business management. It is possible that Washington got from him the inspiration to turn Mount Vernon and his other plantations into self-contained communities, as far as possible.

At Gunston Hall there were, among the slaves, shoemakers, spinners, weavers, blacksmiths, tanners, carpenters, coopers, and even a distiller. Nothing whatever was purchased if it could be made on the place. The woods furnished timber and plank for the carpenters; the cooper made hogsheads for the tobacco and casks for the cider and other liquors. All the ploughs, chains and bolts were forged by the blacksmiths; cotton and flax were grown for the weavers and spinners; stockings were produced by the knitters; and every Fall the distiller made a quantity of peach and apple brandy. There were five hundred people on Colonel Mason's place, but he had no manager nor steward, and attended to everything himself with the aid of a few intelligent slave assistants.

In this respect Washington followed his example, as in many other ways. The five plantations that belonged to the Mount Vernon property had each a hired white overseer—with most of whom there was always a good deal of trouble—but the estate as a whole was handled by Washington personally, without a steward, until the beginning of the Revolution, when his continued absence made it necessary to appoint a superintendent whose authority extended over the entire property.

§ 9

Coldly reserved men, like Washington, are often stern and forbidding in manner, but he was not. His feeling of courtesy was strong; his manners were good, and he never forgot them.

It would be too much to say that he was a charming person. He was too serious to have the fluid quality of charm, but he could be pleasant and agreeable; and his conversation even with people whom he detested left the impression of quiet urbanity.

Beneath the gripping materialism of his nature there ran a warm current of affection for children. He remembered the names of children he had met, and his pockets were often full of presents for them.

He never had any children of his own.

He loved his step-children, John Parke Custis and Martha (called "Patsy") Custis, as if they had been his own. The boy, who turned out to be a stupid youth, was raised in a sort of juvenile splendour, with a young negro in livery attending him on all occasions.

Something for these children was always included in the orders for goods from London, and the orders were numerous. One sent in the summer of 1759, not long after his marriage, included among other things:

A small Bible, bound in Turkey, with Martha Parke Custis written inside in gilt letters.

A fashionable dressed doll to cost 1 guinea and one at 5s.

A good spinet, to be made by Mr. Phinnis, Grosvenor Square.

A small Bible, bound in Turkey, with John Parke Custis written inside in gilt letters.

Things ordered for Mrs. Washington included:

> 1 salmon colored tabby velvet of the enclosed **pattern**, with satin flowers to be made in a sack and coat.

Tabby was a soft plain velvet or silk.

> 1 cap, handkerchief, tucker, and ruffles, to be made of Brussels lace on Point proper to be worn with the above negligee, to cost twenty pounds.

A very high price, it seems, for such an **outfit**.

> 2 prs. of woman's white silk hose and
> 6 prs. of cotton hose.
> 1 fashionable dress or bonnet.
> 1 doz. round silk stay-laces.
> 1 black mask.

The mask was no doubt to be worn at masquerade balls, which Washington and his wife frequently attended. Among the other items in this order were "1 doz. most fashionable cambric pocket handkerchiefs," "1000 minikins"—which were small pins, "8 lbs. perfumed powder," and "2 handsome breast-flowers."

§ 10

On Jan. 29, 1769, he wrote a letter to William Ramsay about Ramsay's son William. In this letter he suggests that Ramsay send his son to college, and he suggests "the Jersey College"—now Princeton University. He expected, evidently, that Ramsay would not be able to finance such a project, so he proposed to contribute twenty-five pounds annually toward the son's education.

This Ramsay belonged to the Alexandria lodge of Freemasons to which Washington belonged. It would be interesting to know what manner of youth the son was, and why he attracted Washington's favourable attention, but here we are lacking in information.

In the Diary record for Feb. 13, 1785, we read of Washington's attendance at William Ramsay's funeral, walking "in a procession as a free mason, Mr. Ramsay in his life being one, and now buried with the ceremonies and honours due to one."

CHAPTER IX

THE COLONIAL PEOPLE

§ 1

In a vague sense the pre-Revolutionary colonials considered themselves Englishmen. It was a feeble conception, about as flabby as the average man's recognition of the fact that he is an Aryan. It had no potency, no real force, and was brought out, staggering and blinking, into the sunlight only when English aid was needed.

There was, however, an extremely thin upper crust of society to which England bulked large. In this class were most of the people of culture, the government officials, the wealthy merchants, the readers of books, the ship-owners, the people of fashion.

But to the ordinary unkempt American of that epoch England had become merely an abstraction which materialised, on occasion, in the shape of a British hunting knife or a suit of Lancashire woolen goods. These uninspiring symbols of overlordship gave place now and then to a glimpse of some entirely human governor, royally appointed. He would arrive in the pomp of an authority which had acquired the pallid features of a half-veiled political mysticism.

Provincial patriotism crystallised about the individual colony. There was no American nation, even as a figure of speech. Wealthy colonials, travelling in foreign lands—as some of them did—never thought of calling themselves Americans. They were Virginians, or Rhode Islanders, or Carolinians, as the case might be. Years after the Revolution Washington still referred to Virginia as "my country."

115

In the history of the time there is a criss-cross of provincial rancours and jealousies. New York and Connecticut had a long-standing quarrel, and Virginia and Pennsylvania almost started a war of their own in 1774 over a question of boundaries. Georgia was afraid of South Carolina, and Rhode Island—the most truculent of the colonies—defied Massachusetts. Maryland was sorely disappointed with her neighbours, and had interminable disputes with Virginia and Pennsylvania.

The colonial point of view was parochial in its limitations—I am speaking now of the ordinary average man—and immensely foreshortened by the difficulties of communication. The world's intelligence came, if at all, in a muddy trickle of unreliable news. Travel was so expensive and precarious that people usually stayed at home. The average man knew nothing of the outside world. Geography was the Cinderella of the sciences. It was not taught at all in the schools; nobody needed it. In 1815, fifty years after the time we are discussing, a knowledge of geography was for the first time made a condition for entering Harvard.

It is surprising to learn that the later colonial population was almost wholly colonial born. In 1760, the thirteen colonies had about one million six hundred thousand inhabitants, including four hundred thousand negro slaves. The number of the foreign-born—including the English—in this total is unknown, but it was quite small. The people of the colonies, in the decade before the Revolution, and for a generation afterwards, constituted the most thoroughly American stock that has ever inhabited this continent.

Immigration in large numbers had come to an end in the seventeenth century. Thereafter, newcomers arrived only in driblets. Ships loaded with London wares frequently brought two or three passengers; and now and then a shipload of indented servants arrived. But there was no organized passenger travel, and there were only feeble attempts to induce immigration; except, of course, the immigration of negro slaves from

Africa, where they were captured and imported in large numbers to America.

An authority [1] on the subject of colonial population declares that the entire pre-Revolutionary population of whites grew from a total immigration of about one hundred thousand.

It was not a new land, though the illusion of historical perspective is apt to make us think it was. At the outbreak of the Revolution the colony of Virginia was one hundred and sixty-eight years of age. Massachusetts had struggled with its internal Puritan inhibitions for more than a hundred and fifty years. New York had been Dutch for forty years and English for ninety. Georgia, the infant among the colonies, was nevertheless old enough to have middle-aged children of its own, for it had been settled in 1733.

Thousands of families ran back through an American ancestry of four or five generations. We have seen that George Washington belonged to the third generation of American Washingtons.

These people spoke of "old times." They thought of the early settlers as faraway, antiquated characters. Looking backward in time, the men of the Revolution saw John Smith and Pocahontas, Myles Standish and Priscilla Alden, Roger Williams and Peter Stuyvesant dimly through the haze of distance. These were considered remote historical figures, and they were indeed further away from the Revolutionary people in thought and outlook than Washington is from us.

§ 2

By the middle of the eighteenth century life in the colonies had stratified into a clearly defined social geology. There were three layers, broadly speaking, which for convenience in classification we may call the Very Best People, the Best People,

[1] F. B. Dexter, *Estimates of Population in the American Colonies.*

and the Common People—who, in the literature of the day, were termed "the mob."

Naturally, the Very Best People would be those who did no work at all. There were not many of them in the colonies. They had lands, horses, slaves and investments, which they hired other people to look after. In this class were most of the higher government officials and the possessors of huge land grants, such as Lord Fairfax of Virginia and the Van Rensselaers, Livingstons and Schuylers of New York.

The Best People were not as idle and parasitic as the Very Best People, but they did not work nearly as hard as the Common People. The Best People in every colony were the traders and merchants, shipowners and planters. They looked after their financial interests personally, but in other respects they resembled the Very Best People. The pick of the lawyers and the fashionable ministers were among the Best People, too.

To reach the Common People we must slide down-hill quite a bit from these loftier levels. The Common People were those who worked with their hands, and kept the country alive. Work was plentiful, but was insipid from lack of variety. It had to do with the soil, with heavy logs, with ships and fish. It was back-breaking and sweaty, and had a close resemblance to the daily work of a horse.

Beneath the Common People there was another class which was even commoner, that consisted of the slaves and white indented servants.

There is a sharp ring of modernism about these colonial distinctions. Indeed, if we melt the negro slaves and indented servants into the mass of common people, we have the same classifications that exist to-day. Money, or land—which was the eighteenth century equivalent of money—had displaced both noble birth and pious works as a passport to gentility. Feudal rights and shadowy assumptions of power were fading, and an aristocracy based on wealth was moving into positions of authority.

The whole population in the older communities, with the exception of a few romantic idealists and born rebels, consisted of go-getters. Every one was trying to improve his situation in life—his *material situation*, I mean, though a few here and there went in for mental improvement. The prevailing idea was to get the best of one's neighbour, if possible, by selling him something—generally land—at a large profit. Shares in new settlements were bought and sold on speculation, as one deals in stocks, and were passed from hand to hand among the moneyed classes in the older towns.

"Wealth was increasing," says James Truslow Adams, in his *Revolutionary New England*, "but with even more rapidity it was concentrating. In Boston, in 1758, Charles Apthorp died leaving over £50,000 and there were others equally or even more wealthy. . . . In New Hampshire Benning Wentworth, who had been bankrupt in 1740, had acquired 100,000 acres of land and a fortune in money twenty years later, and was living in princely style in a palatial mansion of fifty-two rooms."

There was a keen sense of class consciousness in the higher ranks of society, for the Best People and the Very Best People were afraid of "the mob," and they were held together from Massachusetts to South Carolina by this imaginary danger. We have long since learned that the common people are entirely docile and may be led by a ring in the nose as a trainer leads performing bears, but our aristocratic land-speculating forefathers had not found it out, and a fear of "the mob" runs quivering through their letters and diaries. In the general designation of "mob" they meant such people as the mechanics and carpenters and labourers of the coast towns, the small ignorant farmers and the landless poor.

This consciousness of class showed itself in a continual and almost instinctive effort to elect or appoint none but men of the upper class to positions of authority. In the Revolution Washington advised that "none but gentlemen" be taken as officers. General Montgomery, who was a brother-in-law of the wealthy Robert R. Livingston, thought that a lack of "gentlemen" was the main defect of the Continental army, and he tried to think of some way of "engaging gentlemen to serve."

John Adams, bubbling over with Revolutionary passion as he returned from the Continental Congress, rode along a country road and met one of the common herd. In his democratic fervour Mr. Adams drew the fellow into conversation, and found that he was "grateful" to Mr. Adams and to the Continental Congress. "There are no courts of justice now in this province," he said, "and I hope there will never be another."

This artless hope made the brilliant Mr. Adams, leading member of the bar and frequenter of the courts of justice, very despondent.

For a moment the Revolutionary cause tottered in his mind. When he reached home he wrote his reflections:

> Is this the object for which I have been contending, said I to myself, for I rode along without any answer to this wretch. . . . If the power of the country should get into such hands, and there is a great danger that it will, to what purpose have we sacrificed our time, health and everything else?

§ 3

The well-to-do families in the larger towns lived in fine houses in a sort of mahogany-and-silver elegance. They liked polished floors and flowered fabrics, powdered hair and snuff-boxes, roast venison and Madeira wine. These Best People were utterly unlike the rough settlers of the back country in appearance, character and manners. They were few in number, for at least five-sixths of the population were farmers, backwoodsmen, labourers and slaves.

Boston was the largest city in 1765, but its trade was

dwindling, and its 16,000 population was to remain almost stationary for twenty years. Like all the large coast towns, Boston was a mercantile centre for the back country.

The largest manufacturing industry in the colonies in the pre-Revolutionary period was distilling—the making of rum from molasses. The principal centres of the distilling trade were Boston and Newport. The highly profitable African slave trade also centred in Rhode Island.

Philadelphia was the second city in size, and was soon to be the first. At the close of the Revolution it contained about twenty-five thousand inhabitants. New York was the third town in importance. Charleston was the fourth; and Newport was the fifth.

It was before the day of standardisation. There had not been any broad mingling of the various colonial peoples, and the large towns differed strikingly in appearance. Each of the colonies, founded by some distinct wave of settlers, grew up in a close atmosphere of insularity, and developed peculiarities of its own.

Boston, sitting on its hilly peninsula, was a closely packed town with narrow, twisting streets. At first impression it appears to have been inhabited only by fierce-eyed lawyers and preachers who turned themselves, on the slightest impulse, into furious writers of pamphlets in which they discussed politics and theology with an incredible virulence.

New Yorkers, on the other hand, applied themselves strictly to business and had an unconquerable faith in money as a solvent of human misery.

In Charleston all was sea wind, wide verandahs and scarlet flowers. Upon arriving in that sun-smitten land travellers fell readily into languor and reminiscence, and decided to do to-morrow whatever should be done to-day.

The largest of the Jewish communities was at Charleston. At the outbreak of the Revolution Charleston had six hundred Jews among its inhabitants. With pride they recorded the fact that not one of their number was a Tory. Another group of Jews lived at Newport. Spanish Jews they were—the Sephardim—dark people with black curly hair and black eyes. They were among the prominent merchants at both Newport and Charleston.

Philadelphia was wide-spreading and quiet, of a large clear spaciousness. In the 1760's it was the fastest growing city on the American continent.

Many women were engaged in business, and in the activities connected with ownership. One is surprised at the number. Mrs. Elizabeth Anthony Dexter has written a book about them entitled *Colonial Women of Affairs*, in which she has given most interesting details of the ways of she-merchants, feminine managers of estates, inn-keepers, writers and actresses.

Around the time of the Revolution Mrs. Mercy Warren was a celebrated literary lady and the great blue stocking of her day. A sister of the radical orator, James Otis, she was a thorough patriot. Her drama, *The Group*, which appeared on the eve of the Revolution, is a satirical play in which the leading loyalists of the time are shown up, to their disadvantage, in their disguises.

Mrs. Warren's satire is heavy. It reminds one of Mark Twain's characterisation of the Mormon Bible, which he called "chloroform in print." Literature was hardly a feminine occupation.

Life was slow-moving, almost indolent in its leisure. The wealthy played cards with great decorum and flirted by means of fans and handkerchiefs.

They wrote each other ponderous "Sir" and "Madam" letters. Crystal bowls of rum-punch stood all day long awaiting any casual caller. Black slave boys followed meekly behind the great ladies, carrying the toilet case, the bon-bon box and an extra wrap. In the wide rooms, lined with damask and pictures of the Fall of Troy, the candle light was reflected from a

Mrs. Mercy Warren
From the painting by John S. Copley

multitude of mirrors and fell on white-powdered heads bent in kissing obeisance over ladies' delicate hands.

§ 4

These are the high lights of the colonial scene. They do not represent the whole, but only a part. There was no air of elegant leisure about most of the people. Their mahogany had turned to pine and their silver to pewter. The average colonial American was a wiry farmer with an ignorant mind and a tough hide, living on an impassable road, and existing on rough food, hard work and an urgent spirit of self-reliance.

Nearly all the rich lands were in possession of the great land-owners. The small farmer struggled in his stony fields for small reward, as he does to-day. But as we go back from the coast the farms are further and further apart, and the backwoodsman finally takes the farmer's place.

Pioneers, or backwoodsmen, are always social rebels. They are at odds with civilisation, and never at home among its intangible restrictions. In them a sense of inferiority mingles with an incurable shyness. They move before an oncoming civilisation as the first wave of an advancing tide runs up a beach. Long after the pioneer is dead, and his bones are dust, his spirit lingers in the places where he has been and colours its civilisation. We may discern the spirit of the harsh pioneer even in the current life of our own times.

Backwoodsmen on the Appalachian frontier were almost as savage as the Indians. Their moral and economic standards had receded through the downward gravitational pull of deprivation until they rested on the primitive conceptions of the early Saxons. In the life and manners of these frontier people we see the tenth century, folded over in time and laid along the western fringe of colonial civilisation.

They were not only equal to the Indians as fighting men, but far superior to them in staying power. As their life became by degrees more and more fierce and primitive, they adopted various Indian customs—among them the rather messy practice of scalping one's enemies. They took Indian scalps whenever they could and dried them on the walls of their cabins as the farmers of to-day dry the skins of rabbits.

An interesting document appears in the Pennsylvania archives. The western inhabitants of the province, in 1764, considered themselves neglected, so they indited a memorial to "The Honourable John Penn, Esquire, Governor of the Province of Pennsylvania." These humble folk did not pray the honourable governor for more and better schools or for good roads, or for any of the things which burden the grievances of this day and time.

What they wanted was to be paid for Indian scalps, and this is what they said:

> In the late Indian War [2] this province, with others of his Majesty's Colonies, gave rewards for Indian scalps, to encourage the seeking them in their own country, as the most likely means of destroying or reducing them to reason; but no such encouragement has been given in this war, which has damped the spirits of many brave men who are willing to venture their lives in parties against the enemy. We therefore pray that public rewards may be proposed for Indian scalps, which may be adequate to the dangers attending enterprises of this nature.

The people who lived in this fashion were callous and rough to a degree almost beyond our modern conception. The life of our cowboys in the early days on the western plains was a mere youth's frolic compared to the daily hardships of these pioneers. Virtually everything they used or consumed was made with their own hands.

They raised small patches of corn, wheat and flax. There were no mills to grind their corn and wheat. These cereals

[2] That of 1755-1763, in which Washington was engaged.

were pounded into coarse meal and flour in stone or wooden mortars.

There was plenty of animal food, for the woods swarmed with game. Hollow trees dripped with wild honey. Wild turkeys were plentiful, too, but it was extremely difficult to get close enough to them to shoot them.

Deer meat furnished venison, fresh and dried, and deerskins crudely tanned became moccasins and leather coats. The scrappy patch of flax, and sometimes an acre of cotton, and a few sheep, provided raw material for the spinning wheel and the hand loom. Tallow from deer or slaughtered cattle was melted into candles.

Existence was always so close to the knife edge of disaster that the smallest accident would frequently lead to tragic consequences. The man and meat-provider of the house sometimes set out with his gun into the trackless woods and never returned. Waylaid and scalped by Indians, perhaps; or killed by some furious rushing animal when his gun failed to fire. Even when the surrounding Indians were friendly there was no security against Indian attacks, as marauding bands from faraway tribes often passed up and down this border, sometimes going a thousand miles from their own land.

In time of sickness the backwoodsman had to rely on whatever remedies he could concoct at home. Fresh wounds were sucked dry and plastered with hartshorn leaves. An aching tooth was extracted by tying a string around it and giving the string a jerk. Broken limbs had to mend the best they could; there were no surgeons to set them.

Existence was hard, but these frontier people were so tough and leathery that a life which seems impossible to us did not cause them a great deal of discomfort. A woman in childbirth often called for her pipe and tobacco as a solace for labour pains. Next day she would be up and about, sitting lankily by the fire with the new-born child in her lap.

They were not simple people; they were merely primitive,

and the primitive life is a most complicated condition of circumstances. Simplicity can only be attained in old and rich civilisations where the mechanism of life runs so smoothly that it is hardly noticed. On the colonial frontier life consisted of nothing but mechanism. Existence resolved itself into a perpetual committee of ways and means. There could be no place for culture, for the flowering of the finer human sympathies. The sensitive and the delicate, from whom genius springs, all died young.

The primitiveness of these pioneers was destructive. It ate like a cancer through the fragile tissues of the soul. It reduced the equation of life to factors which could be expressed only in pounds of lead and pounds of beef. Its spirit spread from the frontier and saturated the body of colonial civilisation. It was like some burrowing animal gnawing at the roots of imagination and fancy. It barked its harsh verdict in seaport towns where backwoodsmen were never seen, and spoke with the tongues of people who would hardly have recognised a backwoodsman if they had ever met one.

§ 5

Colonial civilisation, as a whole, was harsh, shrill and defiant. It was strikingly bare of graciousness, of charm—even of good manners—but it was not lacking in lurid drama or in a strain of hard-fibred romance.

§ 6

There was the Indian. . . .

His murky shadow lies, red and insistent, across the whole picture of colonial life.

In the beginning the early settlers considered the Indians simply a part of the landscape. They were ignorant of the Indian character, of course, and looked upon these savages as poor, helpless people who wandered half-naked about the woods because they knew nothing better to do. To get the Indians decently clothed, to teach them Christianity, and then to put them to work at low wages, seemed to be the beneficent duty of the hour. Attempts were made in the early days to make slaves of them, with deplorable results.

The colonists were not long in finding out that their ideas about the Indian were totally wrong. They soon learned that they were facing an utterly warlike race whose individuality was inflexible, and whose views on almost every conceivable subject were directly contrary to the accepted opinions of white men.

There were never many Indians on the American continent, as we measure population to-day. Theodore Roosevelt, whose close studies of Indian life entitle him to consideration as an authority of the first rank, estimated that the Six Nations at the time of the Revolution numbered only ten or twelve thousand; and the Six Nations, or Iroquois confederacy, was unquestionably the most powerful of all the Indian aggrega-tions of tribes. This estimate of ten or twelve thousand in-cludes women and children. Their effective fighting force, counting every able-bodied man, may have been about four thousand. As a matter of fact they were never able to put anything approaching that number in the field.

In the latter half of the eighteenth century the Indian tribes on our Appalachian border, from Canada to Florida, probably had a total population of one hundred thousand. If this estimate is in error, it errs by being too high.

Opposed to these hundred thousand Indians were approxi-mately two million white people. This overwhelming disparity in numbers and resources carried to the Indian heart no feel-ing of terror or of subjection. In treaty-making and in con-ferences they considered themselves as equals of the whites. The representatives of diminutive tribes acted like the envoys of haughty empires.

The white preponderance was, in fact, not nearly as effective as the comparison of numbers would indicate. Contact with
the Indians was only on the frontier where the population
was thin. There was no longer any fear that a combination
of savage tribes would crush colonial civilisation. An inhabitant of New York or Boston might live for many years without setting eyes on a wild Indian; he might indeed never see
one.

People are usually indifferent to dangers to which they are
not personally exposed. Somebody else's danger takes on the
quality of romance. It becomes dissolved in flabby sentiment;
it has all the unreality of printed words. In the older colonies
—in the long-settled districts of the coast—there was much
talk of heroic Indian fighters, and some sighs over Indian outrages, but not much assistance in the way of troops or money.
Whenever military aid was given it was sent grudgingly, with
many complaints about expense. The successive defeats of
the Indians, and the rolling back of the tribes, were accomplished chiefly by the backwoodsmen alone.

§ 7

Cruelty with the Indian was not merely the result of an outburst of rage. It was a cold, almost unemotional quality.
He studied the infliction of pain with all the patience and ingenuity of a scientist on the scent of a discovery. His love
of cruelty was leading him, with strange indirection, to a knowledge of anatomy, for he had learned that certain mutilations
brought death too quickly. In Indian communities small animals were tortured by the children as a training for the larger
affairs of life . . . dogs and rabbits mutilated and burned
alive by the boys and girls while their elders sat around in
pleasant, laughing conversation.

This profound love of cruelty was mixed with a strain of
easy good nature. The Indian was not the taciturn, silent

being of popular myth. He put on this air of grim reserve
when he was in the presence of white people. An Indian community was always stirring with gossip and banter. There
was a great deal of laughter at jokes and stories. The stories
were generally obscene, and the jokes filthy, but the laughter
was hearty and good-natured.

Although he was unspeakably cruel the Indian did not shrink
from pain. On all occasions he fought well; and if captured
by an enemy tribe he submitted without a whine to the most
hideous tortures.

The dealings of the colonists with the Indians were greatly
complicated by the fact that the Indian mind was ten thousand
miles away from every form of Caucasian thought. It is not
sufficient to assert that they were far behind us in civilisation.
They were not only behind, but were travelling on an entirely
different road.

The Indian had no clear idea of property. The tribes were
generally, though not always, communal in respect to ownership. They did not understand the possession of land in the
way we understand it. Whenever a tribe sold, with gaudy
formality, an enormous mileage of territory for a few European gewgaws the Indian skull seldom contained a true conception of the transaction. This was not because they were
fools—for many of them were intelligent in their way—but
because the entire current of Indian ideas hardly touched our
own.

Most of the confused wars between the white man and the
red man originated in disputes over land transactions. The
white man nearly always got the better of the savage in these
business dealings, until the Indian resentment reached the
explosive point. William Penn bought land from the Indians
in large areas and never had any difficulty with them. He paid
the Indians what they considered a good price, though it was
very little; and the purchased lands were surveyed with the
boundaries marked. Penn explained carefully what land own-

ership meant, and took the time to make the Indians understand it.

Both parties to land transactions often went through the business with their tongues in their cheeks. The Indians frequently sold land which they had no right to claim. They had hunted over it, perhaps, a few times. On the other hand, white men engaged in these dealings knew that they were not buying a substantial title. They merely wanted something which would look well in a legal record.

§ 8

The Indian tribe was not a political community in any sharply defined sense. In superficial appearance it seemed to be a sort of loosely jointed democracy, without an executive head or a legislative body which could make its decisions effective, but in reality it was an anarchy, tempered by tradition. The tribal government had no means to compel any of its members to do anything against their will.

Each tribe had two chiefs. One was the peace chief, or sachem, and the other was the war chief. The peace chief, who was sometimes a woman, was elected usually for life, and was not really a chief but a counsellor. He gave advice, but nobody was obliged to follow it.

The war chief was a temporary leader in time of war. He was supposed to be the best warrior in the tribe, and his fitness for leadership was generally decided by the number of his enemies' scalps suspended from the ridge pole of his lodge.

Indian renegades, or warriors far away from home, often pretended to be chiefs, and the whites sometimes made treaties with these irresponsible wanderers. The object in pretending to be a chief was to get the presents which the colonial representatives habitually gave to the Indians whom they met in conferences. In these subterfuges they were aided by the interpreters.

Washington mentions this variety of deception in a letter from the border to Governor Dinwiddie in 1755. Under instructions from the governor he was making efforts to alienate the Indians from the French. He wrote that he had heard "from undoubted authority, that some of the Cherokees, who have been introduced to us as sachems and princes by this interpreter, who shares the profits, have been no other than common hunters, and bloodthirsty villains."

The Indian practice in declaring war was to take a tribal vote, but this weighty proceeding was not binding on any individual. The vote expressed merely the trend of opinion. If the sense of the tribal meeting was against war, there was nevertheless no way of preventing the war enthusiasts from starting a war anyway, and they frequently did. This naturally involved the whole tribe. If, on the other hand, the vote was for war the disgruntled opponents of the measure might refuse to fight, and they often did.

At first impression the tribal community would appear to have been a paradise for pacifists; but these reluctances were not due to pacifism. They came from expediency, or pique, or some other similar cause.

Pacifism as a principle among the Indians was as unthinkable as professed cannibalism would be to-day on Manhattan Island.

To get a clear picture of their life we must understand that social prestige in the tribe was based on murder. The Indian's preoccupation was constantly with murder as a career, for murder represented to him the highest possible achievement.

Of course no Indian spent his whole time in committing murders. He had work to do. The Indians planted crops; they built rude houses—the wigwam was used only by the less advanced tribes; they hunted; they tanned skins. There is a popular belief that the warriors never worked, but this is an error. They labored in the fields by the side of the squaws, though one must admit that this labour bore about the same relation to the brave's real career as golf bears to the career of a business man.

A man who had taken no scalps—and I fancy these men were very few in number—was an object of derision. The warriors would joke about him coarsely and throw filth in his face. They would suggest that he put on trousers, a garment which stood for effeminacy among them. (The conventional Indian brave wore a hunting shirt of leather, with moccasins and a breech cloth which resembled a baby's diaper.)

With these social standards in vogue it is needless to say that every young man went on a scalping expedition—even if he had to go alone—as soon as he was old enough to use a tomahawk. When the tribe was at peace with the neighbouring tribes and with the bordering white colony the young men were sternly forbidden by the chiefs to take scalps in that vicinity. Sometimes these admonitions were effective, but that did not prevent the young men from going a long distance from home for the coveted scalps. They were sometimes gone for months, and would return eventually with the fair-haired scalps of some far-distant white family dangling from their belts.

But the white men could not distinguish between the Indians of various tribes, and an outrage of this kind had the effect of infuriating the people of the border community where it had occurred against the nearby Indians, although they might have been wholly innocent of this particular crime.

The result was a constantly simmering border warfare, which would boil over now and then into a conglomeration of fighting that almost makes the hair stand on end with its tales of horror.

In a society constituted on such a basis intellectual stagnation is certain. Indian thought had crystallised into custom and tradition. As utterly unbending and intractable as the Indian was, it is strange, nevertheless, that he never showed any interest in the white man's superior devices and made no effort to imitate them. The triumphs of mechanical inven-

tion—a form of progress which usually appeals to crude intellects—hardly ever aroused a spark of curiosity among the
Indians, or any attempt at imitation. It is true, indeed, that
they adopted the white man's firearms as superior instruments for killing, but I have looked in vain for a mention of
an Indian gunsmith. They needed gunpowder urgently in their
wars against the colonists. If any Indian ever attempted
to make gunpowder I have not been able to find a reference to it.

§ 9

Their intense love of cruelty often defeated their own interests. In the first place, it put them outside the great court
of human sympathy. One cannot consider or discuss the
rights of men whose lives are one long trail of murder, who
torture their captives, who tear innocent little children to
pieces before their parents' eyes, whose greatest pleasure is in
the infliction of unspeakable agonies on the weak and strong
alike.

There are frequent instances of the torturing of captives
who would have been ransomed on terms which would have
been very favourable to the Indians. Sometimes people
of distinction who fell into their hands were put cruelly to
death. A notable instance of this was the burning alive of
Colonel William Crawford, who commanded the expedition
against the Shawnees and Delawares in 1782, just after the
close of the Revolutionary War.

Colonel Crawford, then fifty years of age, had been a
personal friend of Washington for twenty-five years. It was
he who had located Washington's western lands, and he had
accompanied Washington on his land-inspection tour to the
Ohio in 1770. He had served as a colonel in the Continental army; and at the close of the Revolution was given command of a regiment of militia which had been raised for the pur-

pose of putting an end to the Indian outrages in the Ohio
territory. At the first skirmish with the Indians the militia
deserted their commander and took their way home in panic-
stricken flight. Colonel Crawford and Dr. Knight, surgeon
of the expedition, were captured.

They soon knew that their fate was to be burned at the
stake, as their faces were painted black by the Indians. The
colonel was burned, but Dr. Knight was held for torture on
another day, and escaped. The doctor then wrote a narrative
of the colonel's execution. I quote from it:

When we went to the fire the colonel was stripped
naked, ordered to sit down by the fire and then they
beat him with sticks and their fists. Presently after I
was treated in the same manner. They then tied a rope
to the foot of a post about fifteen feet high, bound the
colonel's hands behind his back and fastened the rope
to the ligature between his wrists. The rope was long
enough for him to sit down or walk around the post once
or twice and return the same way. The Colonel then
called to Simon Girty [3] and asked if they intended to
burn him? Girty answered, yes. The Colonel said he
would take it all patiently. . . .

The Indian men then took up their guns and shot
powder into the colonel's body, from his feet as far up
as his neck. I think not less than seventy loads were discharged upon his naked body. They then crowded about
him, and to the best of my observation, cut off his ears;
when the throng had dispersed a little I saw the blood
running from both sides of his head. . . .

The fire was about six or seven yards from the post
to which the colonel was tied; it was made of small
hickory poles, burnt quite through in the middle, each
end of the poles remaining about six feet in length. Three
or four Indians by turns would take up, individually, one

[3] Simon Girty was a renegade white man who lived among the Indians
and acted as their interpreter.

of these burning pieces of wood and apply it to his naked
body, already burnt black with the powder. These tor-
mentors presented themselves on every side of him with
the burning faggots and poles. Some of the squaws took
broad boards, upon which they would carry a quantity
of burning coals and hot embers and throw on him, so
that in a short time he had nothing but coals of fire and
hot ashes to walk upon.

In the midst of these extreme tortures, he called to
Simon Girty and begged to him to shoot him. . . . Girty
then, by way of derision, told the colonel he had no gun,
at the same time turning about to an Indian who was
behind him, laughed heartily. . . .

Colonel Crawford at this period of his sufferings be-
sought the Almighty to have mercy on his soul, spoke
very low, and bore his torments with the most manly
fortitude. He continued in all the extremities of pain
for an hour and three-quarters or two hours longer, as
near as I can judge, when at last, being almost exhausted,
he lay down on his belly; they then scalped him and
repeatedly threw the scalp in my face, telling me that
was my great captain. An old squaw . . . got a board,
took a parcel of coals and ashes and laid them on his
back and head, after he had been scalped. He then raised
himself on his feet and began to walk around the
post. . . .

But enough of this nightmare. Let us turn to a more agreeable subject.

Before turning, however, it is necessary, in the interest of
truth, to record the fact that our colonial forefathers burned
people, too. Burning alive was a legal punishment for negro
slaves convicted of insurrection against their masters and it
was sometimes carried out.

As late as 1741 eleven negroes were burned alive at one
time in New York City for participation in a slave uprising.
which gave the city a dreadful spasm of fright. One of the

eleven was not burned, but roasted. His sentence reads (I quote from the record): "to be burned with a slow fire that he may continue in torment for eight or ten hours, and continue burning in the said fire until he be dead and consumed to ashes."

CHAPTER X

PURITAN AND OTHER MORALS

§ 1

PURITANISM was the most powerful and the most significant of all the social forces that went into the making of the American spirit.

It was more than a religion; it embodied the English radical thought of the early seventeenth century. It was a revolt against the authority—temporal and spiritual—which emanated from the King and ran down through the veins of the Established Church of England.

In its vision of beatitude Puritanism beheld the Kingdom of God on earth. Its ideal was a theocracy in which man would govern himself by God's bare word . . . not the word of God transmogrified by interpretation and dressed in frills to suit the prevailing taste, but the Holy Word coming from the Bible like the blow of a fist.

To the Puritan the Bible was not an inspiration but a threat. He worshipped the God of the Hebrews; his spiritual conceptions went back to Moses.

At the bottom it was an economic and political rebellion. In the Puritan under-consciousness there were dim pools of thought in which may be discerned revolutionary conceptions of government, of taxation, of human rights. These submerged ideas came to the surface on the theological plane, for in the seventeenth century civilised men thought of social problems in terms of theology, as they think to-day in terms of money and mechanics.

The Puritan believed in the letter of God's word at a time when nearly everybody else believed in fleshly lust. He hated sin and sinners; but he conjugated the verb *to sin* in terms of

137

pleasure, and so naïvely exposed his own unconscious desires.

His bitterness at life flowed into and coloured his idea of God, but his bitterness arose from a complex of causes that had but little relation to religion. He had acquired a religion before he had acquired a morality; and, consequently, he was never as good nor as virtuous as he imagined himself to be. He was tangled in his religious faith as in a coil of barbed wire. He could not move in any direction without lacerating himself with its prickly inhibitions.

The undergrowth of this dark wilderness of ideas consisted of political opinions which were so modern that we stare in amazement when we run across them. The early Puritan believed in the political equality of men. He asserted that by "naturall birth all men are equally and alike born to like propriety, liberty and freedom." He was a democrat before any one else had ever thought of giving the underdog a voice in affairs. His democratic notions were extremely revolutionary; they were tinged with communism.

This was the attitude of the early Puritans, but not of the later ones. Their faith degenerated in transplantation. The Christian virtues were rubbed pretty thin by the vicissitudes of colonial life, by head-on collisions with the Indian tribes, by greed for land, by Medford rum, by the profits of the slave trade.

In the prosperity of the New World the economic necessity that had been the inspiration of Puritanism melted away. Nothing remained of its primitive urge but the rough mould in which it had been cast. It existed thereafter only as a ghost, and was as disagreeable and nasty in manner as ghosts usually are.

As a doctrine, by means of which men could shape their daily lives, Puritanism was bound to fail. It was lopsided and full of internal contradictions from the start. In its political ideas it was centuries too early, and in its theology it was centuries too late.

Before the beginning of the eighteenth century Puritanism had deteriorated into mere cantankerous bear-baiting. Its chief delights were in the repression of free speech and in the persecution of competing religions. Quakers were whipped and hanged, and poor demented old women were stoned to death as witches. Love-making on the Sabbath was prohibited. Eager faces peered from night-darkness into candle-lit rooms to see what husbands and wives were doing.

The strain that Puritanism in its raw state put on human nature was too great for endurance. Its ideals curdled into tacit hypocrisy, into recognised compromises with the flesh and the devil. When a sin became too strong to resist it was given a sort of pious dignity of its own. The slave trade bore a hymn-book on its black escutcheon, for it performed the holy work of bringing the heathen negro into the light of Christianity.

§ 2

The sexual morality of the Puritan was too good to be true—and, in fact, was not true. The high tension of sexual morals was eased considerably by the diverting practice of bundling.

Bundling means simply the lying in bed together of an unmarried young man and an unmarried young woman. The theory behind the institution was that, in homes of small dimensions, a girl had no place to entertain her beau except in bed. The nights were cold; there was usually only one fire-place, before which all the family sat. Squalling children and prosy old men cluttered the stage and made love's tender passages very difficult, if not impossible. But, under the warm blankets in the darkness of the bedroom, conversation was decidedly easier and much more pleasant.

Bundlers were not supposed to remove their clothing, though the learned books on this subject declare that the prohibition against undressing was held by accomplished practitioners to be merely theoretical, not to be taken literally, but in its broader and more constructive sense.

Chastity was implied, for both man and woman were supposed to be already sanctified by grace. Indeed, in one aspect, bundling was considered a test of virtue.

Dr. Henry Reed Stiles, who has written informatively on the practice of bundling, says that it reached the height of its popularity between 1750 and 1780. Among the common people it was a recognised institution. The girl's mother frequently tucked in the young couple and made them comfortable. The better class considered bundling a vicious practice—too public and too vulgar. Their own bundling was carried on with more circumspection.

As bundling grew into almost universal popularity New England communities were full of expert bundlers, who went around bundling from one place to another.

The moralists were hot on their trail, and the practice was a subject of acrimonious controversy in the latter half of the eighteenth century. The temper of these reformers is indicated in this quotation from a long poem against bundling:

> Hail, giddy youth, inclined to mirth,
> To guilty amours prone,
> Come blush with me, to think and see
> How shameless you are grown.

> *   *   *

> Dogs and bitches wear no breeches,
> Clothing for man was made,
> Yet men and women strip to their linen,
> And tumble into bed.

> Yes, brutal youth, it is the truth,
> Your modesty is gone,
> And could you blush, you'd think as much,
> And curse what you have done.

A poet with an evil imagination, undoubtedly, who put the worst possible construction on this pastime.

But bundling had its defenders—poets of broader views and cleaner minds. One of them states his argument of morality combined with economy in verses of metrical precision:

> Since in a bed a man and maid,
> May bundle and be chaste,
> It does no good to burn out wood,
> It is a needless waste.
>
> Let coats and gowns be laid aside,
> And breeches take their flight,
> An honest man and woman can
> Lay quiet all the night.

Bundling was one of the symptoms of the breaking up of austere Puritan standards. There were others . . . the rum trade . . . speculation in land . . . the business of slavery. . . .

But let us look for a moment at the other side, where there is much to be said. We must never forget that the Puritan brought the germ of liberty to the New World. He was a harsh, tyrannical person, and he cared nothing for other people's liberty, but he cared a lot for his own, and he was pugnacious in defending his rights. Independence cannot be *conferred* on a race; it must be won; it must come from the inner consciousness. It is not a gift, but a state of mind, with the courage to sustain it. The Puritan had an independent mind; he was a rebel by instinct.

He believed in education. His feet were hardly planted o American soil before he founded a college which was kep going in that struggling colony by keen and cutting sacrifices on the part of the people. Every one gave something. Even the poorest farmers brought donations of butter and vegetables to Harvard to keep it alive.

At the beginning of the Revolution there were hardly any

illiterates in Massachusetts. There were probably more read-ing people there in proportion to the population than in any other part of the world. A hundred years before Virginia and South Carolina had even dreamed of having a free school of any kind there was a school that was virtually free in every Massachusetts township.

What a pity it is that human institutions continue to exist after their inspiration has ceased! Puritanism died, its day was over, but it continued to function as if it were still alive. Out into the American people flowed—not its blood—but the virus from its dead body; and to-day it still runs through our current life, breaking out now and then in strange and potent hypocrisies.

This transfusion of acidulous Puritan conceptions into the whole of American civilisation took place after the Revolution. In colonial times Puritanical ideas existed only in New England, but with the end of the war Massachusetts and Connecticut people began to migrate to the West and South. With them they carried the dead shell of Puritanism, and set it up osten-tatiously in their new homes.

§ 3

Turning now to Virginia we must note that George Wash-ington, wealthy planter and fox-hunting sportsman, was with-out a trace of Puritanism. He was so completely indifferent to its pious irascibilities that he appears never to have made any comment on them. Indeed, he seemed, according to the evidence, to have had no instinct or feeling for religion, al-though he attended church twelve or fifteen times a year.

The name of Jesus Christ is not mentioned even once in the vast collection of Washington's published letters. He refers to Providence in numerous letters, but he used the term in such a way as to indicate that he considered Providence as a synonym for Destiny or Fate. Bishop White, who knew him well for many years, wrote after Washington's death that he had never heard him express an opinion on any religious subject. He added that although Washington was "serious and attentive" in church he never saw him kneel in prayer.

Nevertheless, he believed in the stabilising power of religion. He had no religious feeling himself, but thought religion was a good thing for other people—especially for the common people. Any one who understands American life will recognise the modern captain-of-industry attitude in this point of view.

In his Farewell Address, which unquestionably represents Washington's most mature opinions, the name of God does not appear, but he had a good word for religion, to wit: "Of all the dispositions and habits which lead to political prosperity, religion and morality are indispensable supports."

Reading this, we pause and reflect. He considers religion a matter of policy. Of that we might have been sure—knowing, as we do, his type of mind. But the statement does not come up to expectations; he has not tied religion up to property. Any modern captain of industry would do that. How ever, we are not yet at the end of the statement. In th same paragraph, a few lines further on, he says:

> Let it simply be asked, where is the security for property, for reputation, for life, if the sense of religious obligation desert the oaths which are the instruments of investigation in courts of justice? And let us with caution indulge the supposition that morality can be maintained without religion.

Washington had the inestimable faculty of being able to say nothing. He said nothing about religion—nothing very definite—and was willing to let people think whatever they pleased. Jefferson, on the contrary, talked a great deal about religion. His intellect was expansive, prolific, full of ideas. He was a deist, like Washington, and he wanted to convince others. He attempted to rewrite the Bible. When he was elected President old maids in New England hid their Bibles, for the rumour had gone out that the infidel Jefferson, now in the White House, intended to put through a law which would confiscate all the Bibles and put his own in their place.

But when Washington was President no one hid a Bible. As he never discussed religion at all, and went to church occasionally, he was considered by most people to be a quietly religious man. It was something of a shock, therefore, to the people of Philadelphia when the reverend Dr. Abercrombie, Washington's pastor, criticised him from the pulpit. He told him that, as President, he should not belong to a church unless he could set a good example to others. He reminded Washington that he never took communion, and in short, that his example was bad.

Washington listened to these reproaches in silence, and never went to that church again. His only comment was that he would not annoy Dr. Abercrombie by his presence.

In colonial Virginia religion was a social formality. The fashionable faith was that of the Established Church of England. It was as different from the faith of the Puritans as a religion could possibly be and still remain in the Christian category. The Virginia parson was, in many instances, a jovial drinker and gambler, too busy with the lighter pleasures to inflict a sermon of more than twenty minutes in length on his congregation.

Nevertheless, with the attachment to phrases and forms which has always been a characteristic of the American mind, the statutes of Virginia made a denial of the Trinity a crime subject to a penalty of three years' imprisonment. The law was not enforced. There were laws against witchcraft. Free thinkers were excluded from office, and even from the custody of their own children. That is, they were supposed to be, but this law was also a dead letter. Its retention on the statute books was probably not an oversight, however. We have observed in our own times that such obsolete laws are frequently retained for the purpose of persecution in individual cases.

§ 4

By the middle of the eighteenth century the Puritan church and state had quietly separated. Theocracy was on its death bed. But the movement of separation had been so gradual, and so much in the natural order of things, that the religious party did not realise its loss of authority until it was too late to regain it.

Theology ceased to be the chief topic of literary dialectics and politics took its place. Such agonising pamphlets as *The Gospel Order Revived* and *Sanctification through Works* went out of style, and essays on taxation and the natural rights of man swarmed into literature.

Yet, in this hour of its decay, Puritanism produced its most profound intellect—its great philosopher—like one of those curious flowers which bloom only when their roots are dying. Jonathan Edwards was to Puritanism what Herbert Spencer was to the philosophy of rationalisation. On the narrow plane of a bigoted religion he displayed an almost overwhelming intellectual vigour.

A queer strain ran through his family. His grandson was the Aaron Burr who killed Alexander Hamilton. His own grandmother was Elizabeth Tuttle, who was divorced by her husband for adultery, an unspeakably scandalous occurrence in that epoch. Elizabeth's sister murdered her child, and her brother was a murderer, too.

His mind moved with speed. He was quick and vivid, and somewhat erratic in behaviour. When he was on his travels, and a new idea occurred to him—as many did—he would write it down on a slip of paper and pin the slip to his coat. At the end of a thoughtful day he would ride up to his stopping place for the night with paper streamers fluttering from his garments.

There was more than a touch of Dante in him. He was a

"hell-fire" preacher of such blazing fervour that he sent his hearers home in hysterics. He told them that God would make blood squirt out of them, that He would hold them over the mouth of hell as one holds a spider over a fire; that the holy redeemed would lean over the parapets of heaven and chuckle merrily at the sight of the wicked writhing in the flames. All this sounds like the crack of doom, but it is simply the reaction of a poetic soul into which a gross religious materialism has been poured.

Jonathan Edwards was a religious sadist, which is a state of being that is always associated with some form of suppressed sex. But he was much more than a religious sadist . . . much more, indeed.

At heart he was a mystic and a poet. His sadism was confined to his religion. In the ordinary affairs of life, in contact with people, he was a gentle-hearted person. His writings contain passages of rare charm. He fell in love with Sarah Pierrepont and wrote of her as Dante wrote of Beatrice.

The sombre spirit of the Florentine flowed into poems which have the iridescence of liquid bronze; that of Jonathan Edwards in a colder land and among a harsher people, went into a philosophical work, called *The Freedom of the Will.*

This metaphysical treatise remains to-day, after time has sifted the chaff from the wheat, the ablest literary production of the colonial period. The author's conceptions have a crystalline lucidity. They are knitted together by a logic of marvellous texture. Even if one does not agree with him one must admire his book as an intellectual feat. He was a keen metaphysician . . . but, nevertheless, a metaphysician intoxicated with the glory of God; a Spinoza smitten by the fear of sin and laden with a New England conscience.

This stream of Puritan culture flowed through Washington's early years without attracting his serious attention. Undoubtedly he knew who Jonathan Edwards was, but it is not likely that he ever read one of his books.

§ 5

The colonies before the Revolution produced only two men of the first intellectual rank. One of them was Jonathan Edwards and the other was Benjamin Franklin. Neither of them had the mental grasp or the vision of Thomas Jefferson, but Jefferson attained his intellectual maturity after the Revolution.

It is now nearly a century and a half since the death of Benjamin Franklin, but we may still reach across the years and touch him without feeling the sense of distance. He is so modern in character that everything he wrote sounds as if it might have appeared in last Sunday's newspaper.

His most interesting biographer called him "many-sided," as indeed he was. His range and versatility were extraordinary. He was the first American go-getter, the first of our shrewd countrymen who began life with no capital but "a pair of socks and a headache" and rose to money and fame.

In his youth Franklin's character had not been entirely admirable, and many of his fellow-citizens thought it always lacked some indispensable qualities. His father was an humble candle-maker in Boston, and Benjamin was apprenticed to an elder brother who was a printer. He became an egotistical and cocky youth, and a poor apprentice . . . had a knock-down fight with his brother . . . ran away from home . . . went to Philadelphia . . . seduced girls . . . embezzled thirty pounds.

Then he threw off these evil ways as one throws off a cloak, and set out to make a fortune and a career.

His printing business prospered. He published newspapers, books and an annual periodical called "Poor Richard's Almanac," in which he printed commonsense observations and wise maxims, most of which he had paraphrased from Rabelais, Swift and Sterne. He was the inventor of the great American Short Cut to Wisdom, the founder of the School of Thumbnail Philosophy. He understood the common people; he had been one of them. He was the first American writer of renown to discover that the average man cannot follow any line of reasoning, unless it has to do with money or sex, for more than three minutes continuously. Everything he wrote, with a few exceptions, was in the form of three-minute essays, so he became a sort of eighteenth century Confucius, with a dash of Elbert Hubbard.

But he was of much heavier weight than this observation implies. At the age of forty-three he retired from business to devote the remainder of his life to scientific research.

This devotion to science was interrupted by long spells of political and diplomatic activity—he was a colonial representative in England for ten years and was for nine years in France as our first envoy—but notwithstanding interruptions, he applied himself to science with such success that he was the leader of the eighteenth century world in electrical discovery.

He had four distinct careers. In all of them his figure is monumental. He was the greatest of the early publishers, the most renowned scientific investigator of his day, an important American statesman, and by far the most successful of American diplomats. As a politician he had discovered, as Stuart Sherman says, "the great secret of converting private desires into public demands," and that is the essence of American politics. And there was his literary career, besides. In that field he attained such a luminous celebrity that his mantle, worn rather thin, has been passed on from one generation of authors to another. To-day, torn into scraps, it adorns the persons of forty or fifty newspaper column writers.

In this prodigious life there is hardly a trace of effort. He was indolent by disposition and calm in manner. His scientific experiments were really a kind of play, and he went about the solution of problems with the utmost simplicity and directness. Everything he knew had been gathered by reading or observation. He was without intellectual traditions. In their place

BENJAMIN FRANKLIN
Painting by M. Chamberlin

he had the indestructible sanity of the self-taught. His most striking characteristic was a flaming curiosity. But he was never interested in an idea simply as an idea. He cared only for conceptions that could be turned to practical use. His mind stood permanently at the metaphysical zero.

Physically, he was a large, broad-shouldered man without sharp angles. A smooth, rounded sort of man. There was probably a good deal of the feminine in him.

Franklin and Jonathan Edwards, both powerfully intellectual, existed in different intellectual worlds. Like Washington and Jefferson, Franklin was a deist; which means that he had no religion at all, but only a code of behaviour.

He was a firm believer in chastity and moderation, but he was not a fanatic. Like Samuel Butler, he believed that vice has a purpose, and that its true function is to keep virtue within reasonable bounds. During the year his illegitimate son was born Franklin was deeply absorbed in a plan which he had conceived of writing a literary work to be called *The Art of Virtue*. He intended to indicate how the virtues might be acquired—the way to be frugal, chaste, temperate. But the plan was never carried out, though he fumbled with it for years.

Instinctively a ladies' man, his love affairs run through his life side by side with his homely philosophy and his scientific experiments. He admired women and understood them thoroughly. He was the kind of man to whom women tell their troubles on first acquaintance. Many women, who would not think ordinarily of any kind of philandering, allow men of this type to make love to them as a matter of course.

Despite his wide popularity many Americans considered Franklin and his friends a lewd lot of people. To the end of his days the aristocratic section of Philadelphia called him "a sly old rogue" and would have nothing to do with him socially. Such a posture seems rather absurd, for when Franklin returned from France at the close of the Revolution he was undoubtedly one of the most illustrious persons in the world. Washington was the only man in America who was on his level, and Franklin was received everywhere in Europe, and in America—outside of Philadelphia—by people in the highest social circles.

He is said to have been one of those who recommended Washington to General Braddock, though he knew Washington only by reputation at that time.

§ 6

Pre-Revolutionary literature was all sharp angles, and consisted chiefly of tirades. Irate men seized their pens as one seizes an axe. No man of backbone was satisfied with calling his political opponent a scoundrel; he had to be some kind of elaborate scoundrel.

Writers were clumsy with words. They attempted satire, which is an utterly disastrous field of adventure for an awkward writer. Their satires, starting out bravely in imitation of Swift, soon sank head and ears in a morass of burlesque, the cheapest of all literary devices.

Everything was an imitation. Poets, floating easily on a current of doggerel, imitated the biting jingles of Butler's *Hudibras*. Solemn political disputants imitated the style of the Bible. Others heard the rolling thunder of Milton's lines, and tried to roll a little thunder of their own, but produced only growls.

Primitive lands sometimes produce men of talent; they almost never give birth to a genius. The human race, like other species of living organisms, creates in the long run the individuals it needs. It develops types to fit the circumstances of existence, and in a primitive society nobody has any particular need for a genius. There the prime necessity is physical action; consequently, individuals whose personalities are rooted in the soil of action are produced and rise to eminence.

The genius is a symptom of ebbing racial vitality. The genius type begins to appear in a civilisation only when the inner force of the race has reached its apex and is subsiding, though this may be long before there is any diminution of its outer, exterior force.

Colonial America produced a handful of talented men, but men with the unmistakable touch of genius do not begin to appear until long after the Revolution.

CHAPTER XI

LOGGERHEADS AND PEWTER DOLLARS

§ 1

WASHINGTON's political career began in 1758 with his election to the House of Burgesses as a member from Frederick county. He had kept his eye on the office for several years. In 1755 he wrote to his brother that he would like to be a candidate that year if Colonel Fairfax did not want the place. Some of the Fairfaxes evidently had a candidate, for Washington's brother let the matter drop. Two years later he was a candidate, but received only forty votes. Then, in 1758, he appeared on the list again, with the Fairfaxes behind him. Powerful as these great land-owners were, they did not make his success at the polls an assured matter, for shortly before the election Lord Fairfax wrote to William Fairfax, "I fear Col. Washington will be very hard pushed."

Needless fears . . . it all turned out well. Washington received three hundred and one votes, which was the largest number cast for any candidate. He did not appear personally at the election, as he was on the Virginia frontier in the war against the French and Indians, but he was well known to all the voters, either by acquaintance or reputation. There were no campaign speeches; liquor was freely distributed and took the place of political eloquence.

With a generous hand he provided refreshments for the tired voters. This is what the election cost him:

	£	s	d
40 gallons of Rum Punch at 3/6 per galn.	7	0	0
15 gallons of Wine at 10/ per galn.	7	10	0
Dinner for your Friends	3	0	0

	£	s	d
13½ gallons of Wine at 10/	6	15	0
3½ pts. of Brandy at 1/3		4	4½
13 gallons of Beer at 1/3		16	3
8 qts. Cyder Royal at 1/6		12	0
30 gallons of strong beer at 8d	1	0	0
1 hhd. & 1 Barrell of Punch, consisting of			
26 gals. best Barbados rum at 5/	6	10	0
12 lbs. S. Refd. Sugar at 1/6		18	9
10 Bowls of Punch at 2/6 each	1	5	0
9 half pints of rum at 7½d each	0	5	7½
1 pint of wine	0	1	6

Confronted with this comprehensive list, one mentally calculates . . . three hundred and one Washington voters . . . and enough liquor to stock a barroom. They must have been formidable indeed in their carrying capacity. But let us keep in mind that drinking was not a furtive sin, as it is with us; nor was it a pastime. It was a sort of athletic sport. Men tried for records as one-bottle men or two-bottle men. Three-bottle men (and there were a few) were looked up to with the reverence that we show nowadays only to champion prize-fighters and noted preachers.

Washington was a one-bottle man. This means that at dinner he customarily drank a pint of Madeira, besides rum punch and beer. He preferred Madeira to all other beverages, but he was catholic in his drinking habits, and often drank cider, champagne and brandy. If he was ever intoxicated I have never read of it; and, judging from what I know of his character, I am inclined to think he never was.

§ 2

The amount of drinking that was done by all classes of society is almost beyond belief. A stranger in Philadelphia in 1744 wrote in his diary that he was "given cider and punch

for lunch; rum and brandy before dinner; punch, **Madeira,**
port, and sherry at dinner; punch and liqueurs with the ladies;
and wine, spirit and punch till bedtime; all in punch bowls big
enough for a goose to swim in."

They were bold drinkers, too—ready to snap their fingers
before the bleary face of Silenus—for they thought nothing
of mixing gin with beer, and rum with beer. Every amateur
drinker knows that this mixing of distant cousins in the family
of beverages is a heroic venture. Our stalwart ancestors would
stir gin, beer and molasses together and drink the menacing
concoction as carelessly as one drinks a cup of coffee.

Flip was the most popular of the rum and beer drinks. It
is mentioned so frequently in the chronicles of the time that
one gets an impression of it having been almost as common as
soda-water is to-day. Mrs. Alice Morse Earle, in her diverting
Stage-coach and Tavern Days, gives a recipe for it. In
a pitcher two-thirds full of strong beer they put enough sugar
or molasses to make the beer sweet. To this mess they added
about a gill of New England rum, and stirred it all together.
Then a poker of special shape—with a large head on it—
was heated red-hot and plunged into the pitcher. This red-
hot iron, which was called a loggerhead, made the concoction
boil, and gave it a burnt, bitter taste.

A loggerhead was part of the mechanical equipment of every
fireside. At times it was used in controversy to take the place
of the logical syllogism. In the debates which followed the
convivial absorption of flip or rum-fustian the disputants
would often seize loggerheads for the purpose of bringing
their opponents to a state of material, if not mental, conviction.
Thus, the expression "to be at loggerheads" arose.

The common name for rum was "Kill-devil." It was made
from West Indian molasses, and the centre of the distilling
trade was Rhode Island, though there were many distilleries
throughout New England and some in New York. As far back

as 1731 the annual production of rum by Boston distilleries was estimated at one million two hundred gallons.

By 1771 the business of rum distilling had grown into an industry of large dimensions. In that year more than four million gallons of molasses were imported. Part of this quantity was used for sweetening instead of sugar—Professor Channing thinks fifty per cent—but the remainder (say two million gallons) was made into rum on the basis of one gallon of rum for one gallon of molasses. In addition to this domestic output the British West Indies sent something more than two million gallons of rum to the North American colonies. Altogether let us say, four million gallons of rum for 1771, including both the domestic and imported products. Of this total, about three hundred thousand gallons were exported. The rest, which we may estimate at three million seven hundred thousand gallons, was the ordinary colonial consumption for one year.

Labourers and mechanics expected their employers to supply them with rum while they were at work. After the Revolution, when Washington was president of the Potomac Canal Company, we find him negotiating with merchants to furnish rum for the workmen at two shillings a gallon.

Any attempt to prohibit the sale of liquor would have caused a more determined patriot uprising than that aroused by the battle of Bunker Hill, and no such attempt was ever made.

The drinking of rum was almost universal, but the consumption of it was not really so great in volume as that of hard cider, which practically every one drank daily in quantities, with their meals and at odd times during the day. It was even given to children of four or five years of age. A New England minister who had laid in forty barrels of hard cider for the use of his family and guests during the winter, wrote that he was afraid of running short before the next cider season.

Mrs. Earle mentions a minister's ordination at which the eighty people in attendance drank thirty bowls of punch before going to meeting; and the sixty-eight who had dinner disposed of forty-four bowls of punch, eighteen bottles of wine, eight bowls of brandy, and a quantity of cherry rum. If the ordination sermon was not well received under these conditions, the new minister must have been indeed a poor sermoniser.

Among the gin-beer mixtures was one called by the strange name of rum-fustian, although it had no rum in it. It was almost as popular as flip, the rum-beer mixture. Rum-fustian is easy to make. Half a pint of gin, a quart of beer, a bottle of sherry, the yolks of a dozen eggs, sugar and nutmeg. It turns out to be a queer-tasting drink . . . makes one think somehow of liquid leather—but it carries authority like a man carrying a club.

Bumbo, sometimes called mimbo, was made of rum, hot water and sugar. This was also called grog. It was precisely the same aromatic drink that one gets to-day at the sidewalk cafés in Paris under the name of *grog américain*.

§ 3

For all this drinking the towns were well supplied with taverns. Most of them were places with rickety furniture and a bad smell, but some were clean and handsome. Very English, these better taverns were . . . sanded floors . . . oak beams . . . stuffed parrots . . . windows with leaded panes. The fire in the roomy stone fireplace would send its light flickering over iridescent glass and pewter mugs and jolly faces, while the air was full of tobacco smoke and politics.

All the taverns had gaudy signs; and every other kind of establishment had them, too. The business quarters of the towns were lively and colourful.

It was the golden age of the picture-sign. Most of the common people were illiterate; they remembered the merchant's shop by the picture over his door. Looking along a busy mercantile street, one would see, swinging in the breeze, a line of king's heads, dogs and eagles, nuns, crowns and swords, pine-trees and Indian chiefs, all painted in bright colours on wood. The art of sign-painting was highly developed. Men of talent went in for it. Many of the tavern signs around Philadelphia were—according to tradition—the work of Benjamin West before he attained his world-wide celebrity as a portrait painter.

Some of the taverns became historic through their connection with the revolutionary movement. The Raleigh Tavern at Williamsburg was the Faneuil Hall of Virginia. It was there that the Virginia delegates met when the House of Burgesses was dissolved by the royal governor.

Another historic tavern was that of Richard Woodward at Dedham, Massachusetts. There the famous Suffolk convention met in 1774 and abolished the administration of British law in Massachusetts—the first definite step in the separation of the colonies from the mother country.

The Woodward tavern was renowned in another way. For about fifty years it had been the home of the Ameses, father and son, who published Ames' *Almanack*. They ran the tavern and wrote the *Almanack*. This publication was as popular as Benjamin Franklin's "Poor Richard" though its circulation was limited chiefly to New England. When the elder Nathaniel Ames died his son continued the *Almanack*, and his mother became the tavern-keeper. In a few years the widow Ames married Richard Woodward.

Young Ames did not like his step-father. He wrote a scrappy diary on the blank leaves of one of his own *Almanacks* in which he sets forth his trials. In frankness and self-revelation he is an American Pepys.

> *May 9.* Old Dick Woodward struck me with his saw.
> *May 12.* Dick Woodward fined for striking me and bound to good Behaviour.

Young Ames soon leaves home and sets up in a house for himself. He still finds the world full of woe:

> *Nov. 25.* Annual Thanksgiving which I celebrated with much Thankfulness in a little boiled Rice at home alone, then came in my Brother William who had good provisions sent him from his Mother and dind here at my House upon it, of which I could not so much as taste. Mrs. Whiting my Housekeeper prevented my having Provisions of my own cooked and went among her Relations to dine leaving me to cook for my Self.

His grievances extended to the journalistic tribe:

> *Sept. 24.* Never let me write again to the Printers of Boston News Papers for they are all Knaves Liars, Villains to serve their Intrest and when they appear most Friendly have most of the Devil in their Hearts.

Now and then mystery and drama wing through the chilly air:

> *Oct. 12.* The Fair Lady here at my House is said to be a german Princess in disguise.

But Old Dick Woodward takes all the joy out of life:

> Old Richard Woodward has declared that he will fleece our Estate as much as possible & accordingly Oct. 12th carried off several Loads of unthrashed Rye & carried off all the last years Corn & threatens to carry away the Hay out of the Barn in defiance of Law & Equity threatens to strip & waste as much as possible.

So there they are . . . Mr. Ames groaning and complaining, Mr. Woodward stripping and wasting, the Boston newspapers uttering lies, and a tow-haired lady sitting in haughty reserve in the parlor . . . all transfixed in their attitudes, as motionless as figures in a doll's house.

§ 4

The colonials had a love of colour which amounted to a passion. They painted everything they could lay their hands on. Their preference was not for the softer tones, for the pastel shades, but for colors that were sharp, bright and hot.

Their carriages were painted yellow, green, red or blue—in Philadelphia brown was favoured—with shiny wheels.

They went in for coloured fabrics. Women wore enormous puffy gowns of satin, in bright colours, with shoulder veils of green or lavender. Well-dressed men usually appeared in blue coats, with gold or silver buttons on which the wearer's monogram was engraved. Under this was a yellow waistcoat, cut long in front, with large pockets in which huge watches were carried. Sometimes a dandy was provided with two watches, one for each pocket, with a connecting gold chain running across the waistcoat. When any one asked him what time it was, he would look ostentatiously at both watches, and average their respective tallies. For ordinary occasions the knee breeches were of blue or tan velvet, but for highly formal affairs these garments were of white gleaming satin. There were lace ruffles on the shirt front and lace cuffs, which were weighted with shot to keep them hanging down—otherwise they would have interfered with the movements of the hands. Wealthy people, both men and women, wore stockings of silk. The men's stockings were usually striped.

Boots did not come into general use until the Revolution. They were never worn except on horseback, or in rainy weather. Men's hats were broad-brimmed—some of the brims were seven inches wide—but the brims were pinned up in triangular shape.

Of course, none of this description applies to the dress of the poor. They could not afford silks or laces. Coarse woolen, with linen for petticoats and shirts, provided material for their outfits. The men frequently wore leather coats—and a single suit, with a leather coat, would last a man for many years. But they wore bright colours whenever they could, particularly in the shape of gaily printed handkerchiefs which the men put around their necks and the women pinned over their breasts.

The colonials loved warm colours, but there was no gleam of the genial Mediterranean in the colonial soul. Our forefathers' hard, unrelenting character shows itself in the bitter quarrels which wrangle endlessly through the files of their newspapers. There were libels, charges and countercharges. When an aggrieved person could not get his grievance into the newspapers, or if he lived in a place where no newspaper was published, he sometimes assailed his enemy in a vituperative handbill or broadside. This document was distributed gratis, the creator of it often standing on the street and giving it away himself.

They had an inordinate fondness for lawsuits. The colonies were full of maladjusted, turbulent people; restless groups which did not fit into the scheme of things. And, besides, I fancy they were greatly bored for lack of amusement. At any rate, they appeared to enjoy lawsuits, and at the slightest incentive they went to court with the elation of guests attending a garden party.

Long before the Revolution both lawyers and lawsuits were multiplying, and lawyers had assumed a prominent place in American life.

Patrick Henry, a country lawyer who had studied law for only six weeks before his admission to the bar, conducted 557 lawsuits in the year 1765—an average year. Nearly all of these suits were in the inferior courts—mere trifling squabbles— but the great scholarly lawyers were busy, too. Thomas Jefferson, who had grilled himself on law-books for four years as a student in the office of the profoundly legal George Wythe, represented two hundred clients at the bar of the General Court in the course of twelve months.

§ 5

The desire to have a lot of famous ancestors—especially "well-born" ancestors—is one of the most interesting of human traits, and one of the most illogical. If one does not amount to much, then a distinguished ancestry ought really to be a standing reproach, for if a man cannot measure up to his forefathers, it is obvious that he is a degenerate specimen of the race.

On the other hand, if a man amounts to a great deal, a common breed of ancestors ought to be highly esteemed, for that proves beyond doubt that the family has made some progress since its forebears displayed their peasant illiteracy on this rolling planet.

Such reasoning, sound as it is, does not impress the American people very much. Most of our well-to-do families have managed, by the aid of skilful genealogists, to locate a collection of distinguished progenitors; and indigent portrait painters have become prosperous on the creation of imaginary pictures of men in armour and women in Elizabethan ruffs.

In fact, with the invention of romantic literature and the remarkable success of the stock and bond business the ancestor hunt has been carried on so thoroughly that the whole American nation appears now, in popular belief, to have descended from the "best" families of Europe.

The historians who are most widely read have helped along this pleasant illusion. Through them we see the Cavaliers of Virginia, with plumed hats and swords which "leap from the scabbard"; the sedate Dutch founders of New Amsterdam, their pockets filled with gold doubloons and their hearts with courage, separating themselves strangely from their noble estates in the Netherlands to settle in our barbarous land; the scholarly Puritans of New England; and the haughty *noblesse* of South Carolina, who are supposed to have brought to that forest-covered colony a punctilious honour which was

so touchy and irritable that it can be compared only with
poison ivy in its practical effects.

This picture, with its trailing perspective of English squires
and sons of lords, is romantic but untrue.

As a matter of historical fact, America was settled by the
ordinary run of poor and illiterate folks. Its great prosperity is the achievement of their descendants; it stands to-day
as monumental evidence of the ability of ordinary, common
people to create material wealth.

The colony of Virginia was peopled mainly by day labourers
and indented servants. There was no Cavalier emigration. In
every colony there were a few families who had been gentlefolk
in England—the Washingtons and Lees in Virginia, the
Calverts in Maryland, the Winthrops in Massachusetts—but
their number was so small as to be insignificant. The aristocracy of colonial Virginia, like the aristocracy of every other
colony, was self-made and arose in the colony itself. Hendrik
Willem Van Loon says, "Dukes don't emigrate," and Mr. Van
Loon is right.

It would have been as unreasonable for a seventeenth century Englishman of culture and social standing to have come
to America to live as it would be for one of our wealthy idlers
to take up a residence in Siberia.

If the Cavaliers of Virginia are imaginary, it may be said
with equal truth that there was no pick of God's children in
New England, either, even though the words "sturdy" and
"God-fearing" have been worn thin in describing them.

Many of the Puritans were lazy and some were drunken.
They had to set up stocks for offenders almost as soon as
they arrived; and James Woodward, the first man put in
them, was sentenced "for being drunk at the Newetowne."

The settlers of New York were plain Dutch farmers of the
lower class. Their Knickerbocker aristocracy, which they
formed later when they grew rich, consisted of people whose

names were unknown in the puffy little *beau monde* of Holland.

Georgia was founded to provide a refuge for poor debtors and converted criminals. Georgia and Pennsylvania are the only two of the thirteen original states that make no claim to a strong admixture of high-class blood. The Quakers of Pennsylvania were common people, and said so; and their descendants say they were, too, greatly to everybody else's surprise.

§ 6

Besides the free white people and the negro slaves there was another class, among the inhabitants of the colonies, known as indented servants.

The indented servant was a white person held in slavery. His servitude differed from that of the negro slave in that it was not perpetual, but only for a definite term—usually for three or four years, but in some cases it was much longer. Indented servants, or "redemptioners," were usually immigrants . . . poor people who could not pay their passage to the New World, and who gave an indenture to the captain of the ship that brought them. This indenture was a legal instrument which bound the immigrant to servitude for a certain time. Upon arriving at a colonial port the captain would sell the indenture to some tradesman or planter for the passage money that was due him, and the indented servant was turned over to the purchaser of the instrument.

While the servitude lasted the indented servant was in reality a slave. He received no wages, but only his board and clothes. He could not leave his master's plantation or shop without permission; he could be put at any work that suited his master's purpose. Indented servants were whipped for disobedience just as slaves were whipped.

Among the indented servants were many convicted criminals. The English jails, always overcrowded in the eighteenth cen-

tury, were emptied occasionally by sending gangs of prisoners
to the colonies. Some of these convicts were persons of rank.
A baronet was brought to America for stealing a ring; and
Fiske mentions a certain Henry Justice, Esq., barrister of the
Middle Temple, who was sent to America for seven years for
purloining a book from the library of Trinity College, Cambridge.

There is a tradition still current in Virginia that the sexton
Hobby, who taught young George Washington to read and
write, was a convict who had been brought from England and
sold as an indented servant. According to this story his name
was Grove, and he was called "Hobby" as a nickname. How
true or false this is I do not know; anyway, it is a matter of
no importance.

Washington bought these white slaves now and then. There
were always a few of them about Mount Vernon among the
carpenters and other skilled workmen. A Mr. McGachen wrote
to him, from Baltimore, in 1774:

> I have purchased for you four men convicts, four
> indented servants for three years, and a man and his wife
> for four years. The price is, I think, rather high; but as
> they are country, likely people . . . Mr. Crawford
> imagined you would be well satisfied with our bargain. I
> have agreed to pay £110 sterling for them.

Criminals were not deported to America after the colonies
became independent, but the traffic in indented servants continued for some years after the Revolution. In 1786 Washington wrote in his Diary:

> *Sunday, June 4th.* Received on board the Brig Ann
> from Ireland, two Servant Men for whom I had agreed
> yesterday, viz. Thomas Ryan, a shoemaker, and Caven
> Bowes, a Taylor, redemptioners for 3 years service by
> Indenture if they could not pay Each, the Sum of £12
> Sterg. which sum I agreed to pay.

§ 7

Slaves in colonial America were sold in about the same way as second-hand automobiles are sold nowadays. One brightens up the old car and takes it to a dealer who puts a sign on it, stating the price and emphasising its good points. After awhile somebody comes along, looks over the motor, haggles with the dealer and takes the car away. Change the automobiles to negroes and you have a slave market.

Washington, with his habitual care for details, took pains to "brighten up" his negroes when he offered them for sale, though he was too frank to conceal their faults. In sending a sullen and refractory negro named Tom to the West Indies to be sold he wrote to the captain of the ship:

> This fellow is both a rogue and a runaway (tho he was by no means remarkable for the former, and never practiced the latter till of late) I shall not pretend to deny. But that he is exceedingly healthy, strong, and good at the hoe . . . which gives me reason to hope that he may with your good management sell well, if kept clean and trim'd up a little when offered for sale.

He expected his slaves to do their full share of work, and he held them rigidly to the regulations of his plantations. There was a good deal of the martinet in Washington; we see this quality appearing in all his relations with inferiors.

But he seems to have treated his slaves very well—not exactly as one treats human beings, but as one treats a stable of valuable horses. He established a small hospital at Mount Vernon for them. There are many instances in his diary of his attention to sick negroes. His slaves were whipped on occasion, after repeated disobedience, but these occasions were rare. One day he came unexpectedly upon a white overseer giving a slave a thrashing. The sight enraged Washington, and he fell into one of his furious tempers. He seized his horse-whip and approached the overseer, his eyes blazing. The overseer, realising that he was about to take the negro's place as an object of castigation, kept walking backward and saying, "Remember your character, General—remember your character!" Washington remembered his character and rode off with a few words of rebuke.

The literary tactics which Henry Cabot Lodge employed in his biography of Washington to conceal the fact that Washington bought and sold slaves are amusing.

Mr. Lodge knew very well that Washington bought slaves and sold them, on occasion. But he did not want to say so, for Washington was one of his political deities. If he said that Washington did not buy and sell negroes he would be telling a lie; and that would not do. So he reflected about it, not knowing what to say, until he ran across a book by an English traveller named Parkinson. This person had visited Mount Vernon for a day, and wrote something in his book about Washington. Lodge quotes Parkinson as saying that "Washington never bought or sold a slave" . . . and Lodge adds that this is "a proof of the highest and most intelligent humanity."

Parkinson did write that Washington never bought or sold a slave, but Parkinson was mistaken. Lodge knew that Parkinson was in error, but he did not feel obliged to say so, and this slippery statement appears in Lodge's book. If confronted with the facts, Mr. Lodge could assert that he was merely quoting Parkinson. There is a strain of shrewdness in history-writing, as there is in law and business.

In the generation that preceded the Revolution the opposition to slavery was strong throughout the South. As many as twenty-three distinct acts to limit the slave trade were passed by the Virginia House of Burgesses between 1699 and 1772, but all of them were vetoed by the Crown. The English government thought that any restriction of the slave traffic would injure the business of the Liverpool slave ships.

In 1761 the assembly of South Carolina attempted to stop slave importation by imposing a heavy duty on negroes brought into the colony. That measure, too, was disapproved by the King.

Washington was opposed, in theory, to slavery. He thought it uneconomic. We have many expressions of his opinion to that effect, but he never took any active steps to put an end to it; and, in fact, he added largely to the number of his slaves by purchase. In the year of his marriage he bought thirteen slaves with some of the money that came to him from Mrs. Custis, and we find him both buying and selling for several years thereafter.

The ownership of slaves was a practical necessity to a Virginia planter. There was no way of cultivating a large estate without them. Some Virginia planters detested slavery to such a point that they gave up their estates. Arthur Lee went to England to live, declaring that he could not bear to own slaves or live in a community where there were slaves.

Haworth says that if Washington "took any special pains to develop the mental and moral nature of 'My People' as he usually called his slaves, I have found no record of it. Nor is there any evidence that their sexual relations were other than promiscuous—if they so desired. Marriage had no legal basis among slaves and children took the status of their mother."

In this respect Washington was not like many planters of the time who made their slaves go to church on Sundays and attempted to encourage chastity and marriage among them.

The focus of African slave importation was in Rhode Island. Great fortunes were founded in that little colony on the profits of slave-catching; and it is hardly necessary to say that in Rhode Island the business of slavery wore a look of beneficence.

At times it assumed an air of piety . . . negroes reclaimed from savagery . . . led to Christianity and eternal salvation . . . and so on.

The Rhode Island slave ships were sent to the African coast with rum or other goods, sometimes with money, with which they bought negroes from the chiefs.

Slave-trading appears to have been the only human activity of the eighteenth century from which nobody has ever been able to extract a particle of romance. Slave-ship captains were almost wholly without charm. Yet they had their troubles; and some of them deserve at least a sigh, if not a tear, of sympathy. Consider the plight of Captain Samuel Moore. This sturdy slaver captain sailed merrily away to the African coast for negroes and dropped anchor at a place which had the romantic name of Yamayamacunda. He had supplied himself with pewter dollars to pay the chiefs for the slaves. The bluff old soul had shrewdly reasoned that the savages would not know the difference between pewter and silver; and they didn't. They accepted the pewter dollars with artless smiles of joy after the slaves, men, women and children—all in fetters—had been brought on board and deposited in the dark and crowded hold.

The captain was rather absent-minded, and he so far forget himself as to sail back again, in two or three years, to sweet-sounding Yamayamacunda. The irate chiefs dashed the pewter dollars in his face, and he was mobbed, robbed, and stripped of everything without the least consideration.

Unfortunate . . . but such incidents did not often happen. There were other and more subtle ways of handling these exorbitant savages. For example, we find a letter from the owners of a slave ship (which was departing for Africa with rum) to its master, Captain Potter, in which there appears this sound advice: "Worter yr. Rum as much as possible and sell as much by the short measure as you can."

CHAPTER XII

STORM CENTRES

§ 1

ENGLAND's world policy in the first half of the eighteenth century may be described as an alert opportunism. In a sentimental era addicted to Venice and masquerades she went in for slave-carrying and bank accounts. Her policy was very simple. It was not anchored to any kind of emotional conception, and it possessed all the supple flexibility of a grasping hand. In dealing with the inconsistencies of geography and the prejudices of men such an attitude had its points, even though it did lack a philosophy.

§ 2

Early in the century she strangled romance to death in its cradle.

While the other highly respected powers of Europe were doing their best to live up to the martial prowess so gloriously depicted by their authors, England tried to persuade somebody else to do her fighting, and usually succeeded. In the whole range of her modern history she has never gone to war to please a King's mistress, nor to win a medal, nor to hear the trumpets blow. Whenever she has done any fighting it has always been for some very substantial object, such as a lot of zinc mines, or for a place to catch codfish and keep others from catching them.

In the eighteenth century she looked out from her narrow island on a world as full of prizes as little Jack Horner's pie was full of plums.

She sat in the game of international politics as one sits at a card table. Occasionally a lucky deal would fill her hand with trumps. Shifts could be made, however, to do without trumps, for even in the most arid pauses there were trick cards concealed in her pocket, and her technique was rich in evasions, in bluffs, in false bids.

It was a century of change. Old empires and old ideals were about to pass away. Beyond the foggy horizon of the future stood the ghost of Machinery. Before long it was to emerge and go striding across the world in a grotesque materialisation of iron and steel. On its way it would trample down the immemorial philosophies and traditions of power. There was to be an empire of machines. Machinery and the money it creates were to be the instruments of authority, and the men in control of them were to say Yes and No.

A premonition of this was growing in the hearts of men. Commerce and industry, which had lain for centuries dozing at the feet of power, woke up and began to make terrifying gestures. Business men became cocky in manner. They developed rights of their own, and invaded palaces with declarations of this and that. Irresponsible authority, once so sure of itself, fell into stammered excuses. Personages and events had an air of amiable make-believe, as if they were merely killing time on the stage until the curtain should be rung down. Senseless armies wandered across the face of Europe and fought wars which began and ended in riddles. International disputes assumed the puzzling features of a game of anagrams.

In these complications England was at home. Her finger was in every pie. She inspired Continental wars, and fought in them sometimes—but not much. Though she was usually absent from the battlefield, she never failed to attend treaty-making conferences. From them she always came back home with both glory and profit, though the profit in most cases was considerably larger in volume than the glory.

France thought that the leadership of the world should be French. Her justification for this assumption was her own size and inherent strength. Around the time of the American Revolution there were twenty million people in France, while England's population was only eight million. But French world policy was checkmated in every direction by England. Preponderant France and little sea-washed England stood facing each other for a hundred years with daggers up their sleeves.

The English had the knack of securing strategic points in geography as well as in diplomacy. They captured Quebec and throttled the French empire in America by a tight grip on the St. Lawrence. They got hold of Gibraltar and turned the Mediterranean into a British lake. At the Peace of Paris in 1763 they forced France to surrender the whole of her gigantic North American territory. By that time the conviction that England was the world's greatest nuisance had become firmly fixed in the French mind. We shall see further on how this conviction, with a bayonet in its hand, walked right into the midst of our fading Revolution and brought it to a glorious conclusion.

§ 3

Among the shuffling cards of England's opportunism two aces appeared. One of the aces was India and the other was North America, and she held them both. Their importance was so enormous that they ceased to be cards in a game. Opportunism dwindled, faded away. India and America became the magnetic poles of England's empire. She resolved to hold them at all cost, come what may, for her new conception of international power rested upon them.

These two dependencies, separated from each other by the width of the world, had drifted into England's solar system from totally different directions.

The North American colonies had grown up in the British empire as unkempt and disorderly children grow up in a household. In their infantile years they had received almost no attention from the English government except in the way of reproof. Translate into the high-sounding language of state documents such ordinary expressions as *you mustn't do that . . . stop that now . . . and behave yourself . . .* and you have in a few words the kernel of the English government's messages to the colonies for the first hundred and fifty years of their existence.

England never founded a college in colonial America, never gave a library to a colonial institution, never made an effort to enrich the mental and spiritual life of the colonial people. If her child learned to read and write, it happened only because he traced the letters crudely for himself.

But in time disorderly children become men, and then who shall do the spanking? The colonial infant had grown into an awkward, iron-muscled youth with an alarming tendency to talk back and knock people down. England saw her child sprawling in the Atlantic sunshine . . . huge, lowering, smiting at flies with a mighty fist . . and the thought occurred to her that his wages would make a pleasant addition to the family budget of empire.

Cheerful thought! The only difficulty was that the grown-up colonial child did not have the faintest notion of turning over a penny, if he could help himself. We shall see that for ten years England used every artifice, from kind words to threats, for the purpose of wheedling money from her offspring. Then, finding nothing of avail, in the heat of exasperation she decided—when it was far too late—to give him a good hearty beating.

§ 4

America, struggling through the grime of a hard-bitten youth, held defiantly to every shilling.

India, on the other hand, burst upon England in a torrent of gold and diamonds.

For a century or so the English, French, Dutch and Portuguese had maintained trading stations on the coast of the Indian peninsula. A monopoly of the English commercial interests was vested in a semi-governmental trading corporation called the East India Company. This concern had unusual powers. It possessed a small army of its own in India; it had a fleet of ships; it coined money; it made treaties with native rulers; it was empowered to transact any kind of mercantile or financial business. In England the company had been given a legal monopoly of practically all the products of the Orient. Silks, teas, spices, Indian woods, camphor—in all these, and in some other Eastern commodities, it held the exclusive right to trade.

The company's position in India was weak. Its power did not extend beyond its stations on the coast. Company officials spent most of their time in an effort to placate temperamental Indian rulers. Business was carried on under harassing regulations. Sometimes a capricious rajah would despoil the company's warehouses and murder its servants.

In 1743 a young man of eighteen named Robert Clive obtained a position in the company's service as a clerk—or "writer," as the job was called—and departed for India.

His family of quiet gentlefolk resided in the rural Shropshire village of Market-Drayton, where young Clive had acquired a reputation which left much to be desired. As a boy he had a habit of climbing to the top of the church steeple and throwing pebbles at people.

Later on, as an older youth, he developed considerable organising ability. He organised the lawless boys of the village into a gang which levied tribute on the shop-keepers. Any one who refused to pay had his windows mysteriously broken by stones. In the beginning the enterprise made little headway; most of the merchants declined to contribute, but after their windows had been smashed ten or twelve times they grasped the laudable nature of the undertaking, and paid up. After all, it was a kind of insurance.

Thereupon, there was no more excitement. The adventure settled down into a humdrum bill-collector's job, and the youthful Clive was excessively bored.

At the age of eighteen, when a young man looks life squarely in the face, and considers his future career, Clive took up the question of highway robbery as a profession, and examined its good and bad points, its emoluments and its drawbacks. Before he had time to decide, his family obtained a writership in the East India Company for him, and he was sent hurriedly away, with tears and embraces . . . *good-bye son; and good luck, but don't write; we've heard too much bad news as it is.*

Upon arriving in India Clive, friendless and despondent, attempted twice to take his own life. Then he picked himself up, went to work, and after awhile was put in charge of some faraway, insignificant post. There he had a quarrel with a native prince, made war on him, and defeated him. With that success (I am, of course, leaving out the details) he set out to conquer India.

Clive's conquest of India, which he accomplished almost singlehanded, is a story that belongs to the Arabian Nights. One must treat it as history, incredible though it may be, for there are the witnesses in black and white; and there is the patent fact of India in the British empire.

In the early part of his Indian career he acted usually without authority—and without support. With a handful of men at his back he walked through warlike Indian states as one walks through a field of corn. He fought against odds which were not merely overwhelming, but grotesque.

He appears to have been altogether devoid of a moral sense, for he forged names, broke treaties and instigated wholesale murder. Without a trace of compunction he turned treacherously against native allies. What he wanted was money, and he waded victoriously through the diamond-encrusted wealth of India. One of his biographers, putting the best possible face on sordid circumstances, mentions Clive's generosity. Very generous person. As an instance of this generosity, he says that once when the loot of a captured city amounted to about three hundred thousand pounds, Clive kept only one hundred thousand pounds for himself, and gave the remainder to his subordinates.

Bengal conquered and Englishmen strutting about in lordly fashion, this highwayman sailed back to England. No longer Robert Clive, clerk . . . but Lord Clive . . . millionaire . . . nabob. He purchased a magnificent estate, and littered its ground with queer Eastern images—

> As if a shipwrecked pagan, safe in port,
> His guardian sea-god to commemorate,
> Should set a sculptured porpoise, gills a-snort,
> And vibrant tail, within the temple gate.

Clive's conquest, with its exaltation of pillage, coloured the whole fabric of English life in the latter half of the eighteenth century. There was a glamour about the success of its bold unscrupulousness. Other men tried their hand at the same game, and came back to England on a wave of money and bad manners. Office-holding in India was an approved form of public graft. Men of low birth and obscure talents rose at a bound in the sunshine of that opulent land. A waiter in White's Club in London named Thomas Rumbold went to India and became governor of Madras. After three years of office he returned to England with £164,000 and, as Sir Thomas Rumbold, entered Parliament on the Conservative side.

The rich East India Company itself was robbed right and left by its underlings. Its officials were forbidden to trade on their own account; nevertheless, a number of them cleaned up £1,500,000 in five years in the salt trade, which was sup-

posed to be a monopoly of the company. Sir George Pigot
came back and bought an estate for £100,000. Another nabob
paid £28,000 for a collection of pictures which were worth
only £3000.

Contact with the supine East India twisted insensibly, and
by slow degrees, the judgment of the English governing classes.
A whole row of seats in the House of Commons was occupied
by Anglo-Indians who had purchased their elections at exorbitant prices. Lord Chesterfield complained bitterly that,
in trying to buy a place in Parliament for his son, he found
that the prices had risen to three, four and five thousand
pounds. The nabobs in Parliament must have looked with
peculiar resentment on the refusal of the American colonies to
be taxed.

As for Clive, his barbaric splendour was the talk of London.
His prodigious vanity impelled him to pay enormous prices
for everything he acquired. In his house he had a huge chest
of gold coins, which he would open ostentatiously and then invite his guests to take a handful. Walpole wrote: "You
would be frightened at the dearness of everything. . . . I expect that a pint of milk will not be sold under a diamond, and
then nobody can keep a cow but my Lord Clive."

The impact of India upon England was tremendous, yet
its effect at first was felt only by the comparatively small upper
class in politics and society. Indirectly, and in devious ways,
its poison eventually seeped through the entire British population, and showed itself in a weakening of ethical standards,
and in feverish activities connected with money.

But for a long time the conquest of India meant very little
to English merchants and manufacturers. The East Indians
did not purchase English manufactures to any great extent.
The American trade was the largest overseas trade in the
empire; it formed a substantial factor in British commerce.

Both India and America were priceless, but had England
been obliged to choose between the two there can be no

doubt that she would have held on to America and let India go.

Besides the value of its trade, the American colonies had great political importance in the line of Britain's international policy. The colonials belonged to the same race and spoke the same language as England herself. They could defend themselves, and England felt that she could rely on them for aid if she ever became involved in a back-to-the-wall struggle in Europe. India, on the other hand, was inert and alien; and it was clearly realised in England that the Indian empire might be readily lost to any power with a superior navy.

These conditions serve to explain the mildness of the mother country in dealing with the American colonies despite the crass urge for exploitation which was at that time the leading motive in English public life.

§ 5

In governing her North American colonies England had never used force, and never thought of using it until just before the Revolution. She relied partly on her constitutional authority; and partly on the fact that the colonies had needed her protection. Englishmen reasoned from this that as long as protection was needed obedience was implied.

But her chief reliance was in keeping the colonies in economic subjection. Here we see the bedrock of English political thought in colonial affairs. To the empire-building mind the whole colonial question is a worthless riddle unless it can be solved in terms which may be translated favourably on a ledger. That was true then, and is true now. There was no reason whatever for possessing colonies which could not furnish a market for English manufacturers and a profitable investment for English funds, unless they were conquered and dusky dependencies like India that could be despoiled without resistance.

The Mercantile System which tied the colonies economically to the mother country was not an English invention, but a French one, and its right name was Colbertism. I shall call it Mercantilism, for that is what the colonials and the English called it.

The central idea of Mercantilism was the erroneous conception that in dealing with a foreign country—in buying or selling—half the profit of the transaction passes to the foreigner, therefore foreign trade should not be permitted in any commodity which could be produced at home, even if the foreigner could produce and sell it for less money.

In one respect it included the principle of the protective tariff, carried to extreme limits; but in its bearing on the colonies it went much further. Under Mercantilism the colonies, through restriction of their market to England, were forced to pay a steady tribute to British merchants and middlemen.

The modern conception of commerce—and undoubtedly the correct conception—is that both parties to an equitable business transaction are benefited. Its basic idea is that goods should be purchased in the cheapest market, and that in the long run this procedure benefits all parties. This view is now accepted, in the main, by all enlightened nations.

Mercantilism was legally expressed in a series of Navigation Acts, the first of which ran back to the time of Charles II.

The maritime transportation of colonial goods was restricted to vessels built either in England or the colonies, and manned by crews of which two-thirds at least had to be British subjects.

The colonials were required by the Navigation Acts to export certain colonial products only to Great Britain, and to no other country whatsoever. These products, enumerated in a list, were called Enumerated Articles.

The enumerated list was short, but it included most of the commodities which were produced in large volume in the colonies, such as tobacco, indigo, pitch, tar and turpentine, hemp, beaver and other furs, hides and skins, masts, rice, pot and pearl ashes, and whale fins.

To keep foreign trade out of the colonies customs duties of a prohibitive nature were imposed on most products that were not of English origin. In cases where the tariff was not prohibitive in amount the goods had to be bought through London. In short, the whole import of mercantilism was to prevent direct trade between the colonies and foreign nations.

The English mercantilists realised that England could not consume the total exportable volume of the enumerated articles produced in America. They insisted, nevertheless, that the goods be sent to England and be unloaded there, to be reshipped later on to some foreign purchaser. This was a device to keep colonial commerce in English hands, and to provide profits for London middlemen.

Non-enumerated articles could be shipped to any country, but the trade in them was small, with the exception of dried and salted fish, cereals and lumber—all of which were products of the northern colonies. It was for this reason that the restriction as to exports was not much of a hardship to any colony north of Virginia, for the products of these colonies were mostly "non-enumerated." It is true that the "Corn Laws" of England—enacted to protect the British farmer—forbade the importation into Great Britain of colonial cereals or meats, but a ready market was found for them elsewhere. The principal grievance of the New England colonies revolved around the question of imports—the restrictions on importing molasses for their rum distilleries from the French West Indies.

Some of the colonials believed Mercantilism to be a good thing for the colonies, though it is difficult to grasp their argument. Among them was James Otis, the Boston orator and radical, whose attitude on this question was grotesquely inconsistent with the rest of his political opinions. In 1764 he said: "The Act of Navigation is a good act, so are all that exclude foreign manufactures from the plantations, and every honest man will readily subscribe to them."

The weight of colonial thinking was, however, on the other side. Long before the agitation that led to the Revolution, the enforced mercantile tribute to Great Britain was felt as a grievance. Rev. Andrew Burnaby, Vicar of Greenwich, who was in Virginia in 1759, wrote, "They think it a hardship not to have an unlimited trade to every part of the world." He added: "Many of them [the Virginians] consider the colonies as independent states, not connected with Great Britain otherwise than by having the same common King and being bound to her with natural affection."

The rigidity of the system was softened in some instances by the practice of giving bounties or subsidies on certain colonial products. These bounties were paid by the British government. They were allowed on very few articles, and in the aggregate were not large.

In the English theory of commercial empire the place of the American colonials was fixed as producers of raw material—as farmers, fishermen, trappers, and timber-cutters.

Manufacturing in the colonies was forbidden by various acts of Parliament, though in some cases the prohibition was not literally enforced. Rum distilling was allowed. It became the leading manufacturing industry, and the only important one. The colonials were allowed to produce pig iron, but were not permitted to work it up into finished articles. The raw iron was sent to England and came back in the form of knives and ploughs and muskets.

An attempt to set up mills for the spinning and weaving of wool was made in the early years of the century, but the effort was repressed by Parliament, and was never revived. By the time of the Revolution half the imports of British merchandise into the colonies consisted of woollen goods.

With a strange intellectual myopia the colonials looked upon the prohibition of manufacturing as the least of their grievances. It is hardly mentioned in the long wrangle with the successive British ministries.

Where issues and energies are so confused it is difficult to maintain any hypothesis with certainty; however, it is entirely probable—and a good case can be made for it—that the lack of manufactures was the most serious defect of the colonial system. The domestic production of a variety of manufactured articles would have given the colonials a large degree of commercial independence, despite the Navigation Acts. It would have restored the balance of trade, which had run steadily against the colonies for years before the Revolution.

The Mercantile System bore heavily on the southern colonies. Consider the traffic in tobacco. As it was one of the enumerated articles the tobacco growers of Virginia and Maryland were required to send their product to England. But the British government excluded all tobacco except that of American growth from Great Britain, so this gave the American grower a monopoly of the British market. The underlying supposition was that the right of monopoly offset the burdensome restraint on free trade. Superficially this appears sound reasoning, but it is deceptive. The effect was to put a practical control of the tobacco trade in the hands of English tobacco merchants, to the detriment of the planter.

The tobacco grower, at the end of his harvest season, would ship his crop to London or Glasgow consigned to a factor. This agent would sell the tobacco, and put the proceeds to the planter's credit on his books. There was nothing, however, to prevent the factor selling the tobacco to himself, or to a confederate, at a low price; that is, there was nothing to prevent him except a sense of honesty, which is often put to a severe strain under such circumstances.

The proceeds of the sale would be credited to the planter's account, but the money was usually not sent to him. He was

always in need of British-made goods, and with each consignment of tobacco he would forward a list of articles to be
purchased. When the tobacco was sold the factor would sally
forth into the shopping streets of London and buy whatever his
planter-correspondent, three thousand miles away, had put on
the list. Was there anything to keep the factor from giving a
false and higher value to the purchased articles? Or from
getting a commission from the dealers who sold them to him?
Nothing at all, except his conscientious scruples. The meagre
profits of tobacco-planting eventually produced a general conviction in Virginia that the conscientious scruples of London
agents were rather feeble.

Daniel Dulany, a keen Maryland lawyer, wrote in 1765 that
with English profits, freight charges, commissions and taxes,
British goods sent to America were raised to six times their
real value. The tobacco-planters of Virginia got more and
more in debt to their London factors. Debts were inherited,
and passed from father to son like family heirlooms. At the
beginning of the Revolution almost the whole of Virginia was
on the verge of bankruptcy.

In Britain large fortunes were made in the tobacco trade.
The Glasgow importers, says Trevelyan, "known as Tobacco
Lords, strutted in business hours in front of the Trongate
Piazza, clad in scarlet cloaks, cocked hats and powdered wigs,
bearing with portly grace gold-headed canes in their hands."

The experience of Washington was similar to that of other
tobacco planters, though he came through it better than most,
with his wife's fortune behind him. His hot letters of complaint, written to Robert Cary & Company, his London factors, prove that he knew something was wrong. But he did
not express any theories on the subject, for he was lacking
in the sense of theory, and very seldom did any theorising
about anything.

His ways of handling the situation was to get out of the
tobacco-planting business, and we find him gradually turning

his land to the cultivation of wheat, which he ground at his own mill for the West Indian market.

In 1763 he raised his largest tobacco crop—eighty-nine thousand pounds. By 1773 his production had fallen to five thousand pounds, and he had become so implacably opposed to tobacco-raising, that in leasing a farm he stipulated that the tenant should not grow more tobacco than was needed for "chewing and smoking in his own family."

§ 6

The colonies did not face one another. They all faced England, with some thousands of miles of water in between. In the beginning their isolation in respect to one another was simply the result of unavoidable circumstances, but as they grew in size and importance it became the settled policy of England to keep them separate and distinct.

Intercolonial barriers were being broken down, however, by natural economic processes. Business, with its talent for expansion and combination, was moving in that direction.

In the annals of 1762 we find an interesting item which deserves a larger place in history than it has been given. In that year the makers of spermaceti candles in Rhode Island met and considered their state of being. They differed on many subjects, for they were men of various capacities and of diverse degrees of moral virtue. But to a man they agreed on one question, which you ought to be able to name at the first guess, even though you may not be good at guessing.

They were unanimously of the opinion that spermaceti candles were being sold at too low a price.

Thereupon they made a mutual covenant, one with every one, and all together, to raise the price of wax candles, and to keep it raised. Thus the first American "trust" came into existence. They called themselves the United Company of Spermaceti Candlers. In a short while they had enlisted all the important manufacturers of the humble but necessary candle in the northern colonies.

The United Company was a flat-footed little trust. It had no apology to make for its price-raising. It does not appear to have made the usual announcement that raw material had gone up fourteen percent and that labour's demands had become exorbitant. There was no fiddling with either whine or apology. There was not even a declaration of Service, an omission which would be nothing less than deplorable in any benevolent trust of to-day. In vain one turns the pages of the senile newspapers of 1762, hoping to light upon an advertisement of "Sealed-in-the-package Candles. . . . Direct from the Whale to You!"

These spermaceti candlers merely announced an increase in the prices of their product. They also stated—rather impudently—that they did not intend to pay any more than they had been paying for raw material. Nothing was said about labour, but one may fairly assume from the foregoing that if there was to be any change in wages, the trend would be downward.

In the opinion of James Truslow Adams this combination of candle-makers "is of great interest as showing how colonial boundaries were being eliminated in the minds of the moneyed group as contrasted with the as yet extremely provincial outlook and provincial patriotism of the smaller people of town and country. The combination cornered the entire North American supply, and by mere threat of its power seems to have controlled the trade successfully. . . . "

§ 7

Notwithstanding its maladjustment, its palpable unfairness, and its clumsiness, the Mercantile System worked tolerably well for awhile. For two generations it worked very well, and for another generation it still worked, but rather jerkily. Finally, it developed an incurable locomotor ataxia, and although every political quack in England had a remedy, no amount of doctoring did any good.

The fact that a social system works is no proof whatever of its excellence, for everything from the ancient Turkish form of government by murder down to the modern form of government by bank credits has worked, and at times all of them have worked satisfactorily. But a faulty system of collective human relations produces storm centres which reveal themselves after awhile in sudden outbursts.

§ 8

The colonial governments were political organisms of low vitality. Their charters—or basic constitutions—were nothing more than makeshift drafts of what was supposed hazily to be their relations to the mother country and to their own citizens.

The charter of Massachusetts was merely that of a trading corporation—a stock company—which the Puritan exploit was intended to be at first. In course of time it evolved into the fundamental law of the province.

In all the colonies citizenship was tinctured with the stockholder quality. The political literature of the day continually harps on "men who have no stake in the colony," and therefore not entitled to a voice in its affairs. By "stake in the colony" ownership of land was meant. Our forefathers had not gone deep enough into economic thought to realise that labour justifies its own existence, and that a man's "stake" in a community does not grow out of his ownership of anything, but is the result of his usefulness to society.

In each of the colonies there were property qualifications for voters which excluded from the polls all but a small percentage of the population. About one-fourth of the adult males had a right to vote in Massachusetts, but the percentage was much less in some of the other colonies.

Most of the colonies denied the right of suffrage to Jews and Catholics; this proscription was overlooked, however, when the Jew or Catholic happened to be wealthy. Catholics could not vote in Maryland, for instance; but Charles Carroll, who was one of the wealthiest men in America and an ardent Catholic, represented Maryland in the Continental Congress, and was a signer of the Declaration of Independence.

These restrictions as to suffrage were not of British origin. The colonies decided all such matters for themselves.

There were three different kinds of government in the thirteen colonies. Nine of them—New Hampshire, Massachusetts, New York, New Jersey, Maryland, Virginia, North Carolina, South Carolina and Georgia—were royal provinces. In general terms, the governments of the royal provinces consisted of three branches. At the head of the colony was a governor, appointed by the Crown and sent out from England. The legislative assembly was elected by the people—that is, by the small restricted list of property owners who had the right of suffrage.

Between the governor and the assembly there stood a Privy Council, which in most cases was appointed by the governor. In Massachusetts the Council was elected by the members of the lower house.

The veto power of a royal governor was unlimited, and could be sustained against the unanimous vote of the assembly, though an appeal might be made to the British government.

The defective nature of this governmental machine may be readily discerned. There was nothing resembling the cabinet system; the executive was not elected, and was therefore without responsibility to the people; and his autocratic veto power had the practical effect of turning the assembly into an innocuous debating society.

Two of the colonies—Pennsylvania and Delaware—had proprietary governments. Curious survivals of feudalism these proprietaries were. Pennsylvania and Delaware had been granted to William Penn as his personal property. He had owned these provinces as one owns a farm, except in this case his proprietorship implied the responsibility of settling the land and giving his tenants a form of government which would not be contrary to the laws of England. Up to the Revolution the Penn heirs were the lord proprietors of these provinces. They appointed the governor and had an absolute veto power over all legislative proceedings. After the Revolution the state of Pennsylvania paid the Penns the sum of one hundred and thirty thousand pounds to release their claims.

In all the colonies south of New England, except Georgia, the quit-rent system was a feudal nuisance of the first rank. A quit-rent was, in effect, a perpetual ground-rent, usually small in amount, running beneath titles and transfers in cases where the land had originally been part of one of the large grants made by the Crown to individuals. There was no difference between the quit-rent and a land tax, except that the quit-rent was not usually paid to the government but to private individuals who, in many instances, were generations away from all connection with the land. Although it closely resembled a land tax, it did not take the place of a tax. The owner who was subject to a quit-rent had to pay both rent and tax, notwithstanding the fact that he owned the land outright, and could sell it or lease it.

George Washington, as we have seen in a preceeding chapter, paid a quit-rent on some of his lands to Lord Fairfax.

The wrangling, the turmoil, the infinite disorder brought into colonial affairs by the quit-rent system would fill volumes. For example, in 1744 the King gave Lord Granville a grant of land sixty miles wide across the province of North Carolina. The history of the colony for the next thirty years is simply a history of this Granville grant, with the disputes which clustered around it.

Among the colonial governments were two—Connecticut and Rhode Island—which were, in reality, free republics inside the British empire. Perhaps the closest parallel with which we are familiar is that of the Irish Free State as it exists to-day. The voters of these two colonies elected their entire colonial administration, from governor down. No reports were made to the Lords of Trade, and these superintendents of colonial affairs complained just before the Revolution that they did not know what the laws of Connecticut were, and had no official means of finding out.

§ 9

What I have said of the colonial state of mind applies to the early 1760's. In 1764 the revolutionary agitation began, and a new state of mind evolved.

In the ten years preceding the Revolution the resistance to English sovereignty took many diverse shapes, and sprang from a variety of grievances. But underneath them all lay the economic injustice of the mercantile system.

Still deeper, and more fundamental, was the colonial feeling that the colonies were grown-up children, that they had no longer a need of England, that they were tired of sitting below the salt in English councils. They were grown-up children and they wanted a house of their own.

British statesmen did not understand this situation until it was too late to provide a remedy. They thought all along that they were dealing with a problem in the mechanics of empire, when it was in reality a problem of psychology and economics.

CHAPTER XIII

THE WRATH OF MERCHANTS

§ 1

In 1763 the Seven Years War came to an end, and the English nation found itself in possession of the largest empire in the world. In England all was jingoism and joy. Britannia ruled the waves . . . one Englishman could whip five Frenchmen . . . and God saved England's King with the smooth unction of a daily habit.

There was only one fly in this ointment of chauvinism, and that fly was unfortunately of large size. Britain had not only the biggest empire, but also the biggest national debt, in the world. Over the rejoicing stood the sheeted ghost of Money Worries, its bony finger pointing to a total of one hundred and forty million pounds—which represented the funded debt—and another total of about five million pounds, which stood for the annual interest charges.

Englishmen at that time were not as experienced in empire-building as they are to-day; else they would have known that empire and debt go hand in hand; the bigger the empire, the bigger the debt.

The pressing need of the time was the raising of revenue and a reduction of governmental expense. Despite the wealth of the Indies which was pouring into England, many intelligent men thought the government on the verge of bankruptcy. Everything that was considered taxable in England was already taxed to the limit. Windowpanes were taxed; hairdressers were taxed; the wheels of wagons were taxed; the newspapers carried tax stamps; liquor was taxed; lawyers were taxed.

The urgent debt question was, however, only a part of the even larger problem of recasting the empire.

The empire, in truth, needed considerable recasting. It consisted of a geography full of heterogeneous islands, nose-ring savages, conquered dependencies, fawning rajahs, fur-trappers, fighting Irishmen and luxurious sugar-planters. Its inhabitants included every variety of human being. Among other varieties it included a large number of white men on this side of the Atlantic who could bring down a squirrel with a worn-out smooth-bore shotgun at seventy-five yards, and who had no hesitation whatever in shooting at anything that displeased them.

The Pitt ministry, which had carried the French war to such a glorious conclusion, went out in 1763 and Pitt was succeeded by George Grenville, his brother-in-law (but his political opponent) who was a dogmatic person, "desperately well-informed about many things, and desperately in earnest." The job of empire-recasting fell to him. It appears now, in the light of history, that although he was very much in earnest, he was not so desperately well-informed about American affairs.

Almost half of the funded debt, or approximately sixty million pounds, had been incurred in defending the American colonies against the French, according to English computation. There was a general conviction prevalent in England that the colonies should sustain part of this financial burden; that, in any case, they ought to support the British officials in the colonies, and pay for all, or a large part, of the expense of their own military garrisons.

The most popular view of the matter in the colonies was that England had already been paid for her war expenditure by the acquisition of Canada; while the colonies had not acquired anything—except possibly a sense of security—although they had taken part in the war, had furnished twenty-five thousand men, and had almost ruined themselves financially.

The quality of truth was a little strained in this colonial argument. The colonies had not furnished twenty-five thousand men, nor anything approaching that number, unless one counts the men who attended one or two drills and then went home. Nor was it true that the colonies had gone "deeply into debt in doing this"—to use Benjamin Franklin's words—"and all their estates and taxes are mortgaged for many years to come for discharging that debt." Many of their estates were deeply mortgaged, indeed, but this deplorable situation came out of causes which far antedated the war.

As a matter of fact, the funded debts of the colonies were quite small. Great Britain had reimbursed them to the extent of nine hundred thousand pounds, and in 1765 the entire thirteen owed only seven hundred and fifty thousand pounds. In some respects the war had been of financial benefit. The British troops had brought a large amount of money to the colonies, and many shrewd traders had made wartime fortunes.

The loss of colonial shipping had run into a heavy total, but this had been offset in part, if not wholly, by the rich prizes taken by colonial privateers. Rhode Island ship-owners had lost nearly a hundred ships, but the loss, as James Truslow Adams says, "must be considered in the light of the enormous profits they were making. For example, one prize in 1757 netted seventy-eight thousand pounds and another, a few months later, ninety-three thousand pounds, these two alone bringing into the colony profits amounting to the entire war cost in Massachusetts in her year of heaviest military expense."

§ 2

The British ministerial mind eventually came to the conclusion that the American colonies ought at least to contribute toward the support of the British military and civil establishments within their own borders. With that end in view Grenville devised a plan of taxation. It was proposed, at the same time, to station ten thousand of the King's regulars in the colonies for their protection. It was hoped that their presence would prevent Indian outrages.

It appears that many leading Americans thought the troops were needed. Franklin advocated the idea, and said the colonies should contribute something toward the cost of maintaining them. Washington too, was in favour of the plan— no doubt with his own Ohio lands in the corner of his eye.

Grenville's project was divulged in sections. The first proposal that emanated from him had to do with the Acts of Navigation, that fossilised backbone of mercantilism.

Some of the provisions of the Navigation Acts had been conceived with such small regard for colonial necessities that it had been impossible to carry them out. Their only visible effect had been to breed a race of smugglers. So few merchants paid any duty at all that the custom-houses had become quiet dozing places for gentlemen in need of salaries.

David A. Wells says:

> Nine-tenths of their merchants were smugglers. One-quarter of all the signers of the Declaration of Independence were bred to commerce, to the command of ships and to contraband trade. Hancock, Trumbull (Brother Jonathan), and Hamilton were all known to be cognisant of contraband transactions and approved of them. John Hancock was the prince of contraband traders, and, with John Adams as his counsel, was appointed for trial before the admiralty court in Boston, at the exact hour of the shedding of blood at Lexington, in a suit for $500,000 penalties alleged to have been incurred by him as a smuggler.

Grenville realised that the Navigation Acts could not be enforced as they stood, but he thought that a reduction of the tariff, with a vigorous effort to detect and punish smugglers, would put the customs on a productive basis.

Among the chief offenders at that time were the smugglers of molasses from the French West Indies. In 1733 Parliament had passed what was known in the colonies as the "Old Molasses Act," which admitted molasses from the British West Indies free of duty, but imposed a tariff of sixpence a gallon on molasses imported into the colonies from foreign countries.

This Act had never been enforced. The total molasses production of the British West Indies was not sufficient to supply raw material for one-fourth of the New England rum distilleries. Smuggling operations with the French islands had become an industry of immense proportions.

Grenville had a new law put through Parliament, reducing the molasses duty to threepence a gallon, with provisions for its strict enforcement. This law was called the Sugar Act, or the "New Molasses Act."

The purpose of this law was not only to produce revenue but also to restrain the natural tendency to free trade. It was, in fact, a large-scale effort to tighten the British monopoly.

§ 3

To understand the attitude of the Americans we must realise that they were almost wholly without a sense of empire, while the British thought and spoke in terms of a world-wide imperialism.

A new race had grown up in America; a new race with a new outlook, with new horizons, with a new creed. This was the determining fact in the controversy with Great Britain, yet this aspect of the situation seems not to have been clear either to the colonials or to the English. An instant recognition of this fact might have saved America for the empire. But it was not understood, and the British continued to legislate for the Americans as they legislated for Yorkshire farmers . . . and the Americans in their letters of protest continued to refer to themselves as Englishmen, when they were not Englishmen at all.

Practical people are excessively bored by any discussion of principles; they hate abstractions. The result is that their mutual understandings hardly ever get to the root of anything. They like to take up each question as it comes along and decide it superficially and temporarily in respect to its immediate material consequences. Abstract principle is left far behind, and comes trotting along after events as a dog runs after a wagon, without ever quite catching up. The result of this propensity is that large questions, left in the hands of practical men, are almost invariably tangled into hopeless snarls. In all communities of practical people the race of lawyers thrives enormously; they are needed to elucidate the misunderstandings of practicality.

Both the Americans and the British were highly practical. The British government had allowed the Old Molasses Act to become a dead letter. As a practical government, they had realised that it was impossible to collect a sixpence a gallon on molasses, so they did not try to collect it. There the British practical mind came to the end of its road. The act was still a law, but not enforced. The effect of the situation was to make smuggling a recognised industry. It would have been better for the British to have rescinded the dead law away back in the 1730's, and to have put in its place a duty— even if it had been infinitesimal—which the colonists would have paid.

To the American of practical mind the effort of the British ministry to tax molasses even as much as threepence seemed to be a piece of pure stupidity that ought to be resisted to the limit. The rum industry—the life-blood of New England—had grown up on smuggled molasses. The least tinkering with it would be fatal to its prosperity—or so they thought—and yet the English were willing to ruin it to get a trifling revenue of threepence a gallon. Preposterous! They declared that the rum industry could not stand such a duty. It was not a matter of principle; it was a matter of threepence.

Now let us glance for a moment at another body of colonial opinion . . . the doctrinaires . . . the men who think in abstractions. There were not many of them, but what they lacked in number they made up in vehemence. The doctrinaires were born rebels . . . their heads full of philosophic notions and their pockets full of vitriolic pamphlets and scribbled ideas.

The great outstanding figures in this field of thought and propaganda were Samuel Adams of Massachusetts; Patrick. Henry of Virginia; and Christopher Gadsden of South Carolina. In direction of ideas, in texture of thought, in intellectual technique, they were immensely remote from George Washington, who never thought of anything in its abstract sense, but only in its practical aspect.

Yet, notwithstanding such an extreme divergence of intellectual highways, eventually their road and that of Washington came together for awhile . . . for a short distance . . . and forked again.

These men contended that England had no right to tax the colonies in any manner whatsoever, or under any circumstances. If one reflects a moment on this contention it appears in its true light as a renunciation of British sovereignty. In a political sense sovereignty implies the power of taxation.

There is no doubt that, from the beginning, both Adams and Gadsden were thorough rebels and were for independence. Their political philosophy was founded on the inalienable right of a community to govern itself. But Adams' public arguments, in these early years of controversy, were picayune discussions of "charter rights." He was a politician by instinct, and felt very likely that the time had not come to disclose publicly the full measure of his opinions.

§ 4

Another group laid stress on the argument that Anglo-Saxons—free-born and nobody's slaves—could not be taxed without representation. They were willing to be taxed, if only they were represented in the legislative body that levied the tax. They pointed out that the right to be represented wherever taxation was voted was part of the very blood and fibre of the Anglo-Saxon race.

The flaw in this argument was that it had no foundation whatever in history or in fact. The Anglo-Saxon had always been taxed without representation. At that very time, as Trevelyan points out, suffrage was so restricted in England that one hundred and sixty thousand voters—out of two million adults—elected all the members of Parliament. The large towns of Manchester and Birmingham had no representatives in Parliament at all.

In the colonies only a small percentage of the people were allowed to vote. The mobs that swirled through the streets of Boston and New York, setting up Liberty poles and tarring and feathering loyalists, consisted for the most part of unenfranchised mechanics and labourers. We look in vain through the whole of Revolutionary propagandist literature for any serious proposal to give them the right of suffrage.

The colonial controversialists plastered up this prominent wormhole in their argument with the assertion that the landless and disfranchised were represented in the colonial assemblies by the votes of their employers, by the merchants and dignitaries of the community, who acted in their interest. In other words, they were "virtually" represented.

Very well, said the British, we must call your attention to the fact that the colonies are "virtually" represented in Parliament. The merchants and exporters of England are represented in Parliament and they stand for you. Besides, you have powerful friends among the statesmen—Mr. Pitt, our

great Whig, and Colonel Barré, and Lord Camden, to name
a few.

Soon after this exchange of hypocrisies the no-taxation-
without-representation argument died of anemia. A few of
its friends gathered around its dying couch and held up its
feeble head until life was extinct. After its death there was
found among its pitiful effects the neatly engraved slogan,
"Taxation without representation is tyranny."

This slogan was immediately cast in bronze and handed
down the ages. It appears in our school histories as one of the
clarion calls of the patriots, by the side of Patrick Henry's
"Give me liberty or give me death."

The keenly alert radical leaders, such as Samuel Adams,
were opposed to any plan which would give the colonies a representation in Parliament. They saw that with thirty or forty
American members sitting in goggle-eyed silence in their seats,
or rising now and then to emit spread-eagle declarations for
the edification of their constituents, Parliament would be in a
splendid strategic position to impose any taxes it pleased—
America having been fully represented at the time.

The truth is that the colonial merchants who instigated the
revolutionary movement in its early years did not want to be
taxed at all, with representation or without it, and they did
not care a pistareen whether they were represented or not.

But there was still another body of opinion. A very respectable body it was, too, and a very important one . . . the
legal luminaries, the hair-splitters . . . the worshippers of
phrase. These gentlemen made a distinction between external
and internal taxes. Great Britain had an undoubted right,
they said to regulate the ocean commerce of the empire and to
impose tariffs—called external taxes—in the way of such
regulations, but not to produce revenue.

Britain's taxing power, they thought, should begin and end
at the custom house, at the water's edge.

These ridiculous distinctions bear a striking resemblance

to the rules of a child's game of tag. Take any toll you please
on the water, but just put both feet on shore and you are out
of bounds.

Anyway, who was to decide where taxation for regulation
ended and taxation for revenue began?

The most interesting fact in this connection is that the ex-
ternal-internal tax theory made a tremendous impression. It
was accepted by so many colonials that the British government, always trying to placate American sentiment and get
money at the same time, took these theorists at their word.
The Grenville Molasses Act was certainly a measure for an
external tax, and the British governing classes were astonished
when it failed to please.

§ 5

The opponents of any established system that is approaching a crisis in its history always make more noise than its
defenders. The defence of the conventional is such a negative
affair; it must rest its case on antecedent facts, about which
there is always a cloud of querulous disappointment. On the
other hand the rebels and innovators have at their back the
entire world of ideas.

That is why we do not hear much of the thoroughly pro-
British colonials—and there was an astonishingly large number of them. Many American-born colonials sincerely believed
that a place in the British empire on any terms was essential
to the welfare of the colonies; and, of course, such an attitude
implied subservience to British taxation.

The political creed of these men was almost religious in
character. It consisted in a blind faith in the sagacity and
benevolence of three or four hundred beefy English squires,
members of a legislative body in which nearly every seat had
been bought openly at auction.

§ 6

The time was unpropitious for any tampering with colonial affairs. During the war the northern colonies had been active in selling supplies to the troops, as well as in contraband trade with the enemy. In this atmosphere of false prosperity debts were contracted and extended, merchants laid in huge stocks of goods, every one had employment.

With the coming of peace there was a sudden collapse of inflated commerce. Business was stagnant, men were out of employment, goods became shop-worn on the merchants' shelves.

In the southern colonies conditions were the worst in years. There were many bankruptcies among tobacco-planters of Virginia and the rice planters of South Carolina. In 1763 Washington wrote to his London agents that he could not pay the balance which he owed them, and asked for time.

In April of the same year a friend of Washington named Robert Stewart tried to borrow some money from him. In reply Washington wrote that his own affairs were in bad condition, and goes on to say that he was land-poor and negro-poor. He said that his purchases of lands and negroes "swallowed up, before I well knew where I was, all the money I got by marriage, nay more, brought me in debt, and I believe I may appeal to your own knowledge of my circumstances before" [his marriage].

In this statement we discern the origin of some of the financial troubles of Virginia as a whole. The planters endeavoured to secure more and more land, when they could not cultivate profitably the land they already owned.

But the crux of their difficulties lay deeper. The British mercantile system was slowly impoverishing all the colonies, despite their astounding wealth in natural resources. In Virginia the effect of this drain was vividly apparent in the run-down condition of the colony. The aristocratic planters were becoming a little shabby. Their stately homes began to have the moth-eaten look that oozes from a depleted bank account. About the plantations there were mouldy fences, and deep, rain-washed gullies, and tumble-down sheds and a lack of paint.

Tobacco production had increased to the point where Great Britain was glutted with American tobacco and the price had gone down steadily. Not more than one-fifth of the crop was consumed in England, but the tobacco had to be shipped there just the same. Even the packages of smoking tobacco sold in the shops of Boston and New York, although of Virginia production, had made the trip to England. Four-fifths of the tobacco that was sent from Virginia and Maryland to England was re-exported to the European Continent and to other English colonies. English tobacco factors made their own purchase prices, and the profits of re-exportation went to them. Every packet ship from England brought bundles of dunning letters from English merchants. A Parliamentary committee obtained evidence in 1766 that American debts owing in England amounted to at least £4,450,000. Of this immense total more than nine-tenths were debts of inhabitants of the Southern colonies.

Even under these onerous conditions the tobacco-planters could have helped themselves. Why did they not organise a co-operative marketing association, something in the nature of the California Fruit Growers' Exchange? In that case they could have put their own price on tobacco. The fact is that neither co-operation nor economic principles were clearly understood, and business was a vague affair. Men looked to political, rather than to commercial, action for relief. Oliver Wolcott wrote in respect to Virginia: "It is a firmly established opinion of men well versed in the history of our Revolution that the whiggism of Virginia was chiefly owing to the debts of the planters."

The financial difficulties of the Southern colonies were greatly augmented, in 1764, by an act of Parliament which prohibited the use of colonial paper currency. This did not affect the New England colonies—they had been on a hard money basis for several years—but the effect in all the colonies south of New York was disastrous. There was almost no metallic money. Gold and silver flowed to England to cover the debit balances of planters and merchants. Paper had always been used for internal currency. When Parliament abolished paper it failed to provide anything to take its place, and in many communities business went back to a primitive system of barter.

§ 7

Now, from this thousand miles of colonial lands there rises a confused murmur, deepening into a roar. Apostles of discontent, like martyrs in robes of flame, go here and there setting the minds of men ablaze.

§ 8

If George Washington was the Father of Our Country we may say with equal truth that Samuel Adams was the Father of the American Revolution. The paternity in both cases is fanciful. Revolutions and countries have no fathers. They are created by the mass movements of a race; they are the composite results of a thousand separate causes, all woven into a single pattern.

If there had been no Samuel Adams the Revolution would have occurred, perhaps in a different form, but a Revolution nevertheless. Had Washington never lived, the United States would undoubtedly be here to-day. The mass impulses that lead to such enormous results are enormous impulses; they pile up to mountainous height beside even the most gigantic of human figures.

Nevertheless, individuals of great will power whose personalities are in tune with the spirit of their times do have an influence on the mass movements of men. They cannot stop the flow of impulse, but if they happen to be in a strategic position they are sometimes able to accelerate it, to impede it, or turn it in a different direction. No man can stop a river, but a capable engineer can divert it into canals and manipulate its course.

Samuel Adams was a capable engineer of rebellion. It was the one capacity he possessed, for he was a failure at everything else. He was undoubtedly a neurotic; his hands were tremulous, and he stuttered at times of excitement. His graduation thesis at Harvard, when he received his master's degree in 1743, at the age of twenty-one was "Whether it be lawful to resist the Supreme Magistrate, if the Commonwealth cannot be otherwise preserved"—and this question haunted him all his life.

He failed in business; he had no head for figures; he lost a thousand pounds that his father had loaned him; he lost this and that; he had a knack of losing. Eventually he managed to secure an appointment as local tax collector in Boston. In that position he had a wider field; he surpassed all his previous records at losing; he showed what a really first-class loser could do when given a free hand. In a few years his accounts as tax collector revealed a shortage of eight thousand pounds. He was so notoriously honest that nobody accused him of stealing the money. Investigation uncovered the fact that his shortage had come about through his failure to collect tax arrears which had been charged against his office; in other words, it was due to his incompetence. In time he and his friends managed to repay part of the shortage, which was, after all, technical and legal, rather than actual.

At the age of forty-two he was a shabby, disappointed man, bitter with experience, and almost smothered under a sense of inferiority. He had the neurotic's urge for power, and the neurotic capacity to dream. Over his burning dreams lay the

SAMUEL ADAMS

From a painting by John S. Copley owned by the City of Boston

heavy shell of his harsh Puritan training. He was tortured, inhibited, irascible.

The lives of such men are always at the hour of sunrise. There is no noon in their careers. Life is a state of permanent expectation. Things as they are will not do, but a new day is on the horizon, and the old stars are waning overhead.

Many a John o'Dreams walks the streets in broken shoes. Most of them can do nothing but dream, and they dream their lives away. But the shabby dreamer that was Samuel Adams had an ability for political organisation, for propaganda, that was unsurpassed in the British empire. He possessed an uncanny faculty for understanding men in their political aspect.

Already, run-down at the heel as he was, he was at the head of the Caucus Club, a Tammany-like organisation that played a prominent part in Boston affairs. He was an utterly implacable rebel, a mass of indignations, combined with a shrewd, calculating sense of ways and means.

In his relation to British rule in America he was simply a piece of human dynamite.

§ 9

A bright idea shone among the Boston merchants. Its source is now historically anonymous, unfortunately. It would be interesting to know the name of the American originator of the great commercial weapon of boycott. His name may have been Samuel Adams.

As a practical measure of protest against the Grenville taxation programme fifty business men got together and signed an agreement not to buy any more English cloth but at a fixed price, to discourage the elaborate funeral displays which were the custom of the time, and to discard lace and ruffles. The Caucus Club was the pivot of this non-importation movement. Its members were in it whole heart and soul. Samuel Adams began to radiate advice. He wrote letters, addressed meetings in his stammering voice, and sent rasping articles on British tyranny to the newspapers.

This was the first of the boycotts. During the next ten years this form of tacit rebellion was to play a prominent part in the resistance to British sovereignty. The first non-importation agreement died out in a couple of years, but in 1765 it was in full career. Local to Boston at first, it spread to New York, to Philadelphia. By the end of 1765, people in all the colonies were circulating agreements of non-importation and watching their neighbours to see that the agreements were kept.

As to the effect of the boycott in England Macaulay says, "The Exchange of London was in dismay. Half the firms of Bristol and Liverpool were threatened with bankruptcy. In Manchester and Nottingham it was said that three artisans out of every ten had been turned adrift."

It was found impossible to collect the molasses duty. The rum distillers declared that they could not pay even the three-pence a gallon duty on molasses without being brought to ruin. Smuggling went on as usual. The smugglers, a determined lot, fought the armed vessels sent against them; and men struggled on decks that were not slippery with blood, but sticky with molasses.

The non-importation agreement had one cheerful aspect. It enabled colonial merchants to dispose of the unsaleable goods which had been accumulating on their shelves for years. Around the autumn of 1766 most of them had got down to the bare shelves. It was just about that time that sentiment seemed to change, and the best mercantile minds came to the conclusion that the boycott had gone far enough.

CHAPTER XIV

THE IRON-FISTED PATRIOTS

§ 1

In the midst of the turmoil the British government unveiled, with a charming gesture, the second section of its colonial taxation programme. At the unveiling ceremonies George Grenville displayed a frankness and an amiability which were greatly admired. Pandora at the opening of her illustrious box could have hardly been more gracious.

He called together the commissioners of the various colonies and announced that the government proposed to extend the Stamp Act to America. Revenue stamps had been used in England for two generations, and the English people were as accustomed to putting stamps on documents as they were to paying postage on letters.

The British government realised, however, that a stamp tax imposed by Britain on the colonies would belong to the objectionable category of internal taxation from the colonial standpoint, and the government moved cautiously. Upon any strong protest from the colonies Grenville was ready to withdraw his plan. Parliamentary action on the measure was deferred for a year, that the colonies might have time to deliberate and offer objections.

There was practically no protest, and the Stamp Act became a law in 1765. The failure of the colonies to make an emphatic objection in this interval is one of the inexplicable lapses that occur so often in collective human action. The proposal upon reaching America seems to have drifted into a sort of political fourth dimension.

One may surmise that the more radical of the leaders really

wanted the Act passed, that it might stiffen the resentment of the people.

Anyway, the Stamp Act became a law . . . and the storm broke.

The tax was small, and bore with such light pressure on the daily life of the ordinary man, that in normal times it might have been put in effect without being noticed at all by the common people. All legal documents were required to carry stamps to make them valid. The lawyers were among the most vehement opponents of the Act.

Merchants, too, opposed it.

John Hancock declared that he could not continue to carry on his large mercantile business and pay the Stamp Tax. His evidence, I suspect, was *ex parte*. I have taken the trouble to make an estimate of the total amount of stamps he would have had to purchase in the course of a year, considering the known turnover of his business, and its character. My estimate is obviously a guess, but it does not seem possible for the tax to have fallen on him for much more than one hundred and fifty pounds a year. In the volume of his large commercial operations this sum would have been insignificant. One must remember that incomes were not taxed, nor were excess profits.

The whole of England, with its huge trade, bought only three hundred thousand pounds of revenue stamps annually. The estimated total return expected from the American colonies was about one-fifth of that amount. According to the terms of the Act the stamp for a bill of lading was fourpence; for a mortgage, two shillings threepence; for a deed to three hundred acres, five shillings.

In part, the opposition to the Act—and the violent reception it received—arose as a matter of principle. But as one goes deeper into the question this principle loses something of its golden lustre and begins to emit the hollow sound of a campaign slogan. Some of the stamp distributors were thorough-going patriots whose indignation must have been superficial, as they were glad to get the jobs. Richard Henry Lee, who was afterwards president of the Continental Congress, tried to get himself appointed stamp distributor for Virginia.

As an evidence of the chaotic state of public opinion it is interesting to note that the uproar caused by the attempt to enforce the Act was a great surprise to many intelligent Americans. It certainly was to Franklin—perhaps the most intelligent of them all—for he persuaded the British government to give the job of distributor in Pennsylvania to his old friend John Hughes, thus unwittingly leading his friend into a peck of trouble.

The tax could not have been much of a burden as a whole, but the heaviest burden would have fallen on the newspapers if the Act had ever been carried out.

Each copy of every newspaper was to carry a penny stamp, and advertisers were required to pay two shillings an insertion for their advertisements, irrespective of size. A merchant, running an advertisement weekly in a newspaper for a year would have been called upon therefore to pay a sum equivalent to about twenty-six dollars a year. These stamps were carried by English newspapers and advertisements, without complaint. In the colonies it was a different matter. Here the newspapers were tiny publications, weak in resources, and usually the by-products of job printing offices.

The stolidity of the British has a way of curdling into stupidity now and then. In this tax on newspapers the process of curdling seems to have been pretty far advanced.

The Stamp Act set the thirty-odd newspapers of the colonies to barking with a unanimity they had never before displayed.

Roman history, already worn to a frazzle, was pawed over feverishly; but, unfortunately, there were no newspapers in Roman times. Parallels were lacking. Still, Nero would do. . . . Nero always came in handy on a pinch. George III as Nero . . . George III, with his protruding eyes and his mild German countenance, sitting in his green silk coat and eating his dinner of boiled mutton, with one foot, Nero-like, on the neck of the prostrate journals.

If the press be throttled, shouted the newspapers, then where are the liberties of mankind? Crush the newspapers under the weight of stamps, and freedom curls up and dies.

Freedom had not curled up yet, however. The first consignment of stamps for Pennsylvania arrived in Philadelphia on Oct. 5, 1765, and was met by several thousand indignant citizens, who forced Hughes, the stamp distributor, to resign.

In New York Major James was alleged to have said: "I will cram the stamps down the throats of the people with the point of my sword." The patriots thought that remark required a practical demonstration. A large number of them went to his house and demanded an exhibition of his skill in cramming stamps down people's throats. Upon his refusal to give such a performance, they decided to take his house to pieces. It was taken to pieces so impetuously that it could never be put together again. Without a house, they reasoned that he would not need a garden or any furniture, so they broke his furniture to bits and pulled up his garden, leaving him nothing but his sword and his stamps.

The Boston stamp distributor was made to resign; and the Sons of Liberty—a patriotic organisation—tore down Lieutenant-Governor Hutchinson's house and scattered his library in the street.

House-wrecking rose from the condition of a trade and assumed the dignity of a sport. A mob collected in front of Benjamin Franklin's house in Philadelphia and threatened to tear it down because Franklin, who represented the colony in England, had not prevented the passage of the Stamp Act. "Cousin Davenport"—whoever he was—came to protect Mrs. Franklin. She wrote: "I said he should fetch a gun or two, as we had none. I sent to my brother to come and bring his gun also, so we turned one room into a magazine; I ordered some sort of defence upstairs such as I could manage myself."

The rioters were awed by these preparations, and so nothing happened.

When the news of all this stir reached England Franklin wrote home that he had tried to prevent the passage of the Act, "but the tide was too strong against me. . . . The nation was provoked by American claims of independence."

Tar and feathers began to play a part in the political forum. Men who had nothing to do with the stamps, but who were merely adherents of the King, and lovers of law, order, and ten per cent interest, were taken out of their beds at night and coated with tar; after which, feathers were sprinkled over them and they were allowed to go home. Upon investigation it was almost invariably discovered that the men who had been subjected to these outrages were the prominent mortgage-holders of the neighbourhood.

In North Carolina the patriots visited the stamp distributor's house with drums beating and colours flying. The tar bucket and bag of feathers were kept out of sight as a matter of politeness until the honourable gentleman had divulged his intentions. It turned out that his only intention was to resign his office with all possible speed. The resignation having been effected, and witnessed, the meeting became a festive occasion, and the late distributor of His Majesty's stamps drank toasts with his belligerent guests.

Jared Ingersoll, of Connecticut, was that colony's agent in England. He opposed the passage of the Act, but probably not very vigorously, for immediately after its passage he applied for the office of Connecticut stamp distributor, and was appointed.

Then he sailed home to Connecticut, loaded down with stamps and eager to see his old friends. The Sons of Liberty took a hand in the home-coming celebration. An effigy of Mr. Ingersoll with one of the devil beside it decorated a gallows. His popularity was sadly diminished. Children met him in the streets and said "there is a traitor."

The house-wreckers arrived with plans and specifications for tearing down Mr. Ingersoll's dwelling. The governor, elected by the people in Connecticut, came in haste to protect Mr. Ingersoll, but the Sons of Liberty declared that they would not take orders from anybody. Mr. Ingersoll decided to resign. He said that the cause was not worth dying for.

A few stamps were used in Georgia. This circumstance provoked the South Carolina radicals, mostly tradesmen and mechanics who had been organised by Christopher Gadsden, to resolve that all dealings with "that infamous Colony Georgia" must cease.

Yet the wealthy Henry Laurens, South Carolina planter and merchant, later to play a large role in the Continental Congress, disapproved of these coarse expressions of discontent. He was opposed to the Stamp Act, but he thought that since it had become a law it must be carried out. He was all for law, and demanded what "would become of our estates without law, particularly ours who depend upon commerce?" He saw in the zeal of the rioters, as Schlesinger remarks, "only a desire to postpone the payment of their debts."

Let us record the fact, and reflect upon it, that the pre-Revolutionary mobs, parading and tearing down houses for liberty's sake, were composed almost entirely of workingmen, of the landless and the voteless. To such people the Stamp Act was of no moment; most of them would never be required to use a revenue stamp in any form.

§ 2

Why, then, the rioting and the bitterness? The answer to this question is that the disorder was to some extent inspired by the merchants and lawyers—at first. But a stronger incentive was in the condition of the working class. Their discontent was very real, and very bitter, though it had long been inarticulate. This dissatisfaction had nothing to do with the British rule, except indirectly and in the remote sense that the mercantile system affected all classes in the community, rich and poor alike. The protest of the working class was, in reality, an unconscious protest against their local economic status. It was nourished by the cloudy sense of ill-being which always surrounded the colonial proletariat.

The colonial governing classes had never made any serious attempt to regulate the working hours of labouring people, to establish a minimum wage, or to consider the poor as anything else than servile dependents on the rich. Except in New England there were no schools for poor children. In the large towns rents were excessively high, and the laws were conceived and carried out by landlords. Wages were, in money terms, higher than they were in England, but living was much dearer, and labouring people as a class were in a perpetual state of impoverishment.

In the courts a workingman, without land or a vote, had practically no standing when his opponent was his employer or any one else of property or distinction. There was a feudal atmosphere about the later colonial civilisation. It was beginning to take on some of the meaner aspects of feudalism without acquiring the patriarchal kindliness of the feudal age.

Its chief social defect was not over-regulation; the free white man of the time had as much personal liberty as any one could possibly desire. Its deficiency lay rather in under-regulation, in a general disregard of all social problems, with a corresponding fixation of attention on land and property.

The revolutionary movement was started by the merchants and the lawyers. It was purely a commercial dispute which had nothing to do with personal liberty. To make their grievances more alarming to the British government the aggrieved merchants organised the common people—the voteless and landless—into mobs which made it impossible for the British to carry on the peaceful administration of affairs, or to protect life and property.

The common people threatened for awhile to capture the entire revolutionary movement. They would have captured it, in all probability, if the great conservative figures—such as Washington—had not appeared on the scene and pushed the common people down to the bottom of the ladder and kept them there.

§ 3

Now all eyes turned to Virginia, where the Stamp Act was a subject of hot discussion, as it was everywhere else. Some of the members of the House of Burgesses think a protest should be made . . . a dignified remonstrance.

The House is in a state of suppressed—almost hysterical—excitement, but not because of the Stamp Act . . . another reason altogether. A scandal in the management of the Colony's funds is about to come to light; an aristocratic treasurer has loaned public money to his aristocratic friends, and they, bankrupted by tobacco-planting, never repaid him. Some hint of it has floated around for months. There has been an election, and half of the aristocrats have been dumped out unceremoniously. There is a new set of delegates from the western counties; rough, badly dressed men, unaccustomed to polite usage. A rule is put through the House that no member "shall chew tobacco while the speaker is in the chair," nor shall any member spit on the floor at any time.

Washington is there, cool and reflective. He has been a member for six years, though hardly ever speaking a word in the running debates . . . a listening member. He wears handsome clothes and he never spits on the floor, but he is a rough citizen, nevertheless . . . a curious mixture of aristocrat and backwoodsman.

On this beautiful May morning history is to bloom. Some of the more learned members arise and make remarks derogatory to the Stamp Act, but the sense of indignation dribbles away somehow in the wilderness of Latin quotations.

One of the new members named Patrick Henry gets the floor and begins what appears to be a shy and rambling speech. The delegates lean forward, their hands cupped behind their ears; they can hardly hear him. Many of them do not know his name—he is an uncouth person—and the name is whispered from one to another. In his hand there is a fly-leaf torn from a book, with some scribbled "resolves" which he wishes to introduce.

There is a schoolboy diffidence about his halting words and awkward gestures. The Burgesses wonder how long he is going to talk.

Now his voice changes.

It is louder and clearer; it has a tone of gold; it leaves in the air the vibrant tang of a bell ringing in the sky. It goes to the heart like the flaming glory of an autumn sunset. He is saying something about the rights of men; and his listeners see Man, new-born from the earth, standing before the face of Destiny.

The delegates are silent . . . no more whispering . . . they are strangely thrilled, and annoyed at themselves for being thrilled.

The marvellous voice falls to a lower key.

The room is filled with an infinite sad wistfulness . . . far-off, forgotten things and the tears of ages. He is telling of the colonies' struggles, of their simple longing to be free and happy. Under this spell men could not think of Patrick Henry; they thought only of Voice. Yet there he stands, his shoulders drooping lower as his voice falls. His hands hang limply. He is Labour . . . he is the Spirit of Toil . . . he is Aspiration beaten down by Tyranny.

Spectators crowd the doors. From an office across the way comes running Thomas Jefferson, a young law student. He stands listening, breathless. "Patrick Henry spoke as Homer wrote," he said.

The Voice rises; sadness is over. Like an eagle the Voice rises sweeping through the air. Again it has the tone of bells, but these are harsh, iron bells ringing on a night of wind and fire. There is an undertone of rolling drums and crackling muskets. Defiance melts into exultation. The delegates can hardly keep their feet still.

Henry plays with the paper in his hand. "Tarquin and Cæsar had each his Brutus," he says, "Charles the First his Cromwell, and George the Third—"

Peyton Randolph, acting as Speaker, shouts "Treason," and brings his gavel down with a whack. Heavy-jowled Peyton Randolph, his pink jowls turned now to a bloodless white. Henry turns toward the Speaker and finishes the sentence—

"—may profit by their example! If *this* be treason, make the most of it."

Of Henry's seven resolves the last two were undoubtedly treasonable, as they denied flatly the authority of the King of England over Virginia. These two resolves were voted down, but the rest were carried, including one which asserted that "the general assembly of this colony have the only and sole exclusive right and power to lay taxes and impositions upon the inhabitants of this colony. . . ."

Strong language . . . a little too strong, in fact. Next day the House met and hastily rescinded the resolutions. The members were no longer under the spell of Henry's eloquence; he had departed for home.

He appears to have been somewhat frightened by the commotion he had caused. He was a hasty person; his resolves had been hastily written; they were framed in intemperate language. His audiences in the back counties had been composed of disorderly and obtuse people who did not understand mild words.

The resolves were expunged from the record; the House cleaned its slate and fortified itself against another attack of emotionalism. But the story of his speech and its defiant ending, and the wording of his resolves, ran like a flame to the most remote settlement in every colony.

Patrick Henry was the man of the hour.

There can be no doubt that he was one of the greatest orators of all time. His art was dramatic. In spirit he was an actor of genius. But he was more than an actor. His subtle dramatic quality was balanced—perhaps a trifle overbalanced —by the rasping attributes of an indignant ward politician.

He believed in democracy to the bottom of his soul. In his opinions he was utterly honest, utterly sincere, though he was something of a charlatan in his oratorical manner, for he endeavoured to sway his audiences by leading them into states of emotional hysteria. That is why his brief career as a member of the Continental Congress is a blank. The atmosphere of the Congress was not congenial to revivalist tactics.

His personality was so full of rhythm, of cadence, of sobbing violins, of soaring flights, that his career might readily be set to music. But it would have to be the music of a brass band.

Notwithstanding these strictures upon his sharply limited personality, which his admirers must admit to be true, the dramatic story of his Treason speech, as it flew through the colonies, did more to awaken the revolutionary spirit than anything that had happened up to that time. Its boldness penetrated the average mind.

§ 4

Washington's diary for May 30, 1765—the day the House acted on Henry's resolves—records nothing but the fact that Peter Green came to him as a gardener; and the entry for May 31st is, "Cut my Clover for Hay."

We know, however, that he was present in the House of Burgesses when Henry made his speech. The vote on the resolves was not recorded, and no one knows how Washington voted. How singularly unrevealing his letters are! He wrote to Francis Dandridge in 1765 that he was opposed to the

Stamp Act—this letter was written after the Patrick Henry episode—but he does not say how he voted on the Henry resolutions.

At that time he was not a revolutionist; revolutionary thought had gone far beyond him, and he did not catch up with it for ten years.

He was not yet a rebel in a definite sense, but he was even then a bitter antagonist of Great Britain and all her works. Behind his antagonism stood the memory of men and events —of the foolish Braddock, England's picked soldier, and the craven flight of red-coated men—of his own laboured application for a British military commission, and its casual refusal —of the high-flown proclamations of British governors—of the crisp letters from tobacco agents in London, pointing out overdue debit balances. Still further back in time was the memory of brother Lawrence and his story of flat-headed stupidity at the siege of Cartagena.

Power of any kind creates enemies by its mere existence. When it is stupid power it creates them in masses. Many men in the colonies, no more revolutionary in spirit than Washington, thought of Great Britain as he thought.

Yet, indifferent as he was to abstractions, it is probable that none of these prickly memories would have stirred within him any feeling deeper than a hazy resentment if something else had not occurred to arouse his latent sense of wrong and turn it into an active grievance.

In 1763 the King had issued a proclamation forbidding any further encroachment, by individuals or private land enterprises, on the territory west of the Alleghenies. This measure was part of a large plan for the regulation of Indian affairs. Negotiation with the Indian tribes was taken out of the hands of the colonists and turned over to royal commissioners. The colonials were not only forbidden to settle, squatter fashion, on these lands; they were even prohibited from purchasing them from the Indians.

Lands were to be bought from the Indians, if bought at all, by the King's representatives. They in turn were to resell them to actual settlers at a fair price.

What a blow this was to Washington's land schemes! He had long been in the Ohio Company, and in May of 1763 he had been one of the organisers of the Mississippi Company, which had its hand reached out toward the rich lands in the Mississippi basin.

He thought the law might be evaded, or that it would become a dead letter. We find a letter from him to William Crawford, his land agent (this was the Colonel Crawford who was burned at the stake), in which he directs Crawford to go on his account to the Ohio territory and

> secure some of the most valuable lands in the King's part, which I think may be accomplished after a while, notwithstanding the proclamation, that restrains it at present, and prohibits the settling of them at all; for I can never look upon that proclamation in any other light (but this I say between ourselves), than as a temporary expedient to quiet the minds of the Indians. . . .

During the same year (1763) he turned his attention to another land speculation, this time nearer home. A company was organised to reclaim the Great Dismal Swamp, that large area of tangled bogs and dark lakes which lies on the southeastern edge of Virginia. Washington was the prime mover in this enterprise, but his actual investment was small. It was a successful venture—at least, he thought it was—for he listed his Dismal Swamp shares in 1799 as worth twenty thousand dollars.

During the 1760's he spent a great deal of time in looking after the land claims of the soldiers who had served under him in the French and Indian War. In the eagerness for volunteers at the outbreak of hostilities Governor Dinwiddie had offered bounties of land, two hundred thousand acres in all, of which Washington's own share was to be twenty thousand acres.

After the war was over and Dinwiddie had gone back to England, innumerable difficulties arose over this bounty, according to the traditional custom in respect to promises made to soldiers at the time of enlistment. Some of the land, it turned out, was on Pennsylvania soil; other portions had already been granted to other people, none of it was properly defined.

Washington gave his time, without charge, to the straightening out of these snarls. Most of the awards were utterly worthless. To hold a valid title the soldier had to have his land surveyed and staked, and the title recorded. Kentucky, where the land was finally located, was about as far away from tidewater Virginia at that time as Mexico is from New York to-day. To the average ex-soldier the process of getting the land was a monstrous impossibility. Many of them sold their claims for small amounts of cash. Washington picked up some of these claims at low prices. He wrote to his brother Charles: "As you are situated in a good place for seeing many of the Officers at different times I should be glad if you would (in a joking way rather than in earnest, at first) see what value they set on their lands."

Rather interesting light on his trading methods, that letter to brother Charles.

To his old friend Captain Posey, who appears to have been perpetually hard up, he paid the modest sum of £11. 11s. 3d. for a soldier's claim for three thousand acres. This figures out at a price of about two cents an acre.

His habit of making shrewd bargains was well known among his neighbours. One time Henry Lee, who was dining at Mount Vernon, mentioned that he wanted to sell a certain blooded horse.

"I'll buy him from you," Washington said.

"Oh no, I shall not sell him to you," was Lee's reply.

"Why not?"

"Because you never pay what anything is worth," Lee explained.

§ 5

At the height of the Stamp Act excitement Massachusetts invited all the other colonies to send delegates to New York to meet her own delegates for the purpose of considering colonial affairs.

This Stamp Act Congress was a piffling affair. Virginia was one of four colonies that did not send delegates. The delegates fluttered through a number of sessions, drew up a fluttering protest, and fluttered home.

In their petition to Parliament they referred to George III as "the best of sovereigns," an unfortunate phrase which was to come back and haunt the patriots.

It was hardly worth while anyway, for His Majesty's government, weary of controversy and considerably alarmed at the violence, decided to repeal the Stamp Act in its entirety.

Not only that—

They went even further; they wanted to clear up the whole subject matter of dispute at one sweep. The duty on molasses was reduced from threepence to one penny a gallon, but the duty was to be assessed on molasses imported from the British colonies as well as from the French West Indies. Before this was done the government had assurances from the colonial agents in London that this duty would be satisfactory.

The repeal of the Stamp Act was accompanied, however, by the passage of another measure, known as the Declaratory Act, in which the British government declared its perpetual right to "bind the colonies in any case whatsoever." This Declaratory Act was considered, in the colonies, nothing but a meaningless gesture, a face-saving effort on the part of the mother country.

The news of the repeal caused immense rejoicing in

America, with a wave of emotional hysteria over love for the good old mother country. There was hardly a dry eye among the crowds that set off fire-works and waved flags. The assembly of New York voted a statue to King George. This statue, made of lead, was pulled down some years later and melted into bullets to shoot the King's soldiers.

Merchants sighed with relief. Remonstrance was all right in its way . . . but the mobs had been getting ugly and beyond control. John Hancock, patriot and wealthy merchant, strolled around in his handsome velvet coat and rejoiced. "You may rest assured," he wrote, "that the people of this country will exert themselves to show their Loyalty & attachment to Great Britain."

Charles Thomson, who was to be for many years the secretary of the Continental Congress, said that a heartfelt joy was to be read in every countenance. Mr. Thomson probably did not see the countenance of Mr. Samuel Adams, for certainly no heartfelt joy was to be read there.

CHAPTER XV

GEORGE WASHINGTON AND SAMUEL ADAMS

§ 1

WASHINGTON's fame, so luminous in 1759, was growing dimmer with the years. The saviour of Braddock's army, the dramatic hero of Fort Necessity, the fearless soldier of the Virginia border, had become a stolid tobacco-planter who thought incessantly of land. For a month or so each year he sat silently in the House of Burgesses. The revolutionary movement, now aflame, North and South, did not expect much, if anything, of him.

In the natural course of events, considering the forgetfulness of men, his renown would have dwindled in any case, but it was rapidly paling into insignificance beside the new luminaries.

In Massachusetts there were Samuel Adams, and John Hancock, and James Otis; in Pennsylvania there was Dickinson; in New York there were Sears and Macdougal; in South Carolina there was Gadsden—to mention only a few of those who were distinguishing themselves by revolutionary agitation. In his own Virginia there was Patrick Henry, who shone for a time like the sun.

Washington's name seldom appears in the vast record of the ten years' controversy that preceded the Revolution. It was a time of eloquence and argument, but he was neither an orator nor a writer. Back-biting commentators have hinted that Washington was really pro-British until the bullets began to fly, and that he took up the revolutionary cause only when he came to the conclusion that the patriots would win.

Nothing could be further from the truth. If it were worth while it would be easy to prove that he was anti-British as

early as 1760. In his case one may tack *anti* and *British*
together with a neat sense of accuracy, for he was more
thoroughly anti-British in these early years than many others
who held prominent posts on the patriotic side during the
Revolution.

His antipathies are easy to discern, but when we come to
his preferences we find ourselves in doubt. He was anti-British,
but *pro* what? The idle determinative *pro* goes dangling about
in the air, endeavouring to hook on to something.

Finally we think of land, and then we have it. He was
pro-Land and anti-British . . . and pro-Land meant the
American side. A map of his political views in the pre-Revolutionary period would be simply a map of the Western
Territory, with a few disappointing financial statements from
his London agents tacked on to one corner.

Albert Jay Nock says, in his *Jefferson:*

> As a desire for free trade was the animating spirit of
> the Revolution in one section of the country—that is to
> say among the merchants and traders of New England—
> so free land was the desideratum among Virginians. They
> wanted to see the great royal land-grants broken up; they
> hated this monopoly as much as the Massachusetts mer-
> chant hated the British monopoly of his trade, and for
> the same reason; the merchant would be better in a free
> competitive market, and the Virginian would do better if
> he could get hold of some of the monopolised land for
> himself.

§ 2

Distrusting his own intellectual powers, Washington moved
with extreme caution in political affairs. In the course of his
career there were several men who had at various times an
advisory relation to him which was somewhat similar to Colonel
E. M. House's relation to President Wilson.

Though he consulted his friends, and frequently adopted

their views even when they were contrary to his own, we may declare with assurance that nobody but himself had a hand in shaping his fundamental ideas. It would not have been possible for any one, however persuasive he might have been, to have turned Washington into a radical. Beneath all his political conceptions there ran a sense of property. He was a Virginia land-owning aristocrat from beginning to end.

In the heat of the Revolution he was simply a conservative land-owner fighting for independence from Great Britain, and for nothing else. The difference between him and the French revolutionists was profound. They revolted against an order of civilisation; their ideal was a new conception of human society. Washington had no such ideas. He was satisfied with the social structure of Virginia. What he wanted to do was to get rid of dependence on a government three thousand miles away.

The Colonel House of this part of Washington's career was George Mason of Gunston Hall. George Mason was seven years older than Washington. He was a wealthy scholar, a man who read books and reflected profoundly on events and men. These qualities doubtless impressed Washington, but I imagine that he was more impressed by the fact that Colonel Mason was the owner of an enormous estate and was himself a highly efficient plantation manager.

The outstanding feature of Mason's political views was a fear of centralised power which was almost morbid in range and intensity. He was an original states-rights' man; and in this quality he went even further than Thomas Jefferson himself.

As a young man he had served in the Virginia assembly, but he was disgusted by the restraint imposed on the colonial burgesses by a foreign governor and council, and he found small satisfaction in making laws for foreigners to approve and administer.

From about 1765 to the beginning of the Revolution the ideas of George Mason were the ideas of George Washington.

He wrote the Fairfax Resolves which Washington introduced in the House of Burgesses, and he was the author of the non-importation agreement of 1769. On all important measures in the House of Burgesses Washington consulted him. After the Revolution they disagreed, and ceased to be friends—for Washington came, at that time, under the influence of the Hamilton coterie, whose ideas were diametrically opposed to those of Mason.

Washington possessed only ordinary intellectual ability. The myth-making process which has given him the attributes of a modern Solomon began with the Federalists in the 1790's. The motive behind it was simple enough. He was the god of their party, and they felt that their party, in its pursuit of power, had to stand or fall on Washington's reputation for unimpeachable wisdom.

The Federalists constituted the party of property. Their entire philosophy rested on the conception that the possession of property implies both intellectual capacity and high moral quality. They spread industriously the legend of the Best People . . . Dollars, Brains, Purity, Land, Holiness, Efficiency, all walking through the ages hand in hand. Under this impulse they lifted Washington to an incredible altitude of legendary wisdom and virtue and left him suspended there while they turned to something else.

I have no desire to belittle Washington; I am merely trying to present the truth, good or bad. The truth is that he was entirely devoid of original ideas. He had no overpowering intellectual urge, no passion for making novel mental combinations. He was without mysticism, without fancy. In the dim regions of his soul there were no lonely beaches where the ocean of infinity sent its rolling surf. His ideas were all plain, conventional and as familiar to the perception as slabs of granite. He never announced a belief in anything that was not already believed in by many other people. Although he assisted in forming the American government there is not a single important feature of the governmental structure that was contributed by him.

The keynote of his personality was Character . . . not Intellect, nor Imagination, nor Feeling. He was a perfect pattern of will and self-discipline. He possessed fortitude, steadfastness, dignity, courage, honesty and self-respect.

One searches the *Diaries* in vain for some hint of revolutionary activity, yet he did take part, now and then, in the movement. He was opposed to the Stamp Act, and probably voted for Patrick Henry's Resolves; and, in 1769 and 1770, he was active in promoting the new non-importation movement.

Washington, with a set of non-importation resolutions which had been drawn up by George Mason, rose in the House of Burgesses and attempted to get the resolutions passed by that assembly. The governor thought some of the resolutions dangerous to the prerogative of the King and dissolved the House. The Burgesses went over to the Raleigh Tavern and passed them unofficially. This was in 1769. The Virginians, as a whole, failed to live up to this agreement, but Washington kept it religiously.

Occasionally he wrote a letter about political affairs. In one of them to Francis Dandridge, an uncle of Mrs. Washington in London, he shows that he has a clear notion of the evil effects of the mercantile system in this passage:

> What may be the result of this [the Stamp Act], and of some other (I think I may add) ill-judged measures, I will not undertake to determine; but this I may venture to affirm, that the advantage accruing to the mother country will fall greatly short of the expectations of the ministry; for certain it is, that our whole substance does already in a manner flow to Great Britain, and that whatsoever contributes to lessen our importations must be hurtful to their manufacturers.

But this was all mere by-play in Washington's life at this period. He was occupied with his own affairs . . . with the acquisition of land . . . with improvements in its cultivation . . . with fox-hunting and card-playing . . . with his step-children . . . with the purchase and sale of horses and negroes. These were his placid years, and the only quiet years he was ever to have.

It is interesting to reflect that while the hum and stir of propaganda went on, that while the country drifted crazily through riot and disorder to revolution, the man who was to emerge as the majestic world figure of the epoch was enjoying the serene life of a country squire. Who would have dreamed in 1765 that George Washington—then busy with his mulberry trees and his dogs—was to become the symbol and embodiment of the American Revolution?

At Mount Vernon his life was simple. He rose invariably at daybreak, which in the summer was at about four in the morning. Without waking Martha, or any of the guests, he would go softly downstairs to his breakfast. This consisted of cornmeal hoe-cakes (these are thin, flat cakes of moistened cornmeal, baked and served hot), honey and several cups of tea.

After breakfast his custom was to ride around his plantations. On these morning rides he wore "plain dark clothes, a broad-brimmed white hat, and attached to his saddle-bow was an umbrella with a long staff." He must have made a quaint, sober and Quakerish appearance.

In the course of the morning he would return, and change his clothes. Then he ate a second breakfast, consisting of ham and eggs, or fresh fish, with corn-cakes, honey and tea. Dinner at Mount Vernon in colonial times was at two o'clock. After the Revolution it was changed to three o'clock. In the afternoon he would appear among the ladies and tea-cups on the verandah in one of the handsome suits which were made for him by his London tailor. His stockings were of silk, and his shoe-buckles of silver. His reddish-brown hair was powdered and tied in a queue.

Card-playing was the great indoor sport of the age, and Washington played almost daily. At Mount Vernon they always played for small sums. His winnings and losings were so evenly balanced that his total losses—after deducting the sums won—were only £6.3s.3d. in four years.

On fox-hunting days, which were frequent, he would occasionally hunt all day, getting a snack at a neighbour's house. Sometimes negroes came following the hunt on jogging mules with picnic baskets crammed full of food and bottles of wine.

Outside of fox-hunting, he appears to have loved the theatre more than any other form of amusement. He went to every play, good or bad, that was produced within his reach. The theatres of the day were rough, barnlike affairs, and there were not many of them. However, the acting was usually good; the actors were English, almost invariably, and well-trained.

The Virginians had a passion for the theatre which reminds one of the Elizabethan English. Lewis Hallam's company which, I believe, was the first professional dramatic enterprise of the time in America, went to Williamsburg in 1752, and remained in Virginia for eleven months, playing to profitable houses. The astonishing character of this exploit is shown best by the fact that Williamsburg had less than a thousand inhabitants. Washington saw Hallam's company in 1752—mostly in Shakespeare's plays—and in later years we find him attending the theatre in Williamsburg several evenings a week.

The dramatic criticisms which appeared in the Virginia and Maryland newspapers are amusing in their solemnity. In them these candle-lit performances in barns are treated as if they were the weightiest affairs in the world. One of the reviewers of the drama, who saw Miss Hallam for the first time, was so stunned by her beauty that nothing could restrain his frenzy. "Ye Gods! 'Tis Cytherea's face!" he exclaimed in print.

Dancing was another pleasure of which Washington never tired. With him it was a form of physical exercise, and probably without much, or any, emotional or æsthetic significance. He had the active, outdoors temperament which loves movement for its own sake. During the Revolution, when he was about fifty years of age, he danced once with Catherine Greene —the wife of General Greene—for three hours without stopping. All the other dancers paused and looked on; it seems to have been a kind of endurance contest between him and Mrs. Greene.

The Virginia balls were stately entertainments. Quadrilles and minuets, men and women bowing and curtseying to the music of violins and tambours. The dances had such quaint names as High Betty Martin and Leather-the-Strap. Intricate figures, the dancers weaving in and out, barely touching fingertips in passing; the dancing school precision of evolution kept amid the gaiety of laughter and the flutter of fans. Perfume and powdered hair, silks and laces, glancing eyes and words with subtle meanings, all under the soft yellow light of candles.

Washington usually devoted his Sundays at Mount Vernon to letter-writing. He was a most methodical correspondent. In writing he would first sketch a draft of the letter he intended to write, and then copy it neatly, making alterations as he went along. The draft was then filed as a record. Occasionally he went to church—about one Sunday in four on an average— but he never mentions the text of the sermon in his *Diaries*, nor does he give the subject of the discourse.

The Virginia aristocrats were fond of visiting one another. Mount Vernon was seldom without guests. People came and went, sometimes staying for one meal, but frequently making a sojourn of several days.

As Washington's step-son, "Jacky" Custis, grew up this influx of the neighbouring gentry was increased by his friends.

§ 3

"Jacky" Custis was good-natured and popular, though he did not have much brains. He was spoiled, no doubt, by wealth and lack of restraint. In Washington's *Diaries* he appears as "Jacky" Custis; then as John Parke Custis; then as Mr. Custis. We may trace his growing up in the shape of his name.

When he was a stripling youth he rode with Washington in helter-skelter fox hunts over hills and gullies. In fancy one may see him, sitting on his sleek, superb horse before the mansion, waiting for the hunt to assemble. Yelping dogs run about the horses' legs; "Jacky" wears his scarlet hunting coat; the ladies look on from the terrace; the rim of clear sky falls sharply on the distant hills; the breeze rustles the leaves of the ever-verdant laurel. Negroes, all white teeth and ebony skin, pass back and forth. "Jacky" flicks at them teasingly with his whip.

Mr. Custis sat on top of the world. His only trouble seems to have been some little difficulty about book learning. When he was seventeen years of age Washington wrote of him to Rev. Jonathan Boucher, head of a famous school at Annapolis: "He has little or no knowledge of arithmetic, and is totally ignorant of the mathematics." He knew a few words of Latin, but "nothing of Greek," nor of French. He was sent from one school to another with his horses and his liveried negro servant; and to King's College, in New York. But education failed to take, and his stay in the haunts of learning was brief.

If he had known any French he might have read, and adopted as his own, the query which Louis XIV made to a cardinal. Louis, then the Dauphin, was thirteen and as ignorant as a carp. This cardinal pestered him about his inability to read.

"*Mais à quoi sert de lire?*" the prince inquired, and put the cardinal on the defensive. History, in its stupid inconclusiveness, omits the cardinal's reply; but if he was honest he an-

swered probably that there is no good whatever in reading
when one sits on top of the world.

Perhaps Mr. Custis, too, with the uncanny intuition of
youth, felt the uselessness of it all.

His sister Martha was an epileptic. From contemporary
accounts she is made to appear very beautiful and charming;
a delicate, fragile, dark child, with eerie, suffering eyes.
Everything known to the medical science of the time was tried,
but her fits continued. Then George and Martha went into
the realms of quackery and put iron rings on her hands, and
made her swallow strange and barbarous compounds. She
died in 1773.

During these years Washington kept a large pack of hunting dogs, and he looked upon the breeding of dogs as such a
serious matter that he kept a record of it in his diary. One
comes frequently upon entries like this:

> Oct. 1st: The hound bitch Tipsey was lined by the
> little Spaniel dog Pompey, before she was shut up in the
> House with old Harry.

On one occasion there seems to have been a catastrophe in
his nicely calculated dog-breeding programme. He was away
from home at the time or it would not have happened. He records it in these words:

> Returned home from my journey to Frederick, etca.,
> and found that the Hound Bitch Maiden had taken Dog
> promiscuously: That the Bitch Lady was in Heat and
> had also been promiscuously lined, and therefore I did not
> shut her up; that Dutchess was shut up, and had been
> lined twice by Drunkard, but was out one night in her
> heat, and supposed to be lined by other Dogs; That True-
> love was also in the House, as was Mopsy likewise (who
> had been seen lined to Pilot before she was shut up).

While these dog-breeding disasters were happening at Mount
Vernon the Sons of Liberty were spreading over the colonies,

committees were forming, legislatures were resisting royal governors, and men were putting pen to paper to prove one thing or another.

§ 4

Over in England a highly intelligent gentleman named Charles Townshend had become chancellor of the exchequer. He was hardly settled in his seat before he began to tinker with taxation. The Townshend scheme of taxation was announced as a "logical" plan. The logic of it consisted in taking the Americans at their word—as Grenville had done before —on the distinction between external and internal taxation.

There was to be a custom-house duty on glass, paper, lead and paints. There was also to be a duty on tea of threepence a pound.

Another section of the plan provided for the establishment of a board of customs commissioners in Boston, with supreme authority over the Atlantic seaboard. This was for the convenience of colonial importers, who had been obliged to carry their disputes to London for adjudication.

The Townshend Acts were called collectively by the colonials the "Paint, Paper and Glass Act." The ministry, in putting these measures through, was greatly encouraged by the success of the one-penny duty on molasses, which was being paid by the colonials, though with considerable grumbling.

The money to be raised by Townshend's logical plan, it was carefully explained, was to be expended entirely in America. The salaries of the royal governors and judges were to be provided by this fund.

Remonstrance had grown into a habit. As soon as the Paint, Paper and Glass Act was announced Parliament was flooded with American petitions. Nevertheless, it became a law in November, 1767.

The Boston merchants decided to do their own protesting this time. The petitioners "humbly pray." They had had enough of mobs. Samuel Adams, specialist in British tyranny, was not even called in consultation. Dignity was the order of the day. James Otis declared that "no possible circumstances, though ever so oppressive, could be supposed to justify private tumults and disorders."

The conservatives had somehow got into the saddle. Intellect displaced tar and feathers as an instrument of controversy. Merchants, planters and lawyers, opposed to Britain, began to feel that dependence on England was, after all, better than dependence on a home-grown mob. So the petitioners "humbly pray."

Pamphlets poured from the presses. "Senex," "Cunctator," "Amico Publico" and "Brutus" filled the newspapers with argument and anonymity. The whole dispute seemed likely to fritter itself away on fine interpretations of colonial charters and superficial arguments.

Letter-writing went on a tremendous pace—people writing to convince other people. Even Washington took a hand at it. He wrote of "our lordly masters of Great Britain," of "bashaws," of "maintaining the liberty which we have derived from our ancestors."

With the local bashaw, Lord Botetourt, governor of Virginia, he seems to have been on very friendly terms. His *Diaries* contain numerous records of his dining at the governor's house.

The best of the pamphleteers was John Dickinson, of Philadelphia. *His Letters of a Pennsylvania Farmer* were published serially in 1767, and later in a book that went through eight or ten editions. It was the ablest statement of the colonial cause that had appeared. The *Letters* were supposed to be addressed to some one in England. They were not revolutionary, but loyal, in tone; they appealed to the good sense and good-will of England. Their arguments on the rights of the colonies were considered sound, though a little too legal and historical in their setting to get down to the ordinary, semi-illiterate colonial. They got to the cultured people, however. Throughout the intellectual stratum of the patriot party they were universally read and praised.

The *Letters* appear to me to be full of hazy contradictions. The author asserts loyalty to England and says "there must exist a power somewhere, to preside," and declares that power to be Parliament. But he goes on to deny the right of Parliament to levy any kind of taxes. Then he says that the colonies are free, and should be free, of external control. In other words, Parliament had, in his opinion, some vague power over the colonies, but must not, under any circumstances, attempt to put it in practice.

Dickinson came within a hair's breadth of being the greatest figure of Revolutionary times. He was a wealthy man of culture and standing. In intellectual force he was much superior to Washington. His acquaintance was large, and he was thoroughly in touch with every phase of public affairs. In the late 1760's no sensible person would have compared Washington with him, for a moment, as a bearer of potential renown.

Yet the name of John Dickinson means nothing to the American people to-day; one has to thumb the pages of history to find out who he was.

He had become a rebel through meditation, and not through instinct, like Samuel Adams; nor through resentment, like Washington. His failing was the incapacity to make irrevocable decisions. He had a typically open mind, he was willing to be convinced of anything that was reasonable.

Revolutions are made by men whose minds are not open, who are not willing to be convinced.

He meditated so long on the Declaration of Independence, and saw the arguments of both sides so clearly, that he could not make up his mind to sign it. At the time of signing he absented himself from the Congress, and so lost his one remaining chance of immortality.

Intellect sat on her throne, reason and moderation were in

the air. The merchants' genteel boycott of British goods had
stiffened into non-importation agreements which extended from
Boston to Charleston. Moderation ruled, although under-cur-
rents in which moderation was sadly lacking slipped along un-
obtrusively beneath the surface of affairs.

Early in 1768 Samuel Adams, then a member of the Massachusetts Assembly, persuaded the legislature to send what is
known in history as the Massachusetts Circular Letter to all
the other colonies. Adams had written the letter himself.

Very mild, this letter is. It discusses the Townshend Acts,
says trouble will probably result from them, deplores trouble,
and suggests that the colonies discuss their rights with one
another by correspondence. Then it says that the Townshend
duties are objectionable because they infringe on "natural and
constitutional rights," in that they take away property without the consent of the people.

Ah, there we have it . . . the fine, smooth hand of the
shabby man in Boston. The Townshend Acts were concerned
only with external taxes, and it was understood generally that
Parliament had a right to levy such duties.

But Adams had contrived things so that Massachusetts put
herself flatly in opposition to external taxes. The distinction
between internal and external is dropped: All taxes are now an
imposition. Through this deft manœuvre Adams had edged the
colonies one step further toward the conflict.

In this widening of the field of argument we have a clear
epitome of the agitation that led straight to the Revolution.

There was a good deal of widening in other ways, too. The
gentility of protest was rudely jarred when a customs official
at Providence was decorated with a coat of tar and feathers
by unknown parties; when three men, in crestfallen tar-and-
feather apparel, were led through the streets of New York
by unknown parties; when a British revenue sloop was burned
to the water's edge by unknown parties.

The Sons of Liberty and Unknown Parties were synonymous

terms. Nobody knew who the Sons of Liberty were—at least, nobody in authority knew—and their organisation was always a mystery. Usually they appeared with their faces blacked, or in some kind of thin disguise. Citizens whose powers of observation were good enough to recognise them generally received anonymous warning letters. After the receipt of a few letters the capacity for recognition invariably waned.

The Ku Klux of the present day are almost a perfect replica of the Sons of Liberty. In organisation, in pretended ideals, in mystery of movement, in passwords and disguises, the Ku Klux and the Sons of Liberty are as much alike as two peas.

The tendency to form lawless secret organisations has always been a characteristic of the American people. In a certain sense the history of the country might be written in the activities of the Sons of Liberty, and their successors, the Barn-burners, the Night-riders, and the Ku Klux.

The crisis, hovering in the horizon, drew nearer when John Hancock—patriot leader and friend of Samuel Adams—smuggled a cargo of Madeira wine into Boston almost before the eyes of the customs officials. The wine got in, but the sloop was seized. "Unknown parties" arrived on the scene with the alacrity of firemen hastening to a fire. They knocked down the King's officers, threw stones, dragged people around by the hair, and broke windows. The customs men, thoroughly frightened, fled to a fort in the harbour, and the governor of Massachusetts wrote an urgent request for troops.

Two regiments came from Halifax and camped on Boston Common. In a short time their camp was the hanging-out place of every trollop and blackleg in town.

§ 5

The amiability of the working people was at a low ebb. Bad manners ran with easy fluency into abuse and blows. In the lighter moods of the populace the soldiers were called "bloody backs" and "lobsters." In more irascible tempers they were shouted at in terms which a decent historian cannot print.

The soldiers were permitted to do odd jobs about the town to piece out their miserable pay. In March 2, 1770, a redcoat came by Gray's ropewalk and was asked by some one if he wanted to work. He said he did, and the workmen told him with a laugh to clean out the privy.

The soldier's feelings were hurt, and he remained before the place for an hour or two, standing in the windy street, muttering to himself and talking to the closed windows. One may see him, in fancy, his hands blue with cold, his rough shoes covered with mud, and his coarse scarlet coat glowing like a flame against the grey houses. After awhile a workman came out and knocked him down. Soldiers ran to help their comrade. For the next two days there was a succession of street brawls in the town.

On March 5th the sentry before the custom-house was set upon by a mob. Captain Preston with eight men came to his assistance. This squad stood with fixed bayonets around the sentry-box. For a while the crowd stood off and shouted obscenity at the redcoats, daring them to fire, and calling them cowards. Then the mob came closer and began to throw stones.

Crispus Attucks, a town character who was half negro and half Indian, attempted to take a soldier's gun away from him, and the soldier shot him dead. Immediately the squad began to fire into the crowd, apparently without orders to do so. Six Bostonians were killed, and several wounded.

This was the celebrated Boston Massacre.

The Revolution was at last down to the level of the common people. Men to whom the Townshend Acts were economic Greek, and who smiled indulgently at the Stamp Act, could understand Murder . . . plain, vile Murder. Samuel Adams was the busiest man in Boston. Get Paul Revere, the engraver! A picture of the carnage must be made—at once! Where are the poets! Let them begin their ballads! And the journalists—call it *A Short Narrative of the Horrid Massacre in Boston!* Troops shooting men down like dogs! That's right! Put a dog in the picture to show the contrast! Shot down like dogs! Redcoats running all over Boston, shooting in every direction! No, no—not a black-and-white picture! Put red in it; soldiers' coats must be red! The negro? Leave him out . . . no, put him in, but make him white! It won't do any good to have a negro in it when it gets to South Carolina!

Perhaps you have seen the picture by Paul Revere. It is one of the best known of the Revolutionary prints. Soldiers in close, neat ranks, firing a volley into a crowd of decent-looking citizens. A dog stands in the foreground, evidently undisturbed by the commotion. Under the engraving there is a jingling poem, beginning—

> Unhappy Boston! See thy Sons deplore,
> Thy hallow'd Walks besmear'd with guiltless Gore.

Copies of the picture flew like the wind to every Son of Liberty in America. If Britain ever needed a publicity agent she needed him at that moment.

The Massacre did not turn out, in the end, as well as the radicals expected. The soldiers were tried in a Boston court, and every effort was made—to the credit of the leading patriots—to give them an unbiassed trial. John Adams volunteered to defend them. All of them were finally released.

§ 6

While this uproar was reverberating down the long backbone of America, the British government magnanimously repealed all the Townshend duties except that on tea. They would have repealed the tea duty also, but the King wanted some small duty kept to maintain the right.

The patriot party suddenly found itself without a cause. The Boston Massacre was a fizzle, and the duties had been repealed. Many of the intellectual patriots thought the dispute was settled for good. The British thought so, too. They sat back to watch the colonies purr in contentment.

There was not much purring done. The superficial grievances had been removed, but the situation at the bottom was unchanged. Disorder continued. Britain had already lost her colonies, and was not aware of it.

Governor Bernard of Massachusetts, cynical observer of men, ventured in his reports to the British ministry to suggest the creation of an American order of nobility. He thought that would go far toward bringing about peace and order.

One wonders what the effect of such a policy would have been. We may be pretty sure that Samuel Adams would have declined his honours; he was that kind of person. We may be equally sure that John Adams, with his passionate love of titles, would have accepted his.

With George Washington as Lord Mount Vernon, John Hancock as the Earl of Dorchester, Patrick Henry as Baron Henry of Rivanna, John Adams as Viscount Something-or-other, and Thomas Jefferson as the Marquis of Monticello, would the Revolution have occurred? One can never tell. My own conjecture is that it would have broken out eventually, and that it would have been different in form.

CHAPTER XVI

§ 1

THE pleasant white flag of conciliation was hardly raised to the mast-head of British policy before it was ripped into shreds by the patriot tornado, which at the moment was blowing at some unheard-of miles an hour. The colonial leaders declared that the British government had repealed the Paint, Paper and Glass Act only because manufacturing of the dutiable articles had begun in America, and that the government wanted to kill American industry.

The government was unable to turn around without putting somebody "on the brink of ruin." The rum-distillers were again on the brink. They had been paying the duty of one penny a gallon on molasses, but now they claimed that even this small duty was too high, and that Danish rum was underselling theirs on the coast of Africa.

It was evident that deft revolutionary minds were moving under the surface of American affairs.

The disorder of the Stamp Act period broadened into anarchy. The government was not able to convict offenders in cases tried before juries; it made an effort to abolish juries in certain cases by increasing the powers of the admiralty courts. The only result of this move was to add another grievance to the colonial list.

Debts were repudiated, houses wrecked, ships burned, men mobbed. General Gage, commander of the British troops in Boston, on one of his meditative afternoon strolls came across a tarred and feathered man who was being ridden on a rail by unknown parties.

In the excess of movement our sensations are blurred. The records of the time, like an overspeeded motion picture film, are all flash and stir, waving arms, trampling feet and drifting smoke.

Now and then the flying scene stands still, like Joshua's sun in Ajalon, while the colonial world watches the evolution of British stupidity. A strong party in the House of Commons urges the government to bring the entire Massachusetts legislature over to England to be tried on a charge of treason. Wonderful idea, in view of the fact that the British government is unable to arrest anybody, or to keep order in a single township.

Another genius of the governing party suggests to General Gage that the best way to pacify Massachusetts is to disarm every man in the province. Gage had a defective sense of humour, else he would have replied: *Come over and try it.* Being a stolid soldier, all he can think of as an answer is that, in his opinion, such a procedure is not practicable.

In all the Southern colonies, from Pennsylvania to South Carolina, there is an intense sectional struggle between the wealthy people on the coast and the poorer people of the uplands. Political power is in the hands of the wealthy; the uplands are inadequately represented in the colonial legislatures, though in the slave states the uplands have the majority of the white population.

A civil war between East and West breaks out in North Carolina; there are armies and a pitched battle. This strife has nothing to do with the British-Colonial dispute; it is an outgrowth of sectionalism, and revolves around the exorbitant fees of court-house officials.

Merchants who import English goods are forced to send them back, and to make public apologies. Nevertheless, importing goes on, as the figures show, and it appears to be a pretty safe occupation when the importer stands in solidly with the patriots.

John Hancock, hot patriot and sworn signer of the non-importation agreement, is accused by John Mein, publisher of the Boston *Chronicle*, of importing forbidden goods in quantities. Terrible commotion. Hancock denies it; thereupon Mein astonishes Boston by printing custom-house manifests in detail, with a long list of Hancock's imports. In some way he has access to the secret records of the custom-house, probably through connivance of officials. Somebody feebly replies to Mein, but now the Boston *Chronicle* is in full swing. Every week its front page is covered with lists of imports. Mein proves that many of the merchants who are loud in non-importing talk are bringing in goods.

Logic reels; reason weeps. The patriotic party drops its poor little wisp of denials and picks up a brickbat. Mein's house is plastered with filth; his windows are broken; his printing plant is wrecked; his papers are torn up in the streets by angry citizens. Then Mein fades out of the American Revolution. Years afterward we see him in London, begging Parliament to reimburse him on account of his losses.

§ 2

In all this muddled strife one may discern two streams of revolutionary impulse.

One was the revolt of the proprietary class—the merchants, planters, lawyers, ship-owners and distillers—against the economic and political domination of the English.

The other was a muscular, inarticulate rebellion of the working people—the small farmers, the mechanics, the voteless, the landless—against the growing power of wealth, either British or colonial.

For the purpose of clarity I shall call the revolt of the proprietary class the Imperial Civil War, as this term seems to describe it with fair accuracy. One may explore this revolt in vain for any new conception of human rights. The planters and merchants wanted to get rid of Great Britain so they might run American affairs in their own way. They were out for land and profit, and Britain interfered with the pursuit of these ends, for the British wanted land and profit themselves.

It is true that those who conducted the Imperial Civil War used phrases, borrowed from Locke and Burlamaqui and Montesquieu, about *equality* and *liberty* and *natural rights,* but these were mere slogans, not to be taken literally, and intended only to influence the lower classes.

The common herd was expected to do most of the fighting, of course; but even the common herd with its exquisite sensibility to suggestion from above, can hardly have been thrilled over the woes of a planter who wanted to get more public land for nothing, or of a ship-owner who had been caught smuggling, or of a lawyer who had had to buy a sixpenny stamp to put on an attachment which would enable him to seize some poor debtor's furniture.

So Locke and the great liberal thinkers were searched for advertising material. It appeared, from a perusal of Locke's essays, that all men, "by nature, are free, equal and independent," and the advertising campaign was tied to that phrase.

Men may be created free and equal, but when it came to practical matters, most of the patriots were not considered free enough nor equal enough to be allowed to vote for delegates to any of the Continental Congresses, or to have any hand in the patriotic governments.

Under the revolutionary constitutions the old qualifications for the right to vote still held good—fifty acres or its equivalent, in most cases—and Washington insisted that "only gentlemen be made officers," though ungentlemanly patriots were quite welcome as common soldiers.

I have said that there were two main streams of the revolutionary movement. One impulse I have called the Imperial

Civil War. The other—that of the working people—I shall call the People's Revolution.

Both of these movements, taken together, form the composite which is known in history as the American Revolution. Besides the main streams there were many cross-currents—the war on the loyalists, or tories, for example, which was a civil strife of large dimensions.

At times the Imperial Civil War and the People's Revolution ran together in a single stream. At other times they divided and ran in different directions. The course of the People's Revolution can be traced only in its acts of blind resistance, for it was unorganised, without a spokesman, without a leader, and only half-conscious of its own existence.

Samuel Adams might have been its leader, but his horizon was too close. He lacked breadth and vision; he was never anything but a specialist in British tyranny. Possessing no property himself, he was nevertheless unable to free his mind of the conception that property and good citizenship were synonymous terms. Patrick Henry was a thorough democrat, but his capacity for leadership was small. Circumstances restricted Gadsden to local activities in his faraway South Carolina, or he might have been the voice of the People's Revolution. Yet, here again, we have the limited vision, the shut-in personality, the specialist in British tyranny.

But what of Jefferson? He had a profound belief in democracy. His mental voltage was higher than that of any American of the eighteenth century, except Franklin; and there is no doubt that he was greatly superior to any other man of his time in breadth of political understanding.

Jefferson was late in attaining his intellectual maturity. At the beginning of the Revolution he was thirty-two years old, and still a believer in phrases, like some bearded giant of a boy who still believes in Santa Claus. His great political vision was to come to him years after the People's Revolution had

expired, and the latter half of his life was spent in his efforts
to revive it.

Without a directing mind the People's Revolution flowed and
eddied through the colonies, revealing itself in senseless mobs;
in bitter class resentments; in blind, fanatic outbursts of sectionalism. The shrewd and wealthy leaders of the Imperial
Civil War attempted—and often succeeded—in putting themselves at its head, and in turning its strength to their own uses.

§ 3

In 1772 a small British warship—the *Gaspee*, Captain Dudingston—was used by the Customs Commissioners to patrol
Narragansett Bay and watch for smugglers. The *Gaspee* was
active in this business; so active, indeed, that there were
numerous seizures of smugglers' vessels. The Rhode Islanders
contended that this armed ship had no right to be in their
waters. Their argument was highly involved, and legal, but
one cannot think of it otherwise than as essentially flimsy, for
if the British government was not allowed to enforce its laws
with its own war vessel in its own waters—what then? This
contention could mean nothing else than that Rhode Island
considered herself outside the British empire.

News came to Providence on June 9, 1772, that the *Gaspee*
was ashore on a sand bar, a few miles below the town. The
smuggling merchants decided to destroy her, and this was accomplished that night. One of the participants named
Ephraim Bowen has left a first-hand account of this incident.
He says that during the afternoon the report was spread around
Providence that the *Gaspee* was helplessly aground.

> Mr. Brown [a leading merchant of Providence] resolved
> on her destruction. . . . Soon after sunset, a man passed
> along the main street, beating a drum . . . and inviting
> those persons who felt a disposition to destroy that
> troublesome vessel, to repair to Mr. James Sabin's house.

About nine o'clock I took my father's gun . . . and went to Mr. Sabin's and found it full of people. . . . Orders were given to embark. . . . A line of boats was soon formed. . . . The party thus proceeded till within about sixty yards of the *Gaspee*, when a sentinel hailed. No answer. . . . In about a minute Dudingston mounted the starboard gunwale, in his shirt, and hailed, "Who comes there?" No answer. He hailed again, when Captain Whipple answered: "I am the sheriff of the county of Kent; I have got a warrant to apprehend you; so surrender, damn you."

I took my seat on the thwart . . . with my gun by my side. . . . Joseph Bucklin, who was standing on the main thwart by my right side, said to me, "Ephe, reach me your gun, and I can kill that fellow." I reached it to him. Bucklin fired, and Dudingston fell. . . . Bucklin exclaimed, "I have killed the rascal!" . . . The men on deck retreated below.

John Mawney, who had for two or three years been studying medicine and surgery, was ordered to dress Dudingston's wound . . . the ball took effect directly below the navel. . . .

How much like a Ku Klux episode this is, with its curious mingling of secrecy, law and order, sheriffs, warrants and assassins in a night attack. The sailors, with their wounded officer, were set ashore, and the ship burned.

The British dillydallying over this incident is illustrative of the government's dazed condition. A commission of inquiry appointed by British officials wasted months in investigation only to report that the *Gaspee* had been destroyed by unknown parties. The commission was unable to find any one in Rhode Island who knew anything whatever about the occurrence. This astounding state of affairs did not cause the government to declare martial law and take over the management of things. On the contrary, the commission was quietly dissolved and the matter was allowed to drop.

It went into the silences so far as the British were concerned, but the Americans held to it as a topic for a long time. Their feelings had been hurt. The mere existence of the commission of inquiry had offended every patriot. If a free people are to be pestered by commissions whenever they shoot a naval officer, or burn a ship, what is the world coming to, anyway?

In Virginia the progress of the investigation was followed with excited interest. The announced intention of the government to try the burners of the *Gaspee* in England aroused hot resentment. Thomas Jefferson, then a member of the Assembly, thought something ought to be done about it. He says in his *Autobiography*: "Not thinking our old and leading members up to the point of forwardness and zeal which the times required, Mr. Henry, R. H. Lee, Francis L. Lee, Mr. Carr and myself agreed to meet in the evening in a private room of the Raleigh to consult on the state of things."

That he did not invite Washington to meet with them is an interesting circumstance. Is it a fair inference that he did not consider Washington "up to the point of forwardness and zeal which the times required"? I think it is. Washington was a "silent" member, and at that time would hardly impress any one as active as Jefferson.

At this informal meeting Richard Henry Lee proposed a system of intercolonial correspondence which would bring the revolutionary elements in all parts of America into a common understanding. The correspondence was to be carried on by revolutionary committees, to be called Committees of Correspondence. The plan included a central committee for each colony, with local committees for towns and counties. This proposal was approved by Mr. Jefferson's little gathering, and was sent at once to the leading revolutionists in all the colonies. In a short time each colony had its Committee of Correspondence.

The plan was not new; it had already appeared in Massachusetts, where Samuel Adams had it in operation among the towns of that province, but to Richard Henry Lee belongs the honour of the continental scheme.

Richard Henry Lee was the kind of man who, early in life, begins to look like a family portrait. Such men usually mummify in their prime. Thereafter they live among the medallions and curios of their race. Surrounded by genealogical tables, time-worn letters, quaint silhouettes, jewelled swords, and unheard-of documents, they spend their lives in making finicky corrections in historical narratives. Richard Henry Lee was spared this fate by the coming-on of the Revolution, where Destiny had given him a rôle about halfway between the star and the chorus.

Gilbert Stuart did his picture; a portrait in profile. In it he reveals an extraordinary resemblance to the Egyptian Pharaohs . . . large thin nose, hollow cheeks, and general convexity of countenance. He was a man without a trace of greatness, yet he inspired events and impressed himself on history through mere pertinacity and insistence. In considering Mr. Lee's revolutionary tendency, it is well to remember that he tried to obtain one appointment after another in the British colonial system. His particular ambition was to be a member of the governor's council, but his letter-writting campaign for that position was unsuccessful.

Mr. Lee was as land hungry as Washington. In 1774 he wrote to his brother William, who lived in London, and urged him to press an application for western land in behalf of the Mississippi Company. "There is plenty of room yet," he wrote, "for us on the North side of Ohio between that & Illinois, on the Wabash, the Miamis, and other waters between Illinois and Ohio."

The British saw at once the immense potential danger in the Committees of Correspondence. William Lee wrote from London that their organisation put the ministry in a panic.

The Committees, by tacit consent of the revolutionary elements, assumed one governmental function after another; and in 1774 they brought the Continental Congress into being.

§ 4

Again the shadow of the ill-omened East India Company falls on American affairs.

In 1769 the Company, almost brought to ruin by the peculations of its own officials, had been obliged to raise the price of tea at its London auctions. The Oriental tea business, as carried on by the Company, was clumsy and roundabout. The tea was brought from China to London. There it was auctioned to London tea merchants. The bidding began at an initial, or upset, price fixed by the Company. The London merchants sold the tea to American importers, who in turn sold it to retailers on its arrival in America.

The increased upset price caused a higher price along the whole line. The increased price, with the threepence duty, made the smuggling of Dutch tea profitable. Tea smuggling developed into a large industry, which is reflected in the custom-house figures. In 1768 the East India Company sold approximately nine hundred thousand pounds of · tea in America; in 1770 this total had dropped to ninety-seven thousand pounds. By 1773 the Company was on the slippery edge of bankruptcy, with seventeen million pounds of tea stored and unsold in its London warehouses.

A thoroughly business-like plan to enable the Company to undersell smuggled tea was conceived by the Company and approved by the government. Its central feature was the elimination of middle-men.

The company proposed to ship the tea direct to America in its own vessels, to establish Company warehouses in America, and sell direct to retailers. It cannot be doubted that this plan, if it had been set in operation, would have put the tea smugglers out of business. It would have left the legitimate tea importers also without an occupation.

How curiously these facts have become twisted in the popular conception of our time. The average American believes that the Boston Tea Party, and other acts of resistance, came about because the British government tried to force our sturdy forefathers to pay a higher price for tea.

The truth is precisely the contrary.

Tea was to be sold at a lower—not at a higher—price.

Then, why?

The explanation is not at all complicated.

The smuggling element was very strong, and smuggling profits were large. Smugglers were among the respected merchants of the seaport communities. They occupied a position in colonial life that was similar to that of the better class of bootleggers in our time. Suppose the Anti-Prohibition movement should become so powerful that prohibition would be really in danger. Does any sensible person think that the bootleggers of America would stand by, in idle indifference, and see their trade swept away and their families brought to ruin? Dollars by the million would pour into the Prohibition treasury; lobbies would besiege Congress, the Ku Klux would be set to work, and in the remote districts the more aggressive opponents of Prohibition would probably be decorated with tar and feathers.

One has only to transfer this picture to an eighteenth century frame, and put tea in place of liquor, to understand the situation. John Hancock, "prince of smugglers," had a warehouse full of tea which would fall in price as soon as the Company's tea was landed.

For awhile the mercantile patriots were in a quandary over this latest instance of despotism. Honest Samuel Adams, specialist in British tyranny, had to think hard. How may one convince even a gullible member of the common herd that a reduction in the cost of living is a hardship?

One necessity of the situation was to keep the tea from being brought ashore. It had to be prevented at all hazards from getting to the people.

Arguments managed to shape themselves into being. Some of them were good. That one about this move on the part of the Company being only an entering wedge was excellent. An entering wedge . . . as soon as the tea trade is established, the Company will open all kinds of stores, sell everything, and drive the entire flock of merchants out of business. Another good one was that the cut in prices was only temporary. When the Company gets everything its own way, then prices will go up. This assertion was invented simply as an argument but in it the patriots probably hit the truth.

When the first shipload of tea reached Boston unknown parties, to the number of several hundred, went on board the vessel and emptied the whole cargo (value £15,000) in the water. In Charleston the tea was landed and stored in a damp place, where it eventually rotted. At other ports the vessels were turned back.

The British government could not stand this insult to its dignity. By act of Parliament the port of Boston was closed. The people of Boston were informed that the port would be opened again whenever the Company's loss of £15,000 was made good. This sum was never paid, though many people in Boston were in favour of paying it as the best method of avoiding trouble.

There was a stir among the Committees of Correspondence. Their sense of collective action evolved the First Continental Congress, which met in Philadelphia on September 5th, 1774. Washington was one of seven delegates from Virginia.

§ 5

The opening of the Congress does not seem to have attracted much attention in Philadelphia. The newspapers of the time say very little about it. Washington rode into Philadelphia on horseback, unnoticed, in company with Patrick Henry and Edmund Pendleton, and took lodgings at a private house.

Both the Adams cousins—John and Samuel—were delegates. John Adams wrote that Dr. Rush, and others, came out from Philadelphia and met them on the road. He says that their purpose in coming was to implore the New England delegates not to mention independence. That would spoil everything. They said the Quakers were utterly opposed to all such bold moves. Because of John Adams' supposed leaning toward independence he was shunned. He says of his early experiences at the Congress: "I was avoided like a man infected with the Leprosy. I walked the streets of Philadelphia in solitude, borne down by the weight of care and unpopularity."

If it was like that with John Adams, what must have been the state of cousin Samuel?

We must mention, however, the fact that Samuel Adams wore a new suit, and had gold coins in his pocket. The Boston patriots had become so accustomed to the shabbiness of Samuel Adams that they had ceased to notice it. After his election as a delegate to the Congress it was learned that he could not go, as he did not have enough money to pay his expenses. This embarrassing situation was relieved by a quiet subscription among the patriot leaders, and at the same time he was provided with a handsome new suit, that he might represent Massachusetts in a manner worthy of her dignity.

In the *Diary* entry for September 28th, Washington says that he "spent the afternoon with the Boston gentlemen." The historians and diarists of the time, with their remarkable talent for leaving out everything of interest, fail to give us even a fragment of the conversation between Washington and these forward-looking progressives.

There are reasonable grounds, however, for the inference that Washington went to see the "Boston gentlemen" to ascertain if they were infected with the poisonous spirit of independence. A Captain Mackenzie, former Virginian and friend of Washington, held a commission in one of the British regiments stationed at Boston. This officer, thoroughly pro-British himself, had written a letter to Washington which was intended to prejudice him against the Massachusetts delegation.

Evidently the Adamses did not disclose their hand to the tall Virginia colonel, for soon after this conference, Washington wrote a long letter to Mackenzie, of which the following is an extract:

. . . and though you are led to believe by venal men,— for such I must take the liberty of calling those new-fangled counsellors, who, for honours or pecuniary gratifications, will lend their aid to overturn the constitution, and introduce a system of arbitrary government,— although you are taught, I say, by discoursing with such men, to believe, that the people of Massachusetts are rebellious, setting up for independence, and what not, give me leave, my good friend, to tell you, that you are abused, grossly abused.

This I advance with a degree of confidence and boldness, which may claim your belief, having better opportunities of knowing the real sentiments of the people you are among, from the leaders of them, in opposition to the present measures of the administration, than you have from those whose business it is, not to describe truths, but to misrepresent facts in order to justify as much as possible to the world their own conduct.

Give me leave to add, and I think I can announce it as a fact, that it is not the wish of that government, or any other upon this continent, separately or collectively, to set up for independence; but this you may at the same time rely on, that none of them will ever submit to the loss of those valuable rights and privileges, which are essential to the happiness of every free state, and without which, life, liberty, and property are rendered totally

PHYSIONOTRACE OF WASHINGTON

This is supposed to be a perfect reproduction of
George Washington's profile. It was made by St. Memin,
a Frenchman, who came to America in the 1790's. He
had invented a machine similar to a pantograph which
made a mechanical production of profiles. He called
the picture produced by his machine a physionotrace.

insecure . . . more blood will be spilled . . . if the ministry are determined to push matters to extremity, than history has ever yet furnished instances of in the annals of North America. . . .

Washington's resentment against the British was deep and genuine, but even as late as October, 1775—months after the battle of Bunker Hill, and while he was in command of the patriot army—he was still opposed to independence. He was not in spirit a revolutionist but a reformer.

The pet theory of the reformers of the time was that the heart of the English people was in the right place; that the English nation, if it had its way, would withdraw all coercive measures; and that the armed resistance of the colonials was not against the English as a people, but only against the ministry. The British force in Boston was referred to by American leaders as "the ministerial army."

This theory, so far as it concerns the sentiments of the English people, was founded on pure fancy. The "friends of America" in Parliament, led by Pitt, Burke, Barré and Lord Camden, were in a hopeless and insignificant minority.

Parliament was filled, as we know, with bought sycophants of George III, and might therefore not be supposed to represent anything but the Hanoverian ideas of the King. In a general sense, such a supposition was correct, but in the case of England against America Parliament seems to have spoken with the voice of the country. Englishmen wrote pamphlets and articles in favour of the American claims, it is true; but not many of them did. The great weight of recorded opinion was on the other side. Even Pitt, who thought that America should not be taxed without her consent, held with brilliant though rather confusing inconsistency that the colonies must always be subject to the will of Parliament. He gloried in the American resistance, he was proud of the Americans for having taken up arms, he spoke of "free-born men," and so on; and in the next breath he said that he, for one, was for putting down every attempt at American independence, cost what it might.

§ 6

The First Continental Congress remained in session fifty-two days. It produced, first, a "Declaration of Rights," intended ostensibly for the perusal of the British government. In this Declaration Congress demanded the repeal of about twenty acts of Parliament. It was, in reality, a campaign document for circulation in America. Most of the delegates thought it would have no effect on Parliament—and it didn't. For the government to have accepted these demands would have meant the abolition of England's colonial empire.

Then the peacemakers had their say. Joseph Galloway, a Pennsylvania delegate of wealth and distinction, brought out a plan for a harmonious union of Great Britain and the colonies. The Galloway plan was an extraordinarily able document. It stands at the high-water mark of the conservative influence in Congress.

I shall not go into the details of Galloway's plan, but its essential feature was an administrative separation of America and England; both, however, to be under the British crown. America was to remain a part of the empire, although a separate political entity. This plan, once accepted by Great Britain and the colonies, would have eliminated the whole question of taxation as a factor of discord, and would have done away with British officials and British edicts.

Galloway's plan gave the radicals in Congress a scare. They voted it down—but by a narrow majority—and attempted, by expunging all mention of it from the record, to keep the people from learning of its existence.

We do not know what Washington thought of this plan; his vote is not recorded. Voting in the Continental Congress was not by individuals, but by colonies, and the votes of the colonies on this measure are not in the record, so we do not know even how Virginia voted. Washington does not refer to the Galloway plan in any of his letters written at the time.

Mr. Galloway's plan was voted down; and from that time the moderate, or conservative, influence in Congress began to subside. Later on Mr. Galloway himself came rather severely under the critical patriotic eye. After hostilities had commenced he found on his doorstep one morning a box containing a hangman's noose, with a polite note to the effect that this noose would soon be used as his necktie. He took the hint and departed for the British lines, abandoning his large fortune in Pennsylvania lands to the patriots.

The First Continental Congress was not very constructive in its measures, but in boycotting its work was thorough. A set of non-importation resolutions, known as the "Continental Association," was put through.

The Continental Association was different from the preceding boycotts, as it included exports as well as imports, though the non-exportation feature was not to go into effect for about a year, in order "not to injure our fellow-subjects in Great Britain, Ireland or the West Indies."

The Congress was without authority; its resolutions were simply recommendations to the colonies. Uncertain as to its own status, it went falteringly through its programme of resolutions and adjourned, to meet again in May of the next year. There is no account of Washington's activities as a delegate, but the presumption is strong that he took no part, except as a member of various committees.

An interesting, though wholly unsympathetic comment on the situation—in Boston, at least—appears in a letter written in November by a British officer, and published in England:

According to my promise I write to you on my arrival here. The troops are just put into quarters. The workmen at Boston were so mulish that the General was obliged to send to Nova Scotia for carpenters and bricklayers to fit up barracks for our accommodation. . . . The inhabitants of this province retain the religious and civil principles brought over by their forefathers in the reign of King Charles I; and are at least a hundred years behind hand with the people of England in every refinement.

With the most austere show of devotion, they are destitute of every principle of religion or common honesty, and are reckoned the most arrant cheats and hypocrites on the whole continent of America.

The women are very handsome, but, like old Mother Eve, very frail. Our camp has been as well supplied in that way since we have been on Boston Common, as if our tents were pitched on Blackheath.

As to what you hear of their taking up arms to resist the force of England, it is mere bullying, and will go no further than words: whenever it comes to blows, he that can run fastest will think himself best off. Believe me, any two regiments here ought to be decimated if they did not beat in the field the whole force of the Massachusetts Province; for tho' they are numerous, they are but a mob without order or discipline, and very awkward at handling their arms.[1]

In this letter we see a partial exposition of the ignorance of America which afflicted the English nation at this critical period.

Awake at last, and conscious of impending disaster, the British ministry planned to send Lord Clive—conqueror of India—out to America as commander-in-chief of the King's forces. This plan came to naught, for on November 22, 1774, Lord Clive escaped from his fierce hungers and his dreams. On that day his life came to an end through suicide.

[1] *Letters on the American Revolution,* edited by Margaret Wheeler Willard, p. 14.

CHAPTER XVII

THE PEOPLE'S REVOLUTION

§ 1

THE colonies were lost to England, though neither England nor America knew it. English colonial policy had become an echo of dead opportunities. Yet petitioners "humbly prayed," as ever before. English officials still went to and fro about their empty business, and patriotic committee-men signed papers with the flourish of confidence.

It was a peculiar situation. The governing power of the provinces had trickled into the hands of unauthorised legislatures and haphazard committees. In Philadelphia a second Congress, vastly more assured in manner than the first one, met on May 10, 1775. Somewhere in the American defiance lay the ectoplasm of a new nation.

The attitude of the Americans revealed all the characteristics of a modern strike. People acted as if Great Britain and her laws were non-existent.

In the loyalists, or Tories, the government had a large body of willing strike-breakers which was never used. The loyalists were sufficiently numerous in almost every community to have taken on the functions of government. But to have done this successfully they would have needed a strong organisation of their own, much boldness, and unquestioning British support. They appear to have lacked all these essentials.

The revolutionists were in a minority at all stages of the Revolution. This fact is conceded by even the patriotic commentators of the time. It is equally true that the loyalists were also in a minority. The larger part of the population was either indifferent, or too fearful of consequences to take sides. The vehemence of the patriots, especially in the physical aspects of their propaganda, helped mightily in drawing citizens to the glowing heart of freedom. We may deplore tar and feathers, as all decent people should; but facts are facts, and there can be no doubt that, in the early stages of the Revolution the unrestricted use of these homely instruments of conviction kept more people from declaring themselves on the English side than did the eloquence of Patrick Henry.

The loyalists did not have the impetuosity, the fervour, the organisation, of their adversaries. As a peace-loving wayfarer, caught in the whirl of a street mob, looks around for a policeman, so the colonial loyalists looked to England for protection. But England hoped that the loyalists would protect themselves. In the early stages of the conflict the English policy was tied to that idea. A few troops were to be sent over, enough to keep decent order and stamp out the more flagrant cases of rebellion, while His Majesty's loyal subjects would put themselves in power.

This policy was visionary. At the first attempt of British troops to seize a handful of the patriots' military supplies at Concord, the redcoats were met by embattled farmers who fired the shot that is supposed to have been heard around the world.

§ 2

It may not have been heard around the world, but it was heard as far as Virginia. Colonel George Washington heard it, and when the Second Continental Congress convened in Philadelphia he appeared in his uniform, the only man on the floor so attired. He had already declared, at the Virginia Convention, that he was willing to raise a thousand men and march them at his own expense to the relief of Boston.

He sat in Congress, day after day, a silent member—silent in speech, but loud in military garments. It was his way of saying that war was inevitable, and that he was ready.

The fox-hunter had come out of his serene noon of land, horses and dogs, to sit in meditation among the large intellects. Rather dramatic, in a way. Every visitor who hung around the door naturally inquired, "And who is the tall gentleman in uniform?"

What a shining target this uniform would have been for a modern cartoonist! Satire and comedy—the bespangled uniform among the buff-and-brown delegates. But it was all sedate and solemn. Comedy never showed her smiling face.

War was indeed inevitable. After Concord, men had come running, some from a distance of three hundred miles, and an impromptu army of twenty thousand farmers in shirt sleeves surrounded Boston. Fierce, uncouth men calling themselves captains marched across the stony hills with nine or ten volunteers behind them.

Men in shirt sleeves, in tag ends of antique uniforms, in garments made of cloth spun and woven by the women folks, in cocked hats, in red worsted caps, in caps of beaver fur. In their hands were old flintlocks, smooth bores; guns seven feet long, of pack-horse weight, and without bayonets. Powderhorns hung at their sides. On their backs many of them carried outlandish bundles of necessities, gunpowder mingling with bacon.

They had come together without compulsion, every man of his own free will. The People's Revolution was in full bloom. But it had no leaders; it never had a leader who understood its meaning.

The Massachusetts Provincial Congress, meeting in hasty session at Watertown, had set General Artemas Ward at the head of this popular uprising. General Ward was a mild village deacon sort of man; and was, besides, too fat to mount a horse.

And there was Israel Putnam, second in command, fifty-six years old. He had been ploughing in a Connecticut field when the news of Concord whirled by. Like another Cincinnatus, he left his oxen standing in the furrow, and started forthwith for the scene of battle. He was all grey hair, boldness and garrulity. He had been in every war that had occurred since he was a child. By nature a private soldier, he was wholly without a sense of authority, and had less brains and more courage than any other officer in the patriot camp.

Among the officers was Joseph Warren, a fashionable Boston physician and friend of Samuel Adams. Dr. Warren was a gentleman of culture; grave, meditative, a philosophic dreamer. In his immaculate satin breeches and wine-coloured coat he went about the camp—a copy of Montesquieu in his pocket—quietly thinking his lofty thoughts and watching the patriots load their muskets with scraps of iron and rusty nails, bullets having run short.

On the morning of June 17th the British generals in Boston had something to talk about. During the night a detachment of the rebel army had fortified an eminence called Breed's Hill which overlooked Boston and commanded it, in a military sense. This elevation, within easy cannon shot of the town, is at the eastern end of Charlestown peninsula, and is separated from Boston by the narrow Charles River. The patriots had intended to occupy Bunker Hill, a higher elevation to the west, but for some unexplained reason their entrenchments were thrown up on Breed's Hill and the battle of Bunker Hill was really an action fought on Breed's Hill.

Why the British had not already occupied this position is a question which History declines to answer—probably because she does not know the reason. So, all of a sudden, the strategic importance of Breed's Hill burst like a thunderclap upon every one in the British army, even upon experienced generals like Howe, Clinton, Burgoyne and Gage, all of whom were in Boston. Unless the Americans could be driven out the British would have to evacuate the city—so Sir William Howe said. "Which will be very disagreeable to us all," he added.

Charlestown peninsula is almost an island—a bloated penin-

sula that bulges enormously and is connected with the main-
land by a narrow neck. On each side of the neck there is, or
was, water deep enough to float small warships. The British
needed only to bring their armed sloops up to this neck, land
their infantry under naval protection, and the patriot force
on Breed's Hill would have been caught in a trap. This most
obvious thing in the world is precisely what they failed to do.
At a council of war they decided to take the position by frontal
attack. The British generals had the utmost contempt for the
embattled farmers; they thought the Americans would not
fight.

A belief that the Americans were cowards was at that time
one of the national superstitions of England. In certain circles
the adjective "American" was a jocular synonym for "cowardly."

Before we lose ourselves in amazement let us remember that
these senseless beliefs are common, even to-day. Before the
World War there was a general conviction among husky, red-
blooded Anglo-Saxons that the French were an effeminate race.

Since the World War we have not heard much about cowardly Frenchmen; and after the Revolution the talk of cowardly Americans died out in England.

The reputation for cowardice that floated around the American name had its origin among British army officers who had
served in campaigns with colonial troops. Wolfe, the hero
of Quebec, thought the colonials a poor fighting lot. Sir Peter
Warren is alleged to have described the conduct of the colonials at the siege of Louisburg as "dastardly." Braddock, too,
considered the Virginians mere skulking cowards, yet they
saved the wreck of his army. There was no place for the
American style of fighting in British army tactics, and every
little thin-brained martinet who saw a man firing from behind
a tree jumped to the conclusion that it was a case of weak
courage.

The colonials were not lacking in stamina. They were

quite as brave, or perhaps a little braver, than men usually
are.

§ 3

There is a throb of drums. Redcoats and bayonets, lines
of silver and scarlet, move swiftly over the green field at the
foot of the hill. In the river lean spars nod above a smoky
haze; there the King's ships fume and growl. Their solid shot
rolls around the hilltop. The ships are all smoke and spars,
but the swarming rowboats are giant beetles. Their oars rise
and fall with rhythmic insect motions. Huge beetles with red
backs, for the soldiers are packed tightly in them.

This is the stage, and all Boston is the audience. The town
rises on its heights as galleries and boxes rise in a theatre.
The roofs are fluttering with people who cling precariously
to chimneys and window-frames.

The effect is not dramatic, but merely theatrical. It is like
a community pageant, where everybody knows it is all make-
believe.

On the summit of the hill there is a ridge of new earth which
lies harsh and yellow against the soft green of the grassy
slope. How silent and harmless it seems. Deserted, maybe?

The village of Charlestown is burning, but that, too, is a
sort of impersonal conflagration, kindly arranged by the directors of the piece. Its flames stand warmly against the sky
like tall red flowers.

The troops have nearly reached the summit, and the audience
holds its breath with excited expectation. The grenadiers are
in perfect step; their red line is as straight as if it had been
drawn by a ruler.

There is a murmur of voices behind the breastworks. The
rebels are saying something to the British . . . perhaps they
are sick of their adventure; perhaps they are asking for a
parley.

One voice is heard above the rest. Its loud nasal twang

stabs the air. "Colonel Abercrombie," the voice cries, "oh, Colonel Abercrombie, are the Yankees cowards?"

How absurd such a question seems. Colonel Abercrombie, advancing at the head of the 22nd, does not reply; it is neither the time nor the place for a public debate.

The British come on until they are within fifteen yards of the works. Then the Americans appear above their entrenchments, and the new earth has a fringe of blazing guns. The British line reels in its tracks, falters a moment, and goes slowly down the hill, a dark red wave of men, seen dimly through the drifting smoke.

All Boston stares. The hill is speckled with dead and wounded men. The scene is no longer theatrical. The spectators have a sensation that something terrible and unexpected has happened. Women are being helped down from the roofs.

The British come again. Sir William Howe, his silk stockings splashed with blood, goes up at the head of a regiment. "I ask no man to go a step further than I go myself," he says. This time the regiments, almost cut to ribbons by the American fire, stand and re-form in the open field, before the trenches. Steady, gallant troops they are. They fire at the heads appearing above the works, but they fire too high, and the damage is slight.

The Americans reply with a hail of bullets, rusty nails, and old iron—the coarse vernacular of colonial warfare. They do not fire too high; the damage is appalling. The British observe a marksman, standing on something in the trench, shoot down twenty officers without missing a shot. They can see that he does not take the time to load; he hands down the empty guns, and some one hands up loaded ones. Finally he is killed by a company of grenadiers firing at him steadily.

The British line trickles back. The troops are a little panicky, but there are reinforcements at the foot of the hill. The commanders hold a council.

This third time they try it in columns—not in line—and they

go over the works. The Americans are out of ammunition; they are running in all directions; mere boys, led by fierce, middle-aged men.

Waiting Boston sees the British flag rise in the limp air, and hears the thin strains of faraway music . . . "God Save the King."

§ 4

The British won the hill, but the Americans won a moral victory of the first magnitude.

Thereafter no one could truthfully say that untrained and undisciplined men would not fight; thereafter no man of sense in England thought that the King's troops would drive the Americans before them like a flock of refractory sheep.

The British force in the engagement amounted to about 3,500 men, and the Americans had approximately an equal number behind their breastworks. The British losses were extraordinary large. They had 228 killed and 826 wounded, or total casualties of nearly one-third their effectives.

The Americans lost 140 killed, among them Dr. Joseph Warren, and 301 wounded and missing.

Prof. Channing points out that in the twenty battles of the war the British had 198 officers killed. Of these 2⁷, or about one-eighth, were killed at Bunker Hill. All the officers of General Howe's staff, without exception, were either killed or wounded. General Howe himself, wet with the blood of his own soldiers, was white-faced and "greatly moved." He said that there had not been an engagement in the Seven Years' War as hot as that of Bunker Hill; and that the attack on Quebec, where he had led the forlorn hope, was mere play compared to it.

§ 5

In the Congressional cacophony of mingled ideas the thought of colonial unity began to assume a preponderant place. It

was pushed forward industriously by the New England delegates, especially after the skirmish at Lexington and Concord,
for the people's army around Boston was a New England
army. The dire thought that the other colonies might eventually leave them in the lurch was always present in their
minds.

One day in the middle of June Cousin John Adams met
Cousin Samuel Adams as they were both about to enter the
door of Congress.

"Well, what for to-day?" said Cousin Samuel.

"I am going to move to-day," replied Cousin John, "that
Congress adopt the army before Boston, and that Colonel
George Washington be appointed its commander-in-chief."

Cousin Samuel was all for the adoption of the army by
Congress; but Colonel Washington's name was not to be found
among his carefully selected enthusiasms. The army is a
New England army—he argued—and Washington is from
Virginia; a wealthy aristocrat from Virginia. Wouldn't his
appointment rather dampen the ardour? . . .

"It is just because he is from Virginia, and aristocratic and
wealthy, that I propose to nominate him," said Cousin John,
in substance. "There is nothing that the revolutionary movement needs quite as much as it needs aristocracy and wealth;
and above all it needs Virginia and the South."

Samuel Adams was as astute in politics as he was democratic
in opinion. His cousin did not have to explain any further.
Astuteness was considerably stronger than democracy at that
moment.

"And I expect you to second the nomination," said Cousin
John.

The New York Provincial Congress had already written to
its delegates that the commander-in-chief should not only be
an experienced soldier; but that he should be so wealthy that
he would rather communicate lustre to his dignities than receive it from them. It seemed to many of the delegates that

the opulent Washington, sitting there every day in his uniform, was ready to communicate a good deal of lustre.

When John Adams got on his feet to nominate a commander-in-chief John Hancock, who, as president of the Congress, was in the chair, thought that Adams intended to name him. Adams portrayed the high qualifications that the new commander must possess; and continuing, he said:

> Gentlemen, I know these qualifications are high, but we all know they are needful in this crisis in this chief. Does any one say they are not to be obtained in this country? In reply, I have to say they are; they reside in one of our own body—

John Hancock was all smiles.

> —and he is the man whom I now nominate—George Washington of Virginia.

Washington, apparently startled, rose hurriedly and left the room. The upturned crescent of Hancock's smile turned into a downward curve of chagrin. John Adams wrote that he had never seen any one's expression change as quickly as Hancock's changed that day.

The nomination was opposed by some of the delegates, even by some of the Virginians. Edmund Pendleton of Virginia spoke against it. In secret session, of course, and while Washington was out of the room. The question was deferred until next day, and then Washington was appointed commander-in-chief by unanimous vote.

He made a modest speech of acceptance, and declined to take any pay for his services. This refusal of money was an effective gesture. More than anything else at that time, it served to make him a popular hero. The idea of a wealthy man doing anything without being paid for it was entirely novel and fascinating.

I suspect that Washington's surprise at being named by Adams was simulated. The matter of appointing a com-

JOHN HANCOCK
Painting by John S. Copley

mander-in-chief had been talked about for some time, and every probability leads to the supposition that he had been approached and his acceptance obtained before Adams rose.

Adams wrote sometime later in his *Diary*:

> Whether this jealousy [that of the Southerners against New England] was sincere, or whether it was mere pride and a haughty ambition of furnishing a Southern general to command the northern army, I cannot say; but the intention was very visible to me that Colonel Washington was their object, and so many of our staunchest men were in the plan, that we could carry nothing without conceding to it. . . .

The reader will doubtless remember that Washington's last military service was sixteen years in the past; and that he had never commanded more than twelve hundred men.

Besides his "skill and experience as an officer," his "independent fortune, great talents and excellent universal character"; all of which were mentioned by John Adams in his nominating speech, there was another reason for his appointment which was not mentioned publicly.

The revolutionary movement as a whole—and, in particular, the army around Boston—had grown entirely too democratic for the taste of the wealthy land-owners, lawyers and merchants who composed the Congress. "The heads of the mobility [1] grow dangerous to the gentry," Gouverneur Morris had written the year before, "and how to keep them down is the question." Morris was an aristocratic revolutionist of the John Jay-Alexander Hamilton type. In another letter of the same period he exclaims with a note of fear that "the mob begin to think and to reason."

Something had to be done about it. In Congress it was felt that the best remedy would be to place at the head of the

---

[1] *Mobility* was an eighteenth-century word meaning the common people; in distinction to *nobility*.

army an iron-willed conservative, a fighting aristocrat, and give him full power to put things in better shape.

§ 6

Now the fox-hunter is on his horse. . . .

The long shadows of sunset are falling on the People's Revolution, on embattled farmers, on milk-and-water phrases.

They have put the fox-hunter on his horse. . . .

Away now with the child's play of dogs and kennels. No more shall we hear of "Mopsey lined by Pilot," or of "a bitch fox killed after 1½ hrs. chace." Red-coated foxes are to go streaking over the hills, with ragged blue-coated hounds after them . . . and the great cannon are to beat and blaze.

The British shall remember the day when Captain George Washington, "a very deserving gentleman," wanted a British army commission and was lightly refused.

The fox-hunter is astride his horse. . . .

And what of the fiery radicals? What of Samuel Adams, and Patrick Henry, and Christopher Gadsden? Oh, these men have lived too long. Already the flesh and blood have left them; they have become nothing but characters in a historical romance. As pale, complaining ghosts they are still to exist for a time, sitting uneasily in the smaller seats of power.

The Virginia aristocrat is on his horse.

§ 7

The patriot army met Washington's eye with the sprawling carelessness of a picture by Hogarth. But Washington's taste was not Hogarthian. The picture was to be painted out and redrawn on a more precise pattern. In a few weeks Washington wrote to Richard Henry Lee, "I have made a pretty good slam among such kind of officers as the Massachusetts government abound in."

To his mind the army appeared to be in a disgraceful state. There was almost no distinction between officers and men. A company consisted, as a rule, of the men of a neighbourhood, and the officers were neighbours and comrades who had been elected to their posts.

At this period of army reform courts-martial were held every day, and their monotone sounds like the buzz of angry bees. Officers were dismissed for ignorance, carelessness, unmilitary behaviour and cowardice. Some of the offences were particularly atrocious. Lieutenant Whitney was tried and convicted of "infamous conduct in degrading himself by voluntarily doing the duty of an orderly sergeant."

As infamous as that was, its infamy was exceeded by that of a cavalry staff officer who was found "unconcernedly shaving one of his men." This officer had probably been a barber back home, and was keeping in practice.

It was all so disgraceful that perhaps the less said of it the better; but before we pass on fairness impels me to call attention to the fact that this disgraceful army had held the British in close confinement in Boston for nearly three months, although the British troops were commanded by four of the most experienced generals in England's service; also, that it had given England's best troops a beating at Bunker Hill that they remember to this day. For some reason, not apparent in the military annals, the Continental army, after having been trained and disciplined, never succeeded in doing so well on any other battlefield.

There came with Washington, as military experts and disciplinarians, General Horatio Gates and General Charles Lee. Both of these gentlemen were professional soldiers, and both had been officers in the British army. Gates had been made adjutant-general of the Continental army by Congress, and Lee was made a major-general, ranking next to the fat Artemas Ward.

Charles Lee, who was not a relative of the Virginia Lees,

was an unbalanced, erratic person, as strange a character as there is in the history of the time. He had left the British army years before because of some slight in the matter of promotion. Since then his career had been that of a military adventurer. He had "basked," as Lossing says, for awhile in the favour of the King of Poland, then he had basked here and there in the favour of other monarchs. As our Revolution opens we find him basking in the favour of Congress, but his basking days are soon to be over.

He considered prudence "a rascally virtue," and said that he preferred the society of dogs to men. In appearance he was exceedingly tall and lank, with a Roman nose of such large size that it appeared to be a deformity. He floated into our history on a stream of sunshine and drifted out of it on a current of Washington's rage at the battle of Monmouth.

Both Lee and Gates were highly proficient soldiers in the technical European sense. From them Washington learned most of whatever he knew of strategy and battle tactics.

Before Washington took command offences went unpunished, men talked back to their officers, and came and went as they pleased. Under his direction this laxity was soon stopped. His vigour in enforcing discipline has always been given high praise by military historians.

A complete system of punishments was established. Some of the penalties were rather quaint. One of them was called "riding the wooden horse." The method of inflicting it was as follows: The patriot was tied a-straddle of the sharp edge of a board, or some similar peaked device, raised about six feet above the ground, and weights were put on his feet. The physical effect was something in the nature of a split, though of course the weights were never heavy enough actually to split the patriot in two. Usually, he would faint after a few minutes, though some of the hardened veterans could stick it out for an hour.

Passing the gauntlet, another form of military punishment, seems to have been a jolly affair for everybody except the offender, for the whole regiment took a hand in it. The command was drawn up in two lines, close together and facing one another. The man to be punished passed slowly between these lines, and was beaten with straps and switches as he made his progress. A sergeant walked before him holding a bayonet to his breast, which prevented him going faster than a walk.

But, after all, these exotic punishments were not common. The more enlightened of the officers opposed the wooden horse. Washington himself pointed out that men were sometimes permanently injured, and he advocated flogging as being equally effective. In time flogging became the central feature of the penal policy.

A patriot sentenced to be flogged was first divested of his shirt, then his hands were tied to a post over his head, and the lashes were laid on his bare back by the drummer of the regiment. These punishments, vigorous as they seem, were carried out with exemplary humane precautions. A surgeon always stood by to revive the patriot in case he should faint.

Thirty-nine lashes were considered a severe punishment, but in looking through Washington's *Orderly Books* I find many instances of one hundred lashes being ordered, and some where the number ran to two hundred.

In May, 1778, for example, John Reynolds struck an officer and received one hundred lashes; John Cline stole a horse and attempted to desert, for which he got two hundred lashes; and a soldier named Lewis, who threatened to take the lives of several officers,. received sixty lashes. But James Whaling, a boy who attempted to run away, was "in consideration of his youth," given only thirty lashes. Michael Nash got drunk, and the sobering influence of fifty lashes was tried on him.

General Stirling, one of the major-generals in the service, was said by many officers who knew him well to get drunk daily. Very likely fifty lashes applied to his bare back occasionally would have kept him sober; but this well-proved remedy was never tried. In consequence, his military genius was not of much use to the cause of liberty.

Flogging was an established institution in all European armies, where the soldiers were either conscripted men and in the service against their will, or riff-raff who preferred the army to a life of beggary.

The Continental army was supposed to be composed of free men, voluntarily enrolled, and fighting for their rights. The introduction of flogging into this army was the stupidest of stupid blunders. It is entirely possible that Washington, who owned gangs of slaves, and was accustomed to consider manual labour degrading, had no understanding of the common people.

In the French Revolution, where the revolutionary army was made up of rebels in mass, flogging was abolished, and it has never been revived in France. Every one knows that the French revolutionary armies, through their victories, upset the calculations of the best generals of the time.

CHAPTER XVIII

THOMAS PAINE AND THOMAS JEFFERSON

§ 1

WASHINGTON was commander-in-chief, and people travelled many miles just to look at him. This semi-obscure land-owner of Virginia became instantly the most prominent man in America. He was discussed at every cross-roads store from Falmouth to Savannah. The ministry in England fingered the forgotten scraps of Braddock's reports, looking for the name of Washington and trying to analyse his character.

As the head of an army which had neither food nor clothes, Washington was in a predicament which was intensely serious, and threatened to become overwhelming. There had been no provision made for supporting the army. It managed to live through 1775 in a hand-to-mouth existence based on voluntary contributions. Congress had authorised the issue of two million dollars of paper currency with "the faith of the colonies" behind it, but this money depreciated instantly, and merchants had to be wheedled into taking it.

The army was without artillery, yet delegates in Congress wrote to Washington that he ought to bombard Boston. Late in the winter cannon were hauled from Ticonderoga on sledges over the snow. The supply of gunpowder ran so low that there were only ten cartridges to a man. Fortunately, captures made at sea eventually furnished enough of this necessary article. Cloth for uniforms could not be procured.

Congress had no legal authority. The delegates met in Philadelphia as a revolutionary committee, and their resolutions were merely recommendations to the colonies.

Washington wrote on October 22nd, "Could I have foreseen what I have, and am likely to experience, no consideration on earth should have induced me to accept this command."

A few months later he wrote, "We are now without any money in our treasury, powder in our magazines, arms in our stores." And then he adds, "The reflection upon my situation and that of this army, produces many an uneasy hour, when all around me are wrapped in sleep. . . . I have often thought how much happier I should have been, if, instead of accepting of a command under such circumstances, I had taken my musket upon my shoulder, and entered the ranks."

It seems a pity that he did not shoulder a musket and enter the ranks. One may reasonably assert that such a gesture would have brought the Revolution to a successful conclusion within one year. Washington going voluntarily into the ranks with a musket would have aroused more enthusiasm, and would have caused more enlistments, than all the resolutions of Congress or the speeches of the orators.

But he would not have done anything of the kind. His declaration was merely a form of speech. With Washington pessimism was a kind of argument, as it is with our men of big business. By depicting the deplorable condition of affairs he endeavoured to impress Congress and the leading patriots with the necessity for action. He was no boaster, but his pessimistic manner was decidedly overdone. It kept many men from having any confidence in the patriot cause until the end of the war.

His letters to Joseph Reed, written about this time, are interesting in the light they shed on his personality. Reed, who had been a member of the staff for a few months, was one of his confidential friends. Washington did not write to him in the pompous, turgid style which he used in letters on political questions.

In the letters to Reed his pessimistic manner is replaced by a curious quality of detachment, in which sarcasm mingles with a heavy humour. Often they have a touch of vivacity. They are always direct and forceful.

He refers to Putnam as "Old Put," and to Governor Trumbull as "Brother Jonathan."

"General Fry, that wonderful man," he writes, "has made a most wonderful hand of it. . . . He has drawn three hundred and seventy-five dollars, never done one day's duty, scarce been three times out of his house, discovered that he was too old and too infirm for a moving camp, but remembers that he has been young, active, and very capable of doing what is now out of his power to accomplish; and therefore has left Congress to find another man capable of making, if possible, a more brilliant figure than he has done."

"The *noble* Colonel Enos," he underscores sarcastically, has left the expedition to Canada without rhyme or reason. Many of the New Englanders, whom he calls "valiant New Englanders," have, he says, an ardent desire to be "chimney-corner heroes."

Anti-Puritan as he was, he detested the Yankees. "Notwithstanding all the public virtue," he wrote, "which is ascribed [to New Englanders], there is no nation under the sun (that I ever came across) pay greater adoration to money than they do."

That was his opinion, but there are two sides to the question. It is a fact that Massachusetts, with less than one-sixth of the total population of the colonies, furnished one-third of the troops that served in the Revolution.

He writes to Reed that if he "could have justified the measure to posterity" he would have retired to the back country and lived in a wigwam rather than command such an army. He was already thinking of his place in history. In his later years this thought seemed never out of his mind. One gets a clear impression that he was consciously playing a part, with posterity as his audience.

He appears, when one knows him well, to be doing something that he does not want to do, but which is expected of him. This reluctance was hidden deeply under his reserves; one catches only a faint gleam of it now and then.

§ 2

The army was composed of volunteers enlisted for short periods. The Connecticut and Rhode Island men were enlisted until December 1, 1775, and none of the other enlistments ran longer than January first.

Early in the autumn Washington began a systematic effort to get the men whose time was about to expire to re-enlist, but with very little result. He wrote to Reed on November 28th:

> We have been till this time enlisting about 3500 men. . . . The Connecticut troops will not be prevailed upon to stay longer than their term . . . and such a dirty, mercenary spirit pervades the whole that I should not be at all surpriz'd at any disaster that may happen.

Persuasion was of no avail. Spellbinders and officers of personal magnetism went among the Connecticut troops and begged them to stay even a short while longer. It was pointed out to them that their departure would leave a large gap in the line around Boston with no troops to fill it.

The Connecticut men departed, nevertheless—forty-five hundred of them—and the local militia and the minute men had to be hurriedly called to fill their places temporarily. This action of the Connecticut troops has been pretty thoroughly execrated in history, but we have never heard their side of it. However, the fact appears on the face of the episode that the Connecticut troops carried out their agreement to the letter. They enlisted until December 1st; they fought at Bunker Hill; they bore the hunger and danger and sickness of camp; and in December they went home. At that time the country was full of men who had done no fighting at all. It was also well sprinkled with war profiteers—they appeared as early as 1775 —who had done no fighting and did not intend to do any.

It became perfectly plain early in the war that Washington's name was not a clarion call to military service. Men did not come flocking from all sides—or from any side—to enroll under his banner. As a matter of fact, as soon as he took command of the army men began to leave it in droves, and the tendency to leave was strong during the eight years of the war. He never had any trouble in getting officers, but after the first burst of enthusiasm at Bunker Hill it became extremely difficult to recruit men for the rank and file.

But Washington's personality was not repelling, and his sincerity and his courage were admired by every one. We must look further than Washington's place in public esteem for an explanation of the general reluctance to serve.

The explanation is, I think, that the common people soon realised the true purpose of the war. They learned that they would gain nothing by it; and it was, in effect, boycotted by most of the men who were expected to do the actual fighting.

Let us consider the possibilities of man-power in the colonies. At the outbreak of the Revolution the total population was about 2,500,000, and of these 500,000 were slaves. Of the remaining 2,000,000 about one-third—say 600,000—were Tories who would not serve under any circumstances. This leaves 1,400,000 as the population from which recruits might be drawn.

About one-fifth of the people in a civilised community are possible soldiers. This gives us 280,000 as the potential military strength of the patriots, but Washington never had more than twenty-five thousand men in his command at any one time; and even that number rarely. On one occasion there seem to have been about forty thousand men in the service, counting all bodies of troops in all parts of the country, though the figures are rather hazy.

The Imperial Civil War needed greatly an intense emotional

issue. Its leaders were never able to develop one, though they
made the most of "British atrocities." The Revolution never
had a *Marseillaise*, but only a *Yankee Doodle*.

> *Yankee Doodle went to town;*
> *He rode upon a pony.*
> *He stuck a feather in his cap,*
> *And called it macaroni.*

> *Yankee Doodle, keep it up;*
> *Yankee Doodle dandy—*
> *Mind the music and the step,*
> *And with the girls be handy.*

That was the war song of the patriot legions. Compare it
with the lofty beat of Mrs. Howe's *Battle Hymn of the Republic* in the Civil War:

Mine eyes have seen the glory of the coming of the Lord;
He is trampling out the vintage where the grapes of wrath
> *are stored;*
He hath loosed the fateful lightning of his terrible swift sword;
> *His truth is marching on.*

*   *   *   *   *

In the beauty of the lilies Christ was born across the sea,
With a glory in his bosom that transfigures you and me;
As he died to make men holy, let us die to make men free,
> *While God is marching on.*

In the American Revolution hardly anybody wanted to die,
either to make men free, or for any other purpose.

§ 3

In December Martha Washington visited her husband at
Cambridge and remained for the winter. She arrived in state
. . . the splendid coach and its four horses; the postillions in

white and scarlet; the harness buckles with Washington's arms engraved on them . . . all whirling through the forlorn camp.

The equipage and its escort stops at the Craigie house—Washington's headquarters—and Martha descends. Young officers in their best blue-and-buff stand bareheaded under the cold sky, bowing and mumbling polite words. "Jacky" Custis comes with his mother . . . "Jacky" and his slender wife, a girlish creature who has nestled among pleasant adjectives all her life. Martha is in silks and furs; she is small, but her manner is that of the *haute noblesse*.

Next day General Nathanael Greene wrote home to Catherine, his wife, that Lady Washington had arrived; and that Catherine must put on her best frock and come to Cambridge.

She was the Mrs. Greene who danced for three hours with Washington without stopping.

The patriots in the trenches, bending over smoky fires and stirring their soup in camp kettles, realised that at last the Revolution was in high society, and gave a sigh of satisfaction.

§ 4

Early in March, 1776, Washington (finally supplied with artillery) advanced to a height in Dorchester which overlooked the town of Boston and the shipping in the harbour, and fortified it. These works were so close to both the town and the vessels that the British position became immediately impossible. The British might have fortified the place themselves, and they never explained why they had not done it.

For a day or two it looked as if there would be another Bunker Hill, but General Howe had had enough of frontal attacks on American positions. He let Washington know that if the bombardment were held up long enough for him to get out of Boston, he would go.

The evacuation was a scene of chaos. The loyalists who

had crowded into Boston pleaded to be taken along with the troops, and Howe agreed to transport them to Halifax. They appeared at the place of embarkation with all their households, with cats, dogs, birds in cages, furniture, bedding, musical instruments. At first these possessions were taken on board the ships; but as the crowd kept coming, and as there was not enough ship room, their belongings were thrown ruthlessly overboard in the harbour.

Washington wrote:

> One or two of them have committed what it would have been happy for mankind if more of them had done, long ago; the act of suicide . . . When the order issued therefore for embarking the troops in Boston, no electric shock, no sudden flash of lightning, in a word, not even the last trump, could have struck them with greater consternation. . . .

He adds magnanimously to this paragraph, "Would it not be good policy to grant a generous amnesty, and conquer these people by a generous forgiveness?"

On the whole, however, taking all his correspondence into consideration, he appears to have hated the loyalists most heartily. "Abominable pests of society" was his favourite description of them.

When Howe had cleared out of Boston there were no British troops remaining in the thirteen colonies. From that time on the war consisted of a series of attempts on the part of the British to reconquer their lost possessions.

It seemed reasonable to expect that the next attempt would be made at New York, and Washington resolved to move his army there. Soon after Boston was taken the army began to spill itself into distance, with New York as its objective. Long, slow-moving columns of straggling men, with wagons and thick pieces of artillery crawled over the New England hills.

There were many desertions on the way. A soldier would stop at a farmhouse and make friends with the people. If the place looked comfortable and there was a pretty girl, the soldier was likely to remain.

During the Fall of 1775 American opinion appeared to be turning away from the idea of independence. Many men of judgment, friendly to the patriot cause, thought the colonies had gone too far in their resistance. The legislatures of North Carolina, New York, Pennsylvania and Maryland passed resolutions against separation.

This conservative sentiment was dissolved with almost dramatic suddenness in the spring of 1776. Several causes combined to bring about the change in opinion. Among them was a proclamation of the King declaring the Americans to be rebels and outside his protection; and another factor was the employment of German mercenaries by the British.

The principal influence, however, was a book entitled *Common Sense*, written by Thomas Paine, the editor of a skimpy little magazine. Paine was an Englishman who had been in America less than two years, and was virtually unknown outside a small circle of patriot leaders.

He wrote in homely words. They march across his pages like muscular, freckle-faced men crossing a field. Behind them there were no cloudy reservations, no unspoken reverences. As we meditate on his bold speech we realise that he was an eighteenth century Lenin without home or traditions, without love or fear. Like Voltaire, he attained intellectual freedom at the cost of respectability. *Common Sense*, as well as his other books, *The American Crisis* and *The Age of Reason*, belongs to the literature of desperate men. Paine was an intellectual desperado of the first rank.

Any one who could understand simple English could understand what he had to say. This is a fair example of his literary style:

I have heard it asserted by some, that as America has flourished under her former connection with Great Britain, the same connection is necessary towards her future happiness, and will always have the same effect. Nothing can be more fallacious than this kind of argument. We may as well assert that because a child has thrived upon milk, that it is never to have meat. . . .

Like all the great propagandists, he met prejudice with prejudice. He realised probably that in large human issues logic falls to pieces with other traditions. One must agree with this attitude, for what is logic, after all, but a tradition which exists on the margin of the emotions?

There was nothing remote about Paine's ideas. While the cooler Revolutionary writers, such as Dickinson, floated above the heads of the crowd and took a bird's-eye view of things in general, Paine stood on the earth and took a bird's-eye view of nothing. His writings were born of grime and dust.

Common Sense was the phenomenal "best seller" of its time. In three months one hundred thousand copies were sold. This is equivalent to a sale of five million to-day, as our population is fifty times larger than it was then.

Paine did not waste argument on the claims of British sovereignty; he treated them with contempt, as if they were preposterous assumptions beneath the level of consideration. He asserted that the colonies ought to be independent because they wanted to be independent; that they were grown-up, that they had no further use for England, and that there was no reason why they should even go to the trouble of justifying their position, except as a matter of courtesy.

Washington, by that time immersed head and ears in the revolutionary movement, was all for separation of the colonies from Great Britain. He said that *Common Sense* contained "sound doctrine and unanswerable reasoning." On April 1st he wrote to Reed:

> My countrymen [meaning the Virginians], I know from their form of government and steady attachment heretofore to royalty, will come reluctantly into the idea of independency, but time and persecution brings many wonderful things to pass; and by private letters which I have lately received from Virginia, I find *Common Sense* is working a powerful change there in the minds of many men.

There was a mystery in Paine's life which it would be interesting to explore if we had the time, but which must be dismissed here with a bare mention.

At the age of thirty-four he married Elizabeth Ollive, the daughter of a Quaker, but there was, in effect, no physical marriage, and in a few years he and his wife parted. "Neither wife nor husband ever revealed why, after three years of make-believe union, they separated forever," says F. J. Gould, one of Paine's biographers. He adds that Paine never again approached any woman on intimate terms, and that "the curtain has never been withdrawn from this mystery of his temperament or physique."

Going back further we find that he was brought up as a workingman—apprenticed at thirteen to a London stay-maker (that is, a maker of corset stays). We may picture him a highly sensitised youth, devoid of physical charm, solitary, and far superior in intellect to the people around him. Bound to a manual trade that he despised, he lived in poverty and spent his time reading books. Destitution, aggressiveness, intellect, sexual impotence, loneliness and sensitiveness went into the composition of this rebel.

After awhile he became a writer for a poor little back-alley newspaper in London. In some way he attracted the attention of Benjamin Franklin, who sent him to America with letters of introduction.

Despite the enormous popularity of *Common Sense,* and despite Paine's high place in the revolutionary roll of honour, he is known to most of our people merely as an infidel, or as Theodore Roosevelt called him, "a dirty little atheist." This slanderous accusation has the tough elasticity of a popular delusion; it survives cheerfully every kind of refutation. Nevertheless, Paine was not an atheist. If he was, then Washington, Jefferson and Franklin were atheists, too, for his belief was the same as theirs. He was a deist, which is precisely the opposite of atheist.

In the first chapter of *The Age of Reason* he wrote: "I believe in one God, and no more; and I hope for happiness beyond this life. I believe in the equality of man; and I believe that religious duties consist in doing justice, loving mercy, and endeavouring to make our fellow creatures happy."

§ 5

Literature does not create public sentiment, though many people think it does. No doubt Paine thought his writings brought about the Declaration of Independence, but this was not the case, though *Common Sense* was enormously important in furnishing a magnetic pole around which revolutionary sentiment might crystallise.

The daily lives of men and women, the actual conditions of existence, the vicissitudes of the average life in their economic aspect—from these circumstances are born the prevailing ideas of an epoch. But most brains are not good at parturition; literature is the midwife which brings half-conscious ideas into being.

Common Sense became the most popular book of its time because it put in plain words what men were already thinking inarticulately.

No longer was the urge for independence concealed. It came out of the category of inhibitions and assumed the rôle of a flaunting virtue instead of a modest vice.

On June 7th Richard Henry Lee introduced in Congress a

resolution declaring the united colonies free and independent states. Dickinson, Robert Morris and others were bitterly opposed to this measure, but the radicals, led by John Adams, managed to get a committee appointed to draft a declaration for consideration.

Thomas Jefferson, a member of the drafting committee, wrote the Declaration of Independence, with suggestions from the other members. In Jefferson's draft there was a paragraph charging the King with having protected the African slave trade against the efforts of the colonies to put a stop to it, and with having thereby violated "the most sacred rights of life and liberty of a distant people, who never offended him, captivating them to slavery in another hemisphere, or to incur miserable death in their transportation thither."

This paragraph was struck out by Congress because most of its members felt that George III could hardly be charged with the iniquities of a traffic which had been carried on in New England ships for the benefit of Southern slave-buyers.

The Declaration was passed by Congress after a hot debate. On the final vote New York remained silent, and the resolution for its approval was carried by the vote of twelve states. John Hancock, president of the Congress, signed the document at once, and most of the members signed it on August 2nd, though among its fifty-six signatures are some which belong to members who came into Congress later, and who had taken no part in the formation of the Declaration, or in the vote which approved it.

Among the signers one may count twenty-two lawyers, ten merchants, and fourteen wealthy land-owners; but practically all the signers were land-owners to some extent. There were four physicians, one or two clergymen and several professional officeholders—one of whom held public office continuously for fifty years.

The management of the Imperial Civil War appears to have been well represented, but there were no representatives of the

People's Revolution among the delegates.   One regrets that a
document which guarantees liberty and equality with such a
lavish hand could not have been signed by at least one workingman or dirt farmer.

§ 6

Thomas Jefferson, who came into national prominence as
the writer of the Declaration of Independence, was at that time
thirty-three years of age.   In mental direction, in personality,
in intellectual preoccupation, he was as different from Washington as a circle is different from a triangle.   Yet, outwardly
they were very much alike.   Both of them belonged to the ruling class in Virginia.   They were both wealthy planters, slave
owners, and fox-hunters.   The art of living had for both of
them an enormous fascination.

Jefferson's force was intellectual and spiritual; Washington's force was economic and moral.

By nature a philosopher and a journalist, Jefferson lived in
a country where philosophy was misunderstood and in a century when journalism was virtually non-existent.   He took to
pen and paper by instinct.   He had a passion for logical forms,
for the arrangement of ideas in sequence, as well as for new
and curious notions.   John Adams says that when Jefferson
came to the Continental Congress his reputation as a writer
had preceded him.   "Writings of his were handed about, remarkable for a peculiar felicity of expression."

On his way to Congress he paused long enough to write out
a constitution for the state of Virginia and send it back.
Wasted labour; it was not adopted.   But to a born writer like
Jefferson the impelling urge is to get the thing written.

Barbé de Marbois, secretary of the French legation, asked
Jefferson—then governor of Virginia—to give him some information about that state.   Thereupon Governor Jefferson
sat down and wrote a complete book on Virginia, its soil, peo-

ple, climate and resources. This production, published under the title of *Notes on Virginia*, is a well-balanced and informative work, and is in circulation to this day.

As Jefferson travels over the face of Europe a stream of descriptive letters come from him. He is an eye . . . a philosophic eye . . . he sees everything, the inside as well as the outside of places and political institutions. He learns the languages; he notes the various methods of planting; he fingers little mechanical contrivances and writes about them; he observes that bricks are laid differently in Holland; he talks with peasants; he sends to America vast bundles of new plants and fruits; he studies French cooking and astronomy. He is at home in France, among a people so intellectually vivid. He is as much of an *encyclopédiste* as Diderot himself, and he has a nose for news equal to that of Saint-Simon. But no *chronique scandaleuse* runs from his pen. He is too much in earnest, too deadly serious, for idle flippancies. His preoccupation is politics, and the relation of man to his cosmos.

Such a personality in the world of thought is like a prism of crystal in sunlight. The flow of ideas spreads itself over an immense spectrum, where every conceivable interest is represented. But if we examine the Jefferson spectrum closely we observe that its deepest colour is around the zone of democratic ideas. He was a pure-blooded believer in democracy; nay, more . . . he was a humanitarian. He saw clearly that all wealth comes from labour, and that the history of the world is nothing more than a history of ruling class schemes to trick labour out of its economic rights . . . and to that end all the institutions of civilisation are turned . . . churches, schools, literature, finance, commerce, morals.

To Washington a mind like Jefferson's could not be anything less than a mystery. Washington, true to the captain-of-industry type, was almost colour-blind to ideas if they were very different from his own. His tendency was to estimate men by what they were rather than by what they thought . . . and it was certain that Jefferson was an aristocrat and one of the Very Best People.

The Continental Congress was also a trifle defective in intellectual vision, else it would have never allowed Jefferson to write the Declaration of Independence and include in it so many sweeping implications.

§ 7

Jefferson's ideas have the subtle permanence of cameos . . . little carved stones which one throws negligently in a drawer, to come upon them many years later, still fresh and vivid in their clear-cut precision.

He thought that one generation had no right to bind another generation, either collectively or individually. A practical acceptance of this point of view would put an end to one of the major evils of capitalism; for capitalism's principal hold on civilisation lies in its capacity to enslave each new generation by documents representing obligations that were incurred by previous generations.

"Merchants have no country," he wrote. "The mere spot they stand on does not constitute so strong an attachment as that from which they draw their gains."

He thought that "The land belongs in usufruct to the living, and the dead have no power over it."

"It is always better to have no ideas," he said, "than false ones; to believe nothing, than to believe what is wrong."

When he founded the University of Virginia he selected its noble motto, which is: *And ye shall know the truth, and the truth shall make you free.*

He thought that generals were usually misfits. "The Creator has not thought proper to mark those in the forehead who are of stuff to make good generals," he said. "We are first, therefore, to seek them blindfolded, and let them learn the trade at the expense of great losses."

CHAPTER XIX

WAS WASHINGTON A GOOD GENERAL?

§ 1

THE object of the British military effort was to establish the imperial authority in a territory a thousand miles in length and from two hundred to three hundred miles in width. Along this coast line there was not a single fortified seaport. There were numerous bays and navigable rivers, such as the Chesapeake, the Hudson, the Delaware, the Potomac and the James.

The entire territory was sparsely settled; it was a land of forests and wretched roads; for foot soldiers the distances were heart-breaking.

The difficulties of the British problem were greatly increased by the necessity of bringing troops and their supplies three thousand miles across the Atlantic. The voyage took about five weeks in good weather; in bad weather it was much longer, often ten or twelve weeks.

On account of the overcrowding of the transports, the long racking voyages, and the impossibility of carrying fresh food on the ships, the mortality among the troops was high. A troopship, less than two hundred feet in length and about fifty feet wide, would sometimes bring as many as five hundred men. Arranged in layers, like salted fish, they slept in the airless spaces under deck. Living in this fashion soldiers sickened and died; and a trail of sheeted dead bodies, weighted and slowly sinking in the green sea, marked the road of empire across the Atlantic.

England's job was herculean; nevertheless, a deficiency in man power was not at first among her troubles. There were plenty of men in England—or they could be hired, as the Hessians were hired—and the English troops were well supplied with armament, food and clothing. Relieved of these material urgencies, the problem boiled itself down into questions involving transportation and strategy. I am referring, of course, to the British military task and not to the political aspect of the war.

The Americans did not possess a navy, and the enormous advantage of sea-power was in the hands of the British. Through control of the sea they could choose the point of attack; they could land large bodies of troops at any place on the American coast. They could move armies by water from one place to another more rapidly than the Americans could move them by land. In such a situation the American advantage of movement by interior lines was nullified, or reversed; the ocean became the interior line on this terrain of strategy.

The potential weight of British sea-power was augmented by the lack of colonial manufacturing industries. The factories of Europe were an absolute necessity to America. Most of the ammunition used in American guns had to be brought from Europe. Even such a common article as salt was imported. There was a constant, urgent need of contact with the rest of the world.

How easy it would have been for the British to have blockaded the entire American coast. The Earl of Sandwich, First Lord of the Admiralty, said in the second year of the war, that there were eighty-seven first-class war vessels on the American station. Not one of them was used for blockading purposes. They swung idly on their cables in New York harbour. These eighty-seven vessels, distributed along the coast, would have meant one blockading ship every twelve miles from Massachusetts to South Carolina.

Wooden sailing vessels were not expensive, and a frigate

could be built in a few months.   The fleet of eighty-seven vessels might readily have been increased to two hundred in a year.

Under this plan of blockade, military operations on land would not have been necessary.   The British need only to have held New York, and perhaps Newport and Charleston, as naval bases.   Small garrisons would have been required to retain these places.

With the coast tightly blockaded the British would have brought the Americans to terms eventually, though it might have taken them two or three years.

Hardly a glimmer of this appears in the British discussion of ways and means.   Lord Barrington may have had a blockade in mind when he declared that the Americans could never be conquered by military operations, but nobody paid much attention to him.

Is it possible that the British ministry did not grasp the first principle of naval strategy, which is that a fleet in being constitutes a military frontier?   A string of warships along the American coast would have meant, in simple speech, that the English frontier had been pushed across the Atlantic.

Some of the Americans understood these possibilities, even if the English did not.   Several years after the war Alexander Hamilton told Pontgibaud that "All the English need have done was to blockade our ports with twenty-five frigates and ten ships of the line.   But, thank God, they did nothing of the sort."

Very likely such a thought did occur to the governing minds of England, and was outweighed by other considerations.   A war of blockade would have seemed in the nature of a confession that all British authority in the colonies was gone, and they were always reluctant to make such an admission.   They had in mind the idea of setting up loyalist governments under the protection of the troops.   To do this effectively they were convinced that it was necessary to defeat and disperse the American armies in battle.   They were obsessed by the thought that the entire trouble had been caused by disorderly persons. Their imperial conceptions were those of a suburban policeman.

England, and the British Empire, though in form a constitutional monarchy, was governed, in fact, by eighty or a hundred aristocratic families. Nearly every one of these families had a general or a colonel among its members. To such sword-bearing gentlemen the idea of a war without battles was preposterous.

Whatever may have been the reason, incompetency or political considerations, the fact remains that Britain did not use her sea-power effectively, or hardly at all, when it was without doubt the central feature of her strategical possibilities. The contest was eventually decided by sea-power, but it was French, and not English.

In one sense the Americans, as poorly equipped as they were, had a distinct advantage. They were already in possession of the theatre of war. Their policy was necessarily a defensive one, and the geography of the country furnished a natural aid to its defence.

The difficulties of the American situation may be summed up as consisting of a lack of men, a lack of supplies, and a lack of effective military ideas. The Americans were never able to overcome these deficiencies; they lasted from the beginning until the end of the war.

§ 2

In 1775 privates were paid six and two-thirds dollars a month. The army was then made up of state troops, loaned to the Continental Congress. Most of the men were enlisted for short terms, and the constant expirations kept the army in a fluid state of disorganisation.

Washington thought the war could not be carried on without a national army of regulars, engaged for long periods, or preferably for the duration of the war. There were many objections to this plan among the members of Congress—they were always jealous of any possible infringement of the powers of the states—but Washington's insistence prevailed, and about the middle of 1776 a Continental army, to consist of about fifty thousand men, was authorised. The soldiers' pay was to remain the same, but if a soldier enlisted for three years he was to get, in addition to his pay, a bounty of ten dollars and one hundred acres of land. The Continental enlistments never reached fifty thousand or anything near that number.

The plan was obstructed, in part, by the competitive efforts of the states to keep their own regiments supplied with recruits. Massachusetts privates were paid thirty-six dollars a month, and all the states paid larger bounties than those offered by Congress. New Jersey gave a bounty of fifty-three dollars, and Massachusetts thereupon raised its reward to the attractive figure of eighty-six dollars. Before the end Virginia was giving a bounty of twelve thousand Continental paper dollars—worth about two hundred dollars in gold.

Washington wrote an interesting letter to the president of Congress in which he said that at the beginning men might have been enlisted for the war without any bounty at all. In other words, the war had become unpopular. Something had happened to the army which made the patriots reluctant to serve in it. The martinet discipline was unsuited to the colonial temperament. The atrocious floggings and the general degradation of the common soldier made the farmer boys resolve that liberty would have to stumble along without them.

If the condition of the army in respect to men was bad, it was even worse in the matter of supplies. The country was full of food, yet there were occasions when the army was on the verge of starvation.

The troops were reasonably well fed during the first year of the war, and at times until the end there was enough food, but the periods of abundance were rare, and short in duration.

Merchants and farmers did not want to take the Continental paper money. It had to be forced on them, but they can hardly be blamed, for it went down and down in value until it became mere trash not worth the white paper on which it was printed.

Another difficulty was that of transportation. The roads were so bad and movement was so slow that it was impracticable to bring food from a distance. The army had to live on the country in its immediate neighbourhood. That was one of the reasons why Washington selected Valley Forge, in the midst of a fruitful agricultural region, as his winter quarters in the fall of 1777. This reasoning looks sound enough when seen from a front, or full-face, view. Its aspect in the rear, however, caught as it passes over the hill of history, is extremely unsatisfactory. The Valley Forge country was, indeed, full of wheat and beef, but the honest Quaker farmers seem to have been lacking in the more impulsive qualities of patriotism. They refused Continental money, which was all that Washington had to give them, and sent their produce into Philadelphia, then occupied by the British, who paid in gold. This commerce was treasonable, but it was not easy to catch them at it.

There were times when the soldiers at Valley Forge were without bread for days. Washington's own Christmas dinner of that year was served without bread, sugar, tea, coffee or milk; a forlorn Christmas dinner of meat and potatoes.

By February of 1778 the army was on the point of dissolution. Washington was informed by Congress, sitting at York, Pennsylvania, since it had been driven out of Philadelphia, that it expected him to seize food and force the farmers to accept the Continental currency. He did make a few small seizures, which "excited the greatest alarm and uneasiness even among our best and warmest friends," as he wrote on January 5th. He wrote to the president of Congress that he was "aware of the prevalent jealousy of military power," and that he "wished to avoid as much as possible any act that might increase it."

The trouble over supplying the army lay fundamentally in the indifference of the general public to the war. The army had the best wishes of a large number of people, but kind regards do not feed soldiers. Instead of being everybody's fervent, daily business the Revolution was gradually becoming nobody's business. The cause was in need of a great and fiery leader, a Mahomet or a Cromwell.

Clothing was even more difficult to obtain than food. Manufacturing was an infantile industry. Shoes, stockings, blankets, cloth for shirts—all these necessities had to be imported from France and Spain. Uncertain and hazardous this method was, for supply ships were frequently captured by the British privateers. In February, 1778, four thousand men—of Washington's force of nine thousand—were unfit for duty on account of having no shoes nor coats. He wrote that many men had to sit by the fire all night for lack of blankets.

The confusion in the matter of distributing supplies is almost unbelievable. Clothing urgently needed by the army lay in distant warehouses and rotted. Shoes intended for troops in Pennsylvania were landed at a port four hundred miles away.

None of this was Washington's fault. His letters are filled with appeals to Congress and to the governors of the states. He endeavoured in every way that his mind could conceive to keep his army in being, and to uphold the sinking fortunes of the Revolution.

His strongest quality was fortitude. The fighter who stays in the ring as long as he can stand on his feet, the man who keeps his business alive while his clothes are threadbare and his stomach empty, the captain who clings to his ship while there is a plank left afloat—that is Washington.

This quality implies sincerity, courage and honesty of purpose, but it does not imply intellect or good judgment.

§ 3

I have said that the third major deficiency of the Revolutionary army was a lack of sound military ideas.

In making this assertion I have no thought of text-book strategy in mind. The French officers observed that Washington's army could not keep step and was poor in the manual of arms, but I do not consider their remarks of any importance. They are the criticisms of drill masters.

When I say that the Revolutionary military leaders were deficient in ideas I mean that Washington and his officers set out from the start to form an army on the British military model; and that such an organisation was wholly impracticable. It was not adapted to the colonial spirit.

Washington did not have much originality. The question as to whether it would be best to imitate the organisation of the British army, or to try something different, appears never to have entered his mind.

The British model was, of course, the European model—an army mathematically parcelled into regiments, and drilled into mechanical precision. Low class men for soldiers, and aristocrats—or "gentlemen," at least—for officers. In battle these armies usually approached the enemy in column and deployed on the field, in the enemy's presence. Firing was by command, and in volleys. The battle line was two or three men deep, the front rank kneeling, with the two rear ranks firing over their heads. Much reliance was placed on the bayonet, owing to the necesssary slowness in reloading the flintlocks, and also because of the poor marksmanship of the British and other European armies.

All this was thoroughly out of tune with the colonial character. The American of 1776 was a marksman without an equal in the world. To him war did not mean evolution; it simply meant shooting somebody. If he was not a marksman he tried to make himself one; his thought was always of putting a bullet

Moun Vernon Feb[y] 3[d] 1770

Rev[d] Sir,

The uncertainty of your return from Maryland (as we heard that Potomack was froze below Cedar Point) added to the difficulty, & indeed danger of crossing the Waters between this and your House are the Reasons of Jacky's detention here so long. — We therefore if he shod be too late in comg hope your excuse for it. —

He brings down several pair of very good London made Shoes, which being too small for him, it woud be acknowledged as a favour if you coud give him any assistance in changing of them for those of larger size. — Our Compliments are offerd & I am Rev[d] Sir Yr most Hble Servt

G[o] Washington

10th The bad weather has detaind Jacky to this time from the date above —

WASHINGTON'S HANDWRITING

This letter was written when Washington was 38 years of age. His writing is rhythmic, careful and orderly. He wastes no space on margins. His signature is strong but showy.

where it ought to go. He liked to fight as an individual, behind trees or rocks. On the approach of a line of bayonets he would run until he could get under cover, and then he would fire again.

Through instruction, discipline and flogging Washington attempted to turn these sharpshooting rangers into an army composed of lines and squares. At the best, the result could be only an imitation highly pleasing to the British generals, for such an American policy would allow them to conduct the war according to rules with which they were familiar.

Charles Francis Adams says, in his *Studies Military and Diplomatic*, that prior to 1776, "warfare as carried on in America had, as the unfortunate Braddock found to his cost, been waged on principles and by methods neither recognised by European students nor understood by its professionals. It was in every sense of the term distinctly irregular. Carried on almost necessarily in heavily wooded regions, it was a conflict between individuals. . . ."

He says further: "The opponent the British officer most dreaded the sight of was the leather-clad ranger; and, of all descriptions of rangers, the organised mounted ranger was the most potentially formidable."

Instead of trying to develop the individuality of the soldier, Washington attempted to repress it. In short, he set out "to whip an army into shape," just as an English general would have done, disregarding the difference in human material. The English general's army would have consisted chiefly of the rakings of the London slums, men vicious in disposition, without any knowledge of firearms, and serving in the army only to be fed and clothed.

No doubt the British system was well adapted for recruits of that type; but in America some other form of organisation, better fitted to the American character, would certainly have accomplished more.

The English statesman Pitt, in one of his anti-war speeches

in the House of Commons exclaimed, "You cannot conquer a map!"

Pitt was not a soldier, but he had the intuition that a great soldier ought to have. He realised that the American strength lay in diffusion; in being as fluid as water and as powerful as water; in being a map. In one sentence he expressed a clearer understanding of American military possibilities than any American general showed during the course of the war.

A Continental army consisting, for the major part, of small commands of fifty or sixty mounted men, would have been very effective, in all probability. These detachments, trained as highly mobile mounted infantry, would have worn the British army to rags and hysteria in the course of a year or two.

Ordinarily, they could have acted as independent units, but at times it would have been desirable to combine them into a larger force. As a nucleus of organisation a central head-quarters army of two or three thousand men would have been sufficient.

The range of the mounted infantry would have been so great that the army could have spread itself rapidly over a large area. This ease of movement would have diminished the diffi-culty of obtaining food and clothing. With such a flexible army Washington could have fed himself at Valley Forge. Not only could he have done that, but the mounted infantry, circling around Philadelphia, would have put Howe's army in a state of blockade, and might have starved it out.

Washington did not understand the use of cavalry. During the first two years of the war the cavalry arm was non-ex-istent, and Washington discouraged every attempt to organise even a single cavalry regiment . . . and this in a country where there was an abundance of horses and forage, and every man was a horseman.

In July, 1776, five hundred citizens of Connecticut, organised and equipped as horsemen, appeared at army headquarters and offered to enlist as a cavalry command. Washington told them that there was nothing for cavalry to do, but suggested that they serve as infantry. They declined; so, in a rather huffy temper, he sent them home, and wrote to their commander that he did not care how soon they were dismissed.

This episode is so amazing that it sends one wandering in a fog of uncertainty as to Washington's motives. After awhile we come to the conclusion that his motives were simple enough . . . he did not know what to do with cavalry. No doubt he thought of the cavalry arm in terms of battle paintings— great waves of horsemen sweeping over level fields to hurl themselves on a hedge of bayonets. In Europe cavalry was reserved for these glittering charges, but in Washington's army the function of horses in mass should have been to convey men with guns in their hands rapidly from one place to another.

His neglect of the possibilities of cavalry offers a curious contrast to his fondness for artillery. During the entire war the American field artillery accomplished hardly anything that was worth while. This is not a reflection on General Knox, the chief of artillery, who was a resourceful officer; but it is a reflection on Washington's policy of developing the artillery arm at the expense of the cavalry arm. The fact is that the field artillery never helped materially in a single one of the pitched battles. It served only to delay the progress of the army. The lumbering, sprawling guns were dragged— with oaths and perspiration—over the gullied roads and stony hills from Boston to New York, from New York to Brandywine, from Brandywine to Morristown, from Morristown to Virginia, when it would have been better if every one of them had been thrown into the first convenient river.

The evidence impels us to the conviction that Washington's conception of an army was a stiff and clumsy conception. The army he had in mind and tried to make was not an army which was suited to the colonial character, nor was it suitable for the work it had to do.

He missed his great opportunity, which was to form an army

on a new model—a highly mobile army of marksmen which would hang on the British flanks and rear, pick off their officers, defeat and capture raiding parties, cut their baggage trains to pieces, and quietly disappear when confronted by the British army in force, unless the odds were greatly in their favour.

As an objection to this argument it may be said that such a fluid army could not have stopped the British from taking any place they might have wanted to occupy. That may be so; but, on the other hand, Washington's conventional military force was never able to prevent them from taking whatever they pleased. They took New York, Philadelphia, Charleston, Savannah. At Saratoga, Gates' army of eighteen thousand stopped Burgoyne's five thousand, but Burgoyne himself thought that Daniel Morgan's five hundred Virginia riflemen did as much execution among the British as all the rest of Gates' army.

Hardly any of Washington's biographers have understood the science of war. Perhaps this is the reason why there has been so little intelligent discussion of his military operations. Many of his biographers have not only been ignorant of military science, but have made themselves mere adulators besides; and to them everything that Washington did, said or thought was absolutely perfect.

However, if we turn to Charles Francis Adams, who was himself an intelligent soldier, we find some interesting observations. I quote one of them here:

> . . . it is curious to reflect on what might, under the general conditions of time, place, season, topography and movement, have been the result had the Americans at this stage of the war [in 1777] resorted to Parthian tactics— anticipated the methods of the Boers instead of constantly recurring to the traditions and practice of Marlborough and Frederick—traditions and practice wholly misleading in America. The military as well as historic

truth is that, on this as on other occasions, Washington measured himself and his army up against his adversary at the point where they were strongest and he was least so. He opposed infantry to infantry; oblivious of the fact that the British infantry were of the most perfectly organised kind, while his own was at best an extemporised force.

Yet, notwithstanding Washington's policy, the tendency to form small and agile groups of fighting horsemen was such an obvious necessity of the situation that it could not be restrained. The partisan bands of Sumter, Marion and Pickens in South Carolina were cavalry groups of this kind. They followed instinctively the American method of warfare; and the results they accomplished were in importance altogether out of proportion to the small number of men engaged.

§ 4

The war was a combat between awkward fighters; a prizering contest in which both gladiators were slow and dull. It was long drawn out and sleepy with delays. The combatants sulked in their corners, rising now and then to scuffle awhile with a sort of sad ferocity.

Both sides had adopted methods which were unsuited to their abilities or to the field of encounter. Under such circumstances hardly anything was, or could have been, clearly thought out. Luck, the deadly parasite of history, swarmed over events both great and small. In the lighting of a fire, in the shoeing of a horse, in a downpour of rain, lay the imponderable elements of destiny.

Nowhere, on either side, was there the clear high intelligence or the sweeping power in mass that smashes luck to bits. The history of the Revolution belongs to the metaphysics of chance; it is a story that ought to be told in terms of philosophy.

Washington and the British War Office were of one mind

in considering the Hudson River the key to the military situation. With both this idea had the intensity of an obsession.

To the end of the war Washington made control of the Hudson the basis of the American plan of strategy, but about
1778 the British began to lose faith in its overwhelming importance. Thereafter they estimated the river and its valley
as objectives worth any reasonable sacrifice, but they no
longer thought that the possession of this amulet would charm
away the rebellion.

The theory behind the Hudson River fallacy was that, with
the river from New York to Albany in British hands, and
fortified, the colonial system would be cut in two; that New
England would be separated from the rest of the colonies and
could be conquered at British leisure.

This reasoning diffuses itself over a good deal of ground,
and is full of baseless assumptions. In the first place, there
was no colonial system. At that time the American nation
was an animal without head or tail. There was really no central government, but merely a committee which called itself a
congress and made recommendations. New England had an
abundance of men, and in all probability they could have defended themselves very well, even if cut off from the Congress
and the rest of the colonies.

In the second place, an effective control of the Hudson was
beyond the means at the disposal of the British commanders.
The distance from New York to Albany is one hundred and
forty miles, and the British never had more than thirty-four
thousand men in America at any one time. To have fortified
the river in such fashion that patriot troops could not cross it
would have required not less than sixty thousand men.

Let us suppose, however, that this large force had been
available. Then, in that case, the whole British army would
have found itself cooped up inactively in forts, and the long
river line would have been continually harassed by the patriots.
To have made the plan effective about thirty thousand addi-

tional men would have been needed for field operations—or approximately ninety thousand men in all. But with ninety thousand troops under British command the possession of the Hudson River would not have been necessary, for such a large force could have made short work of the American Revolution, even if all the British generals had been as incompetent as Howe.

Closely related to this Hudson River strategy was an exaggerated idea of the importance of Canada. It was generally believed by the patriots in 1775 that the people of Canada—then wholly French—were only waiting for some little encouragement to throw off Britain's hateful yoke. In the fall of that year Washington detached fifteen hundred men from his diminishing shoestring army around Boston and sent them under Benedict Arnold to attack Quebec.

This expedition, after astounding hardships, reached Canada in mid-winter and was defeated. A similar invasion started from New York, and succeeded in taking Montreal, which was held for a month or two. Washington thought the capture of Quebec essential to the success of the American cause, so more thousands of men were sent, furnished with Continental paper money and proclamations inviting the French-Canadians to turn against the oppressor and join the patriots in the cause of freedom. The proclamations were a flat failure for the following reason:

In 1774 the British government, for purposes of administration, had turned over to the province of Quebec the region south of the Great Lakes—the land now covered by the states of Ohio, Indiana, Michigan, Illinois and Wisconsin. The French-Canadians were informed that they might settle in this territory, and that they would have full liberty to practise their religion, which was Roman Catholic. This measure of the British ministry was called the Quebec Act. It caused almost as much uproar in the American colonies as the Stamp Act had ever aroused. The Puritan virtues of the indignant patriots rose to the boiling point. It seemed hardly credible, they said, that England, the bulwark and champion of Protestantism, would allow Popery to be practised on American soil. The hideous idolatry of the Roman Catholics! The degeneracy of England! The very hellishness of it all! Not only did England allow Popery to be practised on the English soil of Canada, but she actually had gone so far as to invite the idol-worshipping Canadians to perform their heathenish rites on land consecrated by American blood.

Upon their arrival in Canada with their proclamations inviting the French population to buckle on the armour of freedom the patriots found that the British government had already issued some literature of its own in which it had been mean enough to tell all about the No-Popery views of the patriots.

That was a bad slam, but the Continental money was even worse. The Canadians refused to take it, as it was completely worthless in Canada, so the invaders had to seize supplies or starve.

In a few months the Canadian exploit petered out, and the débris of the little army drifted back, leaving a reputation in Canada as brigands and Catholic-haters. Benedict Arnold had made, however, a brilliant reputation for himself. His conduct before Quebec had shown him to be a soldier of resource and courage.

This military enterprise, carried out at a time when the patriots needed every man and every ounce of powder, has an air of fantastic adventure which is not easy to reconcile with Washington's practicality.

The secret of it is to be found in the series of ideas which circled continually in his mind about the Hudson River. Canada, he thought, was a natural military base for the British. Suppose they should come down the Hudson and meet a British force from New York. Then the colonies would indeed be cut in two.

But there were two hundred miles of tangled forests and rugged hills between Montreal and Albany. This natural obstacle was in itself a first-rate defence. The land was covered with deep snow for four or five months a year, and the St. Lawrence was frozen every winter. Part of this wilderness might be traversed over navigable lakes; but, even so, what could be the sense of invading the colonies through a jungle when it was easy enough to invade them from a comfortable seaport?

In the light of ordinary intelligence the idea of an invasion from Canada seems to have been absurd; nevertheless, it was well-grounded, for in 1777 the British actually did attempt to do that very thing. As a result they lost Burgoyne's entire army.

The capture of Burgoyne gave rise in Europe to a profound and favourable impression of American military strength, and it was the determining fact that brought the French into the war as allies of the United States. It turned out, therefore, that an invasion from Canada, instead of being an event of direful import, was in effect the best thing for the American cause that happened between Bunker Hill and Yorktown.

§ 5

If we walk around the war on the outside and look at it as a whole, we see that it consisted of two distinct parts, with an interval between, like a play in two acts.

The battle of Bunker Hill and its sequential siege of Boston had no place in the strategy of the war. It was in the nature of a prelude; an accidental conflict which happened to take place at Boston because that city was occupied by troops sent there to keep order.

The first act ran from July, 1776, with Howe's arrival at New York, until the battle of Monmouth, in June, 1778. During that time the war was confined virtually to an area which may be shown by putting one point of a pair of dividers on

New York City, and the other point about one hundred and twenty miles distant on the map. Then describe a semi-circle. The top of the semi-circle rests on the Hudson, and its curve sweeps around behind Philadelphia and on to the Atlantic Ocean.

This was the theatre of war for the first two years, while Sir William Howe was in charge of the British operations. The only military event of great importance which occurred outside this area was the attempt of Burgoyne to break through from Canada, and his surrender to Gates at Saratoga, sixteen miles north of Albany.

After the evacuation of Boston the area of New England was untouched by the ravages of war, except for a few brief raids on the Connecticut coast.

No state south of Pennsylvania was invaded until 1780.

When the curtain went down on the first act there was a long pause. The British were at war with France—later with Spain and Holland—and had no initiative left for America. They held New York city, and nothing else. From June, 1778, until the end of 1779 they were inactive.

The second act was played in the South—in South Carolina, North Carolina and Virginia, and the curtain came down at Yorktown, in October, 1781. Washington had no part, personally, in any Southern campaign except the operations around Yorktown. He commanded in seven battles and one siege from June, 1775, until June, 1778. After that, he was not in a battle for three years and four months.

CHAPTER XX

WASHINGTON LUCK

§ 1

Sir William Howe was one of the most deliberate generals in the history of warfare. He belonged to that strange race of men who have somehow overlooked the inexorable urgency of time. He did everything too late. He arrived in America too late, marched too late, fought too late, resigned too late, died too late.

He walked through our Revolution like a slow-paced cardinal walking through the dim corridors of the Vatican.

It was he who was on Destiny's programme as the star in the first act of the British conquest of the colonies. On June 30th, 1776, the curtain went up on Act One when Sir William Howe appeared in New York bay with an army on board transports.

An immense flotilla of five hundred vessels. The lower bay was white with sails and vivid with life and movement. The fleet was under the command of Admiral Lord Howe, who was Sir William's brother.

The troops landed and encamped on Staten Island. Other contingents soon arrived. Sir Henry Clinton came from his unsuccessful attempt to take Charleston and brought another army with him.

Hired soldiers from Hesse-Cassel and Brunswick reached America in July. The employment of these mercenaries did incalculable injury to the British cause. Until then many Americans had looked upon the war as nothing but a fierce little family row .... the mother and her children. But these Hessians were foreigners. They spoke German; they

307

had no ties in America and no sympathy with the country. They were hired by the English to come over and kill Americans, just as one might hire a butcher to come in and kill an unruly bull.

This fierce resentment over the Hessians was a great surprise to George III. They were not foreigners to him. He was as much German as English, and he spent several months of every year in his own Electorate of Hanover. His imagination was too feeble to furnish him with even a rudimentary conception of the American spirit.

The Landgrave of Hesse-Cassel made a very good bargain. He was to receive for every man killed the sum of fifty-five dollars, and twelve dollars for every man wounded. The British agreed to pay the hired troops on the same basis as the English soldiers, and to provide food, clothing and arms. In addition to all this munificence, the Landgrave was to receive $550,000 annually from the British government.

In all, about thirty thousand mercenaries were brought to America, but only seventeen thousand returned to Germany. Five thousand deserted and eight thousand were killed or died. The Hessian troops could not march ten miles in the country without leaving a trail of deserters. The chief ambition of every Hessian soldier was, it seems, to get clear away from the army as soon as possible and be a farm labourer; or to settle down on a little land with a cow and a few pigs.

With his various reinforcements General Howe had under his command about thirty-four thousand men. His army was the largest military force that had ever been sent across an ocean, up to that time, by any European power.

Upon arriving at Staten Island, Howe settled down for seven weeks. He saw that Washington had made up his mind to defend New York City. The patriots were setting up batteries on the water front, and Washington's soldiers thronged the streets. All this came to Howe through his spies. New York was a town full of loyalists; secret codes were passed around; every other man in the place had scribbled memoranda in his pocket.

§ 2

In the ardent spring of that year, before the British expeditionary force had arrived, a few of His Majesty's ships lay uneasily at anchor in New York harbour. On one of them William Tryon, royal governor of the province, sat in a simmering rage. His part in the drama of empire had grown comical . . . a governor without a province . . . and a humourless governor at that, who issued threats and proclamations in a steady stream, while Washington mounted cannon.

His lack of humour, or his baffled spleen, or something, led him after awhile to attempt the part of Macbeth with Washington as Banquo. He was the mainspring of a plot of which the chief features were the murder of Washington, the confusion of the patriots and the seizure of the city.

This conjuration by dirk and poison might have succeeded if the conspirators had not allowed it to leak out by taking so many loyalists into their confidence. As many as five hundred people were said to have been involved, including Matthews, mayor of the city, a jolly fellow, described as "the facetious David Matthews." They bribed one of Washington's life guards, a poor devil named Thomas Hickey. When the exposure came, the facetious mayor was sent to prison and Hickey was tried, convicted and hanged.

There was a Danny Deever air about Hickey's execution . . . troops in line . . . a glitter of bayonets . . . stern commands . . . the populace in swarms . . . files-on-parade. The contemporary newspaper account which I read says that "during the execution, Kip, the moon-curser, suddenly sank down and expired instantly." I do not know who Kip was, or how he cursed moons; but it does seem most extraordinary that a moon-curser should expire so suddenly, under such circumstances, so I pass the fact on for others to elucidate.

With five hundred of the King's ships in the bay, and a patriot army drilling in the streets, and a plot discovered, and the mayor sent to prison, and a man hanged, and a moon-curser who fell dead, the little city of New York was so addled with excitement that it could hardly eat its meals.

Excitement was mixed with worry. . . .

Pale, haggard men walked the floors of their little shops; merchants figured gloomy problems of ribbons and calicoes; householders went about their premises, wondering painfully what a cannon-riddled house really looks like.

§ 3

In the operations around New York in 1776 both the attack and the defence revealed a profound ignorance of the elementary principles of military science. Even more; they revealed an absence of ordinary common sense.

Washington had sent General Charles Lee to New York in February with instructions to fortify the city.

For the benefit of those who are not familiar with the local geography of New York City I will say that the city is on Manhattan Island—a long loaf of an island which runs north and south. On the west of Manhattan is the Hudson River; on the east is the East River. At the southern end of the island New York harbour begins. At the lower end of the harbour is Staten Island—an island as large as an ordinary county. East of New York, across the East River, is Long Island—an island as large as two or three counties. Brooklyn, then a small village, stood on Long Island across the East River from New York. The water on all sides of Manhattan Island was navigable for warships. At the time of the Revolution the town of New York occupied only the southern tip of its huge island.

General Lee strode about New York, followed by the pack

of hunting dogs which he kept always at his heels. Followed also by obsequious citizens and spies. "What to do with the city," he wrote to Washington, "I own, puzzles me. It is so encircled with deep navigable water, that whoever commands the sea must command the town."

There can be no doubt as to the soundness of Lee's statement. It was possible for an enemy to encircle the island with naval vessels, and to invest it so completely as to cut off the retreat of the defending force. Washington instructed Lee to go on with his fortifications, notwithstanding these inherent disadvantages.

On April 13th, Washington himself arrived and took charge of things. The plan of defence was to erect batteries at points which commanded the rivers. But the rivers were wide, and the artillery was of short range. There was not the slightest chance that this pop-gun defence would be able to stop the movement of British vessels. Washington did not believe that the batteries would be of much use, and said so. In the light of his own opinion, his insistence on setting them up with so much expense and trouble is inexplicable.

Lee had called attention to the fact that the town of New York was dominated by the heights of Brooklyn, an elevated ridge on the other side of the East River. Washington decided to occupy these heights, and sent fifty-five hundred men across the river to take possession and throw up breastworks.

When the deliberate Howe was finally ready to make a move, the relative position of the two armies may be summed up:

Washington held Manhattan Island and Brooklyn Heights. He had about twenty thousand men, of whom only fourteen thousand were fit for duty. Of this force nearly half were in Brooklyn, and were separated from the remainder of his army by a river half a mile wide. He had made the naïve strategic mistake of dividing his force—already inferior—into two parts, and putting these parts on opposite sides of a wide, deep river. This idea was conceived with a full knowledge that his opponent controlled the sea and had only to sail up the East River to cut his army in two.

As far as the Howes were concerned their military problem was of such a simple nature that it would hardly tax the intellect of a child.

All they had to do was to keep the American troops on Long Island penned in their position by using Lord Howe's fleet to take possession of the East River. Then, General Howe's army of thirty thousand men could have been landed, under protection of the war vessels, somewhere near the northern end of Manhattan Island. Properly deployed, his force would have stretched across Manhattan. The whole army, moving slowly forward in such overwhelming force, would have driven Washington's army before it into a pocket. In the end the American army would have had to surrender or fight its way out—and the chance of fighting through against such enormous odds would have been pretty slim.

There is no gleam of this naked logic in Howe's strategy. When his plan came out it was so thoroughly swaddled in flounces and gewgaws that nobody has been able to say, to this day, whether the child was white or black.

Now eight days of awkward strategy began. On August 22nd Howe crossed from Staten Island to Long Island with a large number of troops. A simultaneous move by Lord Howe's fleet up the East River would have settled the fate of the American regiments on Brooklyn Heights, but no such move was made.

Washington hurried over to Long Island, and took command. Greene, his best general, was laid on his back with fever. The British attacked Washington's position on August 27th, and succeeded in turning the American left flank. The American defeat was disastrous, almost catastrophic. The British took a large number of prisoners, including ninety-one officers, among whom were Generals Stirling and Sullivan.

In the afternoon of the 27th the American army was in a state of chaotic disorganisation. Washington had lost altogether about two thousand men, including prisoners, and his nervous mob of thirty-five hundred were facing twenty thousand British regulars.

This should have been the great moment of Sir William Howe. The ghost of an unborn peerage and a niche in Westminster Abbey stood at his elbow and stared in his face. But he had no eyes to see; he called off his troops and said that enough had been done for one day. He wrote that the men were too fatigued to continue, but British eye-witnesses said that it was difficult to make the troops desist.

It is interesting to speculate as to what would have happened if the victorious Howe had continued the battle on the afternoon of August 27, 1776. In all probability the entire American force on Long Island, including Washington, would have been forced to surrender.

Would this have broken the back of the Revolution? I think not. But Washington would have disappeared from history, except as an incompetent general who almost ruined the American cause at the beginning.

During the night of the 27th Washington had a chance to take his remaining troops across the river to Manhattan. But instead of doing that perfectly sensible thing, he sent for reinforcements, and twenty-five hundred additional men were brought into the trap.

On the 28th God made it rain and gave General Howe an excuse. The flint-and-powder muskets were useless in a rainstorm, but the bayonet was not. The British might have carried everything with the bayonet, considering their immense numerical superiority. Howe deliberated, and decided to wait. The rain fell in a deluge for two days.

The first recognition of the fact that he was in a trap appears to have come to Washington on the afternoon of the 29th. An impression that was heightened probably by the

dreary downpour; the muddy, frightened men; the cold gray
river at his back; the hum of noises from the encircling British
lines. The situation was truly desperate. The rain, the mud,
and the crowding enemy must have brought the worn but still
gloomy picture of Fort Necessity to his mind.

It was in such heart-breaking circumstances that Washington was at his best. He could look disaster in the face as
coolly as other men look at a dress parade. Slow and dull
of apprehension at other times, he thought with precision and
speed when things were at their worst.

During the day of the 29th, there had been a languid stir
among the British ships. It looked as if they were preparing
to cut off his retreat. Quietly and quickly he had boats
assembled, and at night he got his entire force across to Manhattan without the loss of a man. The regiments were a mere
mob. The men climbed over one another to get into the boats.

§ 4

With the British in possession of Long Island there was
a pause in operations.

The brothers Howe announced that they had come bearing
the olive branch of peace. The captured General Sullivan was
released on parole and sent as their messenger to Congress.
They had conciliatory proposals from the British government,
they said, and would it be possible to meet a few gentlemen
from Congress?

Congress appointed a committee; and Benjamin Franklin,
John Adams and young Edward Rutledge jogged over the
muddy roads from Philadelphia.

The Howes belonged to one of the great Whig families of
England. During the revolutionary agitation they had been
warm friends of America. Franklin had been their house guest
in England, and they knew him well, so there was considerable
talk about chess-playing and Miss Julia—sister of the Howes

—who appears to have been the crack chess-player of the family, and had beaten Franklin.

After awhile this pleasant conversation drifted around to the dispute between England and the colonies. Lord Howe said he felt for America as for a brother. It turned out, however, that his peace offer consisted of nothing but the power to grant pardons to those who would voluntarily lay down their arms. All would be forgiven and everything put back where it was; and Parliament had solemnly agreed to consider any grievance. Franklin said that nothing could be done unless Great Britain was ready to recognise the independence of the states. Lord Howe had no power to do that, and he said he was sorry that he had not arrived before Congress had committed itself to independence. The Commissioners said they were sorry, too. With these mutual condolences this immature peace conference came to an end.

Now the olive branch of peace was laid aside, and the Howe brothers picked up the club of war.

Washington and his army were still on Manhattan Island. The British problem had been further simplified by Howe's possession of Brooklyn. The obviously sensible move for the British would have been to surround Manhattan with their navy and land their army so as to cut off the American retreat.

Some of the American generals realised clearly the hazardous position of the army. Greene wrote Washington a long letter, advising "a general and speedy retreat." Charles Lee told Washington that he considered Manhattan wholly untenable.

Washington was of the opinion that the city should be destroyed if the patriots had to give it up. He wrote:

> If we should be obliged to abandon the town, ought it to stand as winter quarters for the enemy? . . . At present I dare say the enemy mean to preserve it if they

can. If Congress, therefore, should resolve upon the destruction of it, the resolution should be a profound
secret. . . .

The question of burning New York, upon being put up to
Congress, received a most decided negative. By no means.
The town must not be burned under any circumstances. In
the meantime, before the decision of Congress arrived, Washington had been gathering combustibles and storing them in
cellars.

Washington was still in a state of vacillation as to giving
up Manhattan when the British decided the question for him.
On September 15th, they landed at Kip's bay, near the present
East River end of Thirty-fourth Street. Washington, at his
headquarters in Harlem, heard the sound of cannon, and he
came galloping down the island with his staff trailing along
behind him.

Near the spot where the Public Library now stands, at the
corner of Fifth Avenue and Forty-second Street, he met a
stream of wild-eyed fugitives, breathless soldiers in flight, some
of whom had thrown away their arms.

This was one of the occasions when Washington lost his
temper. He lost his hat, too. An ungovernable rage took
possession of him. He struck at the fleeing soldiers with his
sword. He dropped his hat; he was something of a dishevelled
general.

There was a story current at the time that he was within a
hair's breadth of becoming a murderer, though this tale may
be apocryphal. An officer, they said, came panting along in
white-faced terror and recognised Washington. "Save yourself, General," the officer called out, "the redcoats are coming!"
The sight of this officer in craven flight so enraged Washington
that he snapped his pistol at him, and tried to run over him
with his horse. The terrified captain, or lieutenant—or whatever he was—hurried away more frightened than ever, and

probably mortified by this reception of his well-meant effort to do the general a kindness.

§ 5

The story of the battle of Long Island and the evacuation of New York, as I have told it here, is in strict accordance with the facts, though it is only fair to say that the conventional historians interpret it differently.

Fiske says (*American Revolution*, Vol. I, p. 143) that in the whole of Washington's career, "it would be hard to point out a single mistake." He says further (Vol. I, p. 216) that Washington knew it would be "well-nigh impossible" to hold New York, but that he thought it "the part of a good general to take this chance."

This assertion does not agree with what Washington himself said. Immediately after the evacuation of New York he wrote, "Till of late, I had no doubt in my own mind of defending this place." Previous to the disaster he does not reveal, in any of his letters, or reports, the fear that a defence would be "well-nigh impossible."

Fiske says (Vol. I, p. 211) that the "retreat [from Long Island] has always been regarded as one of the most brilliant incidents of Washington's career," but he makes no comment on the brand of military skill that sent Washington's army to Long Island in the first place.

Sydney George Fisher says (*The Struggle for American Independence*, Vol. I, p. 493) that Washington was moved by political considerations; that he thought the effect on the American people would be depressing if New York were abandoned without a blow.

Channing says (*History of the United States*, Vol. III, p. 229) that, "Military considerations, alone, would have dictated its abandonment [of New York], but other reasons demanded that the Americans should attempt to retain it." He does not say what the other reasons were. It is difficult to see what reason could have justified Washington in putting his entire army in a trap. The fact that the trap was not closed on him was due to Howe's timidity and slowness, and not to Washington's foresight.

The good angel that stood at Washington's side all his life had to work pretty hard during this Long Island-New York exploit to keep up the high standard of Washington luck.

§ 6

Five days after the British occupation a great fire occurred in New York, despite the resolution of Congress and the positive orders of Washington. I am confident that the conflagration was not instigated by Washington. It may have been accidental.

Eleven hundred houses, about one-fourth of the town, were destroyed. The burned district was east of Broadway and south of Wall Street. This quarter of the city was not rebuilt until after the war.

Acres of nude chimneys and bony walls stood among the warm, live houses. During the seven years of the British occupation these skeletons held out their stark hands. After awhile they attracted some feeble life of vagrants and wastrels. Hovels of board and tents of old sails grew up around the sterile chimneys as toadstools grow at the foot of dead trees. In these tattered homes lived a swarm of destitute loyalists and the rogues that war breeds.

New York was crowded with British soldiers. For seven years it was a city of litter and bad smells. At night armed patrols stamped through the dark streets. Through the closed windows of taverns came yellow blades of light and the dribblings of ribald songs. Under the windows of generals there was the discreet resonance of the footsteps of spies.

When he was forced out of New York Washington took

a position at White Plains, twenty miles to the north. There he was attacked on October 28th by Howe and defeated, but the engagement was a hot one, and the patriot troops retired after a strong resistance.

Washington's letters to Congress at this time are full of complaints. Their irascible temper and tone of pessimism seem echoes of his hot epistles to Governor Dinwiddie when he was commanding the troops on the Virginia border in 1758.

He wrote to the president of Congress that as long as he is permitted to inflict only thirty-nine lashes for any ordinary offence discipline might as well be abandoned. His idea of developing an *esprit de corps* appears to have been tied up exclusively with the mental picture of a whipping post. Napoleon, the greatest soldier in the world's history, depended on medals, promotions, and an imperial pat on the shoulder.

"The militia," Washington wrote, "instead of calling forth their utmost efforts to a brave and manly opposition . . . are dismayed, intractable and impatient to return. Great numbers of them have gone off. . . . " A body of New York militia, he says, refused to obey their colonel or do their duty because General Howe had promised the American people "peace, liberty and safety, and that is all they want."

§ 7

Although Washington had given up Manhattan he left still occupied an entrenched work on the northern part of the island. This position, called Fort Washington, was held by three thousand American troops. The failure to abandon it is unaccountable. It was isolated, remote from the rest of the patriot army, and its continued retention was of no value whatever. It was surrounded on three sides by ground held by the enemy; and on the fourth side was the Hudson River.

On November 16th the British attacked this outlying work in great force, and compelled its surrender, with its garrison

The gloom caused by this catastrophe was deep and wide. Washington had been defeated every time he had met the British army in the field.　But the surrender of Fort Washington was the greatest disaster of all, for there the patriots were behind breastworks on a height, and it had seemed to many that the stage was set for another Bunker Hill.

The reputation of Washington sank in public esteem. Thousands of people took the oath of allegiance.　Elkanah Watson says in his *Memoirs* that "we looked upon the contest as near its close, and considered ourselves a vanquished people."

Washington wrote:　"If every nerve is not strained to recruit the new army with all possible expedition, I think the game is pretty nearly up."

The pendulum of popular emotion always swings too far. The general depression was hysterical, and without an adequate basis in the facts of the case.　The country was, as yet, virtually untouched by the war.　It was full of riflemen, bad roads, and vast distances.

Howe turned his attention next to Philadelphia.　His subordinate, Lord Cornwallis, drove Washington slowly before him across the State of New Jersey until he reached Trenton on the Delaware River.　Washington crossed the river and hovered on its west bank, and Cornwallis took possession of the town.

The effective patriot force had got down to about thirty-five hundred men.　Washington wrote that "with a handful of men compared to the enemy's force, we have been pushed through the Jerseys without being able to make the smallest opposition and compelled to pass the Delaware."

In another letter he said:

> . . . between you and me I think our affairs are in a very bad condition; not so much from the apprehension of General Howe's army as from the defection of New York,

the Jerseys, and Pennsylvania. In short, the conduct of the Jerseys has been most infamous. Instead of turning out to defend their country and affording aid to our army, they are making their submission as fast they can.

Congress, thinking Philadelphia would be captured, fled to Baltimore with its secretaries and its papers.

All of a sudden the patriot gloom was turned to joy by Washington's attack on Trenton in December. Clear, bright, daring was this adventure.

There were fifteen hundred Hessians in Trenton. To picture the scene one must imagine a snow-covered village on one long street perpendicular to the river. The days are short, icicles drip from the roofs. The gray wood smoke rises from the chimneys, the surrounding hills are a white desolation. Before the town flows the dark Delaware, filled with floating ice. In the streets one hears the deep-throated German speech, the rattle of drums, and the sharp staccato of roll-calls. Across the river the rebel army lies somewhere among the hills.

Washington's plan was carefully calculated, and his instructions were given in secrecy to his officers. The attack was to be made on Christmas night. Washington himself, with one part of his army, was to cross the Delaware above the town, and another column was to cross below. They were to march toward each other, and catch the enemy between them.

The crossing below the town was never made; there was too much ice in the river. But Washington's column got across successfully. Upon reaching the New Jersey side Washington separated his force into two divisions. One under Greene took an inland route so as to reach the head of the village street. The other, under Sullivan, went along the river bank. It was a night of sleet and rain. Progress was painful, for the roads were in utter darkness and the snow was knee deep.

Just at dawn (December 26, 1776) the two columns reached

the village, and the Hessians awoke to find bullets flying through the icy streets. The fight was short and sharp. A thousand Hessians surrendered. The Americans lost only four men; two of them were frozen to death.

During the afternoon Washington recrossed with his prisoners and his entire force to the Pennsylvania side of the river.

Howe and his officers had about come to the conclusion that Washington's army was in the process of disintegration, and his success at Trenton startled them. Cornwallis, about to sail for England, was sent hurriedly back to Princeton to take command of the British force at that place.

On January 2nd, 1777, Cornwallis left Princeton with eight thousand men and moved toward Trenton, which had been occupied again by Washington. At that time the American army had grown in numbers by the arrival of the Pennsylvania militia to about five thousand men.

In the afternoon Washington sent out a regiment of riflemen to delay the advance of Cornwallis. This was done with such effect that the British did not arrive before Trenton until nightfall, and Cornwallis decided to postpone his attack until the next day.

During the night Washington sent his baggage down the river to Burlington. Then he left his camp fires burning, and he and his army withdrew from Cornwallis' front. They marched around his left and rear and started rapidly to Princeton. By daylight they had reached Princeton, which is ten miles from Trenton, and overwhelmingly routed three British regiments which were on their way to join Cornwallis.

Washington was now between the British force and its base at New Brunswick. His intention was to march rapidly to New Brunswick and seize Cornwallis' supplies, but his men were too exhausted to make the attempt, so he turned north while the dazed Cornwallis was hastening to Princeton. By easy marches Washington reached Morristown and went into winter quarters.

The short Trenton-Princeton campaign revealed a military mind of a high order. It was nothing less than masterly in conception and execution. In celerity, daring and vigour it reminds one of the astonishing 1862 campaign of Stonewall Jackson in the Shenandoah Valley.

There is some doubt, however, as to whose plan it was. Greene's friends claimed that it was his. Washington said to a committee of Congress, "I assure you, the other general officers, who assisted me in the plan and execution, have full as good a right to your encomiums as myself."

Alexander Hamilton was serving under Washington at this time, and in 1777 he became Washington's chief secretary, so it is reasonable to assume that he knew the inside history of the campaign. He delivered a funeral oration at Greene's death in 1789, in which he said, "As long as the enterprises of Trenton and Princeton shall be regarded as the dawning of that bright day which afterward broke forth with such independent lustre . . . so long ought the name of Greene to be revered by a grateful country."

CHAPTER XXI

WASHINGTON AND THE PLOTTERS

§ 1

CONGRESS, sitting among the stables and hitching posts of the village of Baltimore, plucked up courage and returned to Philadelphia. There the members amused themselves with sedate pleasures. They drank tea with sedate ladies in drawing rooms of damask, and with other ladies not so sedate in drawing rooms of rose. They read heavy political pamphlets and passed marked paragraphs from hand to hand. They visited the scientific laboratory of the great Rittenhouse, mused solemnly in the Philosophic Society, and examined, at the college, the wonderful orrery which showed mechanically the motions of the earth, moon and planets. Membership in the Congress was in itself a sort of education.

The sessions of the Continental Congress were secret. Closed doors and members pledged to silence. The British managed, however, to obtain a daily transcript of the proceedings, but they have never divulged the source of their information.

Congress meditated in Philadelphia while Washington, among the hills of northern New Jersey, tried to turn his militia into British grenadiers. Howe, with an army already drilled to a feather-edge, burrowed in New York and wondered what to do next. Since arriving in America he had acquired a mistress. Her name was Mrs. Loring, and her husband had been rewarded with the lucrative job of commissary-general.

Loring rhymes with snoring. A fact so pertinent did not escape the perception of the innumerable imitators of Alexander Pope in the British army. New York was littered with

324

poetic handbills—supposed to have been written by British officers—in which General Howe was depicted as snoring by the side of Mrs. Loring while the arch-rebels were still unhung.

It is not likely that General Howe snored all the time. There must have been hours, or moments, which he devoted to military duties. However, nothing was done for six months.

He could have put twenty thousand men on his transports in January and sent them to Virginia, where winter operations were possible. Before June he would have—or, at least, should have—conquered that state from tide-water to mountains. Then, with his army on the transports again, he would have been back in New York to meet Washington in a summer campaign. But he remained on Manhattan Island, doing nothing.

Washington commanded only three thousand men at Morristown, but he had a fine talent for military deception; it was the one department of strategy in which he was an adept. Around Morristown he scattered his men in farmhouses for miles, and kept changing them about. Even the country people, close at hand, thought he had a large army. He instructed the adjutant-general to prepare false returns, showing a force of twelve thousand men, and he contrived to have these papers fall into the hands of a British spy.

In midsummer (this was in 1777) an important movement began. General John Burgoyne was sent by the War Office to Canada for the purpose of invading the rebellious colonies by way of Lake Champlain, the Adirondack wilderness and the Hudson River. Howe was fully informed of this plan, and was expected to co-operate, though there is some doubt as to whether he had positive orders to advance up the Hudson to meet Burgoyne.

Washington thought the long-expected pinching operation had begun. . . . New England was to be pinched off. He held his army in readiness to start hot-foot after Howe as soon as the British began their march up the Hudson.

But that would have been too simple for Howe. He was a most complicated soldier. His mind evolved a piece of strategy which had all the clumsy ingenuity of a child's puzzle.

He loaded his transports with eighteen thousand troops, and let a story leak out that he intended to go to Boston by sea, to meet Burgoyne by crossing New England.

The Americans were not taken in by this yarn. They could not imagine why any general with an ounce of sense would want to go to Boston and fight his way across hostile New England when he could attain his objective by going up the Hudson River, with his war vessels keeping pace with him.

However, his army was on the transports. He kept his men in New York harbour, on crowded ships, under blistering decks, during the month of July. Burgoyne, was, in the meantime, cutting his way through the wilderness. Washington, hovering in New Jersey, could not believe that Howe would desert Burgoyne. He thought the elaborate embarkation was a ruse, and that the troops would be off their ships and up the river before long.

On the contrary, the vast white-sailed fleet swam out of the bay one pleasant summer morning and was soon lost to the view of Washington's spies.

Then came many days of guessing.

In about three weeks—almost long enough to have crossed the ocean—the armada turned up in the Chesapeake, and the shores of that bay were littered with the bodies of horses that had died on the stifling ships and had been thrown overboard.

At the head of Chesapeake Bay, where Howe landed, he found himself forty miles southwest of Philadelphia, and not much more than one hundred miles from his starting point on Staten Island. His base, which was New York, could be reached only by a long, circuitous sailing voyage. At Trenton, where he had been the year before, he was within thirty miles of Philadelphia and his base was only sixty miles distant.

Why he should have decided to start his attack on Philadelphia from the Chesapeake is a matter that cannot be explained to ordinary lay readers, as it belongs to the more occult or mystic branches of military science.

Now, with Howe located, Washington's army was on the move. It went through Philadelphia with drums beating, and the troops arranged to make an appearance of great numbers. The ragged soldiers had sprigs of green in their hats to give the ranks a touch of sprightliness. Some of the men were in British or Hessian uniforms, taken from prisoners, or stripped from the dead. The horde of women camp followers that habitually marched with the soldiers was sent to the rear, and through secluded streets; but many of the women disliked seclusion and poured after the regiments in a shrill, slatternly mob.

Some of these women were wives of the soldiers; but most of them were prostitutes who had a strange love for the rough life of camps. There was an uncanny streak of vampire in them. After battles they would rob the enemy's dead. Forty dead men of Burgoyne's army were buried in one pit, all absolutely naked; the women following the American army had stripped them of everything. At times Washington made efforts to clear the women out of the army, but without success. On the march from Valley Forge to Monmouth he gave strict orders that no women should be allowed to ride in the wagons . . . hoped to discourage them by making them walk in the blazing sun. They followed the army just the same; and one of them named Molly Pitcher distinguished herself on the Monmouth battlefield by serving a fieldpiece.

The pictures which we see in the newspapers of the Mexican army of to-day on its campaigns, give an idea of how Washington's army looked. Long, heavy rifles on the shoulders of boys, mere children; strange, hungry-looking men in moustaches and checked shirts; ragged, laughing desperadoes, frowsy and partly drunk; handsome farmer lads who had never seen a city, and who stared in wonder at the marvels of Philadelphia; grave patriots of middle age, men with bushy eyebrows and stooped shoulders, who walked as if they were stepping over furrows, speaking in gruff voices, hard as nails.

Washington and his staff, and all the generals and field officers, wore splendid uniforms and sat superbly on their sleek horses.

On one side of Washington rode a young man who was to play a considerable part in history, and whose name— somewhat shortened—was to be given to streets, towns, counties, flying squadrons and sleeping cars. He was a French volunteer who had recently arrived in America, and his name was Marie Paul Roche Yves Gilbert du Motier, Marquis de Lafayette.

He was a red-haired, blue-eyed boy of twenty, related to the great family of Noailles. Seen in profile, his head sloped backward in a sharp angle from the tip of his nose, making his forehead non-existent. Lavater, the physiognomist, said that men with heads shaped like that are fools. They may be, but if Lafayette was a fool, it must be said for him that he was a fool with high ideals, sincerity, honesty and courage.

Lafayette had become interested in the American cause through an incident so curiously fortuitous that it reminds one of the subtly conspiring Fate in Greek dramas. He was an officer in a French regiment at Metz when the Duke of Gloucester, brother of George III, was entertained at the officers' mess. This prince told the officers of the American revolt and of a Mr. Washington who was leading it. His wondrous tale shone in the mind of the nineteen-year-old Lafayette as the sun shines on the sea. There was nothing else in sight; the struggling people of America filled his horizon. The memories of his life had grown suddenly dim; feelings and ambitions were washed away. It was like a religious conversion. His father was dead, but he had a young wife and innumerable relatives. The family of Noailles listened to his story of

MARQUIS DE LA FAYETTE

From a painting by P. L. de Bucourt, Peintre du Roi. It shows
Lafayette as a Commander of the Paris National Guard in 1790.

America and his desire to come to our aid as people listen to the mumblings of a lunatic. When they found that he was determined to go to America they endeavoured to have him put in the Bastille. He got away eventually in a ship that he had purchased for the voyage.

When he arrived in the summer of 1777 Congress had become tired of foreign volunteer officers. Most of them were inefficient and roystering adventurers who wanted to be supported at American expense. The committee in charge of such things came pretty close to turning Lafayette away, but their attention was captivated after awhile by Lafayette's assertion that he did not want any pay, and that his desire was to serve as a volunteer in any capacity.

There was the flaming quality of a lighted match about Lafayette's bold face, red hair, blue eyes, and vivacious manner.

Through Philadelphia he rode by Washington's side, at the head of the shabby array of men.

At this time he could speak very little English, and his conversation with Washington was interpreted by a stripling officer of the staff who was also to be a prominent historical character and to have a lot of things, chiefly banks, named after him. This youth was Alexander Hamilton.

Howe was as much impressed by the importance of Philadelphia as the British War Office was by that of the Hudson River. In the back of his head there must have been an idea that the capture of "the rebel capital," as he called it, would bring the war to a close. He thought of war in terms of chess, a common delusion of shallow generals, whereas in fact the science of war is a science of circumstances.

In his sweeping perambulation down the coast and up the Chesapeake we may trace an attempt to develop a major offensive on the side of the board, to use a chess term.

He thought it would sound well in England—his taking of the rebel capital, for there they spoke of capitals in terms of London and Paris. So he marched toward Philadelphia and took it easily enough after he had defeated Washington at the battle of Brandywine, September 11, 1777.

§ 2

What of Burgoyne while this conquest of the capital was going on? We left him entangled in the northern woods; and, turning to him, we find him still more deeply entangled. His force of eight thousand men has leaked away to less than five thousand. His Indian auxiliaries have left him one by one, as the Indians always did when they found the game a losing one. He is opposed by General Gates with eighteen thousand men. Burgoyne is a bagged fox.

Let us grant that some mysterious reasoning made it necessary for Burgoyne to begin his invasion in a wilderness—then, even so, why did not Howe advance up the Hudson to meet him? Howe answered that question, in a way. He said that he considered the capture of Philadelphia more important.

Everybody was looking for glory. There would not have been much glory for Howe in helping Burgoyne, but he thought there would be a lot of glory in taking the rebel capital, the very centre of everything. He saw himself going down in history as the proud but generous conqueror of Philadelphia.

In the later days of October eager messengers, bursting with news, galloped along the colonial highways. As the brown streak of horse and rider flashed by the farmhouses and through the village streets, the man on horseback would shout that Burgoyne had surrendered. No use to ask more—the foam-speckled horse is already going over the hill—but the rider calls back that it is all of Burgoyne's army, and Burgoyne himself.

Electric . . . overwhelming. The King's badges, long kept hidden and awaiting a better day, were silently burned in thousands of homes. Certificates of patriotism, signed by tobacco-chewing committees, were brought out of old trunks, wiped off and neatly framed.

Burgoyne's surrender made a great impression in France, which at that time was sitting on the fence of indecision, unable to decide whether it would be better to join America openly and do England as much harm as possible, or to remain on the fence and keep out of trouble. The leading minds of France finally decided in favour of trouble; and Gates' victory over Burgoyne was the deciding factor.

Benjamin Franklin, then a man of seventy-two, was our representative in France. I am sure it would have been interesting to have seen him, in his sober brown suit, walking among the clipped laurels and rain-beaten roses at Versailles, with a crowd of bored courtiers listening to him explain what it was all about.

Since the autumn of 1776 the French government had been secretly supplying the Americans with arms and supplies. It is characteristic of the French that this contraband traffic should have been entrusted to Caron de Beaumarchais, a playwright and man of lyrics. Beaumarchais, a careerist of obscure parentage and great talent, had enlivened the gay court of Versailles with his satirical dramas. He was the Bernard Shaw of his time.

One day this dramatic person appeared in the rôle of businessman . . . a large exporting establishment . . . goods bought and sold all over the world . . . but principally with America . . . legitimate trade, of course . . . no guns, no ammunition, no supplies for troops. His admirers thought that this commercial venture was merely another proof of his versatility.

Under cover of Beaumarchais' pretended commerce the French government sent us cargoes of military necessities. By September, 1777, the value of the French supplies received by the Americans amounted to more than one million dollars.

In the spring of 1778 they sent us Baron von Steuben, a military technician of experience and skill. He was a Prussian officer who had served under Frederick the Great. The French selected a Prussian rather than a Frenchman partly with the idea of deceiving the English as to French intentions. It was arranged finally that he was to appear in America as a volunteer, and without any apparent connection with the French intrigue.

This secrecy was really unnecessary, for Steuben had hardly arrived at Valley Forge before the news of the French alliance with the United States came out. After that French aid was, of course, open and above board.

Washington and Congress knew of Steuben's official character. He was given a general's rank and appointed inspector of the army. His duties were those of a drillmaster. Major Ganoe in his *History of the United States Army*, says:

> Rising at three in the morning, smoking his pipe and drinking his cup of coffee, Steuben proceeded to the parade ground, where he personally taught drill movements. He would illustrate the manual of arms by using the musket in his own hands. Such a democratic demonstration shocked the higher officers, who were still imbued with the British idea of aristocratic aloofness. . . . Steuben forced the discovery that in a country where caste is obnoxious an officer must gain results by more direct means.

Love of liberty was not Steuben's motive in coming to America. He was not a volunteer in the same sense as Lafayette. Steuben was simply a hired soldier of narrow mind and mediocre ability, though he was a good tactician. At first he did not like us, but after a while he grew to like us a lot; so much, indeed, that he remained here after the war and became an American citizen.

His dream was to live in a free-and-easy baronial style, surrounded by friends and dogs. In the 1780's he bought a house in the country—on Manhattan Island—called "Louvre," and resided there in the odour of whiskey and cigars.

He gave food and drink to all who came. He was eaten out of house and home, got in debt, was threatened with jail, but was rescued by his late comrades-in-arms. For years Steuben's financial entanglements were among the well-known topics of the time.

§ 3

Late in 1777, the British publicity department brought out its masterpiece of propaganda. This achievement was in the form of a volume made up of letters supposed to have been written by Washington.

In these epistles, most of which were addressed to his wife or to his brothers, Washington admitted that the war was a mistake. He deplored his part in it, wished he was out of it, and declared that, after all, British rule was better than the rule of the mob.

The preface sets forth circumstantially how the letters were obtained. It seems that Washington's body servant, a negro named Billy Lee, was left behind in the retreat of the army across New Jersey because he was too sick to be moved. The British captured him, the preface says, and found in his possession a package of drafts of letters written by Washington.

All the letters were forgeries from beginning to end. They had been written, evidently, by some one who was well acquainted with Washington and his affairs; there is a deceptive air of verity about them. In them he called his wife Patsy, which was his intimate nickname for her. The style of the epistles is conceived in Washington's heavy, rolling manner.

The facts are that Billy Lee was never captured at any time, and that he never had any letters of his master in his keeping. Why should he have had charge of correspondence, when Washington was surrounded by a swarm of confidential secretaries?

It is also significant that the London publisher could not

produce a single letter in Washington's handwriting; or in anybody else's handwriting.

Many people believed at the time that the letters were genuine; and it is entirely probable that there are still people who believe in them, despite the flimsiness of their origin.

Washington thought these forgeries were the work of John Randolph, a Tory refugee in London. Randolph, who was a member of the Virginia family of that name, had taken the British side. He knew George and Martha very well, and had been a guest at Mount Vernon.

These letters were spurious; but on another occasion a genuine letter written to Washington by Benjamin Harrison was intercepted and published by the British.

Benjamin Harrison was a friend of Washington of many years' standing. A member of Congress, he was put on a committee which dawdled about the army for awhile. During this jaunt he wrote Washington a letter which contained the following paragraph:

> As I was in the pleasing task of writing to you, a little noise occasioned me to turn my head around, and who should appear but pretty little Kate, the washer-woman's daughter over the way, clean, trim and as rosy as the morning. I snatched the golden, glorious opportunity, and but for the cursed antidote to love, Sukey, I had fitted her for my general against his return. We were obliged to part, but not till we had contrived to meet again; if she keeps the appointment, I shall relish a week's longer stay.

The enemy captured Harrison's messenger and printed the letter. Evil minds seized upon this dry morsel and tried to twist it into evidence that the Father of Our Country led an immoral life. It was made the basis of a rather obscene Tory farce called *The Battle of Brooklyn*.

The British and Tories naturally put the worst possible construction on this epistle. but if we analyse it coolly and carefully we see that it contains no evidence of Washington's immorality.

Ah, yes, one may say, but does not the letter make a fatal admission? On Harrison's part it does. That I grant. It shows that he was not above an affair with a washer-woman's daughter. I am not defending Harrison, although he was a signer of the Declaration of Independence, the father of one president and the great-grandfather of another.

But where is Washington implicated?

Nowhere.

Harrison merely says that if he had had time he would have fitted the girl "for my general against his return." Fitted her for what? Why, for doing the laundry, of course. It seems perfectly obvious. Unfortunately he ran two unrelated ideas together—his philandering and the week's wash—so that people not equipped with analytical minds got a wrong impression.

§ 4

In December, 1777, Washington's army went into winter quarters at Valley Forge, about twenty-two miles from Philadelphia. He had nine thousand men, but before the winter was over three thousand of them had deserted to the British. The deserters came into Philadelphia half-naked, some with no clothing but tattered blankets wrapped around them. So many men were sick as the result of privation, and so many were without coats, blankets, hats or shoes, that one wonders how the army held together at all.

The country seemed to have abandoned Washington and his army. At York, where Congress was in session, his reputation had sunk among the legislators until his friends could keep him in command only by the barest majority.

The opposition to Washington in Congress was led by John Adams, who had nominated him for commander-in-chief, and James Lovell, a waspish delegate from Massachusetts, who appears to have been constitutionally against everybody and everything. But with the opposition we find Washington's old friend, Richard Henry Lee, who said that "Gates was needed to procure the indispensable changes in our army."

Jonathan Trumbull ("Brother Jonathan") declared that "a much exalted character should make way for a *general*." Timothy Pickering, one of the generals of the army, criticised Washington cautiously to Greene and other officers, and managed to convey the impression that he considered Washington's military capacity of a low order. Greene, admired by Washington, and a confidant of the commander-in-chief, admitted that Washington lacked decision. As for himself, he said, "I decide in a moment." This remark had reference to Washington's habit of consulting every general in sight before making a move.

Jonathan D. Sargent, another opponent of Washington, wrote:

Thousands of Lives & Millions of property are yearly sacrificed to the Insufficiency of our Commander-in-chief —Two Battles he has lost for us by two such Blunders as might have disgraced a soldier of three months standing. . . . Such Feebleness, and want of authority, such confusion and Want of Discipline, such Waste. . . .

Gates was the military idol of the day. He had actually compelled the surrender of an entire British army, and that was a pedestal large enough to sustain a popular hero. The fact that Gates had had four times as many men as Burgoyne was not taken into account; nor was the fact that the British at Saratoga were out of food and hopelessly lost in the woods. They would have surrendered if Gates had been in China.

A small-souled man was General Gates, with a head that could be easily turned by flattery. Far-flung ambitions crowded into his mind; he saw himself superseding Washington. With him, as with all inconsequential men, self-assertion was a synonym for arrogance. He began to send his reports direct to Congress, instead of to Washington, his superior officer.

Among the foreign volunteer officers serving in the patriot army at that time was an Irish-Frenchman named Thomas Conway. An Irishman by birth, he had been brought up in France, and had become a colonel in the French army. He had offered his services to Silas Deane, one of the American envoys in Paris, and Deane was so favourably impressed that he promised Conway a position as brigadier-general. Deane had no authority either from Washington or from Congress to make such a promise; nevertheless, that is what he did, and Conway appeared in America. He was a disagreeable, know-it-all person, with a contempt for the American army, and a talent for causing trouble.

Congress made him a brigadier-general, to the great dissatisfaction of a long line of American colonels. But Conway was not satisfied with that; he declared that the welfare of the United States required that he be made a major-general. Bristling with complaint, he sent carping letters right and left. Washington estimated him correctly as an irresponsible adventurer and troublemaker, and received him coldly.

Then Conway entered the Gates party with enthusiasm and eventually wrecked whatever chance Gates may have had. But for the moment they were on the crest of the wave. The Board of War was re-organised, and Congress put Gates at its head, which made him—in a sense—superior to Washington. Conway was made inspector-general of the army.

The Gates faction was in the saddle . . . a little unsecurely, but in the saddle, just the same. They ruined their position by continuing to plot. Dr. Benjamin Rush, a prominent person whose mouth dripped with the sugar of admiration for Washington, took his pen treacherously in hand to write a string of anonymous letters in which he expressed an opinion of the great man that was far from sugary.

One of the letters was sent to Patrick Henry, then governor

of Virginia. The writer declared that "the people of America have been guilty of idolatry by making a man their God. . . . " He said something about "Baal and his worshippers," and implied that Washington was Baal. The God of heaven, he went on, would not let America succeed until the people had put an end to this terrible state of affairs.

Patrick Henry forwarded this silly nameless letter to Washington, who recognised Dr. Rush's handwriting; but Washington did not think the incident worthy of comment.

Conway, too, had the deadly itch of literary composition. He wrote a laudatory epistle to Gates, which that general evidently read to his military family. Major Wilkinson, a member of Gates' staff, got drunk and said that Conway had written: "Heaven has been determined to save your country, or a weak general and bad counsellors would have ruined it." The story reached Washington, who thereupon wrote the words I have quoted above to Conway, merely introducing them with a "Sir," and concluding with "I am your humble servant."

Consternation. Conway sought Washington and insisted that the quotation was not correct. Gates got wind of the incident and turned it around in his mind until he thought he saw a way to throw the odium of the affair on Washington. He wrote a letter to Washington, and another to Congress, in which he hinted that Hamilton had broken open his desk and had made a copy of the letter. The intention behind this rigmarole was, of course, to implicate Washington. To Gates' letter Washington replied that his information had not come from Hamilton.

Conway now got hold of his original letter and wrote to Washington that the quotation was altogether incorrect, but he did not supply the correct wording. He showed the letter rather hurriedly to Henry Laurens, president of Congress . . . Conway holding one corner of the written sheet, while Laurens held the other. Laurens said he remembered the following words: "What a pity there is but one Gates! But the more

I see of this army, the less I think it fit for general action under its actual chiefs and actual discipline."

Then Wilkinson, frightened at his own indiscretion, told Gates that it was not he who had revealed the contents of the letter. Pretty soon Gates found out that Wilkinson was a liar, and spoke to him so severely that Wilkinson challenged his commander to a duel. On the morning set for the duel Gates sought out Wilkinson and burst into tears (according to Wilkinson) and said that he had as lief shoot his own son as Wilkinson. No duel . . . reconciliation for the moment. Not long afterward, however, Wilkinson resigned his position as secretary of the Board of War and wrote to Congress that he had detected General Gates in "acts of treachery and falsehood."

By that time all this mess—which historians call the Conway Cabal—had become ridiculous, and Washington's imperturbable conduct shone by contrast. Gates was ordered back to the army by Congress, and Conway was placed in command of the insignificant post of Albany. From his obscure corner Conway wrote an impertinent letter of resignation to Congress, and his resignation was immediately accepted. It appears that he did not intend really to resign, so he rushed down to Congress and attempted to get a reinstatement but it was too late.

The next thing that happened was that Conway, because of his continued abuse of Washington, had to fight a duel with General Cadwallader. "I have stopped the damned rascal's lying tongue, at any rate," Cadwallader said, as he saw Conway lying on the ground with the blood gushing from his mouth.

Conway recovered and disappeared from our history, but while he was in anticipation of death he wrote to Washington an humble letter of apology.

In this episode one may see how great issues become distorted. Washington's management of affairs was certainly open to criticism, but his critics became so enmeshed in anonymous letters and lies and floods of tears and denials that everything they said increased Washington's reputation and the question of his fitness simply petered out.

It is a striking illustration of Washington's generosity that he never allowed the memory of this plot against himself to interfere in his relations in after years to the men who had taken part in it. When he became President he appointed some of them to important offices.

§ 5

Howe's failure to smash the American army at Valley Forge furnishes an interesting subject for historical speculation. The whole destitute outfit could have been surrounded and driven like a flock of captive sheep into Philadelphia. Howe had twenty thousand well-clothed and well-fed troops. Twenty miles away Washington's army of about three thousand effectives shivered on a wintry hillside.

Sydney George Fisher believes that it was Howe's settled policy to hold towns and fortified positions until the Revolution had worn itself out. Even so, it seems that the wearing-out process would have been accelerated by the capture of Washington's army.

Howe himself wrote in April, 1778, that although the enemy's force was small, "the want of green forage does not yet permit me to take the field. . . ."

A ridiculous excuse . . . he had almost no cavalry, and very little need of green forage.

My own impression is that General Howe was suffering from a neurosis which was not understood at that time, but which is called shell shock to-day. I think that he never recovered from the deadly fire of Bunker Hill. He went up at the head of the troops, his staff was shot down to a man, and he was splashed with blood. At the end of the battle he seemed on the point of collapse. His reluctance to make frontal attacks on American positions begins from that date. Thereafter we observe him circling about the Americans, feeling them gingerly, taking sea voyages, retreating, standing still—doing anything, in fact, to avoid grappling with them.

During that winter in Philadelphia Venus cuddled in the lap of Mars. The mistresses of the British officers constituted a social hierarchy. They dressed in costumes which were feminine replicas of the uniforms of their *chèrs amis*. Patriot spies reported that the whole population appeared to be loyalist. Most of the wealthy people of the town remained there during the British occupation and entertained the officers with balls, routs, dinners and charades. It is amusing to watch their change of sentiment when the British left the place. Nearly all of them became patriots at once.

The mistresses dominated society, and Mrs. Loring was the greatest of the mistresses. Gentlemen preferred blondes. Mrs. Loring's delicate blondeness aroused universal admiration.

The resources of the British empire poured into Philadelphia; the town was full of money, gamblers and unashamed grafters. Gambling tables were set up in fashionable houses. A Hessian officer who ran a gaming establishment enriched himself and ruined a score of young Englishmen. Mrs. Loring set the pace in feminine gambling. She lost three hundred guineas in one evening as nonchalantly as you please.

The connection between war and gambling, and between gambling and sexual vice, are themes which belong to the natural history of man. Some day an inquiring Buffon will explore this river of emotion to its source, and make the subject clear to us.

§ 6

We Americans cannot conceive a war without a moral background. Our purposes are invariably moral. Our history is a moral treatise. We despoiled Mexico of her territory for moral reasons; our motives in holding Haiti against the wishes of its citizens are moral; we are still busy in giving the Filipinos a set of American morals. It may now be accepted as a principle that any weak, saddle-coloured nation that happens to be situated near us, and also happens to possess a lot of mahogany, or hemp, or cocoa nuts, or gold mines, had better look out. We have our moral eye on such people, and are likely to introduce American morality at any moment. But if they have no mahogany, nor hemp, nor cocoanuts, nor gold mines, they may stew in their own immorality, so far as we care.

Our wars have always been conducted by men of piety; or, at least, by men whose motives were highly moral.

The British have got beyond all that. They have had so many wars that it would drive a historian into insanity to provide a moral issue for half of them, so they stopped trying long before the American Revolution.

We have not failed to give the Revolution a moral tone; and a myth of exceptional vitality depicts Washington as engaged in prayer in the woods at Valley Forge.

The origin of this legend is interesting. It began with a Quaker named Isaac Potts. He said that Washington lived in his house at Valley Forge, and that one day while he (Potts) was strolling over the landscape he heard a supplicating voice in a little dale close at hand. Slipping up unperceived, Potts said that he saw General Washington kneeling on the ground, with his horse tied to a near-by tree. The General's hands were clasped, and he was praying loudly for the Lord's help. He did not ask for Divine aid in any vague, indefinite way, according to Potts, but made it perfectly clear to the Divine Understanding that he wanted God's assistance for the special purpose of giving the British a good beating.

To any one who knows Washington the idea of this two-fisted fighting man going about bellowing in the woods is grotesque.

In direct opposition to the pious Valley Forge legend is the fact that Washington was never known to pray in church; that his own pastor said Washington never knelt when there were prayers; that he never took communion, even in the church where he was a member.

Moreover, he did not live in Isaac Potts' house at Valley Forge. The stone house in which he lived belonged to Mrs. Deborah Hewes, and the headquarters account books show that the rent was paid to Mrs. Hewes.

There is much doubt as to whether Potts lived at Valley Forge at all while the army was there. There is no proof that he ever saw Washington there or anywhere else.

This prayer story did not appear until years after the Revolution. It was part of the pietistic attempt to prove that Washington was a deeply religious man. This effort was beset with difficulties, as the religionists had to manufacture all the evidence to sustain their case. They have done very well at it, considering the circumstances. The Valley Forge yarn is pretty crude; nevertheless, it has managed to get itself on several bronze tablets.

There is also a literary composition known as "Washington's Prayer" which has been successful, though where or when this prayer was said, or written, by Washington, is not clear. On every anniversary of Washington's birthday the "Prayer" appears in innumerable newspapers. Experience has shown that, in lying, it is best to avoid all circumstantial details. The anonymous author of "Washington's Prayer" has followed that principle. The "Prayer" comes to us as devoid of pedigree as the Dartmoor curse.

§ 7

By one means or another, Washington kept himself in fairly good spirits during the harsh Valley Forge winter. We find him entertaining companies of gentlemen and their wives at headquarters, in spite of the poor food. He wrote irascibly that he had no wine or brandy, but only "vile whiskey" to give his guests.

Martha Washington arrived in February. She wrote that the officers and men were "chiefly in Hutts, which they say is tolerably comfortable; the army are as healthy as can be well expected in general. The General's apartment is very small; he has had a log cabin built to dine in, which has made our quarters much more tolerable than they were at first."

In May, 1778, food had become plentiful, the snow had melted, sunshine flooded the land, and the officers decided to give a play. Washington thought it a splendid idea. He may have suggested the piece, which was Addison's *Cato*, as he had taken a part in that play once, long ago, with Mrs. Sally Fairfax.

The amateur performance was well received. Colonel William Bradford wrote to his daughter, "The theatre is opened. Last Monday *Cato* was performed before a very numerous and splendid audience. His Excellency and Lady, Lord Stirling, the Countess and Lady, and Mrs. Greene were part of the assembly. The scenery was in taste, and the performance admirable."

The kill-joys of Congress, still saturated with the more exasperating of the Puritan virtues, leaped into their armour of indignation and astonishment. To think that patriotic officers, entrusted with the defence of their country, and the freedom of a race, should fall so deep in dissolute habits as to give a play on the stage! The army was indeed lost to shame.

Chewing over these sober reflections, Congress passed a resolution which began with, "Whereas, true religion and good morals are the only solid foundations of public liberty and happiness." The import of the resolution was that "any person, holding an office under the United States, who shall attend a theatrical performance, shall be dismissed from the service."

The president of Congress sent an official copy of the resolution to Washington. That ended the amateur performances of officers, and it ended Washington's theatre-going until after the war.

CHAPTER XXII

THE RIDDLE OF CHARLES LEE

§ 1

ONE of the most disheartening features of a great career
is the responsibility it implies. Proficiency is expected of all
celebrated persons, from baseball players to Presidents. The
soggy weight of achievement rests on the world. Honours are
nailed to action as a sign is nailed to a house; and very few are
able to pull out the nails. There is no fun left except in being
obscure. Great men are invariably men of gloom. Naturally
enough . . . they have so much on their minds.

It was not so in the happy eighteenth century; then one
might be great and joyous at the same time. One was not
expected to do, but merely to be. In England men whose
minds had never been saddened by thought rose to high eminence. A small group of English county families conducted the
affairs of England and of the Empire. Any member of these
families was an eminent person, and considered capable of
carrying on large affairs.

Sir William Howe was a second cousin of George III. The
first Hanoverian King of England had a frumpy, bread-and-
butter mistress who bore the queer name of Kilmansegge, and
was a baroness. Her daughter, by George I, was the mother
of General Howe; who was, therefore, a great general by birth.
Destiny took special pains with him. The steps to renown
were made wide and easy for his benefit.

His lamentable oversight in failing to go to Burgoyne's aid
put a snarl in Destiny's kindly programme, for Burgoyne also
belonged to England's upper class, and his friends became

peevish when he was made the scapegoat of the American fiasco.
The result was a quarrel in the inner circle of Britain's aristocracy, and the resignation of Howe.

News came, in the spring of 1778, that his resignation had
been finally accepted. His place was to be taken by General
Sir Henry Clinton, who was then in command of the New
York garrison.

Before Howe had departed, there was word of a French
expedition on the sea, bound for America. The British were
greatly perturbed. Clinton decided to evacuate Philadelphia,
as he was convinced that the French fleet would blockade the
mouth of the Delaware and turn the pleasant town of Philadelphia into a nest of disagreeable necessities.

Clinton's ideas were very different from those of Howe.
He was a hard, callous, aggressive soldier who understood war
in its most brutal aspect. His plan was to disregard Washington's army, and to conquer the country piecemeal by towns
and districts. It was to be a war of harassment and extermina-
tion. America was to be turned into another Ireland . . .
indiscriminate hangings, patriots in jail, loyalist governments
set up and supported by British bayonets.

In these conceptions Clinton was upheld not only by the British ministry, but also by the majority of the English people.
Moral indignation at our alliance with France—hereditary
enemy of the English race—glowed in the British soul. Even
our old friend William Pitt, Earl of Chatham, turned his back
on us. On April 7, 1778, he appeared in the House of Lords
to make the last and most dramatic speech of his life. He
was a dying man; and his white face and blazing eyes empha-
sised his words as he spoke against the Americans and the
French.

Around this time we find George III discussing Divine Provi-
dence, and assuring people that God was on the side of the
English. He wrote to his ministers of American duplicity and
English rectitude, and drew up plans for town-burning and the

ravaging of the American coast. He hoped that the Indians would be employed in larger numbers than ever to bring the colonies back to a feeling of their own iniquity.

In the matter of Indian auxiliaries we were no better than the British, though they had more success in employing savages than we had. In May, 1776, Congress authorised General Schuyler to engage two thousand Indians; and in July of that year Washington tried to get five or six hundred Indians for his army. The British got the pick of the savages, as they were able to give them larger rewards . . . more whiskey, blankets, guns and food.

Burgoyne had a large number of Indians with his army. He made speeches to them in which he told them that they were engaged in a civilised war, that they must not take scalps or torture prisoners. It was predicted by experienced Indian connoisseurs who were with Burgoyne that the Indians would not remain long in such a rarefied ethical atmosphere; and these prophets were right. When Burgoyne surrendered there were only twenty-odd braves still with him, and very likely these stayed because they had no home, nor anywhere else to go.

The humane instincts of Burgoyne were not shared by all the British generals. In July, 1778, a force of loyalists and Iroquois was organised to devastate the frontier of New York and Pennsylvania. The raid on these settlements, known as the Wyoming Valley Massacres, was one of the most atrocious in the records of savage warfare. Men, women and children were killed without distinction, and the country was laid waste. One of the incidents of the raid was the tomahawking of a large number of prisoners by a female chief named Queen Esther. It seems that this personage turned the butchery into a formal affair. The prisoners were ranged in a circle and the queen went around among them like the Queen of England at a garden party. After chatting awhile with a prisoner—the conversation was necessarily brief—she would raise her tomahawk and split the prisoner's skull, and pass on to the next person.

At that time the Continental army was too weak to send any help to the settlements; but in 1779, the following year, Washington sent General Sullivan with three thousand men to fight the Iroquois.

Sullivan not only defeated the Six Nations (the Iroquois), but destroyed every trace of their primitive civilisation. Their fruit trees were cut down, their crops ruined, their houses burned; and the whole tribe was driven, virtually naked, into the woods. They made their way to the British fort at Niagara, where they subsisted on British charity for the winter. Later, the small remnant of the Iroquois was taken to Canada . . . and thus this great Indian nation disappears from our history.

§ 2

On the eighteenth of June, 1778, Clinton gave up Philadelphia and began his march across New Jersey to New York. He would have gone by sea but for fear that he might encounter the French fleet.

His army had been considerably reduced by the sending of troops to the British West Indies to protect the islands. He had eleven thousand men, and there were four thousand in New York. The British also held Newport, where there was a garrison of several regiments.

The British baggage train—twelve miles of wagons and carriages filled with food, plunder and mistresses—was sent ahead of the army. It floundered slowly through the loose sand of the New Jersey pine barrens, holding back the troops and, by blocking the road in front, creating a tactical situation of great peril.

The weather was the hottest in the memory of the oldest inhabitant. The army was like a penitential procession in the quivering noon of a desert. Overhead the glowing sun lingered for incredible hours at its stabbing torture. At last would come the miracle of night and the cool white stars, to be followed by another suffering day. Parallel to the route of this crawling army ran the road followed by the Americans. They, too, were as men in a furnace. As the roads converged they found redcoated soldiers lying dead, overcome by sunstroke, their heavy loads still on their backs, their eyes staring upward at the keen blue of the sky.

During the entire war the American military operations were without any definite, coherent plan. The country was never organised to resistance as a unit. Washington never had any clear-cut scheme of campaign. The plans originated with the British, and Washington's idea was simply to prevent the British from doing whatever they tried to do. So when Clinton left Philadelphia Washington started after him.

Washington's army had left Valley Forge and started in pursuit on the same day that Clinton abandoned Philadelphia. The American force was then about as large as that of the British—ten or twelve thousand men. It had been increased by the addition of militiamen who had gone home for the winter. The army contracted and expanded in this way throughout the war. The American soldier had a natural tendency to go about his business when there was no fighting to be done.

On June 27th the head of the American column had caught up with the British rearguard at Monmouth. When night fell the advance troops had reached a position where they half encircled the rear of the British column.

The Battle of Monmouth, which occurred the next day, was the most confused engagement of the Revolutionary War. The commentaries on it, and the disputes about it that have got into print, fill a three-foot bookshelf.

Both sides seem to have anticipated nothing more than a rearguard action. It was reasoned by the Americans that Clinton would get away if he could, so their expectation was to attack and defeat the rearguard; and to cut it off, if possible.

Washington had promised Lafayette that he should lead the attack. The Marquis was sent forward with four thousand men, and instructed to advance against the British at dawn the next morning.

But Lafayette was not to have this post of honour, after all. General Charles Lee claimed that, as senior major-general, he ought to be in the centre of events. As this assertion was reasonable, and in accordance with accepted military practice, Washington finally agreed to this change in plan, with Lafayette's consent.

General Lee had just returned to the army after having spent a year and four months in New York as a prisoner of war. He had been captured in December, 1776, while eating his breakfast in a New Jersey farmhouse outside his own lines, and had been carried into New York in his nightcap and dressing gown. He had been exchanged about a month before the army had left Valley Forge, and had resumed his rank as Washington's second in command.

On the morning of June 28th the American troops under Lee began a vigorous attack on the British rearguard. Lafayette accompanied Lee as a volunteer officer.

As Lee's attack proceeded he observed that the British kept increasing in number. This observation was confirmed by officers who came riding back from the front to say that the main body of Clinton's army was coming up.

Washington, with the bulk of the American army, was five miles in the rear.

Up to this point everything in the record is clear. The contradiction in evidence begins here. Some said—Lafayette among them—that Lee had his troops make a shameful and cowardly retreat. Others who were on the spot declared that the retreat was orderly enough—except such irregularity as was the result of the excessive heat. Lee himself asserted that the movement was not a retreat at all, but merely the shifting of the troops to a new and better position.

He said that as he had just been put in command of this advance division he did not know his subordinate officers by

name or appearance; and that the retreat began without his
knowledge; that some brigadier-general ordered it.   He declared, further, that he saw the necessity of the retirement soon
after it began, and gave instructions to bring off the troops
in an orderly manner.   He sent officers to the rear to select a
position on more advantageous ground.

Clinton's reports, published after the war, show that the
whole British army was about to fall on Lee's four thousand
men.   It seems in the light of this fact that the retirement of
his force was a most necessary thing to do.   At Lee's back
there was a morass which could be crossed only by a road on
a high embankment.   It was a ticklish place for an inferior
force.

Washington arrived in haste as Lee was getting his troops
into the new position.   He had met stragglers and frightened
men on the road, and he had heard from these groups that a
retreat had been ordered.   It seems clear that Washington
did not understand the situation, and was too much annoyed
and too hot to find out what it was.   "My God! General Lee,"
he shouted, "what are you about?"

Lee attempted to explain, but Washington was in such a
rage that his explanation was probably never heard.   Two
red-faced men trying to talk, both at the same time.   The day
was torrid, the sunshine felt like hot lard, the troops were
pouring by, the bullets were zipping overhead . . . it was no
time for logic and diagrams.   Lafayette sat on his horse near
by, a Mona Lisa smile on his face.

The question as to whether Washington swore on this occasion has stirred the American nation for five generations.   I
am altogether unable to appreciate the importance of this
question; in my opinion it does not make a bit of difference
one way or the other.   But, at the same time, I realise that I
cannot evade the issue by being so haughty about it.   Biographers have responsibilities.

Washington may have sworn in his heated interview with

Lee, but it does not appear in the evidence; and I think it a very doubtful legend. The story of his swearing at Monmouth rests on the unofficial testimony of people given years after the occurrence, and in the form of loose reminiscences.

Lafayette said that Washington called Lee a "damned poltroon," but I doubt it. *Poltroon* is a Frenchified word that Washington did not use. He preferred "coward."

In the whole mass of testimony produced at the Lee court-martial there is not one word about swearing. Much of this testimony was given by friends of Lee, and Lee himself presented a defence in writing, in which he said that he endeavoured to reproduce Washington's words literally. At the court-martial he was Washington's mortal enemy, and it seems that if Washington had given him a good cursing—which would have been a breach of military courtesy—Lee would have set down something about it in his paper.

There is no doubt that Washington did swear at times, but he was not an habitual user of oaths. He did not swear much, and he did not like to hear others swear at all. At intervals he issued orders against the use of profanity in the army. That means nothing, so far as his own capacity is concerned, for we find him also issuing stringent orders against card-playing for money, when he was in fact an inveterate card-player for small sums himself.

When he did swear his favourite expletive was a plain *by God*. He did not go in often, if ever, for the florid *goddam* type of swearing; but, on the other hand, he never allowed himself to utter such childish, evasive futilities as "By Godfrey," which was the customary big swear word of Theodore Roosevelt.

Evidently he repented quickly his loss of temper at Monmouth, for shortly after his altercation with Lee he turned to that general, who was still hanging around, swollen with injured pride, and mildly directed him to take command of the rallied troops.

Lee behaved with courage and ability in this post. The troops under his command held their ground until late in the afternoon, when Washington ordered them out to rest.

The battle was a draw. Clinton's action in taking the offensive was a surprise to the Americans, and before they could adjust themselves to this situation the day was nearly over.

During the night Clinton got his troops away, and they reached Sandy Hook and the protection of the fleet without any more fighting.

Washington never needed cavalry more than he needed it that day. With a regiment of horse sweeping around the British flank and appearing in front of the twelve-mile string of wagons, think what would have happened. The picture stirs the fighting heart . . . wrecked and burned wagons . . . teamsters shot dead in the road . . . the column turned back on itself . . . a chaos of piled-up débris and tangled men and horses for miles.

Clinton's army would have been caught in an *impasse;* soldiers cannot climb over a dozen miles of wreckage.

An extraordinary feature of this battle was the large number of spectators who went about among the troops. They added much to the confusion. Some of them were dignitaries of the neighbourhood. They took it on themselves to give orders, and to direct troops here and there.

§ 3

Lee could not let well enough alone. On the day after the battle he sent Washington a letter in which he demanded an apology or its equivalent. He declared that Washington had made use of "very singular expressions" in addressing him at Monmouth, and he hinted that the commander-in-chief was influenced by "dirty ear-wigs who will forever insinuate themselves near persons high in office." It is generally supposed that he meant Hamilton and Lafayette.

If he had not written this letter, it appears probable that the whole affair would have been dropped. Washington wrote in reply:

> Sir: I received your letter, expressed, as I conceive, in terms highly improper. I am not conscious of making use of any very singular expressions at the time of meeting you, as you intimate. What I recollect to have said was dictated by duty and warranted by the occasion. As soon as circumstances will permit, you shall have an opportunity of justifying yourself to the army, to Congress, to America, and to the world in general; or of convincing them that you were guilty of a breach of orders, and of misbehaviour before the enemy on the 28th instant, in not attacking them as you had been directed, and in making an unnecessary, disorderly and shameful retreat.

Lee liked to write sharp, biting letters. To that kind of man a downright, sarcastic letter is equal to a victory . . . especially if it has one or two neatly turned phrases. Again he wrote to Washington, declared that he welcomed an inquiry into the respective merits of himself and the commander-in-chief, and said, "I trust that temporary power of office and the tinsel dignity attending it will not be able, by all the mists they can raise, to obfuscate the bright rays of truth."

Washington had him put under arrest immediately, and preferred charges against him. He was tried by court-martial for disobedience of orders at Monmouth, misbehaviour before the enemy, and disrespect to the commander-in-chief.

The weight of expert opinion was that he was guilty only of disrespect to Washington, but he made a political issue of the incident and discussed Washington's failings as a soldier in public while the trial was going on. In short, his conduct was defiant and silly. The court felt, evidently, that it had to convict him on all three charges . . . which it did. Then it had a stroke of remorse, and lightened his sentence to only one year's suspension from the army.

Lee had never been more than a lieutenant-colonel in the British army, but he had so impressed the Continental Congress that a Virginia plantation worth thirty thousand dollars had been given him. At the time of his appointment Washington wrote:

> He [Charles Lee] is the first officer, in military knowledge and experience, we have in the whole army. He is zealously attached to the cause, honest and well-meaning, but rather fickle and violent, I fear, in his temper. However, as he possesses an uncommon share of good sense and spirit, I congratulate my countrymen upon his appointment. . . .

After his court-martial he retired to his estate, and never made an attempt to re-enter the army.

It was just as well for Lee that the court-martial was not acquainted with a piece of work that he did while he was a prisoner of war in New York. As a prisoner he seems to have had a pretty good time in New York with his old associates of the British service. This good fellowship among old comrades led him one day to display his vanity by writing out a plan for the conquest of America. He knew precisely how to go about it; knew all the weaknesses of the American army—for was he not one of their major-generals? His plan, in his handwriting, and endorsed, "Mr. Lee's Plan," was found among General Howe's papers seventy-five years after the war. No one on the American side knew of this document. If the court had known of it General Lee would have decorated a gallows, in all probability.

Lee is one of the riddles of American history. His suggestions to Howe for the conquest of America were treasonable, of course. On the other hand, his actions at Monmouth do not reveal a traitorous intention. He could have had his

whole command—nearly half of Washington's army—captured
or badly defeated by simply obeying Washington's orders and
remaining where he was. But he saved his troops by retiring
with them; and this retirement led to the quarrel that ended
his career.

I think that he was not so much a traitor as an eccentric.
He was renowned as an extraordinary eccentric in a century
filled with eccentricities.

Eccentricity is the resultant of contradictory qualities
clashing together with great force in the field of personality.
Perception, coming through such a medium, is distorted by a
wide angle of refraction. To the eccentric the whole range
of values is shifted. The most insignificant things become
highly important; and momentous, life-and-death actions frequently seem to him to be too trivial to notice. Lee may not
have attached much importance to his treasonable action in
suggesting a campaign to the British. He may have considered it a kind of amusement, or a sort of impersonal puzzle
which he was vain enough to believe he could solve.

One of his exploits was an encounter with Miss Rebecca
Franks, a young Jewish lady of Philadelphia, daughter of a
wealthy merchant. Miss Franks had a caustic wit, and she
expended part of it in making up a funny story about General
Charles Lee wearing "green riding breeches patched with
leather."

When Lee heard this story he became furious. He sent her
the breeches by a messenger, with a letter in which he asks her
to examine them. In the same letter he calls her a prevaricator,
and a scandal-monger, and winds up by challenging her to a
duel in these words:

> You have injured me in the tenderest part and I demand
> satisfaction; and as you cannot be ignorant of the laws of
> duelling, having conversed with so many Irish officers,
> whose favourite topic it is, particularly in the company
> of ladies, I insist on the privilege of the injured party,

which is to name his hour and weapons; and, as I intend
it to be a very serious affair, will not admit of any second;
as you may depend on it, Miss Franks, that whatever may
be your spirit on the occasion, the world shall never accuse
General Lee of having turned his back on you.   In the
meantime, I am yours,   C. L.

P. S.   I have communicated the affair only to my confidential friend who has mentioned it to no more than
seven members of Congress, and nineteen women, six of
whom were old maids, so there is no danger of its taking
wind on my side, and I hope you will be equally guarded
on your part.

§ 4

The Battle of Monmouth was the end of *Act One* of the war
drama.   There was a pause for a year and a half, punctuated
by a few British raids, and by the French expedition to America
under command of Admiral Count D'Estaing.

The French alliance was disliked by many of the patriots.
Some thought that the French, once landed in America, would
never leave.   In this humid soil of distrust public liars grew
to an amazing stature.   Priests by the hundred were coming,
they said . . . priests and crucifixes, books of mass and consecrated wafers.   A Bastille was to be erected at New York.
Other fabulists, of a more humorous turn, spoke of dried frogs,
dancing masters and garlic.

The French made two military and naval efforts in America
as our allies.   The D'Estaing episode of 1778 was the first
one.   It was a pure fizzle, though it scared the British out of
Philadelphia.   D'Estaing remained outside Sandy Hook for a
few days, and then sailed to Rhode Island, at Washington's
suggestion, to co-operate with Sullivan and Lafayette in an
effort to drive the British out of Newport.

Such a mess was made of this attempt that the French were
accused by Sullivan of deserting him.   There was talk of duels.

French sailors were mobbed in the streets of Boston and a French officer was killed. The French alliance seemed about to fall to pieces. The legislature of Massachusetts voted a monument to the slain officer; Washington wrote pacifying letters, and urged that no one speak of the incident. D'Estaing offered to serve as a colonel in the American army, on any service, however hazardous, just to prove that his heart was in the right place. Lafayette proved that his heart was in the right place by riding seventy miles in seven hours "to smooth out matters."

Nevertheless, everything went wrong. "The whole unlucky career of the French fleet was watched by the Tories with great pleasure," says Van Tyne in *The Loyalists of the American Revolution.*

> The French Admiral, it was declared, had "not even Pantagruel's luck, who conquered two old women and a duck." Lafayette and his countrymen were described as the "frog-eating gentry now capering through your provinces."

Feelings were patched up and the French fleet sailed away to the West Indies . . . later to reappear for a brief moment and make a fiasco at Savannah, where an attempt was made to capture the town and its British garrison.

Nothing more came in the way of men or ships from the French until June of 1780, though a stream of supplies flowed from France to America.

The French alliance was the turn of the war. Its immediate effect was to put England on the defensive. She had to protect her commerce and world-wide possessions.

Long before the French government had come out publicly on the American side privateers commissioned by Franklin had been fitted out in French ports with the connivance of the officials. Most of Dr. Edward Everett Hale's bulky volume on *Franklin in France* is taken up by correspondence relating to

these privateering operations. Some of the letters are very
amusing, particularly those from the French minister Vergennes, who was determined to overlook the existence of the
privateers, even if he had to turn himself into a half-witted
idiot to avoid a perception of the most notorious facts.

The British ambassador seems to have made an irate visit
every day to Vergennes with a handful of reports from English
observers. Vergennes was invariably surprised at these infrac-
tions of neutrality. He told the British representative that
he was greatly annoyed by the American attempt to use France
as a base for privateering and that he intended to stop it at
all cost. He took the British reports eagerly and promised to
act on them. It must be said for him that he kept his promise.
First, he would write to the commandant of the port to learn
if the facts were true . . . if an American vessel had actually
brought an English prize into the harbour. Upon the reply of
the commandant that an American privateer had done that
very thing, Vergennes would refer the matter to Dr. Franklin.
The answer of Franklin was usually to the effect that he knew
nothing about it. Thereupon Vergennes would instruct the
commandant of the port to order the offending privateer out
of the harbour immediately, and to see that no supplies of any
kind were furnished.

By the time Vergennes' letter reached the commandant the
privateer had sold her prize, taken on board a stock of provisions and sailed away. The prize, her name changed to
Belle Fleur or *Sainte Vièrge* and with the French flag at her
masthead, had also departed. Sometimes the letter of international law was observed by the privateer selling her prize just
outside the harbour.

Only a small part of the American privateering was carried
on from European ports. Most of it was done by privateers
belonging to Boston and Philadelphia. It was the great
American industry during the war; it became a business of
colossal proportions.

The Library of Congress has published a list of seventeen hundred vessels to which letters of marque were granted by the Continental Congress. But that does not include all the privateers. The state of Massachusetts alone issued its authorisation to nearly a thousand ships. All the northern states had vessels, owned by their citizens, engaged in these enterprises.

Many large fortunes were made by American owners of privateers. At the close of the war the wealthiest people in the United States were those who had devoted their time and attention to this profitable aspect of the war.

A large number of men were required to man the privateering vessels. Gardner, historian of the navy, thinks that about seventy thousand men were employed on ships mounting an aggregate of eighteen thousand guns. Thousands of men needed in Washington's army were on ships looking for prizes to be sold for the profit of the ship's owners.

With the announcement of the French alliance there was no more subterfuge, and both privateers and Continental war vessels were fitted out openly in France. Among these irregular sea-fighters was Captain Paul Jones. His ship was a ramshackle, leaking old tub christened *Bon Homme Richard*. Most of its guns could not be fired, for the recoil would have sent them crashing through the rotten deck. With this decayed warship he attacked, within sight of the English coast, the fine new frigate *Serapis*. The fight was one of the most thrilling in naval history. In the end he captured the *Serapis* and sailed away in her, though his own ship sank.

This exploit of "the American pirate Jones," as he was called in England, gave the English nation a bad fit of blues. It was understood on all sides that Britannia ruled the waves, and the English counted on their navy as implicitly as Saint Francis counted on salvation. But suppose, after all, that it was a delusion . . . that Britannia did not rule the waves? Gloomy thought for Englishmen.

§ 5

The supplies sent by the French were greatly needed. **By** 1779 American credit had gone nearly to the bottom of the financial scale, and was hovering just above the zero point. Congress had always been afraid to levy taxes. The patriotic cause hung on such a slender thread that the weight of a tax imposition, however light, would have brought it to the ground . . . or, at least, that was the opinion of the patriot leaders. . . . Were they not fighting England because of her attempts at taxation?

Congress attempted to solve its pressing financial problem by issuing paper currency. This money had no backing; there were no metallic reserves behind it; it was simply a promissory note, an obligation based on a rather indefinite belief in payment in the future.

By September 1, 1779, the amount of Continental bills then outstanding was $160,000,000, and the money was passing from hand to hand at about one-twentieth of its face value. Sixty dollars was paid in Philadelphia for two silk handkerchiefs, and beef sold in Boston for ten dollars a pound. Samuel Adams wrote that he had bought a suit of clothes and a hat for two thousand dollars.

Congress issued a circular to the states in which the subject of depreciation was discussed. Depreciation, Congress said, is either artificial or natural; and Continental money—in the opinion of Congress—had been artificially depreciated. In this circular Congress asserted that thirty million dollars was the probable currency requirement of the country. As $160,000,-000 had been issued, the depreciation ought to have been about five to one; but it was actually twenty or thirty to one. Congress thought something ought to be done about it, but did not say what . . . doubtless because it did not know what to say.

In this same year Congress resolved not to issue more than $200,000,000 under any circumstances, and declared that the additional forty million would not be issued if they could help it.

They could not help it, or so it appears, for the additional forty million—and more—was put out and immediately became little more than financial trash. Gérard, agent of the French government, reported to Vergennes that Congress was chiefly occupied by measures against the Tories, and he thought they relied on the confiscation of loyalists' estates as their principal financial resource.

During the last year or two of the war the soldiers received their pay on a basis of forty to one . . . that is, a private soldier was paid about two hundred and fifty paper dollars a month. They complained, however, that they could not buy anything with it at less than three hundred to one. If this is true—and I think it is—a private soldier's pay at this time amounted, in actual purchasing power, to something around eighty cents a month.

The burden of this worthless currency fell as hard on most of the army officers and members of Congress as it did on the common soldiers. Many officers resigned because their families were destitute.

In these dark times the name of Haym Salomon, a Jewish exchange broker, shone with the golden lustre of altruism. He loaned large sums of money to members of Congress, and to officers of the army, without interest. In many cases he never expected to be repaid; and in most cases he never was. His advances were not really loans, but gifts.

Haym Salomon has been strangely neglected by historians. All that I have been able to learn about him has come from obscure pamphlets and old letters; yet it is hardly too much to say that he kept many members of Congress alive during the gloomiest years of the Revolution.

This man was an educated Polish Jew who came to America and established himself in New York a few years before the war. He remained in New York after the British occupied the city, and in 1776 he was taken up and imprisoned for furnishing information to Washington. He managed to escape, and went to Philadelphia, where he became a dealer in foreign exchange.

He seems to have had remarkable business ability, combined with the idealism which, among the Jews, often accompanies a high capacity for money-making. The French employed him in their financial affairs in America. His patriotism was of a most matter-of-fact kind. It affected even his relations with the wealthy French government, for he undertook their disbursements for the extremely small commission of one quarter of one per cent, on account of their aid to the American cause.

James Madison was one of those who was assisted by Salomon. Madison wrote: "The kindness of our friend in Front Street is a fund that will preserve me from extreme necessities, but I never resort to it without extreme mortification, as he obstinately rejects all recompense."

Salomon died in 1785, at the age of forty-five. He had advanced $350,000 to the government which has never been repaid to his heirs, though in the early years of the nineteenth century an effort was made in Congress to have this debt liquidated. Salomon's vouchers from the government were lost by some government official to whom they had been entrusted for the purpose of verification. His descendants, now wealthy New York bankers, long ago abandoned their claim; and the name of Haym Salomon has drifted into a dusty corner of American history.

When Robert Morris became superintendent of finance in 1781, Salomon acted as his exchange broker. Morris was not able to bring much order out of the financial chaos, although his methods were those of a skilled financier. The burden of worthless money was too heavy.

CHAPTER XXIII

ACT TWO

§ 1

CLINTON had the clearest head among the British generals. He was the only one of them to realise that Washington's army did not constitute the main strength of the Revolution. Howe never perceived this important fact; and all of Howe's operations were carried on as war is carried on in Europe . . . strategic positions . . . take the enemy's capital . . . defeat the enemy's army . . . peaceable citizens submit . . . war is over.

That Washington's army was only a symbol of rebellion was plainly seen by Clinton. It was hardly worth while to undertake the risk and trouble of beating such an emblematic military force. The Revolution, in diverse types of revolt, was diffused throughout the body of the American people. Clinton grasped the fact that his problem was not to defeat an army, but to conquer a population. He resolved to go about it by subduing one state at a time. With that state reorganised and held by loyalists and British bayonets, he intended to go on to the next.

All the dazzling glitter had gone out of the war with the departure of Sir William Howe. Clinton was to take the stage as the heavy villain in Act Two, on which the curtain was about to rise.

His part was to include wholesale house-burning, murder, highway robbery, starvation, and tyranny of all kinds and degrees. Rather a depressing programme, one would think; a rôle likely to lead its creator to insomnia and remorse.

Not at all. . . .

Such things do not disturb a soldier's equanimity. They are called "measures of pacification," and that phrase lifts the whole affair to a much higher plane.

Clinton's intention was to pacify South Carolina first, but nothing was done about it for a long time, for the gravitational centre of the war had shifted to the other side of the Atlantic. The Battle of Monmouth took place in June, 1778. Clinton and his army got to New York a few days later. Soon after that, the French fleet under D'Estaing appeared, and then followed the abortive attempt of the French and Americans to take Newport.

Nothing else happened. The sleepy year dragged on through summer, fall and winter, and ran into 1779. During the whole of 1779 there was nothing of great importance. Clinton abandoned Newport because he did not have the troops to retain it. The American foothold of the British had shrunk to the narrow ledge of Manhattan Island. Washington hung about the British position, changing from one bank of the Hudson to the other. His army was too weak to take the initiative, else he might have driven Clinton clear off the American map.

To take the fighting initiative was an instinct with Washington; he was not a fox but a hunter. His inability to act made him restless and moody. This year and a half of pause in the war was his gloomiest time. His letters are querulous and petulant. "Our army, as it now stands," he writes, "is but little more than the skeleton of an army. I hear of no steps that are taking to give it strength and substance." He thought, in this period when the British were giving the patriots a rest, and the country was virtually at peace, that "the common interests of America are mouldering and sinking into irretrievable ruin if a remedy is not soon applied."

The year 1779 was a year of industrial activity and large crops. A great stillness had fallen on the war, broken occasionally by a British raid, but as a whole the country was unmolested, and turned itself to planting and building.

It must have been a comforting fact to the American leaders that the British, after their four years of effort, were just where they had started. The English national debt had grown into a burden of fantastic size. One of the King's armies had been taken bodily and its officers and men were prisoners in America. The French had come into the war, and were keeping England strained to the utmost to find men and money. American privateers had done immense damage to British commerce. In 1779 the Indians had ceased to be a menace; General Sullivan had wiped the Iroquois off the list of troublesome contingencies.

The military situation, it seems, was hardly desperate enough to justify Washington's dark forebodings, although the army had dwindled in numbers and was shabbily supported.

The principal reason for his gloomy views was not the threat of the British army, in my opinion, but a fear that the American social structure was in danger of being overturned by the peculiar development of the financial situation. We must not forget that he was, above all else, a class-conscious, wealthy and conservative property-owner.

Congress, in its anxiety to keep up the fictitious value of the Continental paper money, made it a legal tender for all obligations; and to force the acceptance of this currency it had induced the states to enact enforcing laws which bristled with penalties.

The result was a catastrophe to the creditor class that was doubtless unforeseen by Congress. Mortgages were paid off in depreciated currency; incomes shrivelled up; the wages of labour rose to dizzy, unheard-of altitudes.

Many of the leading patriots who happened to be in financial difficulties took advantage of these laws to get rid of their incumbrances. General Stirling, for one. At the beginning of the war he owed eighty thousand pounds and was virtually bankrupt. He settled this entire obligation in paper worth about one thousand pounds.

In spite of the stringent enforcing act and its penalties, Washington disregarded the law as to paper money, but not until he had taken a considerable amount of the depreciated paper. "I am now receiving," he wrote, "a shilling in the pound in discharge of Bonds which ought to have been paid me, and would have been realised before I left Virginia, but for my indulgence to the debtors." Soon afterward he instructed his manager at Mount Vernon not to accept any more Continental paper in payment of maturing obligations.

At this period of the war Washington's opinion of patriots and patriotism had sunk to its low-water mark. He wrote:

> Men may speculate as they will; they may talk of patriotism; they may draw a few examples from ancient stories of great achievements performed by its influence; but whoever builds upon them as a sufficient basis for conducting a long and bloody war, will find himself deceived in the end. . . . I know patriotism exists . . . but I will venture to assert that a great and lasting war can never be supported on this principle alone. It must be aided by a prospect of interest or some reward.

Well, let us be candid about it. He complains because the common people do not enlist as soldiers. But he overlooks the fact that the common people, although expected to be patriotic, have had no hand in shaping the patriotic programme.

Therefore, why should a workingman of sense interest himself in the woes of a lot of wealthy land-owners who do not intend to allow him to vote? Nor do they intend to better his condition if they can help it. Under these conditions six and two-thirds dollars a month, with free whippings, do not look very attractive; and, as Washington truly said, such a prospect must be aided by "interest or some reward."

In December, 1778, Washington made a visit to Philadelphia, and was astounded at its luxury. The war profiteers were on the horizon, the great privateer fortunes were sailing into sight on a rising tide of dissipation and folly. Washington had, no doubt, his underfed, ragged army in mind when he wrote this letter on December 30th:

> If I were called upon to draw a picture of the times and of men from what I have seen, heard, and in part know, I should say in one word that idleness, dissipation, and extravagance seem to have laid fast hold of most of them; that speculation, peculation, and an insatiable thirst for riches seem to have got the better of every other consideration and almost of every order of men; that party disputes and personal quarrels are the great business of the day. . . .
>
> Our money is now sinking fifty per cent a day in this city, and I shall not be surprised if in the course of a few months a total stop is put to the currency of it; and yet an assembly, a concert, a dinner, or supper, will not only take men off from acting in this business, but even from thinking of it; while a great part of the officers of our army from absolute necessity are quitting the service, and the more virtuous few, rather than do this, are sinking by sure degrees into beggary and want.

This is the letter of a man who is very tired. Washington had reason to be tired. His task was gigantic, though after 1776 he had so organised his military family that much of his work was done by aides acting as secretaries.

These officers, mostly young men, were known as "riding" aides or "writing" aides, according to their inclination for indoor or outdoor duty. A riding aide was a staff officer who could carry a verbal order, or stay on a horse for hours, but who was of little use at a desk. A writing aide was, in effect, a secretary.

The most efficient of the writers on the staff was Alexander

Hamilton. He was twenty years old when he joined Washington's military family in 1777. A slender young man with violet-blue eyes; a spick-and-span young man; a blond young man with reddish hair.

Hamilton was a careerist and go-getter of remarkable talent. Of obscure parentage—he was an illegitimate child—with his own way to make in the world, he was nevertheless as undemocratic as Mussolini, and was one of the Very Best People by instinct. If he had lived to-day we would find him, as a young man, at the snobbiest of the universities, where he would be a member of the most exclusive fraternity. He would make friends with the wealthy among his fellow-students. Graduating with merit and considerable praise, he would hasten to lay his laurel wreath at the feet of a wealthy comrade's sister. Soon after his marriage he would enter his father-in-law's bank as a vice-president. There he would so distinguish himself that he would be invited to become a partner in some great Wall Street establishment. Translate that into the technique of the eighteenth century and you have Alexander Hamilton.

But he was not a hypocrite; he had the courage of his belief. He called the common people "a great brute," and was all for an aristocracy of land, money and intellect.

There is in circulation a story that Hamilton was, in reality, an illegitimate son of Washington. I have never seen this story in print, but I have heard it from many people, and I suppose it was being told by one man to another in Washington's time.

There is not the faintest trace of evidence to support it, but there is a good deal of evidence against it. In fact, it is nothing more than a preposterous yarn, which began probably because of the favouritism shown by Washington to Hamilton, and because the commander-in-chief sometimes loosened his dignity a little and called Hamilton "my boy." I mention this far-fetched legend only because many people believe it to be true.

The skeleton of the story is that Washington, on his trip to Barbados in 1751, met Hamilton's mother, had an illicit affair with her, and as a result Alexander Hamilton was born.

Washington was at Barbados only six weeks. For three weeks he was in bed with smallpox. During the rest of the time he had his dying brother on his hands. There is no evidence that Rachal Levine, Hamilton's mother, was ever on the island of Barbados.

Hamilton was born on the island of Nevis—probably in 1757, as he claimed . . . five years after Washington's trip to Barbados. There is no record of his birth in the public registry office of the island, but this omission came about very likely because his mother disliked to put his illegitimacy on record. Many people thought that he did not tell the truth about his age, and that he was four or five years older than he claimed to be. In support of this theory they cite the existence of a legal document of the year 1766, still preserved in the island of Nevis, on which Alexander Hamilton's name appears as a witness. It seems improbable, they say, that a child of nine would be taken as a witness of a legal paper. It does seem so, but Hamilton was amazingly precocious.

His mother was the wife of a Jewish merchant named Levine. It is said that she was not a Jewess, though this is mere conjecture. Her name was Rachel, a Jewish name, and her husband was a Jew. His father was probably James Hamilton, a wastrel and shabby fellow who held a lifelong position as family black sheep of the Scotch house of Hamilton.

At the age of fourteen Alexander Hamilton was supporting himself as a shipping agent at Nevis. In 1774 he came to New York for the purpose of getting a college education and entered King's College . . . now Columbia University. He had a little money, and he seems to have cut loose entirely from his family. He must have been at King's College during the time that "Jacky" Custis flitted through its halls.

In the Revolutionary agitation of 1775 Hamilton acquired

a local reputation as a "boy orator" . . . also as a patriotic writer. He persuaded the New York patriots to let him have a battery of field pieces, and he organised and drilled a company of artillery.

Writers on Hamilton agree that Washington met this highly capable young man in the spring of 1776, when the patriot army occupied New York City. They say that about this time Washington "discovered Hamilton's merits." Maybe so, but I am inclined to think that Hamilton discovered Washington's merits first. He had a notable faculty for getting a seat in the leading carriage.

He was a valued member of Washington's staff. The commander-in-chief had an enormous correspondence. In writing letters Washington usually indicated the nature of the communication and its main ideas. These were put in words by a staff officer and brought to His Excellency for signing. Sometimes Washington changed a word or two; and on occasions he would write an entire letter or dictate it. The larger part of his wartime correspondence after the middle of 1777 was the work of Hamilton.

In Washington's letters of that period one may trace Hamilton's lucidity of ideas and clarity of phrase. His conceptions of things in general were so much like Washington's that Hamilton could be entrusted with the preparation of most documents with merely a hint from Washington to guide him.

He was conscious of his intellectual ability, and fell readily into attitudes of arrogance and superiority. My impression is that Washington never liked his manner. Men of slow wit in commanding positions are almost invariably disturbed and vaguely ill at ease in the presence of underlings of brilliant capacity.

In February, 1781, they had an open rupture which led to Hamilton's resignation from the staff. "The General and I passed each other on the stairs," Hamilton said; "he told me

ALEXANDER HAMILTON

Painting by John Trumbull. Reproduced through courtesy of the
New York Chamber of Commerce.

he wanted to speak to me. I answered that I would wait on him immediately. . . ."

Hamilton goes on to say that he was stopped by Lafayette, "and we conversed together about a minute on a matter of business."

When he went to Washington's room His Excellency said in an angry tone, "Colonel Hamilton, you have kept me waiting at the head of the stairs these ten minutes; I must tell you, sir, you treat me with disrespect." Hamilton replied, "without petulancy, but with decision," he says: "I am not conscious of it, sir, but since you have thought it necessary to tell me so, we part."

"Very well, sir," Washington replied, "if it be your choice."

Hamilton adds that an officer was sent to him by Washington almost immediately to beg him to come back, but he declined to do it . . . in other words, Hamilton's mind was made up, and Washington would have to stagger along as well as he could without the help of his brilliant young aide.

In a few days Hamilton wrote this supercilious letter to his friend McHenry:

> The Great man and I have come to an open rupture. Proposals of accommodations have been made on his part, but rejected. I pledge my honour to you that he will find me inflexible. He shall for once at least repent his ill humour. Without a shadow of reason and on the slightest grounds—he charged me in the most affrontive manner with treating him with disrespect. . . .
>
> I shall continue to support a popularity that has been essential—is still useful.
>
> Adieu, my friend. May the time come when characters may be Known in their true light.

This coolness did not last long. Washington was too great for Hamilton to ignore; and Hamilton's thoughts on public questions were the thoughts that Washington liked.

§ 2

In December, 1779, Sir Henry Clinton left New York, with a combined military and naval expedition for the purpose of beginning his campaign for pacifying South Carolina.

The second act of the war drama began then and there. In May, 1780, Charleston surrendered after a siege and Clinton returned to New York, leaving the Earl Cornwallis in charge of pacification in all its branches, with power to pacify by hanging, arson, threats or bribes. All these methods were used rather lavishly.

The war had come to an end in the North. For the next two years South Carolina, North Carolina and Virginia were to be the scene of a strife that has hardly ever been equalled for ferocity in warfare carried on by civilised people. The campaigns of Howe and Washington seem nothing more than pleasant tournaments when compared with these throat-cutting ambuscades.

South Carolina was about half loyalist; that is one reason why Clinton selected it as a field for pacification. Another reason was that it could be readily reached by water from New York, but was at such a distance by land that the patriots would find it difficult to send reinforcements to an army in that region.

The struggle became a civil war of the most violent kind. Few prisoners were taken by either side. Men captured in battle were usually hanged or shot immediately.

After Cornwallis had completed the conquest of the state, Congress decided to send an army to South Carolina and General Gates was appointed by Congress to command it. This appointment was made without Washington's approval, or without even asking his opinion . . . one of the many slights which the mercurial, feather-headed Congress gave him during the war.

Gates was beaten so badly by Cornwallis at Camden that

his army was dispersed. Thereupon Congress asked Washington to name a general for the Southern department; and Washington named Nathanael Greene.

The selection of Greene for this post was perhaps Washington's greatest achievement during the war. Greene was an organiser of victory of the first rank, and credit must be given Washington for his ability to appreciate the great military capacity of his subordinate.

Greene created a Southern army out of practically nothing. He had neither money nor credit, and his plans had to be carried out in the stale atmosphere of a losing cause, for the American side was already damned in reputation in the South by its record of defeat.

Notwithstanding these difficulties he contrived to organise an army which was able to stand up before Cornwallis, and which eventually manœuvred him out of South Carolina and North Carolina into that fatal region of lowland Virginia, where he was run down, like a winded fox, by Washington and Rochambeau.

Greene was the son of a well-to-do iron founder of Rhode Island. His father was a crabbed Quaker who did not believe in education, war, or amusement. Greene was put to work at twelve in his father's iron foundry. He educated himself— and his education was a good one—by buying books and reading them secretly in his room. In early youth he began to take an interest in military affairs, probably because his father hated war. After his father's death he was prominent in the Rhode Island militia. He had studied all the classic campaigns; but besides and beyond all that he was a soldier of natural ability.

He was to Washington what Stonewall Jackson was to General R. E. Lee . . . a bearer of burdens, a faithful subordinate of superior skill, a general who could always be depended on and left to his own resources.

The function of the great executive is to select men who are better than himself for the work in hand. Washington was a great executive. His strength lay precisely in that, and in his force of character. His understanding of the great mass of the American people was defective; he did not understand them nor sympathise with them. Nor did he have a correct understanding of military science; of the organisation and conduct of armies. But he had a talent for picking men who could do their work effectively.

Notwithstanding this valuable talent, the situation which he had assisted in developing was so fundamentally in error that his executive ability would have been unavailing if it had not been for the French.

§ 3

The second French effort was under the command of the Comte de Rochambeau. He arrived with an army of fifty-five hundred men in July, 1780, and occupied Newport.

The popular distrust of the French had deepened since the futile attempt of D'Estaing. The Abbé Robin, who came with Rochambeau, said, "The arrival of the French spread terror everywhere . . . the French were generally regarded as slaves to despotism; full of prejudices and superstition; nearly idolaters in their religion, and like kinds of lightweight machines, not well-formed, incapable of firmness or consistency, occupied only with the care of curling their hair and painting their faces. . . ."

Rochambeau's own impression of Newport on disembarking is as strong and alert as an etching by Frank Brangwyn. "The streets are deserted," he wrote, "and there are sad, dismayed glances from the windows."

Instant efforts were made by Washington and Congress to bring about a change in feeling toward our powerful allies. Their letters to people in Rhode Island helped, but French gold was probably a more important friend-maker. Newport was run down and falling to pieces. The French bought supplies in large quantities and paid gold . . . not Continental paper . . . nor any kind of paper . . . but gold.

Rochambeau's army was undoubtedly the most perfectly disciplined military force that has ever been on this continent. The French soldiers were in Newport a year. During that time there was not a single instance of impropriety on the part of a French soldier. There was not even a chicken nor an apple missing.

In a few weeks Newport loved the French. People wore French colours, and had favourite regiments; young ladies practised their French on the officers; everybody who had a horse could sell it at a high price; everybody who had a spare room could rent it. The parlours became salons and were decorated with impromptu drawings made by French officers. The only thing that Newport did not like about the French army was its size; if it had been twice as large it would have given the town more joy.

The officers took pen in hand. Every other man set about writing his impressions of this new land. The officers' mess became a literary school. Within a few years not less than seventy volumes of memoirs of America appeared in France. Comte de Revel was here only twenty-four days, but he managed to write two hundred and eighty-seven pages about us; the Marquis de Chastellux was here several years, and his *Voyage dans l'Amérique Septentrionale* is in two large volumes. The Abbé Robin was the most delightful of the memoir writers. One may amuse oneself for a whole afternoon with his *Nouveau Voyage dans l'Amérique*.

The French helped us a lot with the Revolution, but some of their most valued contributions had nothing to do with the war. They brought us the cocktail—the ancient French *coquetel*—ice cream—and the brass band; three pillars of American civilisation.

Washington met Rochambeau for the first time at Hartford

on September 20, 1780. The purpose of the conference was to devise means of co-operation between the Allies. Washington thought New York might be taken if the French army and fleet would co-operate in a combined effort with the Americans.

He sat at this conference for hours, silent, pensive, looking from one to another, studying their vivid French faces. Lafayette sat by his side as interpreter.

Among Rochambeau's aides was Count Fersen, afterwards famous as the reputed lover of Marie Antoinette. He wrote that Washington's face "was fine and commanding"; but, he adds, "It was unseemly that such a countenance should be veiled with so much sadness."

The conference came to no decision; nothing was done. Washington said he saw that the heart of the French naval officers was not in the enterprise, though Rochambeau thought New York might be taken, and would have co-operated with Washington in trying it if he had not been dissuaded by the naval officers.

On his way back from this conference Washington arrived at the fortress of West Point at the very moment of the discovery of Benedict Arnold's treachery. He took instant charge of things, and sent men to capture Arnold, if possible. Then he attempted to comfort Mrs. Arnold, but she hugged her baby and screamed hysterically that Washington wanted to kill her child. Poor, helpless young woman. . . . The most miserable victim of the spidery Arnold-André mess.

The French army remained at Newport a full year without doing anything whatever. Its presence probably kept Clinton at New York from reducing his force by sending reinforcements to Cornwallis in the South, and in this sense the French were effective.

§ 4

The condition of the common soldier—distressing throughout the war—began to be intolerable near the close. The year

1781, while the war was blazing in the South, was a time of mutinies among the troops in the North.

Not much about the mutinies. . . .

They have the odour of events that are carefully dead.

In the army there were many mutinies. Most of them were sporadic strikes of companies and squads which were quelled by a few vigorous beatings; but two or three were such large affairs that Washington was afraid that they would spread throughout the army.

Most of the men of the Pennsylvania line had enlisted for "three years or the duration of the war." The men interpreted this phrase to mean that if the war ended before three years had expired their service was at an end; but that if it lasted more than three years, their enlistment expired at the end of three years anyway. Their officers held that the enlistments were for three years as a minimum, and as much longer as the war lasted.

The three-year period began to run out around January, 1781. In addition, the pay of the troops was seven or eight months in arrears, and they were in a deplorable condition as to food and clothes.

On January 1st, 1781, there was a mutiny of thirteen hundren men of Wayne's command—then in winter quarters in New Jersey.

The men paraded without officers, under the command of sergeants. The officers drove their horses among the mutineers and used their swords. The soldiers, now denominated as "the mob" in Wayne's dispatches, used bayonets and threw stones. A captain was killed. The men resolved to march to Philadelphia to lay their grievances before Congress. The mutineers were met by a committee from Congress, and in the end most of them got their discharge from the service.

On January 20th there was a revolt in the New Jersey line. They formed without officers and started to Trenton to lay their grievances before the legislature. Colonel Dayton followed them, and finally got them to listen to him. He told them that their grievances would be set right, and he promised a full pardon to all who would return to duty. All of them returned.

Colonel Dayton was afraid that the mutiny might break out again, and he thought an example ought to be made of the ring-leaders. He forgot, apparently, that he had offered pardon to all who returned.

So he wrote to Washington for his assistance in the way of troops to stamp out the spirit of mutiny. "This request was quite in accordance with Washington's own feelings," Hatch says in his *Administration of the American Revolutionary Army*. "He thought that, unless this fatal spirit of insubordination were stamped out at once, the troops of other states would be infected and the whole army ruined."

Accordingly, the American General Howe (Robert H. Howe) was sent to Colonel Dayton's camp with five hundred men. The men had been carefully picked, at Washington's suggestion, from the best-clothed and best-fed regiments at West Point. Washington instructed Howe to enforce unconditional submission, and to execute the leaders of the mutiny.

The mutinous regiments were formed in line, and three men—one from each regiment—were selected for execution. The execution was done by an unwilling firing party made up of leaders of the mutiny. Two of the mutineers were shot. The third was pardoned on the plea of the officers of his regiment.

Washington wrote to Steuben that this mutiny was a fortunate event, as it gave the authorities a chance to put an end to the rebellious spirit before it had gone very far.

However, it does not appear to have been so fortunate after all, as the mutinies kept on occurring. The fact is that by

1781 the soldiers—and working people generally—were completely disillusioned about the war.

The mutiny that took place among the Pennsylvania troops in May, 1781, when they were ordered South, had some interesting features.

The soldiers had been paid in worthless paper money which the inhabitants refused to accept. On the day before their intended departure for Virginia twelve men stepped out of ranks and persuaded the line not to march. They said they wanted to be paid "in real, not ideal, money." These leaders were put under arrest, tried at once, and sentenced to be shot.

General Wayne, their commander, wrote: "Whether by design or accident, the particular friends and messmates of the culprits were their executioners, and while the tears rolled down their cheeks in showers, they silently and faithfully obeyed their orders without a moment's hesitation."

One of the mutineers was not killed by the firing squad, but merely wounded. He lay groaning on the ground. General Wayne called on a soldier to step out of the ranks and put his bayonet through the wounded man. The soldier said he could not do it, as the man on the ground was his friend. Thereupon Wayne put his pistol to the soldier's head and told him that if he did not bayonet the wounded man he would have his own brains blown out. The soldier then killed his comrade. One must say that this soldier had very little spirit, or he would have put his bayonet into General Wayne, right then and there; but before condemning him for his lack of spirit, let us remember that he was ragged, and poor and underfed.

We have got a long way from the People's Revolution, have we not? A long way from the embattled farmers and the elated hum and stir of Bunker Hill. We are wandering in a twilight land of ragged, weeping men . . . men with pistols at their heads . . . and forlorn soldiers being made to shoot their own comrades.

§ 5

Now we come on days big with doom.   The impetuous Cornwallis, hurling himself on South Carolina, had met the deft and implacable Greene, and had been elbowed gradually into Virginia.   There he played hide-and-seek with Lafayete's little command.   Eventually Cornwallis and his army drifted, through their puss-in-the-corner tactics, into the squeezed little corner of Yorktown—a peninsula like a bottle, of which Lafayette made himself the cork.

Messengers went thundering along the country roads from Lafayette to Washington in the distant North; and sloops sailed desperately out of the bay with notes from Cornwallis to Clinton.

The plight of Cornwallis was not bad.   The British ships could take him off or reinforcements might come—but neither ships nor reinforcements ever turned up.   He might have cut his way out—his force was superior to that of Lafayette—but his heart was like water, and he snuggled deeper in his tiny hole. If he had cut through Lafayette, where could he have gone? He thought it better to stay where he was than to face Greene.

Washington consults with Rochambeau and a fast-sailing ship starts to the French West Indies to seek ponderous Admiral De Grasse with a joint message from Washington and Rochambeau.   If he will only come to the Chesapeake with his fleet and block the entrance they will meet him there with their armies, and trap Cornwallis.

But can it be done?   It is all so distant and hazy.   Weeks before they can hear from De Grasse; weeks before their armies can reach Virginia.   By that time Cornwallis may be gone. Nevertheless, Rochambeau and Washington resolve to try it, although it is a hundred to one chance that something may go wrong.

The thundering messengers go thundering back to Lafayette. He must hold on, the cork must stay in the bottle at all hazards. The French army leaves sorrowing Newport and hastens towards the Hudson.

But no news from De Grasse. Suppose he does not come? In the bright West Indies are the gods of Destiny. When the message reached De Grasse he was about to send most of his fleet to France as a convoy for the great squadron of merchant ships that was on the point of departure. But he changed his mind instantly and sent the merchant fleet to France with one frigate. This was a decision of genius. With the rest of his huge naval armament he started for Chesapeake Bay.

The French are across the Hudson, and Clinton sits watching in New York. He suspects a move toward Virginia, but Washington is good at deception. French bakers arrive in New Jersey and begin to build huge bread ovens. All the countryside is told that New York is to be besieged, and Clinton learns it the next day. A whole town of huts to shelter the French officers is going up opposite Staten Island. Washington writes a letter to Rochambeau with instructions as to how the siege of Manhattan is to begin, and contrives to have the bearer intercepted by the British.

Clinton was strengthening his defences when one day his spies told him that the great brick ovens and the city of huts were silent and deserted. Next day he heard that both the French and American armies had passed through Philadelphia. Too late then!

De Grasse arrived on time before Yorktown, and stopped escape by sea. Washington and Rochambeau arrived in time with an overwhelming force. The rarest thing that ever happens in war had happened. Armies and fleets had come together with perfect precision.

The Washington luck was like a high-riding star.

Cornwallis is outnumbered two to one; three to one; four to one. The wide-mouthed French siege guns roar night and day. The village of Yorktown is crumbling beneath his feet.

Trenches are taken in gallant charges. Hamilton leads one and Lafayette leads another.

Smoke-blackened faces. Singing Frenchmen. The great banner of Auvergne stands in a captured redoubt and displays its legend in the wind: *Auvergne sans tache*. Over another re-doubt—once British but now American—floats the young Stars and Stripes. Burning ships; British property going to the flames. The town is a hospital. Cornwallis gazes across the blue water looking for Clinton, but only the tall ships of France lie on the horizon. The fat De Grasse waddles on shore like a duck on land.

Redoubts fall in night attacks. Washington utters a sen-tentious comment. He said, "The work is done and well done." Officers go about telling other officers what Washington has said, and how patly he said it: *The work is done and well done.* It takes its place among the great aphorisms. Everybody knows the war is coming to an end, and that Washington is to be the great man. His every word is treasured as a jewel. No more is heard of Conway or Gates. Hamilton begins to hang around the band wagon.

Cornwallis is willing to surrender. Flags of truce. Firing stops. The Duc de Lauzun goes tripping across the shell-ploughed ground waving a delicate silk handkerchief in the face of the frowning guns.

It was all over on October 19, 1781.

§ 6

The war was over, but a state of war still continued. The definitive treaty of peace was not signed until September 3, 1783.

Washington wrote that these two years of inactivity were the dullest that he had ever spent.

After Yorktown, Washington thought the British would make another effort, and indeed King George wanted to continue the war; but the King had lost his hold on Parliament, and the opposition was in power.

The British still held New York City, Charleston and Savannah, and Washington's army took a position in the highlands of the Hudson.

The spirit of mutiny had spread to the officers. They wanted half pay for life on their discharge from the service. Anonymous addresses were circulated, meetings were held, and threats made. Washington appeared before the discontented officers with a manuscript in his hand. He took out his glasses and said simply: "You see, gentlemen, I have grown both blind and grey in your service."

That impressed everybody so much that the revolt of the officers oozed away. They succeeded finally in getting full pay for five years.

There was no fighting after the surrender of Cornwallis, but things were not as dull as Washington's assertion would lead us to believe. At the army headquarters at Newburgh, on the Hudson, there were dances and dinners; and occasionally a fox-hunt.

At one memorable ball, when Washington appeared on the dancing floor the French officers took the instruments from the musicians and made up an impromptu orchestra of their own.

What a talent the French have for graceful gestures!

Late in 1783 the British evacuated New York, and the American states were free. Washington took leave of his officers, and returned to Mount Vernon just before the close of that year.

CHAPTER XXIV

WASHINGTON AS GRAND SEIGNEUR

§ 1

GEORGE WASHINGTON comes again to Mount Vernon, and there it is as if nothing had happened.

The doves coo under the eaves of the barn; the unwilling slaves trudge over the distant fields; the bees linger among the garden's foxglove and marigold.

In the stable there is the stamp of horses' feet and the smell of hay. In the house there are fragile feminine sounds. The gaunt clock gnaws at the long afternoon.

The surf of green pines beats against the hills; burnished copper quivers on the blue Potomac; the ploughmen throw lazy shadows in the face of the dropping sun; the Maryland shore is azure and uncertain in the failing light. The peaceful day drifts smoothly to its close.

The imperative indifference of these limpid hours rebuked the Revolution as reality rebukes a dream.

But George Washington knew that it was not a dream. He had heard the guns crackle on the Boston heights; he had seen the bayonets and the ragged men. He had seen hot death and cold snow mingled in dark-red writhing. He remembered the babble of tongues and the foreign faces; the shining heroes; young men and old men; and the green poison that drips from the mouths of liars and traitors.

All this had come rushing at him from space and time as a wave rushes at a beach. Now the wave had slipped back; and here was Mount Vernon, and it was 1784.

Nothing had changed, yet all had changed . . . for George

Washington was different inside. Not outside, but inside. He had been lacerated by the sharp teeth of dilemmas.

He had reached the time of life when men of action feel a dull greyness settle within them. It is the wraith of forsaken yesterdays, and it comes to stay for life. After that, there can be no keen new adventure. A man who is grey inside must follow the road that lies before him; he must keep on doing what he has done before; to live means merely to endure.

Observant people who saw Washington after the Revolution said that he acted like an old man. His chilly blue eyes had a look of introspection; they were turned upon himself. He sat in pensive silence, like a man who is trying to solve the riddle of his own soul.

In the maturity of experience did he catch some luminous gleam of the sorcery of events? Did he realise at last that he had not made events, but that events had made him?

§ 2

The American Revolution had become a large uneasy ghost loitering in the corridors of History; and George Washington had become the most famous of living men.

In these days he wrote about "gliding down the stream of life"—a figure of speech which he used frequently; about "tranquil enjoyments"—another Washingtonism; and about being freed from "the busy scenes of public life."

A few days after his return to Mount Vernon he wrote to Governor Clinton, of New York, "The scene is at last closed. I feel myself eased of a load of public care. I hope to spend the remainder of my days in cultivating the affections of good men and in the practice of the domestic virtues."

To Lafayette he said:

> At length, my dear Marquis, I am become a private citizen on the banks of the Potomac; and under the shadow of my own vine and my own fig-tree, free from the

bustle of a camp, and the busy scenes of public life, I am
solacing myself with those tranquil enjoyments, of which
the soldier, who is ever in pursuit of fame, the statesman,
whose watchful days and sleepless nights are spent in devis-
ing schemes to promote the welfare of his own, perhaps
the ruin of other countries, as if this globe was insufficient
for us all, and the courtier, who is always watching the
countenance of his prince, in hopes of catching a gracious
smile, can have very little conception.

There is something musty and unspontaneous about these
convoluted sentences; a faint perfume of the *Elegy in a Country Churchyard*. You will observe that he refers to a soldier
as one "who is ever in pursuit of fame." Not defending freedom, nor winning great causes, but in pursuing fame—in that
we see his mental picture of the soldier's life.

In another letter written during the same year of 1784 he
bids Lafayette good-bye, and says:

I called to mind the days of my youth, and found that
they had long since fled to return no more; that I was
now descending the hill I had been fifty-two years climbing, and that, though I was blest with a good constitution, I was of a short-lived family and might soon expect
to be entombed in the mansion of my fathers. These
thoughts darkened the shades, and gave a gloom to the
picture, and consequently to my prospect of seeing you
again.

How clearly his concealed or unconscious desires and fears
bubble through these letters. He was plainly afraid of death.
This fear is not incompatible with the highest physical courage.
Brave men are often afraid to die. Fear of death lay deep in
his personality, and fear of retirement. To "move gently
down the stream of life," to live tranquilly under his own vine
and fig-tree—these were to him a sort of death; and he constantly associated the idea of death with that of retirement
from public life.

§ 3

Throughout many years of his life Washington's health was not good. Pulmonary weakness ran in his family; several of the Washingtons had died of consumption. He was frequently ill, and several times at the point of death. Yet he speaks of his good constitution in many letters. People have such extraordinary delusions about themselves. It is entirely possible that he believed himself to have "the best of constitutions," or he may have endeavoured to keep in a cheerful frame of mind by attempting to ignore the fact that his lungs were weak, and that he was often laid on his back with malarial fever and other illnesses.

During the Braddock expedition he was desperately ill with violent fevers and pains in the head, and had to be carried in a covered wagon. "I was relieved," he said, "by the General's absolutely ordering the physicians to give me Dr. James' powders (one of the most excellent medicines in the world), for it gave me immediate ease, and removed my fevers and other complaints in four days' time." After his heroic day on Braddock's battlefield he had a relapse; and he says that he was "very near my last gasp."

In 1758 he had a severe illness which incapacitated him for several months. In a previous chapter I have mentioned this sickness, and the mystery that surrounds it. Lossing thought it was some kind of lung trouble, but he was obviously guessing.

People who got through the perils of infancy usually lived long in eighteenth-century America. The country was full of leathery, dried-up nonagenarians who threatened to keep on existing indefinitely. But at the age of fifty-five Washington's handwriting already had a tremour, and his hearing had become so poor that one had to talk very loud to him to make him understand. His eyesight had been feeble for years.

His teeth became defective as early as 1754, and thereafter they always gave him much pain and annoyance. At that time the causal connection between decayed teeth and bad health was unknown. I wonder if his ailments were not partly due to his teeth? We read in his *Diary* of "aching teeth and inflamed gums" on many occasions; and we learn that his teeth were extracted one after another.

He began to use false teeth in 1789. At first these fitted badly and gave a sunken appearance to his mouth. The puffiness of his lips in the Gilbert Stuart Athenæum portrait, and the peasant heaviness of his face in that picture, are not natural, but come from Stuart's attempt to rectify the distortion of the false teeth by placing wads of cotton around his sitter's gums.

Eventually Washington got a set of "sea-horse teeth"— made from hippopotamus ivory—which fitted him much better.

He was subject to colds, as well as to fever and ague, yet he was not ill even once during the Revolution . . . at least, he was not sufficiently ill for the event to get on the records of the time.

In June, 1789, soon after his inauguration as President, he was afflicted with a malignant carbuncle which compelled him to lie on one side for six weeks. This occurred in New York. Dr. Bard, the fashionable physician of the day, did not leave the President's house for nearly a week.

Washington's mother died in 1789 of a cancer of the breast, and in 1794 he had a cancerous growth removed by an operation.

Despite his tendency to illness, his muscular strength was astonishing even in an age of muscular men. This combination of physical strength and susceptibility to disease is a common phenomenon among athletes, who seldom live to an old age. Washington could bend a horseshoe with his hands. Most of the present-day feats of vaudeville strong men could have been done by him with ease. After dinner he would often sit at the table for hours cracking nuts and eating them. Usually he cracked them between his thumb and forefinger.

His horsemanship was superb. Jefferson, who was himself an excellent rider, said that Washington was "the best horseman of his age, and the most magnificent figure that could be seen on horseback."

Americans have always been hero-worshippers, and Washington was the hero of the time. Mount Vernon became the shrine of American glory, the inspiring aim of pilgrimages, the touchstone of adulation. People swarmed around the place, and stayed to dinner . . . governors of states, generals out of service, scientists, diplomats, adoring women, borrowers of money, painters of pictures, applicants for jobs.

I have mentioned the death of Martha's daughter, "Patsy" Custis, which occurred in 1773. In 1781, shortly after the surrender of Cornwallis, she lost her son "Jacky." He had not taken any part in the war, but remained in Virginia amusing himself and protecting his wife and his mother. When the army under Washington came to Virginia, Jacky volunteered as an aide on his stepfather's staff. For awhile he was seen at the siege of Yorktown, ordering people around. This little impromptu soldiering gave him pneumonia, and he died, leaving a widow and four children. His widow soon married again.

Washington adopted two of the children, a boy and a girl. The boy was George Washington Parke Custis; a mediocre, prosy soul who made a lifelong career of being Washington's adopted son. He built Arlington House, near the city of Washington, and wrote a dull book about the Father of Our Country in which he intimates, in a general way, that Washington was a near relative to God. His daughter married Robert E. Lee, who became the famous general of the Confederacy.

The girl's name was Eleanor—known in history as "Nelly" Custis. Martha Washington took charge of Nelly's education, which seems to have consisted principally of practise on the harpsichord. The poor girl had to practise for hours every day.   A visitor describes her as sitting at the instrument, "weeping and playing."

There have been some rather curious speculations as to why Washington and Martha never had any children of their own. In the Washington family there is a tradition—never before published, I believe—that in early manhood Washington had a severe case of mumps which became aggravated by neglect. In these cases mumps frequently results in sterility, a fact well known to physicians.   That is the explanation of his child-lessness current in the Washington family, and it may be the true one.

The tradition is not sufficiently explicit to include the date of this devastating attack of mumps.   It may have been the mysterious illness of 1758; yet that appears improbable, for if the mysterious illness had been the mumps, does it not seem likely that he would have said so?

§ 4

At the close of the war Congress distributed grants of land beyond the Alleghenies to officers and soldiers of the Continental army.   Washington declined to accept any of this land; he held firmly to his determination not to take any compensation for his services as commander-in-chief.   This attitude was a continuation of the heroic role which was in his mind when he declined a salary in 1775.   He wanted land and money, but they were both secondary to his desire for distinction, and for the moral force that flows from distinction.

However patriotic his motive in refusing the land may have been, it was a piece of empty generosity so far as its bearing on the national treasury was concerned.   Under the peace treaty with England the American government obtained all the territory between the Appalachians and the Mississippi river. There was land enough for everybody, land in profusion.   A grant of even one hundred thousand acres to Washington would have been only a drop in the bucket, and it would have cost the American people nothing whatever. But Washington was thinking of posterity; he did not want those who came after him to say that he had sold his services as a patriot.

His altruism as to land was rather limited in its scope. On his return from the war he learned that a large number of squatters had settled on the three thousand acres which he owned at Miller's Run in the western part of Pennsylvania, near the present city of Connellsville. This was land which he had purchased—as the reader may remember—from his destitute friend, Captain Posey, for eleven pounds and some shillings. Washington had never seen this land.

In September, 1784, he made a trip to western Pennsylvania for the purpose of ousting these people. His diary of the expedition is interesting. He was accompanied by his nephew, Bushrod Washington, and by Dr. Craik, his physician and lifelong friend. There were three servants and six horses. The party seems to have been well supplied, as I find among the list of articles carried such luxuries as silver cups, Madeira and port wine, cherry bounce, tents, tea, sugar, spices, and casks of liquor.

The road ran through Great Meadows, where Washington had surrendered to the French thirty years before. He now owned the land on which his fort had stood. The sight of the place aroused no memories of that adventure of the youthful long-ago; or, if so, such meditations did not get into his diary. He says, under date of September 12th:

> . . . stopped awhile at the Great Meadows and viewed a tenament I have there, which appears to have been but little improved, tho' capable of being turned to great advantage, as the whole of the ground called the Meadows may be reclaimed at an easy comparitive expence and is a very good stand for a Tavern.

There was a lot of excitement at Miller's Run as the news

of his approach filtered through the settlement. The pioneers who lived there had apparently taken up the land under the impression that it did not belong to anybody. They had been there for some years, had cleared fourteen farms and had put up a number of dwellings.

On the 14th he writes:

> This day also the People who lives on my land on Miller's Run came here to set forth their pretensions to it; and to enquire into my Right—after much conversation and attempts in them to discover all the flaws they could in my Deed, etc.—and to establish a fair and upright intention in themselves—and after much councelling which proceeded from a division of opinion among themselves—they resolved (as all who lived on the land were not here) to give me their definite determination when I should come to the land, which I told them would probably happen on Friday or Saturday next.

It did not really make any difference what "their definite determination" might be. Washington's mind was already made up; he listened to them simply as a matter of courtesy, for did not one of the "Rules of Civility," which he memorised in youth, say, 'Speak not injurious Words neither in Jest nor Earnest. Scoff at none although they give Occasion"?

He had to scoff a little in private, however, in the secrecy of his diary. He arrived among the squatters on a Sunday, and italic sarcasm appears in his comment on their Sunday piety, which prevents him from settling matters at once:

> *19th.* Being Sunday, and the People living on my Land, *apparently* very religious, it was thought best to postpone going among them till to-morrow.

The Lord's Day over, the discussion began briskly. A committee came to Washington and, after stating their case and saying that they did not believe they could be dispossessed, the committee declared that they were ready, nevertheless, to compromise by buying the land, if the price was low enough.

Washington was willing to sell, but he wanted twenty-five shillings an acre, a high price indeed, considering the fact that the squatters had improved the land themselves. They could not pay any such sum, so he made another proposition. Would they pay rent at the rate of ten pounds a year for a hundred acres? Even this was too much for the settlers, so they decided to stand a lawsuit. Poor judgment on their part.

Washington was disturbed by their defiance. On his way back home we find him wondering, in his diary, how he will go about proving ownership. The surveys and documents had to be looked up.

The lawsuit dragged on for two years, but in the end justice triumphed. The settlers were evicted after much trouble. There was, however, a bright side to this disagreeable episode. The improvements which had been made by the settlers, and the land they had cleared, greatly increased the value of the property. Washington sold it some years later for twelve thousand dollars. As the land had cost only fifty-five dollars and surveying fees the final outcome was, after all, very satisfactory.

His account books are a sort of epic of land speculation. He was always ready to buy and sell.

The year after the Revolution he bought, in partnership with Governor Clinton of New York, six thousand acres on the Mohawk river. Washington paid eighteen hundred and seventy-five pounds for his half. This transaction was highly profitable. In 1793 he sold two-thirds of his share for thirty-four hundred pounds, and in his will he set down the value of the remaining thousand acres at six thousand dollars.

The anti-social nature of land speculation never occurred to him; but, for that matter, it did not occur to any one else in that age, not even to Jefferson. Land, money and food become social problems only when they are scarce, and land was too plentiful in the 1780's for speculation in it to have been a subject of painful meditation.

The speculative impulse, in its spiritual significance, is the desire for conquest transferred to the commercial field. Washington's land transactions and his love for lotteries and card games were all sublimated expressions of his will to power.

But he was not dominated by the speculative instinct. His personality was intensely constructive in the material sense, but not in the intellectual sense. Above all, he was a builder, a producer of material objects.

An interesting picture of this constructive urge is shown in his connection with the Potomac Canal project. He was one of the originators of a plan to make the Potomac navigable from tidewater to Fort Cumberland. The ultimate object was to carry a canal from the head of navigable water to the foot of the hills, and to provide a road or portage that would cross the Alleghenies to the navigable Ohio. With the settlement of Kentucky and the west, it was thought that this highway would be the great commercial transportation route between the seaboard and the back country.

Long before the Revolution he began to talk about this proposed canal, though the idea did not emanate from him. In 1774 a stock company for its construction was organised, and Washington subscribed five hundred pounds. The war came on, and the project was suspended until 1784.

On the trip to his Pennsylvania lands he traced a route for the canal and its continuing road. He was intensely interested in the matter; his diary is crowded with observations and statistics, distances of one place from another, and calculations.

At Bath he met the "ingenious Mr. Rumsey," inventor of the steamboat. This mechanician applied the principle of steam propulsion to navigation long before Robert Fulton. Rumsey showed Washington a model of the boat under "the injunction of Secresy." Washington wrote that it ran on the water "pretty swift," but he thought it rather impracticable.

The Potomac enterprise and a similar project for the James River attracted great public interest in Virginia in the decade following the Revolution; and both projects were semi-officially adopted by the state. Washington, who was president of both companies, was presented by the state with a block of stock in each company. He left this stock in his will to educational institutions.

Jedidiah Morse, writing in 1792, says that the cost of the Potomac canal was estimated at fifty thousand pounds sterling. At that time part of the canal was completed. Its cost ran eventually far above the original estimate. In its final form it became the Chesapeake and Ohio Canal, which—with the coming of railroads—became a secondary appurtenance of a railroad company.

§ 5

It is as an agriculturist that Washington's constructiveness appears in its best light. He was a farmer of exceptional ability. He struggled for a lifetime with the poor soil of his Mount Vernon estate, but his methods were so painstaking, so efficient and so persistent that he managed to make his farming operations pay. Nobody has since been able to work the Mount Vernon lands without losing money on them.

He tried innumerable experiments with fruit trees, and varieties of wheat, and grasses and fertilisers. He thought his land could be improved by spreading Potomac mud over it, but he could never devise an inexpensive way of getting the mud out of the river.

His business as a farmer was well organised. The estate was divided into five farms. Over each farm was an overseer. White men, these overseers were—all except one, a negro slave named Davy. This slave appears to have been as efficient as any of the white overseers. Being a slave, he received no wages, though Washington allowed him more than the ordinary portion of food, and he was given a good deal of freedom in the matter of coming and going. The white overseers were paid about two hundred dollars a year apiece, with a house to live in. They seem to have been partly supplied with provisions by Washington, but the records are rather confusing on this point.

During the Revolution a kinsman, Lund Washington, managed the estate in the owner's absence. Thereafter, the system of managers was continued—and among them were Washington's nephews, Robert and Howell Lewis and George Augustine Washington. The nephew management does not appear to have been a success. After the Lewis *régime* we encounter Anthony Whiting, William Pearce and James Anderson.

Poor little Robert Lewis had a craving for land, in fashion with the time. One day he told his distinguished uncle that he had had a dream. In this dream his uncle had given him a piece of paper. Upon opening the document he discovered that it was a deed to a piece of land which Washington owned at some distance from Mount Vernon.

Upon hearing this dream Washington smiled, and asked Lewis why he did not dream of having received Mount Vernon as a gift while he was about it? However, it ended pleasantly enough. A few days later Washington handed a paper to his nephew, which was in reality a deed to the very land about which he had dreamed. A striking proof that dreams do sometimes come true.

A stranger named Thomas Bruff also had a dream which was not in the least degree a success. He wrote to Washington that he had lost all his property and wanted a loan of five hundred pounds. He said that he was engaged to a beautiful young lady, and that the romance was languishing for lack of money. In a dream his father came to him, he said, and told him to write for aid to·the great and good General Washington.

He wrote once, without a reply, and then his father's spirit appeared again and "toald me to Write again. I made some Objections at first and toald him I thought it presumption in me to trouble your Excellency again on the subject, he then in a Rage drew his Small Sword and toald me if I did not he would run me through. I immediately in a fright consented."

This letter was found among Washington's papers endorsed, "Without date and without success."

James Anderson, the last of the Mount Vernon managers, was a Scotchman who understood the distilling of whiskey. It was he who established Washington's distillery. This whiskey-making enterprise was profitable from the start. Washington soon acquired a reputation for making very good liquor. In 1798 the net profit was eighty-three pounds, with seven hundred and fifty-five gallons of liquor still on hand.

The total profit of the estate that year was a little short of nine hundred pounds. It would have been a great deal more, and usually was in good years, but in 1798 one of the farms showed a net loss of four hundred and sixty-six pounds.

The Mount Vernon estate was not Washington's sole source of income. He did very well at buying and selling land, as we have seen; he loaned money at interest; and he owned houses in Alexandria and Williamsburg and elsewhere which he rented. The Alexandria houses had been built by his carpenter slaves from timber cut at Mount Vernon. They were built virtually without cost.

Haworth thinks that Washington's net cash income was from ten to fifteen thousand dollars a year. This did not represent his gain in wealth, however. Through the rise in land values and the increase in slaves by births he became much wealthier, year by year, than these figures would indicate.

At the time of his death he owned sixty-two thousand acres of land, and was generally thought to be the wealthiest man in the United States.

The best known of the estate managers was William Pearce.

He went to Mount Vernon in 1793 and remained four years, resigning eventually on account of rheumatism. His salary was one hundred guineas, about five hundred and twenty-five dollars, a year; besides which he was furnished with a residence, a horse, and some of the food used by his family.

During the period of Pearce's service Washington was President of the United States. Pearce was required to send his employer weekly reports in great detail, and Washington wrote to him not less than once a week. The letters of Washington to Pearce furnish the contents of an invaluable volume published by the Long Island Historical Society.

These letters are interesting revelations of Washington's perception of details. In December, 1793, he writes:

> There is nothing which stands in greater need of regulation than the Waggons and Carts at the Mansion House. . . . Frequently have I seen a Cart go from the Mansion House, or from the river side to the new Barn with little or no more lime or sand in it, than a man could carry on his back—the consequence of this was that the Brick layers were half their time idle. . . .

The language of an efficiency expert who finds himself in the clumsy, dozing slave years.

The victuals of Ehler, the gardener, were on his mind. (Ehler was a white man.)

> You will perceive by my agreement with Ehler, the Gardener, that he and his wife were to eat of the Victuals that went from my Table (in the Cellar) instead of having it Cooked by his wife as had been the custom with them . . . it would be best, I should conceive, to let them return to their old mode, and for the young Gardener to eat with them. . . .

Some of Washington's political enemies declared that his management was so close that his negroes were half-starved.

When this story reached him he wrote at once to Mount Vernon to increase the allowance of the slaves. Mr. Whiting went too far in that direction, he thought, according to this letter to Pearce:

> From some complaints made by my Negroes, that they had not a sufficient allowance of meal, and from a willingness that they should have enough, the quantity was increased by Mr. Whiting so as to amount (by what I have learnt from Mr. Stuart) to profusion.—This is an error again on the other side—My wish and desire is that they should have as much as they can eat without waste and no more. . . . Davy at Muddy hole, has always had two or three hundred weight of Porke given to him at killing time, and I believe the Insides of the Hogs—that is—the Hastlets, Guts (after the fat is stripped off) etc., is given among the Negroes at the different places. . . .

He believed in conservation. Much of his success in farming at Mount Vernon was owing to the utilisation of waste.

> The hides of the dead cattle (though not good) should be tanned by the old man Jack, who usually attends to this business;—the leather may serve for inner Soals and repairing Shoes—and—something ought also to be done with the skins of the Sheep which have died. . . .

He writes on July 20, 1794, to Pearce to give John the Gardener one dollar on the last day of every month, "provided he behaves well." And he wants to know what is the matter with "Betty Davis, and Doll at Union Farm, that they are—more than half their time—placed on the sick list?"

Betty Davis seems to have been on his mind as he went about august Philadelphia. He wrote in February, 1795:

> By the Reports I perceive also, that for every day Betty Davis works she is laid up two.—If she is indulged in this idleness she will grow worse and worse, for she has a disposition to be one of the most idle creatures upon earth; and is, besides, one of the most deceitful.

This negress evidently continued her deceit and idleness, for a month later he wrote:

> . . . what kind of sickness is Betty Davis's? . . . If pretended ailments, without apparent causes, or visible effects, will screen her from work, I shall get no service at all from her;—for a more lazy, deceitful and impudent huzzy, is not to be found in the United States than she is.

His carpenters were building houses in Alexandria, and he noticed in the reports that one of them took six days to pave and sand a cellar. He wrote hotly to Pearce that any workman in Philadelphia would have done as much in six hours. He does not mention, however, that in Philadelphia workmen are paid wages, while his slaves have no incentive whatever, except the fear of a whipping.

In Lord Charnwood's illuminating *Life of Abraham Lincoln* there is this reference to Washington (page 37):

> Washington's attitude to his slaves is illustrated by a letter which he wrote to secure the return of a black attendant of Mrs. Washington's who had run away (a thing which he boasted could never occur in his household); the runaway was to be brought back if she could be persuaded to return; her master's legal power to compel her was not to be used. She was in fact free, but had foolishly left a good place. . . .

I quote this extract as an illustration of the pitfalls of error which beset the path of even the most truthful of historians. Lord Charnwood is truth itself, in intention. He knows a great deal about Lincoln, but not much about Washington. In this short paragraph he packs an astonishing number of misstatements.

Washington did not say that his own slaves never ran away. Such an assertion coming from him would have been ridiculous. His slaves often ran away, and we find him paying rewards for their capture and return.

MASONIC PORTRAIT OF GEORGE WASHINGTON

Reproduced from a pastel portrait made by William Williams in 1794. This portrait of Washington in Masonic regalia was painted at the request of Alexandria-Washington Lodge, No. 22, A. F. & A. M. of Virginia, to which Washington belonged.

Lord Charnwood says that the runaway slave he mentions was, by Washington's desire, to be brought back if she could be persuaded, but not otherwise. The facts are that this woman fled to New Hampshire, where public sentiment was strongly against slavery. Washington wrote that she was to be seized and brought back if it could be done without arousing a mob. He added: "However well disposed I might be to gradual abolition, or even to an entire emancipation of that description of people (if the latter was in itself practicable), at this moment it would neither be politic nor just to reward unfaithfulness with a premature preference, and thereby discontent beforehand the minds of all her fellow serv'ts who, by their steady attachment, are far more deserving than herself of favour."

Here we have an excellent example of Washington's confused thought when he attempted to express himself on any question of fundamental human rights. He is disposed to gradual abolition of slavery or even to entire emancipation, but a slave girl who emancipates herself is considered unfaithful and ought to be brought back.

Unfaithful to what? He does not say. Perhaps he meant that she was unfaithful to a position where she received no wages and where her body was owned by another person. One might as well speak of a prisoner being unfaithful to a jail.

In such contingencies Washington was not above using guile. While he was President one of his slaves named Paul escaped in company with a slave of Mr. Dulany, a neighbour. Washington wrote: "If Mr. Dulany is disposed to pursue any measure for the purpose of recovering his man, I will join him in the expence so far as it may respect Paul; but I would not have my name appear in any advertisement, or other measure, leading to it."

In short, he wanted to get his slave back, but he also wanted his name kept out of the affair. He was willing to bear his share of the cost if Mr. Dulany would bear the publicity.

On another occasion he brought a number of slaves up from Mount Vernon to act as servants around the Presidential mansion in Philadelphia. He found out soon afterwards that, according to a judicial decision in Pennsylvania, slaves brought into the state were to be considered free.

Thereupon he gave instructions to his secretary to get the slaves out of the state as quietly as possible, so that neither they nor the public would know what was intended until they were back in Virginia.

§ 6

The King of Spain sent him a jackass as a present. It was an enormous creature, of pure Andalusian breed. Washington called this jack "Royal Gift," and used him for breeding mules. He wrote amusing letters to Lafayette and others about the jack's indifference to the charms of mares, and his lazy way of going about his business. One or two of these letters might possibly be called "smutty," if one has that kind of mind.

"Royal Gift" was sent on a tour of the South. Word was circulated in advance of the jack's arrival that he would be in stud on a certain date, and that people might bring their mares. On this trip he earned nearly seven hundred dollars in stud fees.

News of his coming would fly in all directions, and his arrival had the festive aspect of a circus parade. People would come for fifty miles, bringing their families in springless covered wagons, just to get a peep at General Washington's jackass.

CHAPTER XXV

THE FEDERAL CONVENTION

§ 1

THERE were thirteen little free countries in place of the thirteen colonies. Most of the animosities and jealousies of colonial times still continued. There was a political atmosphere of the Balkan states about this aggregation of small republics.

They were flimsily held together by a document known as the Articles of Confederation. It was not a constitution; it did not make a nation; it was a sort of treaty, and was called by the men of the time "a league of friendship."

In the Continental Congress, which consisted of a single legislative chamber, each state had one vote. When a question was put the delegates from a state would get together and agree on the vote from that state, if they could. If they could not agree the state did not vote. The affirmative vote of nine states was required to carry any measure.

The Continental Congress had no power to make laws binding individuals. Its action was upon the states as political entities, and not directly upon the citizens. But, even at that, it could not compel a state to do anything. The Congress was, in fact, not a legislative but a diplomatic body. Its members were really ambassadors, and their attitude toward Congress, and toward each other, bore all the historic distrust and caution which ambassadors are supposed to have.

Many disputes between the states arose, and on numerous occasions between 1783 and 1789 the air was explosive with threats of interstate wars.

New York, for example, considered herself much aggrieved because the farmers of New Jersey brought chickens and vegetables to New York City and sold them there. This took wealth away from New York, so the New Yorkers said, and transferred it to the foreign state of New Jersey. Connecticut people, too, were draining the life-blood from Manhattan. They brought firewood down to the city and sold it from door to door. Then, with New York's money in their pockets, they would go back to the thrifty state of Connecticut, while New Yorkers worried through the sleepless nights wondering how it would all come out in the end. There was a thorough misunderstanding of the principles of trade; and an inordinate value was set on currency.

This narrow provincial sentiment was encouraged by the farmers of New York state. They had produce to sell, and it appeared monstrous to them that the New York state government, which ought to have protected them in their rights, allowed the citizens of other states to get the city trade. They might have got the trade themselves by making their prices lower, but that is exactly what they did not want to do.

After awhile the New York legislature acted. A tariff law was passed. Every chicken that came from New Jersey, every cabbage from Connecticut, had to go through a custom house and pay duty before being allowed to enter the state of New York.

Connecticut and New Jersey applied themselves to ways of retaliation. The Connecticut merchants decided to boycott New York. The New Jersey method was different. On Sandy Hook the state of New York had put up a lighthouse. The New Jersey legislature passed an act for taxing the little scrap of land on which this lighthouse stood, and the tax was made one hundred and fifty dollars a month.

There was another dispute between Connecticut and Pennsylvania which became so bitter that Connecticut was on the verge of declaring war. Long before the Revolution settlers from Connecticut had migrated to lands in northern Pennsylvania. Although they made their homes within the borders of that state they continued to follow the Connecticut laws; and, in fact, considered their communities as a part of the state of Connecticut. After the Revolution Connecticut claimed this Wyoming Valley, notwithstanding the fact that it did not touch the state of Connecticut at any point. In the quarrel that ensued men were killed and the dormant Pennsylvania militia bloomed into uniforms and bayonets. Connecticut was about to send an army to protect the people whom she supposed to be her citizens. Finally the matter came before a special federal court, organised under the Articles of Confederation, and the disputed territory was awarded to Pennsylvania.

Under the Confederation no state could keep a standing army. That was a function of the general government, but the revenue of Congress was so insignificant that it could never afford the luxury of soldiers, and its army was a very small, disarticulated skeleton.

Congress could not levy a tax. Its authority in this direction was limited to requisitions on the states, apportioned on the basis of the real estate value of each state.

The payment of the requisitions was farcical in the extent of its delinquency. In 1781 it was estimated that the continental government would require nine million dollars during the next year. It was thought that four millions might be borrowed, and the remaining five millions raised through requisitions. At the end of the year only $422,000 had been paid in the treasury. Of the requisitions levied in 1783, less than one-fifth had been received in the continental treasury by 1785.

Each state maintained its own custom house and laid duties on foreign goods according to its own notions. In 1781 Congress, worn to despair on the subject of money, asked permis-

sion of the states to collect, for continental expenses, a duty of
five per cent on all imports.

This seemed to be a feasible way out of the money trouble,
but it came to nothing. All the states but New York agreed
to this five per cent impost. New York flatly declined, so
nothing could be done. In the meantime five years had been
consumed in wrangling. There were times when the continental
treasury did not possess a single dollar of coin, though a huge
depreciated volume of continental paper currency was in circulation.

In 1786 New Jersey came out with a statement that she had
been badly treated; and she declared that she did not intend
to pay any more requisitions or to contribute in any manner
to the general scheme of things until New York stopped collect-
ing a tariff on New Jersey goods.

Nothing could be done about it. Congress was entirely lacking in executive authority. The President was merely the
presiding officer of Congress. He had no more power than
the chairman of a mass meeting.

§ 2

To get rid of the army, quietly and without trouble, was
the chief un-public question that disturbed the ruling minds
in 1783. It intruded itself sadly, like a ragged and unwel-
come guest, in the victory festivals of the period. The soldiers
had been treated shamefully, and there was an apprehension in
Congress that these patriotic protectors of the nation might
kick Congress out of doors and take charge of affairs.

Washington managed to disband the army, or most of it,
before it was aware of being disbanded. His method was to
give furloughs to batches of men, to send them away in groups
or singly, and then to send them their discharges later. The
idea behind these tactics was to get rid of the soldiers without
paying them, though Washington himself wanted them to be

paid, as his letters prove. In behalf of Congress it must be said that they had no funds to pay the soldiers; on the other hand it must be said that they made very little effort to raise money for this purpose.

The plain fact is that the commercial element of the country which had come into authoritative prominence was tired of the whole crew of patriots. They wanted to disperse the army as soon as possible. The country was full of business schemes and wartime fortunes were growing in arrogance.

Eighty soldiers mutinied at Lancaster, Pennsylvania, in June, 1783. They marched on Philadelphia and appeared in front of the State House where Congress was in session.

Congress called on the Executive Council of Pennsylvania, meeting in the same building, for protection, but the Council was afraid to bring out the militia, as it was thought that the militia might join the mutineers. The soldiers declared that they wanted their pay and intended to take it from the treasury. They pointed their guns at the Congressional windows but did not fire them. There was a rough play-boy air about the whole proceeding. Congress sent an urgent message for help to Washington—who was then at West Point—and without waiting to see what the result would be, the members of Congress unheroically slipped through the back door and made their way through a golden June sunset to Princeton in New Jersey, thus abandoning the seat of government to eighty mutineers and a sergeant.

Washington was very efficient in cases of mutiny. He sent fifteen hundred troops—best-fed and best-clothed of the army —to Philadelphia at once. That ended the mutiny. Some of the mutineers were whipped, but nobody was shot.

The fleeing Congress, wounded in the sphere of dignity, abjured Philadelphia and decided to remain at Princeton. The members were given tea and liquor by the delighted inhabitants, who assured them of protection.

Notwithstanding its grotesque adventures, the Continental

Congress managed to exist. It held one large asset. The western territory—everything from the Appalachians to the Mississippi—had been turned over to Congress by the states. Nearly all the schemes for financing the government, and for liquidating the public debt, revolved around this western land. It was, indeed, an immense domain. It is interesting to reflect that if the government had held it to this day the entire expense of the national budget could have been met from its rentals.

§ 3

The insignificance of Congress was well known in England. In negotiating the peace treaty the commissioners of the United States, representing Congress, agreed to recommend to the states that no bar or hindrance be placed against the collection of debts due to British merchants by American citizens. They also agreed to recommend that the seizure of loyalists' property be discontinued. At first, the British wanted to be paid for the effects of loyalists taken during the war. Franklin pointed out that sauce for the goose is sauce for the gander; and that, in such a case, he would expect the British government to pay for property destroyed by British troops. The argument was dropped by both sides, and the conclusion was that Congress should urge the states not to molest the loyalists any more.

Such a recommendation was made by Congress, but it had small effect. In some parts of the country, particularly in the South, loyalist property was seized right and left after the conclusion of peace.

As for the collection of debts to British merchants made before the war, it was almost impossible to find either a judge or a jury who would pass favourably on these claims; and their validity drifted into the realm of legal fictions.

The British had agreed, on the signing of the treaty, to give up their forts in the Northwest Territory. Years passed, and they still held on to these posts, declaring that they would give them up when the United States had carried out its part of the compact. This attitude seems reasonable, but it did not appeal to the Americans of the 1780's.

Just at the end of the war, another blow had been given to New England commercial aspirations by a British Order in Council which closed the ports of the British West Indies to American ships. Thus, the question which began the war was lost in its successful conclusion.

But this closing of West Indian ports was a blessing in disguise. New England ships and sailors had to have some occupation, so in the 1780's we see Massachusetts ships sailing timidly to China with goods which it was thought the Chinese might want. By the year 1800 the Chinese trade was a roaring success, and Yankee merchants were cutting the ground from under the English in that faraway market. In closing the West Indian ports they effectually developed a rival for themselves in the Orient.

In the weighty troubles that grew out of the treaty Congress revealed its weakness at every turn. From the first many leading men were dissatisfied with the Confederation, and hoped eventually to replace this feeble "league of friendship" with a closely knit national government.

Washington wrote to Hamilton in 1783:

> It is clearly my opinion, unless Congress have powers competent to all general purposes, that the distresses we have encountered, the expense we have incurred, and the blood we have spilt, will avail us nothing.

A few weeks later he wrote:

> My wish to see the union of these states established upon liberal and permanent principles, and inclination to contribute my mite in pointing out the defects of the present constitution, are equally great. All my private letters have teemed with these sentiments, and whenever

this topic has been the subject of conversation, I have endeavoured to diffuse and enforce them.

There was a body of intelligent opinion in favour of a monarchy. Strange to say, Washington was not considered, so far as we know, by these advocates of monarchy as a possible King, unless Hamilton had him in mind. He was, indeed, written to by an irresponsible colonel who hinted that he ought to be a King, though this man appears to have represented nobody but himself.

Washington was, I think, a republican at heart. What he wanted was a republic—but an aristocratic one—where the suffrage and the authority would be in the hands of the well-born and the wealthy.

The monarchy movement, if such a vague affair can be called a movement, is obscure. It became so unpopular in the end that its originators, among whom was Nathaniel Gorham and Rufus King, buried it as deeply as they could in their memories. These men felt, evidently, that no plebeian American, however distinguished he might be, was of sufficient prestige to occupy the throne. There is a strong probability that Prince Henry of Prussia, a brother of Frederick the Great, was approached on the subject before the matter was dropped.

The spectacle of some gaudy European prince, coming over to occupy a throne in our land of raw liquor and trusty squirrel rifles would have been interesting.

This clumsy playing with the idea of a monarchy was hardly more than a sort of moral nostalgia. Certainly any such attempt would have failed miserably, but there was nevertheless a well-grounded effort to create a permanent nobility by an organisation of former army officers called the Society of the Cincinnati, in which membership was to be hereditary. Washington was the first president of the society, though he accepted the office, I think, without being aware of the society's intention to influence public affairs. He was dis-

pleased with the early conduct of the organisation, and resigned from its leadership, but not until he had persuaded the
society to drop its hereditary feature.   The Society of the
Cincinnati exists to-day as a purely social, and (I suppose)
praiseworthy organisation.

The Confederation was a failure, but commerce and finance
were riding on the crest of the wave.   The close of the war
had found the small farmers, as a class, in acute poverty.   By
taking advantage of the economic needs of these producers the
money-holding groups in the coast cities had been able to
get a tight financial grip on almost the whole of the pro-
ducing class.   There were counties in which nearly every acre
was under mortgage at high rates of interest.   Usury and
profit moulded themselves into large fortunes.   The splendour
of business began to shine.

The discontent of the common people was snapping at
the heels of these primitive money kings.   In every legislature
there were proposals to repudiate debts, to issue floods of paper
money, to impair the value of contracts.   In Rhode Island the
debtors captured the legislative machinery of the state, and
repudiated virtually everything.   They made paper money
a legal tender and forced merchants and mortgage-holders to
take it.   Capital in that little state became so unsafe that it
got out as quickly as it could.   The "shameful conduct" of
Rhode Island was a topic at teas and in counting-houses from
New Hampshire to Georgia.   It was the general opinion that
something ought to be done about it.   The lawbooks were
thumbed, and spectacles rested on learned noses.   It appeared
that nothing could be done under the Articles of Confederation;
Rhode Island was a free state and could act as she pleased.

This was bad enough, but even worse was coming.   In 1786
an armed rebellion broke out in western Massachusetts and
aroused the execration of all who loved peace and profits.
The farmers of that region took up arms against the gaunt

destitution of their lives. Their lands could not produce enough to pay the interest on mortgages and provide the food and raiment for human necessity. In addition to the burden of debt, taxes had gone up in Massachusetts until they were fifty dollars per capita. Compared with this, the taxes which Great Britain had attempted to impose on the colonies were nothing more than trifling small change.

The rebels were mostly veterans of the Revolution. They put themselves under command of Daniel Shays, who had been an officer in the war. Organised with a sort of military discipline, they constituted in fact a formidable force. Lawyers took to their heels, and the frightened judges were ousted from the courts. Debts were to be abolished; everybody was to begin over with a clean slate. On this programme of extreme simplicity the rebellion throve for a brief moment. The rebels invoked the Scriptures and pointed to the ancient Jewish law under which all lands were redistributed every seven years.

Shays' army of "desperate debtors," as these men were called, created terrific excitement, not only in New England, but everywhere else. Henry Knox, the Confederation's Secretary of War, was sent to Massachusetts at once; the militia was called out; the money-lenders of Boston fluttered in agitation. Washington wrote to Henry Lee:

> You talk, my good Sir, of employing influence to appease these present tumults in Massachusetts. I know not where that influence is to be found, or, if attainable, that it would be a proper remedy for the disorders. Influence is not *government*. Let us have a government by which our lives, liberties, and properties will be secured, or let us know the worst at once.

Jefferson, on the contrary, does not appear to have been at all upset by the Shays episode . . . and, in this, he stands alone among the notables. He wrote to W. S. Smith, "God forbid we should ever be twenty years without such a rebellion."

To Mrs. John Adams—of all people—he wrote these disturbing lines:

> I like a little rebellion now and then. . . . The spirit of resistance to government is so valuable on certain occasions that I wish it to be always kept alive. It will often be exercised when wrong, but better so than not to be exercised at all.

The Massachusetts troops eventually drove Shays and his foodless men over the deep-snow hills into New Hampshire. In the meantime Rhode Island sank a notch lower in public estimation by inviting the entire Shays outfit to come to Rhode Island and live.

On a wintry day in the New Hampshire hills Shays' forlorn little army petered out. All the forces of society, represented by a swarm of bayonets, surrounded these rebels as they shivered in the snow. When they were asked by General Lincoln, in command of the Massachusetts troops, what they wanted to do, they said that they wanted to go home. He allowed them to go, and Shays' Rebellion came to an end.

There was some feeble effort to punish the ring-leaders, but nothing came of it. It seems quite clear that the money ring which ruled Massachusetts was afraid to proceed with prosecutions.

After this occurrence the moneyed classes were convinced that affairs were in a sad plight. There was no protection anywhere for capital or investments. A strong, centralised government was urgently needed; the stronger the better.

Now, for the first time in American history we see finance lifting its head above land as an object of attention. It had its origin in the public debt. Let us consider, for a moment, the status of the government's financial obligations in the later 1780's.

First, there was the foreign debt—that is, money borrowed abroad by the commissioners of the Continental Congress.

This amounted, in 1789, to approximately ten million dollars, with arrears of interest of nearly two millions. Second: The domestic continental debt, which ran up to a principal sum of twenty-seven millions; to which must be added unpaid interest amounting to thirteen millions. Thus, the continental obligations, in all, were a little more than fifty millions of dollars.

The precise total of the combined state debts is unknown, owing to the slipshod character of the records, but it was around twenty millions of dollars . . . say, seventy millions for both continental and state debts.

This sum of seventy millions represents only the funded obligations, represented by certificates, or bonds. Besides, there was the enormous volume of continental paper currency, which went down and down until it became entirely worthless and passed out of sight. More than two hundred million dollars of it has been issued. Very little of it was ever redeemed, on any terms.

The holders of the certificates, or interest-bearing obligations, considered them of small worth; they might be bought readily at prices ranging from one-sixth to one-twentieth of their face value.

But, suppose a powerful national government could be put in place of the Confederation . . . a government in complete control of tariffs and indirect taxation. Let us suppose further that it could be done so quietly and so secretly that men with money would be able to buy up this whole mass of depreciated paper before its holders, principally ex-soldiers and very ordinary people, realised the import of the new authority. Then the next step would be a large fiscal operation by which the new and strong government would assume the entire volume of obligations, both state and continental. In a short time these depreciated certificates would rise to par.

Golden dream!

A dream it was . . . but, as the virile, go-getting magazines tell us, there are men who make their dreams come true. The men behind the Constitution made theirs come true, to their great profit.

The first difficulty was how to begin. The Confederation had to be abolished. If a public campaign were started to do away with the government and put a new one in its place the substantial citizens of the country would have the whole pack of the debt-ridden and improvident clawing at them; and every little landless theoriser would put forth his plan. Perhaps there were more Shays than one in the country. Some of them might support their fatuous democratic ideas with armies.

Besides, a general public knowledge of what they intended to do would vitiate the scheme from the outset. Even the most ignorant holder of certificates would hear of it eventually and keep his government paper, or sell it only at a high price.

Into this circle of ideas there came the shrewd notion to call a conference of the states at Annapolis to consider commercial regulations, to devise a uniform system of duties, and so on. After commercial matters had been discussed, then other important matters might be taken up . . . or the convention might simply drift into a discussion of the general welfare. In this way it might be possible to devise a stronger government and one financially able to assume the debts—under the guise of a commercial conference.

The Annapolis convention, which met in September, 1786, did nothing of any consequence. Only five states were represented. Alexander Hamilton was there . . . five states and Hamilton. However, there was a sufficient interchange of views to give the delegates a sense of confidence, so before adjourning they passed a resolution in which they asked Congress to call a convention at Philadelphia, the following May, "to devise such further provisions as shall appear to them necessary to render the constitution of the federal government adequate to the exigencies of the Union, and to report to Congress such an act, as, when agreed to by them, and con-

firmed by the legislature of every state, would effectually provide for the same." This is how the Federal Convention,
which created the Constitution of the United States, came
into being.

§ 4

There was something about the Federal Convention that
makes one think of a meeting of the board of directors of a
large and secretive corporation. Fifty-five sleek, well-to-do
gentlemen sitting carelessly in a closed room. Gentlemen who
know one another very well. Gentlemen of good manners who
apologise for reading their letters in public. Esoteric jokes
pass around with snuff-boxes of engraved silver. Mild and
polite attendants. Tip-toeing doorkeepers, and keys that
crunch loudly in their locks.

In the chair of authority sits the impressive Washington . . .
grey inside, but majestic outside. Boredom flickers in his eyes;
he is grave, serious and bored. But he has the consciousness
of doing his duty, the spiritual uplift of meeting expectations.
Posterity has its eye on that assembly, and he knows it. No
matter how others may act, posterity shall never say—with
truth—that George Washington failed in his part.

At Washington's side sits little Secretary Jackson, fumbling
with his bewildered notes. He left them to posterity, too;
but posterity has never been able to make head or tail of them.

The delegates pledged themselves to secrecy, like a jury in
a murder trial, and for four months they met behind locked
doors with hardly a whisper of their proceedings reaching the
open air. But some of the delegates took notes for their own
use. Among the note-takers was James Madison. It is to
him that we owe the most complete report of what occurred.
During his lifetime he kept his notes in inviolable secrecy.
They were published in 1840 . . . fifty-three years after the
Convention.

The general impression among the people of the country was that the Federal convention's powers were limited to a revision of the Articles of Confederation. This impression did not extend to the men in the Convention, nor to the well-informed elsewhere.

Dr. Charles A. Beard, outspoken and scholarly historian, has given us in his *Economic Interpretation of the Constitution of the United States,* a complete picture of the economic affiliations of each member of the Convention. Dr. Beard's book is based on first-hand research; it is ably documented and is streaming with footnotes and citations; one marvels at the patience of its author with fly-blown records. He has shown that at least five-sixths of the members of the Convention were holders of public securities or in some other economic sense were directly and personally interested in commercial affairs which would benefit by their labours. His data also prove that most of the members were lawyers by profession and that "not one member represented in his immediate personal economic interests the small farming or mechanic classes."

Among the members was Robert Morris, friend of Washington, and by far the most important financial figure of the nation. At that time the position of Robert Morris was something like the position of the elder J. P. Morgan one hundred and twenty-five years later. He was the acknowledged arbiter of American business.

Gouverneur Morris—of the same name but not a relative of Robert Morris—was also a member. This is the Morris, it will be remembered, who complained at the beginning of the Revolution that the people "begin to think and to reason."

Slaveholders and Southern aristocrats were in evidence in numbers. Among them were the two Pinckneys and John Rutledge, of South Carolina.

George Mason, Washington's former political mentor, sat with the Virginia delegates. He and Washington were not so friendly as in the old days.   Mason was a states' rights man, jealous of crystallised authority and looking with a suspicious eye on all kinds of shrewd manipulation.

Land speculation and money-lending were among the economic interests of at least thirty-eight of the delegates, including Washington, Franklin, Gerry, Gorham and Wilson.

Of the fifty-five delegates Dr. Beard says that the names of forty appear on the records of the Treasury Department as holders of public certificates.

The Convention was singularly lacking in doctrinaires, in idealists. Jefferson, the great idealist and humanitarian of the epoch, was in France as the official representative of the government.

It was also lacking in a spirit of inquiry. One would naturally think that a body of men engaged in a constructive work of such immense possibilities would summon before them, day after day, citizens of all degrees and from all sections, in an effort to find out what was wrong and what was required to set it right. But they did not do this; they never summoned anybody. To have done so might have revealed the purport of the Convention, and they could not risk that contingency.

The Constitution was planned like a *coup d'état;* and that was its effect, in truth.

§ 5

As soon as the Convention was organised Edmund Randolph rose and proposed an entirely new plan of government. It had the backing of the Virginia delegates—including Washington, presumably—and was supposed to have been the work of James Madison.

According to the Virginia plan the national legislature was to consist of two houses. The members of the lower house were to be chosen directly by male citizens entitled to vote.

The members of the Senate were to be elected *by the members of the lower house* from a list of persons suggested by the legislatures of the various states. In both the upper and lower houses the votes were to be by individuals, and not by states. The number of representatives from each state was to be in proportion to its wealth, or to its free inhabitants.

An interesting feature was the power of Congress to veto state laws. This would have reduced the state legislatures to rather absurd nonentities.

There was to be a national executive, chosen by Congress for a short term, and ineligible for a second term. The Supreme Court, according to the Virginia plan, was to be chosen by Congress, and was to hold office during good behaviour.

The Virginia plan was, in reality, the basis of the Constitution as it was finally shaped, though it was twisted and turned about so completely in the four months' discussion that it was all but forgotten.

The first dissension occurred over the relative representation of the states. Small states like Delaware and New Jersey saw themselves completely overshadowed and outvoted by the large delegations from the more populous states, if representation on the basis of population or wealth were conceded. Rhode Island would have probably taken this side, too, if that little state had been represented at the Convention. Rhode Island was invited, but declined to send delegates.

A compromise was reached eventually by giving two Senators to each state, irrespective of size.

Alexander Hamilton thought the Virginia plan too liberal. On June 18th, he made a long and interesting speech, in which he set forth his theory of government. His remarks are too extensive for quotation in full, but I shall give a few pertinent extracts:

> My situation is disagreeable, but it would be criminal not to come forward on a question of such magnitude. . . .

I am at a loss to know what must be done—I despair that a republican form of government can remove the difficulties. . . . All communities divide themselves into the few and the many. The first are the rich and well-born, the other the mass of the people. The voice of the people has been said to be the voice of God; and however generally this maxim has been quoted and believed, it is not true in fact. . . .

It is admitted that you cannot have a good executive upon a democratic plan. See the excellency of the British executive—he is placed above temptation—he can have no distinct interests from the public welfare. . . .

He went on to say that he was in favour of having an Executive, or President, elected for life on good behaviour. The lower house to be elected for three years by the voters of the states; and the Senate to be elected by electors who should be chosen for that purpose by the people. The Senators to remain in office during life.

But all that is mere introduction. Here is the milk in this cocoanut:

The Executive to have the power of negativing all laws—to make war or peace with the advice of the Senate —to make treaties with their advice, but to have the sole direction of all military operations, and to send ambassadors and appoint all military officers, and to pardon all offenders, treason excepted, unless by advice of the Senate. On his death or removal, the President of the Senate to officiate with the same powers, until another is elected. Supreme judicial officers to be appointed by the Executive and the Senate. The Legislature to appoint courts in each State, so as to make the State governments unnecessary to it.

All State laws to be absolutely void which contravene the general laws. An officer to be appointed in each State to have a negative on all State laws.

If we look into these ideas we observe that what he proposes is a monarchy with an elected king. The Executive would have an absolute veto power over the acts of Congress; and this veto would extend even to the state legislatures, as he suggests "an officer to be appointed in each state to have a negative on all state laws."

A little too much, this was, for the gentlemen of the Convention. Hamilton never understood the American people, but most of the members of the Convention knew them very well. However attractive Hamilton's plan may have been to some of the delegates, all realised that it could never hope for adoption in its raw form. Something much more evasive and soft-spoken would have to be framed. Hamilton's plan was received so coldly that his feelings were hurt, and he left the Convention and went home, where he stayed until the Convention had nearly finished its work.

Washington felt Hamilton's absence, and wanted him to return. On July 10th Washington wrote to him:

> When I refer you to the state of the counsels which prevailed at the period you left this city, and add that they are now, if possible, in a worse train than ever, you will find but little ground on which the hope of a good establishment can be formed. In a word, I almost despair of seeing a favourable issue to the proceedings of our convention, and do therefore repent having had any agency in the business.

Very characteristic of Washington. He was the most pessimistic great man in all history. Does not this letter remind you of his complaining epistles written during the Revolution, when he wishes that he had never accepted his position, and how much happier he would be as a private soldier?

The letter files of America to-day are full of communications of this type, written by millionaires and heads of large enterprises. No accomplishment is quite good enough to satisfy them, the country is going to the dogs, profits are falling, salaries are high, labour is getting out of bounds, affairs are beginning to look panicky. . . .

The true executive mind is not a mind of optimism. Its tendency is to undervalue, to depreciate. Existing on the achievements of others, on the constructive work of subordinates, it spurs those around it to action by taking a gloomy view of their functions and their future.

On August 7th the Convention considered the qualifications for suffrage under the new Constitution. The wisdom of Mr. Gouverneur Morris spread around the room. He said, "The time is not distant when this Country will abound with mechanics and manufacturers [he means factory hands] who will receive their bread from their employers. Will such men be the secure and faithful Guardians of liberty?"

He concluded that they would not.

Dr. Franklin thought that, "It is of great consequence that we should not depress the virtue and public spirit of our common people, of which they displayed a great deal during the war. . . . "

There was a good deal of talk about "the dangers of the levelling spirit."

Most of the members were of the opinion that there should be a property qualification, but the subject was such a delicate one that they decided to leave the matter to the states.

Charles Pinckney thought there ought tc be a property qualification for members of the national legislature, for the president and the judges—enough property, he said, to make them "independent and respectable."

The trouble with this theory is that experience has shown that wealth does not necessarily make a man either independent or respectable.

Mr. Pinckney's assertion inspired the aged Franklin to struggle to his feet and say that some of the worst rogues he ever knew were the richest rogues.

There was a bitter North-and-South contest over the question as to whether slaves should be counted in apportioning the number of representatives to the states. This discussion eventually broadened out into a general argument on the slavery question. All the states, except South Carolina, wanted to put an end to the importation of slaves. If the slave trade was stopped the South Carolina delegates declared that their state would not enter the Union.

That moment was the opportunity of Washington's life, and he missed it. He had declared on many occasions that he was opposed to slavery—and his influence was incalculably great, What would have happened if he had turned over the chair to some one else for a moment and had said from the floor of the Convention that as far as he was concerned South Carolina could stay out of the Union if she wanted to continue in the slave trade?

Certainly the Union could have existed without South Carolina . . . and it is equally certain that South Carolina could not have existed long without the Union.

Washington said nothing; he did not express an opinion at the Convention but once, and that was on a trifling question of no weight.

What would Jefferson have done in Washington's place? We do not know; we can only guess . . . and guessing is not the province of the historian. Jefferson wrote in opposition to the slave trade before the Revolution. In writing the Declaration of Independence he inserted a clause against the slave trade which was stricken out by Congress. In 1784 he succeeded in putting the Northwest Ordinance through Congress in the face of bitter opposition. The Northwest Ordinance prohibited slavery forever in the territory north of the Ohio. Whether this would have been his attitude in the Federal Convention—had he been there—is a question without a solution.

In the end it was decided that, in determining the population basis for representation, a slave should be counted as three-fifths of a person. The New England delegates were not satisfied. They maintained that, if such a provision was adopted, they wanted every horse in New England to be counted as three-fifths of a person. Their argument seems reasonable, for slaves had no more to say about the government than horses.

In the matter of slave importation a compromise was made to the effect that slave-catching should continue until 1808. This satisfied South Carolina.

The Constitution evolved a series of compromises; everybody was willing to concede something, provided that the main object of a strong government—and one able to cash in the depreciated paper—should be the result.

§ 6

The Constitution is a remarkably able production. The intention of its framers was to create an economic document which would protect established and acquired rights; and this intention has been carried out successfully under the smooth flow of phrases. It is highly self-protective, and is skilfully designed to break up and dissipate radical attacks on any of its fundamental axioms, while at the same time it permits a large freedom of movement to those who are entrenched behind it.

It is full of curious subtleties which are revealed only after an earnest study. The keystone of the conservatism that it embodies is in the judiciary and the Senate. The judiciary—the Supreme Court—possesses a veto power over all acts of Congress which do not fall within the Constitution's narrow limits; and the Supreme Court is a body which maintains an unchanging existence during the lives of its members.

But, even before the Supreme Court is encountered, a radical measure must run the gauntlet of the Senate . . . and the

Senate is elected for six years. In the Senate the smaller states
have an enormous preponderance, owing to the constitutional
principle of equal representation. At the present time (1926)
the Senators from twenty-five small states, having an aggregate
population of less than one-fifth of the total number of inhabitants of the country, can negative any proposition, although it may have passed the House and represents the desire
of four-fifths of the nation's citizens.

The Senate is always subject, more or less, to indirect
manipulation through the ease with which strong financial
interests may control the small states.

Gladstone, who represented commercial interests all his life,
said that the American Constitution is "the most wonderful
work ever struck off at a given time by the brain and purpose of man."

Much of the credit for this wonderful work must be given
to the brain and purpose of Gouverneur Morris. He was a
member of the Committee for Style and Arrangement, which
had charge of the actual drafting of the Constitution. Channing makes an interesting remark about the part played by
Morris: [1]

> The actual phrasing seems to have been left to Morris;
> but he sometimes followed suggestions made by persons
> who were not members of the committee. The draft of
> the Constitution when it reappeared in the Convention was
> widely different in many respects from the project that
> had been committed to it. By changes in phraseology
> and arrangement and by the introduction here and there
> of phrases like "impair the obligation of contracts" the
> friends of strong government accomplished a large part
> of the purpose that had brought them to Philadelphia.

Washington's part in shaping the Constitution was negli-
gible. He was the presiding officer of the Convention, and, as
such, he refrained from taking part in the debates. Lodge and

[1] Channing: *History of the United States*, Vol. III, page 514.

other adulators hazard the opinion that he must have exercised great influence through private conversation, and unofficially, but this is pure assumption. The records of the time do not mention any such conversations. Washington's *Diaries* contain no comment on the work of the Convention, but are given up chiefly to memoranda as to teas and dinners. On one occasion he went on a fishing trip with Gouverneur Morris to Valley Forge. While Morris was fishing, Washington rode around the old Valley Forge encampment, then silent and haunted by memories. What his emotions were—if any—he does not say.

There was considerable difficulty in getting some of the states to adopt the Constitution. Some of the legislatures were unruly, and its adoption wavered in the balance. In this crisis Hamilton, Madison and Jay came forward with a series of masterly essays which were published under the title of *The Federalist*.

We have seen what Hamilton's ideas of government were, but now he was all for the Constitution, though he said in private letters that the plan was as remote from his own ideas as anything could be.

When the question of adoption was in doubt the opponents of the Constitution circulated a report that Washington was not in favour of it. Upon hearing this rumour he came out with a statement—expressed in various letters—that he was for the Constitution, and urged its adoption.

§ 7

One of the most significant facts about Washington's long and distinguished career is that he never formulated any coherent theory of government. Hamilton and Jefferson both worked out distinctly articulated systems of politics. Each stood for a definite, cogent set of ideas of social structure. But there is nothing in the body of American political thought that we can call Washingtonism.

At first impression his political character appears utterly nebulous. His writings are a vast Milky Way of hazy thoughts. We turn their thousands of pages, marking sentences and paragraphs here and there, hoping to assemble them and build up a substantial theory of the common weal.

Can it be that this huge aggregation of words has no impressive import? We are about to think so; however, when we study them in detail we find that his observations are sensible, sane and practical. Yet, somehow, they do not coalesce; they lack a fundamental idea, a spirit that binds them all together.

That was our first conclusion, but then we were thinking in terms of the great philosophies . . . of Rousseau, of Locke, of Adam Smith, of Voltaire, of Ricardo. Later, one day, we thought of the mind of the large city banker, and we saw Washington's political personality in a flash of revelation. Washington thought as almost any able banker who might find himself in the eighteenth century would think.

The banker stands for stability, and Washington was for that. The banker stands for law and order, for land and mortgages, for substantial assets—and Washington believed in them, too.

The banker wants the nation to be prosperous; by that he means that he wants poor people to have plenty of work and wealthy people to have plenty of profits. That was Washington's ideal.

The banker does not want the under-dog to come on top; not that he hates the under-dog, but he is convinced that people who have not accumulated money lack the brains to carry on large affairs, and he is afraid they will disturb values. The banker is not without human sympathy; but he is for property first, and humanity second. He is a well-wisher of mankind, though in a struggle between men and property, he sympathises with property.

In this we see Washington's mind. A coherent political philosophy is not an impelling necessity to this type of intellect.

The banker-mind is for any political party which does not overturn the accepted axioms of valuation.

Washington's ideas of government were not broad nor lucid, but they were very substantial.

CHAPTER XXVI

WASHINGTON AS PRESIDENT

§ 1

WASHINGTON was elected first President of the United States by unanimous choice of the electors. The vote for Vice-President was not at all unanimous, although nearly everybody agreed that, as Washington was a Southerner, a New England man ought to be the Vice-President. What about Samuel Adams, Father of the Revolution? Would it not be fitting and proper for him to sit in one of the seats of the mighty, next to the Father of Our Country? Many people were of that opinion, but it was hardly the time for revolutionists. William Roscoe Thayer says, in his naïve manner, "too many remembered that he had been hostile to the Federalists until almost the end of the preliminary canvass and they did not think that he ought to be chosen."

I should say not. As head of the Senate, what a disaster he would have been to the Federalist financial programme. His cousin, John Adams, likewise a New Englander, was a much safer man. Preferences were divided, and other candidates were considered, but in the end John Adams received a majority of the votes.

Washington's progress from Mount Vernon to New York was a triumphal march. At Philadelphia there were flower-decked maidens and an arch of victory. As he passed under this structure a concealed mechanism was operated so that a wreath was lowered by a wire until it rested on Washington's head.

Trenton had no arch, but it had a poem, which was recited

by thirteen young girls dressed to represent the thirteen states. As Rhode Island was still remaining moodily outside the circle of states, and refusing to have anything to do with the Constitution, it would be interesting to know how the young lady who represented Rhode Island was dressed, and I have turned over innumerable ancient pamphlets in an effort to find out, but without success. Perhaps she appeared as Cinderella.

The lady poetess of the occasion was Mrs. Richard Stockton. She had previously sent Washington some verses about himself as the national hero. His reply to her letter accompanying the verses is one of the few epistles in which he comments on a literary subject. He wrote:

> Fiction is to be sure the very life and soul of Poetry —all Poets and Poetesses have indulged in the free and indisputable use of it, time out of mind. And to oblige you to make such an excellent Poem on such a subject, without any materials but those of simple reality, would be as cruel as the Edict of Pharaoh which compelled the children of Israel to manufacture Bricks without the necessary ingredients.

Amid universal joy he was inaugurated at New York on April 30, 1789. The town quivered with the roar of cannon and the golden voice of bells. Flags and ribbons flashing in the breeze. Sketch artists with pads of paper; and people clinging to roofs. Carriages creeping perilously through the jam of humanity.

Washington appeared on the balcony of the Federal Hall, at the corner of Broad and Wall Streets, and was sworn in office with his hand resting on a "large and elegant Bible." During his inaugural address he appeared to be flustered, or overcome with emotion. He kept putting his hands in his pockets and taking them out again. His hands trembled, and his papers got mixed.

He wore on this occasion a dark-brown suit, with white silk stockings and silver shoe-buckles, while at his side there hung a steel-hilted sword. His hair was powdered and worn in a queue behind. The clothes which he wore were of American manufacture—a fact which was announced proudly by every newspaper.

Congress was then in session in New York, but early the next year the government moved to Philadelphia.

Washington notified Congress that he did not want to accept any pay for his services, but desired to have his expenses paid. After considerable reflection Congress came to the conclusion that it would be best to pay him a salary of twenty-five thousand dollars a year and allow him to spend it as he pleased. Perhaps some little calculation of Washington's expenses during the war helped them to reach this decision. His salary for the eight and one-half years of the Revolution would have amounted to fifty-one thousand dollars. But, as he declined to receive his salary, Congress had paid his expenses—and the sum of expenses was about sixty-four thousand dollars, though this included several thousand dollars chargeable to secret service.

We have a complete, and very interesting, account of the organisation of the Presidential household. There were five white servants who received seven dollars a month each; and they were supplied with liveries costing twenty-nine dollars apiece. There were five black servants—slaves without wages —whose clothes are put down at forty-six dollars a year apiece. Two negro maids—clothes, forty-six dollars a year; a housekeeper at eight dollars a month; three white women at five dollars a month; a valet at one hundred and sixty-two dollars a year; and a steward at twenty-five dollars a month. Eighteen servants in all. They were so numerous that they must have fallen over one another. Besides these house servants there was a coachman. For carrying on his official business he had a secretary, an assistant, and three aides.

The combined salaries of the five were only two thousand dollars a year.

§ 2

Before leaving Virginia Washington had gone to Fredericksburg to tell his mother good-bye. He never saw her again; she died in the fall of 1789.

Washington's relations with his mother do not appear to have been as sentimental as his biographers would have us believe. The fact is that we do not know very much about his mother, or what Washington thought of her; but what we do know leads one to the conclusion that they were not sentimental. Certainly, he was not bothered by anything resembling the Freudian concept of a mother complex.

After the Revolution, when he was a distinguished man, and his house was constantly full of notable visitors, his mother wrote that she would like to visit Mount Vernon and spend some time there with him and Martha. In reply Washington wrote that he did not want her to come; that she would not understand the people who were around him, and that they would not understand her; that she would be miserable in such society, and that it would make him unhappy.

From time to time he went to see her, and occasionally he sent her money, usually accompanying the money with a letter about the many demands made on him. In 1786 he wrote, on sending fifteen guineas, that "I have now demands upon me for more than £500, three hundred and forty odd of which is due for the tax of 1786; and I know not where or when I shall receive one shilling with which to pay it."

The truth is that he was always hard up for ready money. This seems inconsistent with his growing wealth; but it must be remembered that his wealth was principally in land. He was land-poor. Indeed, he was so pressed for cash that he had to borrow money to make the trip to New York to be inaugurated as President, yet at that time his fortune, over and above all obligations, was probably about four hundred thousand dollars.

Bearing on this subject, there is in existence an interesting letter from Washington's mother, which is unfortunately without date. It is addressed to her son John Augustine, who died in 1787, so it must have been written before or during that year. She wrote:

> Dear Johnne,—I am glad to hear you and all the family is well, and should be glad if I could write you the same. I am a going fast, and it, the time, is hard. I am borrowing a little Cornn—no Cornn in the Cornn house. I never lived soe poore in my life. Was it not for Mr. French and your sister Lewis I should be almost starved, but I am like an old almanack quite out of date. Give my love to Mrs. Washington—all the family. I am dear Johnne your loving and affectionate Mother.
>
> P.S. I should be glad to see you as I don't expect to hold out long.

This letter may have been merely a querulous complaint without any basis in fact. There is not sufficient evidence extant to enable us to decide whether it was or not.

It is certainly known, however, that at one time in the 1780's she was accepting gifts from her neighbours. She complained so incessantly of her poverty that a movement was started in the Virginia Assembly to give the old lady a pension. When the news of this reached Washington he wrote to a friend in the Assembly to stop the agitation by all means. He said that he was confident "that she has not a child that would not divide the last sixpence to relieve her from real distress. This she had been repeatedly assured of by me; and all of us, I am certain, would feel much hurt, at having our mother a pensioner, while we had the means of supporting her; but in fact she has an ample income of her own."

Shortly after this he sent his brother to find out the true state of her affairs, and he said that he wanted her to be comfortable, for, "while I have anything I will part with it to make her so."

§ 3

Martha Washington did not like New York and its Presidential splendour. She wrote: "I lead a very dull life here and know nothing that passes in the town. I never goe to any publick place,—indeed I think I am more like a state prisoner than anything else, there is certain bounds set for me which I must not depart from—and as I cannot doe as I like I am obstinate and stay at home a great deal."

There was indeed a lot of formality about those early Presidential years. Martha was called Lady Washington and was expected to act like a queen. Washington wanted to be called "His Mightiness the President of the United States." The speaker of the House laughed at this title, and was never forgiven by Washington. They finally decided to call him simply "The President of the United States."

No matter; titles were of rubber and there were plenty of people to stretch them. Some called Washington "Mr. President"; others preferred "His Excellency"; and still others went as far as to say "His Majesty."

The first Presidential levee, or reception, must have been an awkward affair. It was arranged by Colonel Humphreys, one of Washington's aides. People standing around the sides of a room, gentlemen and ladies in full dress. Humphreys enters the door, which is flung wide open by flunkies, and announces: "The President of the United States." Washington enters, and everybody curtsies. All remain standing in silence. Washington goes around the room, stopping before each person and saying a few words.

That is the way it was, and it displeased Washington. When it was over he said to Humphreys, "By God, you've taken me in once, but you shall never do it again." After that his receptions were not so ceremonious, but they were never informal.

William Sullivan, who had many opportunities for observing him at this period, says: "His deportment was invariably grave; it was sobriety that stopped short of sadness. His presence inspired a veneration, and a feeling of awe, rarely experienced in the presence of any man."

One naturally wonders whether the awe was inspired by Washington, or by the majesty of his position. Even the jolly Mr. Taft inspired awe while he was President. In Washington's case I think the impressiveness was in the man himself, as we find people who met Washington long before he was President making observations similar to Sullivan's. But there is no doubt that his manner of "sobriety that stopped short of sadness" showed itself in a deeper tone after the Revolution, when he had become grey inside, and had lost an irretrievable something from his life.

Sullivan continues: "His mode of speaking was slow and deliberate, not as though he was in search of fine words, but that he might utter those only adapted to his purpose. It was the usage for all persons in good society to attend Mrs. Washington's levee every Friday evening. He was always present. The young ladies used to throng around him and engage him in conversation. These were some of the well-remembered belles of that day, who imagined themselves to be favourites with him. As these were the only opportunities which they had of conversing with him, they were disposed to use them. One would think that a gentleman and a gallant soldier, if he could ever laugh, or dress his countenance in smiles, would do so when surrounded by young and admiring beauties. But this was never so; the countenance of Washington never softened, nor changed its habitual gravity."

The kind of man who doesn't shake hands . . . who has no gossip . . . who is not at all anxious to hear what one has to say . . . who listens to your best jokes with a solemn face, and says coolly, "Is that so?" That was Washington. No wonder he was awe-inspiring.

But he laughed sometimes . . . he laughed once, at any rate, at a play in Dunlap's theatre, called *Poor Soldier* in which he, as a Continental general, was described in good-humoured comic verse. Everybody was looking at his box, and hundreds of people were witnesses of his laughter. Next day the newspapers mentioned the fact that he had laughed.

Philadelphia was at that time the social and financial centre of the country. When the government settled there for its ten years' stay, in 1790, the Washingtons were, of course, on the peak of the social pyramid.

The great society leader of that day was Mrs. William Bingham, the wife of one of the wealthiest speculators in lands and public securities, and a leading Federalist. Mrs. Bingham was a slender, shimmering beauty . . . a skittish lady who shocked her puritanical guests with dainty little oaths . . . a superb hostess . . . a woman of culture and political acumen. She was an admirer of the sedate Washington, and even tried to admire Martha, so thoroughly were she and her husband bound up in Federalist politics.

Mrs. Bingham was of great value to the Federalist cause, to the party of high finance and speculation. In the critical period of Washington's administration her charming entertainments kept many a wavering delegate or Senator in line.

§ 4

When the mechanism of the Washington administration got itself shaped into being it was found that Alexander Hamilton was to be Secretary of the Treasury; Thomas Jefferson, Secretary of State; Henry Knox, Secretary of War; and Edmund Randolph, Attorney-General.

At this distance in time one is puzzled at Washington's

MRS. WILLIAM BINGHAM
Painting by Gilbert Stuart

selection of Jefferson. He and Jefferson were far apart in every fundamental idea. They were not only far apart . . . they moved in different orbits . . . they did not think in the same terms . . . to get an idea, in its bare essence, from one to the other was like signalling to Mars. And there was Hamilton. Jefferson was even further from Hamilton than he was from Washington, for politically Hamilton was simply Washington become vivid and articulate.

But our perspective is historical. We know more about Jefferson than Washington knew; and we know more about Washington and Hamilton than Jefferson knew. The cabinet experiment was new and untried. There were no political parties, in our sense. At that time ideas had not crystallised. This possibly explains Washington's choice of Jefferson . . . then, we must not forget that Jefferson had been five years in France, was presumably familiar with the inwardness of the foreign mind; and Washington thought that this experience ought to make him an excellent Secretary of State.

The only reference to Jefferson that appears in Washington's printed letters before 1789 is in a note to Robert Livingston in 1783, written while peace was being negotiated with Great Britain. He wrote: "What office is Mr. Jefferson appointed to that he has, you say, lately accepted? If it is that of commissioner of peace, I hope he will arrive too late to have any hand in it."

Jefferson had already aroused distrust of himself and his policies among the conservatives by his determined efforts to force liberal ideas into the Virginia constitution. In Washington's appointment of this political antagonist to a place in his cabinet we see, therefore, either a tolerant generosity and breadth of spirit or an ignorance of the profound difference between his opinions and those of Jefferson. I think Washington's motives were mixed. He thought probably that all parties ought to be represented among his advisers.

It was not long before the irreconcilable differences of Ham-

ilton and Jefferson began to appear. Cabinet meetings became
a debating society, the President and the two other secretaries
sitting in idle silence while Hamilton and Jefferson argued
with rancour over even the most superficial questions.

Their ideas were basically so antagonistic that there was
no possibility of an agreement on the smallest matter. Jefferson was for people; Hamilton was for property. In that we
have the essential remoteness of one from the other. Both
were men of great intellectual ability; and both were sincere
and honest, in their way.

In all collective human affairs there is need for both conservative and radical bodies of opinion, but this necessity has
never been recognised in America. It is recognised in England,
where bitter radicals and hardened conservatives settle down in
Parliament side by side, and endeavour to patch up compromises—temporary, perhaps—on which both sides may agree.
They differ on every vital issue, but the itch of dissension is
soothed by respect for each other's opinions.

Politics in Washington's administration was too raw and
sharp to admit of compromise. Hardly anybody appeared to
have a comprehension of the inherent stability of things. Elections do not overthrow civilisation; they merely—and occasionally—overturn governments. But our forefathers thought
all would be lost if an election went against them. Jefferson's supporters were considered half-savage; and Jefferson
himself—one of the most cultured men of his time—was such
a social outcast in Philadelphia that he was very seldom seen
in the houses of people of his own class. Martha Washington,
tactful wife of the President, remarked scornfully that the
walls of her drawing-room were marred by "the dirty fingers
of the democrats."

Hamilton flourished in this flamboyant, aristocratic air.
His views were undiluted by liberalism. He did not think the
common people fit to govern themselves and said so flatly. He
thought, with his friend Gouverneur Morris, that "those who

own the country ought to govern the country." The important question of how the owners of the country had come into its ownership did not seem to trouble him. His opinions were not disturbed by the small souls of money-getters nor by the shabby tricks of money-getting.

There can be no doubt of Hamilton's sincerity, nor of his own personal honesty. In his position as Secretary of the Treasury he could have made a large fortune by methods which would have been only slightly dishonest. But he did not make much money, and virtually all he made came from his law practice.

How then may we account for Hamilton . . . a careerist and a lover of the rich . . . a snob, in truth . . . whose ability was of the first order, but who accumulated no money for himself?

The secret of his personality is that he was haunted forever by the fear of social inferiority. He wanted to be well thought of by the wealthy and well-born. He loved the adulation of important men and women, and he achieved this by being brilliant rather than wealthy. He possessed the extraordinary intellectual capacity which is so often found among those who owe their birth to a voluptuous fancy.

Washington presided with gravity at these recurring cabinet quarrels. We may see the five of them, taut and attentive under the angular light of tall windows in the dull-brown afternoons. The atmosphere was that of a court-room instead of a cabinet. Papers rustled; there were triumphs of statistics, catch questions, and sophistries driven pitilessly into corners and slaughtered in broad daylight. The crisp staccato of Hamilton's words ran in and out among the pauses of Jefferson's Virginia drawl.

Knox, who was devoid of ideas, usually sided with Hamilton . . . as he would, for men without ideas always side with the party that is in power at the time. Edmund Randolph was sometimes on one side and sometimes on the other.

Washington, with the weariness of dialectics pressing heavily upon him, and a little confused by all these fine points, endeavoured to be fair in his decisions; but, after all, he had to decide . . . and did not reason seem to be on Hamilton's side?

He was heartily glad, we may be sure, when Jefferson resigned in 1793. Later, he wrote to Timothy Pickering that he would not appoint to an important position any man "whose political tenets are adverse to measures which the general government are pursuing. . . ."

One such experiment had been enough.

§ 5

When Congress met for the first time after the government was organised Washington drove down to Federal Hall in his own magnificent coach drawn by four horses. His aides in uniform went ahead of his carriage on white horses. Then came a procession of carriages containing his private secretaries and the members of the cabinet. His nephew, Mr. Lewis, rode behind the Presidential carriage on horseback. Rather stately, this approach of the Executive to the halls of legislative wisdom. These ceremonies continued until Jefferson became President. He abolished ceremony and sent his message to Congress by a secretary.

The government had hardly started to work before high finance, through Hamilton, began to play its part. As Secretary of the Treasury he proposed that the government fund all the outstanding certificates of indebtedness of the Continental Congress at par—that is, to issue new six per cent bonds of the government and exchange them at one hundred cents on the dollar for the forty millions of outstanding certificates issued by the defunct Continental Congress. Also he proposed to take over the debts of the states—about twenty millions—and fund them on the same basis.

The document in which he made this proposal is a model of argumentation. In it he refers to the sanctity of the debt—a question on which every one, of all parties, agreed—and he proceeds to outline his scheme in clear and lucid sentences. Then he discusses the possible objections, and answers them. His invariable plan in presenting any proposition was to include the criticisms that were likely to arise. In this way he forestalled argument by answering the objections before they had time to mature.

As soon as the matter came up in Congress the manipulators got busy. Messengers on galloping horses set out to every part of the country. Sailing vessels, the swiftest to be found, turned their noses toward distant Charleston and more distant Savannah. Agents were instructed to buy up every scrap of Continental and state paper; to get it away from its original holders for ten, twenty, forty, fifty cents on the dollar.

Speed was necessary. The news was slow in getting about in those days, but nevertheless before long the discussion in Congress would percolate to the most remote backwoods settlement, and even poor ex-soldiers who could not read would hear of it and hold on to their little wrinkled pieces of paper.

Speed in Congress was necessary, too. Hamilton knew very well that when an issue becomes old and wrangled over it is likely to be defeated. The object here was to jam the measure through. But a hitch in these sprightly proceedings arose in the person of James Madison, who collected a cantankerous party of supporters.

What about the original holders? Madison wanted 'to know why the government should enrich a crew of rich speculators who were buying this paper right and left at twenty cents on the dollar. The funding operation ought to benefit the original owners of the paper, or it should not be done at all.

Large commotion. Uneasy heads lay on speculative pillows through the sleepless nights. It looked as if, after all, the golden dream was to turn into mere pewter.

Madison proposed that in case a certificate should be presented by its original holder he should receive one hundred cents on the dollar; but if it were presented by a purchaser he should get the highest market price at which the depreciated paper had sold in the market, and the difference between that price and par should be given to the original holder. He said he considered that a reasonable plan.

There were many persons high in finance who thought Madison far too reasonable to be a member of Congress. The joy was oozing out of life.

But Hamilton held other cards in his hand.

Most of the opposition came from the South, and at that time there was nothing treasured in the Southern heart more dearly than a hope that the permanent capital of the nation would be established in a Southern state.

It was thought by everybody that the capital of the United States, wherever located, would eventually become the nation's largest city. Washington, Madison, Jefferson—and all the Virginians—wanted the capital on the banks of the Potomac.

Hamilton talked quietly with some of the dissenters, pointing out to them the marvellous beneficence of his funding scheme, and also discussing the advantages of a Southern capital . . . and how the two ideas hung together, in a way. If the funding plan were defeated, Hamilton thought the permanent capital, destined to be the metropolis of the Western Hemisphere, would be located in the northern latitudes. After these informal chats opposition faded into silence.

That explains why the stately capital of our republic was built on a mosquito-ridden morass by the side of the Potomac river.

The golden dream came true. It has been estimated that the speculators cleaned up about forty million dollars on the transaction, and the South got the capital. The original holders of the certificates did not get much, but they were mostly strong, healthy people, with willing hands and hearts, well able to work . . . and labour is good for poor people.

Hamilton's next move was to propose the organisation of a central banking institution, the Bank of the United States, modelled on the Bank of England. Capital, ten million dollars—of which the national government was to subscribe two millions. The remainder was to be sold to the public at the rate of four hundred dollars a share. The Bank was to be a semi-governmental institution.

The object of the Bank was ostensibly to provide fluid capital for the growing business of the country, and to furnish a repository for government funds. These purposes could have been carried out just as well by privately-owned institutions, so the real reason for the establishment of the Bank was something else.

We do not have to look far to see that this move was a part of Hamilton's intention to nullify the liberal features of the Constitution as far as possible; to identify the government with proprietary interests. Mr. Lodge, Hamilton's biographer, says as much. . . . "The full intent of the policy was to array property on the side of the government. . . . He had been unable to introduce a class influence into the Constitution by limiting the suffrage for the President and Senate with a property qualification, but by his financial policy he could bind the existing class of wealthy men, comprising at that day the aristocracy bequeathed by provincial times to the new system, and thus, if at all, assure to the property of the country a powerful influence on the government" (Lodge's *Hamilton*, p. 90).

Hamilton was the rising star of the era. The loudly aggressive business element was for him. Every possessor of a mushroom fortune made by buying depreciated paper believed in him. All the little toads that hop around the roots of the money-tree, hoping to pick up something for nothing, were Hamiltonians.

Washington was the greatest Hamiltonian of them all, because he saw that Hamilton stood for financial stability and the development of the wealthy class. Mr. Lodge says, "He [Washington] met every criticism on Hamilton's policy without concession, and defended it when it was attacked. To Hamilton's genius that policy must be credited, but it gained its success and strength largely from the firm support of Washington." The Bank bill overrode the opposition of the Jeffersonians, passed Congress, and the Bank was organised. It paid a ten per cent dividend in the first six months of its operation.

High finance in America was born at that time. Speculation became the chief activity of the day. Land gave way to money. Paper fortunes came into existence . . . wealth created through sleight-of-hand tricks with paper and ink. The Age of Raw Money and Commercialised Men began, and has continued from that day to this.

If we examine Hamilton's work we find that much of it was based on constructive ideas which became curiously distorted through his manipulation. The Continental debt should have been paid, of course, as a matter of honesty, and Hamilton's funding plan was excellent, save for the fact that he paid the debt to the wrong people, and turned the whole affair into a mere swindle.

Banking and a stable currency are needed in a commercial country. Hamilton brought them into existence, though in doing so he managed to identify the idea of government with that of property so thoroughly that it has never been disentangled.

George Mason—the former friend of Washington—said that Alexander Hamilton had done more harm to America than the British armies.

§ 6

What of Washington while these great events were happening? Was he, too, engaged in shaping the American mind?

He seems to have been principally a figure-head, a symbol. He was almost as impersonal at the top of the government as a statue on top of a monument would have been. We see his hand in appointments to office, in routine affairs, in a vast correspondence.

In 1789 he made a trip through the New England states; and in 1791 he made a great Southern tour which carried him as far south as Charleston, Savannah and Augusta. The story of these pilgrimages is hardly worth the telling; it would be a monotonous repetition of addresses of welcome, banquets, poems, arches, and young girls with flowers.

His never-failing notes made on these tours, and appearing in his *Diaries*, give us an opportunity of seeing the country through his eyes. According to them, his vision was filled principally by material objects. Here is an extract from the first entry on the Eastern trip, made at Rye, New York:

> The Road for the greater part, indeed the whole way, was very rough and stoney, but the Land strong, well covered with grass and a luxuriant crop of Indian Corn intermixed with Pompions [pumpkins] (which were yet ungathered) in the fields. We met four droves of Beef Cattle for the New York Market, (about 30 in a drove) some of which were very fine—also a flock of Sheep for the same place. We scarcely passed a farm that did not abd. in Geese.

The American people had not become accustomed to Presidents; they thought of Washington in terms of royalty. A merchant named Barrell wrote a letter describing Washington's visit to Boston, in which he said: "His Majesty, while here, went to the manufactory of oilcloth, and was exceedingly pleased. The spinning for the manufactory is done by a number of girls who were dressed clean, and in general are likely. His Majesty made himself merry on this occasion, telling the overseer he believed they collected the prettiest girls in Boston."

Very much like a modern President, despite the burden of "His Majesty." Washington was determined to please and handed out compliments on these jaunts, but there is no record of him kissing babies.

§ 7

Under the treaty made with France in 1778 the United States guaranteed the possessions of France in the West Indies. The treaty also contained a provision which might be construed as allowing France, in time of war, to use our harbours as shelters for her privateers.

This treaty, with its concessions to France, was based on American gratitude for French aid in the Revolution. In 1793 an assertive person named Charles Genêt, representing the revolutionary French government, landed on our shores and demanded in the name of France that we live up to our treaty obligations. He and his brother revolutionists were to learn that gratitude does not go far when it conflicts with interest.

France was then at war with England, and any attempt on our part to protect the French West Indies would have involved us at once in a new war with Great Britain. But there was the plain wording of the treaty. Washington was disturbed and confused. The cabinet, including Jefferson, thought we ought to maintain a position of neutrality; but the question was on what excuse could the treaty be disregarded?

Excuses are always found when they are urgently needed. In this case the excuse was that the treaty had been made with Louis XVI, and that as that king had lost his head and his monarchy had been destroyed, the treaty no longer existed. The excuse was poor, but the reason behind neutrality was sound.

The dormant antagonism to Washington began to crystallise around Genêt. He found himself suddenly, and probably to his surprise, a prominent figure in American public life. A strong party in favour of France appeared among the people. Hamilton was known to be an Anglophile, and besides, the story of the funding episode had spread over the country, with exaggerations and distortions. A great many people believed that the entire transaction had been accomplished by the use of English gold.

Genêt was something of a fool. He thought the huzzaing around him was inspired by his own personal charms. The dinners and brass bands and tri-coloured cockades were accepted by him as tributes to France and himself, when in fact they were expressions of bitter discontent against the administration.

John Adams wrote that "ten thousand people in the streets of Philadelphia, day after day, threatened to drag Washington out of his house, and effect a revolution in the government, or compel it to declare war in favour of the French revolution and against England."

Genêt thought the country was all for Genêt, so he went over Washington's head and appealed directly to the people. This brazen insult could not be endured. Genêt's papers were returned to him, and he was told to go home.

He was afraid to go home; was afraid the fierce revolutionists would cut off his head because of the mess he had made: so he subsided at once, became a quiet American citizen, married George Clinton's daughter, and his descendants live in mild Poughkeepsie to this day.

The Genêt episode had revealed a turbulent current of dissatisfaction under the smooth surface of affairs. This discontent was greatly augmented by the Jay Treaty with England.

John Jay, aristocrat and Anglomaniac, who was described by Thomas Paine as "the sycophant of everything in power," was detached by Washington from his important duties as Chief Justice of the Supreme Court and sent as a special envoy to

England to negotiate a new treaty which would clear up all outstanding disputes.

Mr. Jay became a sort of social lion in London. After associating agreeably with Lord Grenville of the Foreign Office for a few months he came back to the United States with a treaty which was the wonder of the age.

He had obtained England's agreement to give up the Northwest territory, and to turn the question of debts over to a commission; also he had secured for American ships the right to trade with the British West Indies. But while this West Indian privilege existed, no cotton, sugar, rum or other product which might compete with the West Indies was to be exported by the United States to Europe. Almost incredible . . . but nevertheless true.

The plain truth is that John Jay was a third-rate statesman in a first-rate position. He had been completely blinded by the glitter of the British aristocracy.

The uproar over the treaty was terrific. Washington had to put it through the Senate, or at least he thought so. His popularity went to its lowest mark. With the aid of Hamilton and the leading Federalists he contrived to get the treaty approved by the Senate on a majority of one vote, though even at that the Senate's approval was on condition the West Indian clause be stricken out.

§ 8

By the end of 1795 Washington was near the end of his second term, and his administration was on the rocks. It had lost prestige everywhere and the country was waiting for it to end, as one might wait for a person to die.

Most of the bitter opponents of the administration thought that Washington, though honest and well-meaning, had not been equal to his task, and had become a tool in the hands of unscrupulous people.

Others, not so generous, included Washington himself in a campaign of personal vilification.

Benjamin Franklin's grandson was one of the leaders in the personal abuse. This man, named Bache, was editor of *The Aurora* newspaper. He declared that Washington was "inefficient," "treacherous," had "little passions" and was in "search of personal incense."

"If ever a nation was debauched by a man," said *The Aurora*, "the American nation has been debauched by Washington."

William Duane, another editor, wrote a pamphlet addressed to Washington, in which he asserted "that had you obtained promotion . . . after Braddock's defeat, your sword would have been drawn against your country."

One of his most violent opponents among the editors was Philip Freneau, a clerk in the State Department under Jefferson. Washington wanted this clerk, whom he called "the rascally Freneau," discharged, but Jefferson declined to do it. It was supposed by well-informed people at the time that Jefferson had inspired some of Freneau's articles, but Freneau swore on oath that Jefferson had nothing to do with them.

Thomas Paine wrote to Washington an open letter of criticism. He says that he was "opposed to almost the whole of your administration; for I know it to have been deceitful, if not even perfidious."

> Monopolies of every kind marked your administration almost in the moment of its commencement. The lands obtained by the Revolution were lavished on partisans; the interest of the disbanded soldier was sold to the speculator; injustice was acted under the pretence of faith, and the chief of the army became the patron of the fraud.

Most of these violently bitter letters and pamphlets against Washington were mere diatribes. Some of them contained an element of truth; others were lies inspired by people without a rudimentary sense of honesty.

Washington never took any public notice of these attacks. But he spoke of them in private conversation, sometimes with great heat.

The esteem in which he had long been held by the people came back almost instantly as soon as he was out of office. On his way back to Mount Vernon in March, 1797, he was escorted through every town by groups of the leading citizens.

Before leaving office he issued a Farewell Address which has become one of the classics of American political literature. The Farewell Address was not written by Washington, but by Hamilton, at Washington's suggestion. According to the accepted story of its preparation Washington submitted a rough draft to Hamilton with a suggestion that Hamilton go over it and improve it, but Hamilton rewrote it from beginning to end. Washington wrote to Hamilton that there ought to be something about education in it, but Hamilton thought the topic of education should be reserved for a speech by Washington. I cannot find any trace of Washington's style in this document; throughout it bears the marks of Hamilton's crisp literary touch.

The Farewell Address contains Washington's final advice to the American people. . . . We must, of course, accept it as coming from him, as he signed it . . . and therefore it represents his mature wisdom.

It is narrow in its scope, and is, in fact, largely a plea for closer union between the states and an admonition against foreign entanglements. It contains nothing about slavery, which was to be the bitter question of the next two generations; and nothing about the basic rights of men under republican institutions.

CHAPTER XXVII

DUST AND ASHES

§ 1

AMERICA has always felt a little awkward in the presence of its retired heroes. To keep on living after all is over is as embarrassing as to be an actor who has to remain on the stage after his part has been played. Most of our surviving heroes know this well, and keep as quiet as possible.

Washington kept quiet indeed after going home to Mount Vernon. He was then very grey inside, his interest in life had melted away, he was no longer a hero in his own mind; he was merely a sad, disillusioned old man who felt himself nearing the horizon of life.

§ 2

He has been considered the least understood of our great men, when in truth he is the best understood. People have thought that they did not understand him because they could not see in him anything that was not in themselves.

It was just in that quality that his greatness lay. He was the American common denominator, the average man deified and raised to the nth power.

His preoccupations were with material success, with practical details, with money, land, authority . . . and these are the preoccupations of the average American.

He was great in all ordinary qualities. Courage was, I think, his most significant trait, and courage is a most ordinary phenomenon. He was utterly honest, but his honesty was combined with shrewdness; and that is the kind of honesty admired by the average American. Washington would not commit a dishonest act on any consideration, but he would get the better of another man in a trade, if he could.

Ideas had only a small part in his life. He did not consider them important, nor does the average American. He respected ideas only when they had the force of authority, or of money, or of a political party. Then one must take notice of them. Here we see the typical captain of industry attitude. The American millionaire employer is willing to let labour talk as much as it pleases and to spout radical speeches. No objection to that . . . but when it organises and goes on a strike—that is another and much more serious matter.

He was thoroughly undemocratic . . . and this, too, is typically American, for our country is the most undemocratic of all the great free nations. He did not understand the economic status of labour. He thought all his life that employers "provide bread" for their workers, when the economic truth is that the workers provide bread for their employers.

His life melts into the background of his time. It is impossible to write his biography without writing history—not because he made history, but because history, in its making, made him. He was so much a part of his epoch that he evolved with it. At times he is all background, and his personality almost disappears in the immense panorama of events.

He was vain, fond of adulation and power, and greatly disturbed by criticism, but he was—so I think—a little ashamed of his vanity, and concealed it under an appearance of great modesty.

There were hard, harsh streaks in his personality, though on the whole he was magnanimous and kindly. Any one who knows the long resentments of human nature cannot help being impressed by his generosity toward his personal enemies.

He was not a man of first-rate ability, but in many ways he was a great man . . . not only great, but very great.

I do not think that he was a good general. By this I mean that he did not know how to bring out the potential military resources of the American people, nor how to build up an army that would fit the American spirit. Nevertheless, I feel that at times he held the Revolution together by his force of character.

His mind was of the executive type. That is, his ability expressed itself in the selection of subordinates, and in getting results through them. Yet, at times, his selections were exceedingly poor. He chose Benedict Arnold to command the most important military post in America; and he picked John Jay as an envoy to negotiate a treaty with Great Britain.

His spiritual life was dim. He thought in material terms. The inner significance of people and events was beyond his range.

§ 3

In the later years of his life, after his retirement from the Presidency, he spent much time in going over his papers and correspondence, putting it in order, annotating it, and doubtless suppressing a part of it.

He saw clearly that he was a great figure on the world's stage, to be talked about and written about. Posterity hovered in the distance. He was eagerly intent on making a good impression on people yet to come. So we see him at Mount Vernon, in his last days, correcting his musty documents, revising his early quaint spelling and punctuation, and inserting high-sounding words to take the place of the lusty vocabulary of his youth.

This gave Jared Sparks his unfortunate inspiration. Mr. Sparks was president of Harvard and a historian of note. In the 1830's he published a twelve-volume *Life and Writings of Washington* in which he had edited, changed and dignified Washington's language. Into Washington's writings he put words which are used only by pompous schoolmasters. Not only did he edit—he suppressed letters and parts of letters.

When Sparks had finished his job of revising Washington's letters he copied out his revisions and destroyed some of Washington's originals or gave them away. His excuse was that many of the letters were mere imperfect drafts. From a biographical standpoint this is both interesting and important. It was without a doubt in part an attempt to conceal Washington's personality.

In a letter to McHenry, then Secretary of War, Washington described his life at Mount Vernon after his retirement from public life:

> You are at the source of information, and can find many things to relate, while I have nothing to say that would . . . amuse a secretary of war at Philadelphia. I might tell him that I begin my diurnal course with the sun; that if my hirelings are not in their places by that time I send them messages of sorrow for their indisposition; that having put these wheels in motion I examine the state of things further . . . that by the time I have accomplished these matters breakfast (a little after seven o'clock, about the time I presume that you are taking leave of Mrs. McHenry) is ready; that this being over I mount my horse and ride round my farms, which employs me until it is time to dress for dinner, at which I rarely miss seeing strange faces, come, as they say, out of respect for me. Pray, would not the word curiosity answer as well? And how different this is from having a few cheerful friends at a cheerful board. . . . I resolve that as soon as the glimmering taper supplies the place of the great luminary I will retire to my writing-table and acknowledge the letters I have received; that when the lights are brought I feel tired and disinclined to engage in this work, conceiving that the next night will do as well. . . .

But it may strike you that in this detail no mention is made of any portion of time allotted for reading. The remark would be just, for I have not looked into a book since I came home; nor shall I be able to do it until I have discharged my workmen; probably not before the nights grow longer, when possibly I may be looking into Doomsday book.

§ 4

On December 12, 1799, he rode around his plantations as usual. The day was stormy, with a fall of snow, which turned into a cold rain. When he reached home he complained of chilliness. His secretary, Tobias Lear, said he saw snow in his hair, but Washington remarked that his greatcoat had kept him dry.

The next day, which was Friday, he complained of a severe cold, but he sat up until late that evening reading the newspapers. Lear read aloud to him the debates in the Virginia Assembly.

Between two and three o'clock on Saturday morning he awoke Mrs. Washington and told her that he was very ill. He could hardly speak. His physician, Dr. Craik, came early in the morning; but before he arrived the people at the house had prepared a mixture of molasses, vinegar and butter, which they tried to get him to take, but he could not swallow a drop.

Bleeding was the universal remedy for everything in those days. Before the physician arrived he was bled by an overseer. Dr. Craik, upon his arrival, saw that he was dealing with a case of quinsy. He put a blister on the General's throat and bled him again. Two more physicians came. They realised that Washington's condition was serious; and Washington realised it, too.

At about four o'clock in the afternoon he said to Lear, "I find I am going, my breath cannot continue long; I believed from the first attack it would be fatal—do you arrange and record all my late military letters and papers—arrange my accounts and settle my books."

Some of Washington's biographers, moved by moral senti-ment, no doubt, describe an affecting scene of the Bible being read to the dying man. This assertion is not borne out by the narratives of Tobias Lear or Dr. Craik, both of whom were continuously in his bedroom on his last day, and were witnesses of his death. Lear's account is very circumstantial. No mention is made in these accounts of the Bible being read to Washington, or of a Bible in the room, or of his dying with his hand on a Bible, as one writer says he did. No minister was present at his death. None was summoned, although there was plenty of time to have brought a minister if he had wanted one.

During the afternoon he was bled a third time. The general opinion of modern physicians is that he was killed by bleeding.

As night was falling, and the candles were being brought in the room, he pressed Dr. Craik's hand and said, "Doctor, I die hard, but I am not afraid to go."

To his negro body servant Christopher, who was in at-tendance on him, and had been standing for hours, the dying man—considerate of others to the last—motioned feebly with his hand and whispered, "Sit down."

Just before his death he placed the fingers of his left hand on his right wrist, and Lear, watching him closely, saw his lips move in counting his own pulse.

He died about ten o'clock at night, Saturday, December 14th. Mrs. Washington, bowed at the foot of the bed, asked "Is he gone?"

Upon being told that he was, she said " 'Tis well. All is now over. I have no more trials to pass through. I shall soon fol-low him."

§ 4

On the next Wednesday he was buried in the vault at the foot of the hill.

A bright, clear day. A high wind sings in the bare trees, and the wintry Potomac is like a sheet of cold blue steel. The people and the troops on the lawn are statues in their silence. Martha, a little bowed old lady in black, leans on the arm of a young man as the procession moves slowly down the river slope. There is the casket with its sheathed sword and its flowers, creeping slowly, as men creep to eternity. Bareheaded, in white lawn sleeves and fluttering black, a man paces by the coffin, his eyes on an open book. Above the wind and the creaking branches rises the deep and vibrant voice of the Church:

"O spare me a little, that I may recover my strength; before I go hence, and be no more seen.

"Lord, thou hast been our refuge, from one generation to another.

"Before the mountains were brought forth, or ever the earth and the world were made, thou art God from everlasting, and world without end.

"Thou turnest man to destruction; again thou sayest, Come again, ye children of men.

"For a thousand years in thy sight are but as yesterday; seeing that is past as a watch in the night.

"As soon as thou scatterest them, they are even as asleep; and fade away suddenly like the grass.

"In the morning it is green, and groweth up; but in the evening it is cut down, dried up, and withered.

"For we consume away in thy displeasure; and are afraid at thy wrathful indignation.

"Thou hast set our misdeeds before thee; and our secret sins in the light of thy countenance.

"For when thou art angry, all our days are gone; we bring our years to an end, as it were a tale that is told.

"The days of our age are three-score years and ten; and though men be so strong that they come to four-score years, yet is their strength then but labour and sorrow; so soon passeth it away, and we are gone.

"So teach us to number our days, that we may apply our hearts unto wisdom.

"Glory be to the Father, and to the Son, and to the Holy Ghost. As it was in the beginning, is now, and ever shall be, world without end. *Amen.*"

BIBLIOGRAPHY

The following works have been read or consulted in writing this book:

Adams, Charles Francis, *Studies Military and Diplomatic*. New York, 1911.
Serene essays on doubtful points in American history. The papers on "Bunker Hill," "The Battle of Long Island," "Washington and Cavalry" and "The Campaign of 1777" will be found interesting by students of the American Revolution.

Adams, James Truslow, *Revolutionary New England, 1691-1776*.
Outspoken, conscientious, interesting. His picture of New England revolutionary thought is without a superior in literature.

Adams, John, *The Works of John Adams, With Life of John Adams by Charles Francis Adams*. 10 vols. Boston, 1856.
John Adams was intelligent, wise, foolish, queer, vain, irascible, lovable, big and small. His letters and comments are fresh, vivid—and his point of view is usually sensible.

Adams, John and Abigail. *Familiar Letters of John Adams and His Wife, Abigail Adams, During the Revolution*. Boston, 1875.
They wrote to each other as if they were writing to sympathetic strangers. With the exception of two or three letters, the book reads like a series of school compositions on the events of the day. But they both set forth many interesting facts in these starchy epistles.

Allen, Gardner W., *A Naval History of the American Revolution*. 2 vols. Boston, 1913.
The most satisfactory book I have found on the early development of the American navy.

Andrews, Charles M., *Colonial Self-Government*. New York, 1904.

Austin, Mary S., *Philip Freneau, The Poet of the Revolution*. New York, 1901.
Freneau was a ship captain who left the sea and became a journalist and poet. His poems are poor effusions; and his journalism was of

Bibliography

the hair-raising, vehement style. He hated Washington as president, and his attacks were supposed to have been inspired by Jefferson, but both Freneau and Jefferson said they were not.

Baker, William S., *Washington After the Revolution*. Philadelphia, 1898.

Ball, G. W., *The Maternal Ancestry and Nearest of Kin of Washington*. Washington, 1885.

Bayard, Martha P., *Her Journal 1794-1797*. Edited by S. Bayard Dod. New York, 1894.

Beard, Charles A., *An Economic Interpretation of the Constitution of the United States*. New York, 1923.

Beard, Charles A., *Economic Origins of Jeffersonian Democracy*. New York, 1915.
These two volumes by Dr. Beard are able contributions to the history of class-conscious political groups.

Beveridge, Albert J., *Life of John Marshall*. 4 vols. Boston, 1916.
The best legal statement of the Fairfax land case is in this work.

Blanchard, Claude, *Journal de Campagne, Guerre d'Amerique* (1778-1783). Paris, 1881.
Lively memoirs by the commissary-general of Rochambeau's army.

Bond, B. W., Jr., *The Quit-Rent System in the American Colonies*. New Haven, 1919.
The most informative treatment of the quit-rent system that I have come across.

Botsford, Jay Barrett, *English Society in the Eighteenth Century as Influenced from Oversea*. New York, 1924.

Bowden, Witt, *Industrial Society in England Towards the End of the Eighteenth Century*. New York, 1925.
A compact statement of the changes brought about in English industrial life by the late eighteenth century development of steam-power and other inventions.

Bowers, Claude G., *Jefferson and Hamilton*. Boston, 1925.
A splendidly written book, excellent throughout. It begins with the inauguration of Washington as President, and its theme is the

Bibliography

conflict between the ideas of Jefferson and Hamilton during the first years of the republic.

Brissot de Warville, *Nouveau Voyage dans les Etats-Unis.* 3 vols. Paris, 1791.

Brown, A. E., *John Hancock, His Book.* Boston, 1898.
A laudatory life of the famous Hancock, without depth or any real understanding of Hancock's character. It presents a good picture, however, of the superficial aspects of big business in the eighteenth century.

Channing, Edward, *A History of the United States.* 6 vols. New York, 1926.
Prof. Channing is a coldly scientific historian with a fine sense of proportion. He is contemplative rather than argumentative. His work is intentionally colorless. The period of the Revolution and time of George Washington form the subject matter of Vols. *II, III* and *IV.*

Chastellux, Marquis de, *Voyages de M. le Marquis de Chastellux dans l'Amerique Septentrionale.* 2 vols. Paris, 1788.
This is the most helpful of all the French books of travel in eighteenth century America. Chastellux was a member of the French Academy. He came to America in 1780 with Rochambeau as a major-general and remained for about three years.

Clark, George L., *Silas Deane,* New York, 1913.

Coman, Katharine, *Industrial History of the United States.* New York, 1925.
A text-book for colleges. Useful because of its compactness.

Conway, Moncure D., *George Washington and Mount Vernon.* Published as Vol. IV of the *Memoirs of the Long Island Historical Society.* Brooklyn, 1889.
Contains much curious and little-known information, some of which is not true.

Crawford, Mary Caroline, *Social Life in Old New England* Boston, 1914.

Curtis, William Eleroy, *The True Thomas Jefferson.* Philadelphia, 1901.

Curwen, Samuel, *Journal and Letters.* Boston, 1864.
Mr. Curwen was a well-to-do merchant of Salem, who was sixty years old when the Revolution began. He appears to have become a

Bibliography

loyalist by mistake. That is the only way I know to describe his attitude. In his *Journal* his sympathies are divided; he hopes the British will win, and that the Americans will not be beaten. He fled to England and was there for nine years. His mind was inquisitive and quaint, with a strain of superstition. He gives some interesting pictures of refugee loyalists in England.

Custis, George Washington Parke, *Recollections and Private Memoirs of Washington.* New York, 1860.
    Not to be relied upon. Rambling reminiscences of Washington flavored with high-flown adoration.

Dexter, Elisabeth Anthony, *Colonial Women of Affairs.* Boston, 1924.

Doniol, Henri, *Histoire de la participation de la France à l'établissement des Etats-Unis d'Amerique.* 5 vols. Paris, 1886.
    By far the best history of the French alliance, but it is quite too long, with its documents and references, for the ordinary reader. Anyone who wishes to write a biography of Vergennes will find all the necessary material in these volumes.

Dunbar, Seymour, *A History of Travel in America.* 4 vols. Indianapolis, 1915.
    The first volume is the only one that deals with travel before the end of the eighteenth century. Written evidently for the general reader. Is very interesting. Contains many quaint old wood-cuts.

Earle, Alice Morse, *Curious Punishments of Bygone Days.* New York, 1896.

Earle, Alice Morse, *Stage-Coach and Tavern Days.* New York, 1922.

Ellet, Mrs., *The Queens of American Society.* New York, 1868.
    Sketches of thirteen American ladies, of whom only two (Mrs. John Jay and Mrs. John Hancock) belong to the Revolutionary period.

Farnsworth, Lieut. Amos, *Diary.* Cambridge, 1898.
    Of small value, except as a revelation of the narrowest type of Puritan mind. Farnsworth was a soldier in Washington's army, and was wounded, but there is not much about military or political affairs in his diary. Now and then he committed some kind of secret sin— he did not say what it was—and his mind was always sopping with remorse.

Farrand, Max, *The Records of the Federal Convention.* 3 vols. New Haven, 1911.

Bibliography

Carefully compiled report of the Federal Convention of 1787. Very helpful in studying the formation of the Constitution.

Faulkner, Harold Underwood, *American Economic History*. New York, 1924.

Fersen, Comte Axel, *Diary and Correspondence*. Boston, 1902.
Useful because of the author's comments on Washington and other officers.

Fisher, Sydney George, *The Struggle for American Independence*. 2 vols. Philadelphia, 1908.
The best history of the American Revolution, in my opinion. The author has breadth of perception, and a luminous understanding of men and events. The length of the work—nearly four hundred thousand words—makes it rather heavy unless one is greatly interested in details.

Fisher, Sydney George, *The Legendary and Myth-Making Process in Histories of the American Revolution*.

Fiske, John, *Old Virginia and Her Neighbors*. 2 vols. Boston, 1897.

Fiske, John, *The Critical Period of American History, 1783-1789*. Boston, 1892.

Fiske, John, *The American Revolution*. 2 vols. Boston, 1891.
Does not compare as a historical study with Sydney George Fisher's *Struggle for American Independence*. Mr. Fiske starts out with too many unquestioning assumptions as to the purity of the patriots and the greatness of George Washington. These assumptions prevent him from discussing many doubtful points in Revolutionary history.

Ford, Paul Leicester, *The True George Washington*. Philadelphia, 1909.
Describes George Washington, in short, vivid chapters, as one would see him and his career from the outside. Not much effort at an analysis of his personality.

Ford, Worthington Chauncey, *George Washington*. 2 vols. New York, 1900.

Franklin, Benjamin, *Autobiography*. Compiled and edited, with notes, by John Bigelow. New York, 1909.

French, Allen, *The Day of Concord and Lexington*. Boston, 1925.

Bibliography

Gay, Sydney Howard, *James Madison*. Boston, 1884.

Gibbs, George, *Memoirs of the Administration of Washington and John Adams*. Edited from the papers of Oliver Wolcott. 2 vols. New York, 1846.

Gibbes, R. W., *Documentary History of the American Revolution*. 2 vols. New York, 1855.
> Letters and documents relating to the Revolution in the South, chiefly in South Carolina.

Giesecke, Albert Anthony, *American Commercial Legislation Before 1789*. New York, 1910.
> A fair piece of work. Careful research and many illuminating facts. It is a historical monograph, intended more for the student of the period than for the general reader.

Gould, F. J., *Thomas Paine*. London, 1925.
> The best biography of Thomas Paine.

Graydon, Alexander, *Memoirs of His Own Time*. Philadelphia, 1846.
> A sprightly young man at the time of the Revolution. He grew up in Philadelphia, entered Washington's army as an officer, was captured by the British and was a prisoner in New York for some time. He had the bad literary habit of telling almost everything of importance in his footnotes, which are voluminous.

Greene, Francis Vinton, *General Greene*. New York, 1913.
> This biography, helpful as it is, would have been better if Nathanael Greene had not been an ancestor of Francis Vinton Greene.

Griffin, A. P. C., *A Catalogue of the Washington Collection in the Boston Athenum*. Boston, 1897.

Griswold, Rufus W., *The Republican Court, or Society in the Days of Washington*. New York, 1854.
> I have found this book very useful. The illustrations, which are handsome steel engravings of post-Revolutionary ladies, are not to be relied upon. The frontispiece, supposed to be a picture of Martha Washington, is really a picture of Washington's sister, Betty Lewis.

Hale, Edward Everett, *Franklin in France*. Boston, 1887.
> A comprehensive study of Franklin's activities in France, told mainly through the letters written by Franklin and the letters written to him. It has the fairest account of the Arthur Lee-Silas Deane squabble that I have seen.

Bibliography

Hamilton, Allan McLane, *The Intimate Life of Alexander Hamilton*. New York, 1910.
> Written by one of Hamilton's descendants. That is both its virtue and its vice. It is quite interesting and as fair, I expect, as such a work can be.

Hamilton, and Others, *The Federalist* (Selections). Chicago, 1898.

Harlow, Ralph Volney, *Samuel Adams, Promoter of the American Revolution*. New York, 1923.
> Psychoanalytical. Mr. Harlow's thesis is that Samuel Adams was afflicted with a lifelong inferiority complex which made him irascible and defiant.

Hatch, Louis Clinton, *The Administration of the American Revolutionary Army*. New York, 1904.
> A historical work of merit. It deals with the Revolutionary Army as a collection of men under rules and regulations. The book is broad in outline, splendid in its fairness, and of great informative value.

Haworth, Paul Leland, *George Washington, Country Gentleman*. Indianapolis, 1915.
> Should be read by every close student of Washington's affairs. The author confines his attention to Washington as a farmer, and it is, I think, the only book on this particular subject.

Hudson, Frederic, *Journalism in the United States*. New York, 1873.
> Too much detail. Too many insignificant facts, and not enough about the underlying motives that inspired the development of journalism.

Irving, Washington, *Life of George Washington*. 5 vols. New York.

Hunt, Freeman, *Lives of American Merchants*. 2 vols. New York, 1858.
> The author of this work was a physician who amused himself by pouring literary adulation over the great figures of the commercial world. The biography of John Hancock contains some interesting facts.

Jefferson, Thomas, *Autobiography*. New York, 1914.
> Interesting as a personal document, but not to be depended upon for historical material. Jefferson wrote it in his old age, and as it was probably written from memory, it contains many unintentional misstatements.

Bibliography

Knight and Slover, *Indian Atrocities. Narratives of the Perils and and Sufferings of Dr. Knight and John Slover among the Indians.* Cincinnati, 1867.

Lee, Henry, *Memoirs of the War in the Southern Department of the United States.* 2 vols. Philadelphia, 1812.

Lee, Richard Henry, *The Letters of Richard Henry Lee.* Edited by James Curtis Ballagh. 2 vols. New York, 1912.

Lecky, W. E. H., *The American Revolution.* Being the Chapters and Passages relating to America from the Author's History of England in the Eighteenth century. New York, 1898.

Letters from General Washington to Several of his Friends. Anonymous, London, 1777.
These letters are spurious, and were supposed by Washington to have been the work of the Tory, John Randolph. They were reprinted in America under the title: *Epistles Domestic, Confidential and Official.*

Lodge, Henry Cabot, *Alexander Hamilton.* Boston, 1910.

Lodge, Henry Cabot, *George Washington.* 2 vols. Boston, 1889.

Mr. Lodge was a politician who wrote biography as a politician would. His work is not sincere; he avoids telling the truth, if possible, whenever the truth would be damaging to his heroes.

Lossing Benson J., *The Pictorial Field-Book of the Revolution.* 2 vols. New York, 1850.
A huge collection of Revolutionary data in two large volumes (in small type) with several thousand illustrations drawn by the author, who was a very good artist. About the year 1848 he made a leisurely trip to nearly every Revolutionary battlefield in preparing this work. It cannot be wholly relied upon, as it is filled with every variety of old man's tale and current gossip.

Lossing, Benson J., *Mary and Martha: The Mother and the Wife of George Washington.* New York, 1886.

McIlwain, Charles Howard, *The American Revolution: A Constitutional Interpretation.* New York, 1924.
A legal study of the relations of Great Britain to the American colonies. The title is misleading. It contains no account of the Revo-

Bibliography

lution; it is a scholarly summing up of the causes of the Revolution.

McMaster, John B., *A History of the People of the United States.* 5 vols. New York, 1893.

With all his scholarship McMaster was the old type of partisan historian. To him, Washington was a demi-god and Thomas Paine was a vile brute hardly fit for association with human beings. His five volumes are, nevertheless, exceedingly helpful in the way of facts. Volume *I* begins at the close of the Revolution.

Marshall, John, *Life of George Washington.* 5 vols. Philadelphia, 1804.

Written by John Marshall in collaboration with Bushrod Washington. It was the first serious attempt at a biography of George Washington, the Weems' book (published in 1802) being a mass of fables. The first volume is called "The Introduction." It contains more than one hundred thousand words, and the name of Washington is mentioned only once, near the end. Washington's courtship of Mrs. Custis and his marriage are discussed and dismissed in four or five lines.

Moore, George H., *Libels on Washington, with a Critical Examination Thereof.* New York, 1889.

A thin affair, consisting mainly of a solemn disquisition on the stories that Washington swore on occasion.

Morgan, George, *The True Patrick Henry.* Philadelphia, 1907.

Morison, S. E., *Sources and Documents Illustrating the American Revolution.* Oxford, 1923.

A helpful book. Reproduces original documents. Its only fault, in my judgment, is its brevity. In order to produce a small volume—which seems to have been Mr. Morison's intention—many important documents are omitted.

Morse, Jedidiah, *The American Geography.* London, 1792.

The first American geography. Contains only two maps, neither of them good, but as a compendium of facts it is invaluable.

Muzzey, David Saville, *Thomas Jefferson.* New York, 1918.

Myers, Gustavus, *History of the Supreme Court of the United States.* Chicago, 1918.

Neill, Edward D., *The Ancestry and Earlier Life of George Washington.* Philadelphia, 1892.

Bibliography

A monograph in the MacAlaster collection. Concise and definite statement of Washington's ancestry.

Nevins, Allan, *The American States During and After the Revolution*. New York, 1924.
  Mr. Nevins has packed into this volume an immense number of facts concerning the political structure of the thirteen colonies and their history during the Revolution and after it. Reading it is difficult because of the small type, and because of the author's evident inability to assemble his information in logical order.

Nock, Albert Jay, *Jefferson*. New York, 1926.

Osgood, Herbert L., *The American Colonies in the Eighteenth Century*. 4 vols. New York, 1924.

Paine, Thomas, *Common Sense* and *The American Crisis*. New York, n. d.

Paine, Thomas, *Letter to General George Washington*, dated Paris, 1795. New York, 1803.

Pellew, George, *John Jay*. Boston, 1890.

Perkins, James B., *France in the American Revolution*. France, 1911.
  The best book on the French alliance. Very readable and interesting.

Peters, Madison C., *Haym Salomon*. New York, 1911.

Phillips, U. B., *American Negro Slavery*. New York, 1918.
  The best book on slavery, its development, and its political and economic aspects, that I have been able to find.

Pickell, John, *A New Chapter in the Early Life of Washington*. New York, 1856.
  The story of the Potomac Company, and Washington's connection with that enterprise.

Pontgibaud, Le Chevalier de., *A French Volunteer of the War of Independence*. Translated by Robert B. Douglas. New York, 1897.

Bibliography

Porter, Kirk H., *A History of Suffrage in the United States.* Chicago, 1918.

Quinn, Arthur Hobson, *A History of the American Drama from the Beginning to the Civil War.* New York, 1923.

Ramsay, David, *The Life of George Washington.* Baltimore, 1825.
Dry facts and hearsay, poorly written. The ancient woodcuts are worth looking at. The frontispiece is a picture of what seems to be the Rock of Ages, in a stormy sea. Washington's name is lettered across the face of the rock.

Randolph, Sarah N., *The Domestic Life of Thomas Jefferson.* New York, 1871.
Letters from Jefferson to his daughters.

Reed, W. B., *Reprint of the Original Letters from Washington to Joseph Reed During the American Revolution.* Philadelphia, 1852.
In this little book the changes made by Jared Sparks are clearly shown by marginal annotations.

Remsburg, John E., *Six Historic Americans.* New York, 1906
The production of a free-thinker who has written a thesis to prove that a number of celebrated Americans were not Christians. It contains interesting sketches of the religious views of Washington, Paine, Jefferson, Franklin and Grant.

Rochefoucauld-Liancourt, Duc de la, *Voyage dans les Etats-Unis d'Amerique.* 8 vols. Paris, 1799.

Roosevelt, Theodore, *Gouverneur Morris.* Boston, 1888.

Roosevelt, Theodore, *The Winning of the West.* 3 vols. New York, 1889.
An excellent contribution to American history. The portion dealing with the conquest of the Northwest Territory by George Rogers Clark during the Revolution is particularly good.

Rush, Richard, *Washington in Domestic Life.* Philadelphia, 1857.

Letters written by Washington to Tobias Lear between 1790 and 1799, and anecdotes about Washington by Lear, form the basis of this volume. The only thing of real value in it is Washington's own account of Benedict Arnold's treason.

Bibliography

Sabine, Lorenzo, *Biographical Sketches of Loyalists of the American Revolution.* 2 vols. Boston, 1864.

A large amount of biographical material is in these two volumes. The sketches are arranged in alphabetical order, and have the dry, direct style of "Who's Who." Van Tyne's book on the loyalists is much more interesting and informative, though a great deal of its matter has been taken from Sabine's work.

Schlesinger, A. M., *The Colonial Merchants and the Revolution.* New York, 1918.

Mr. Schlesinger is evidently convinced that the first duty of the historian is to tell the truth. His first-hand study of the relation of colonial merchants to the revolutionary movement is not merely an excellent piece of work; it is much more than excellent—it is invaluable.

Sherrill, Charles H., *French Memoirs of Eighteenth Century America.* New York, 1915.

Smith, Thomas E. V., *The City of New York in 1789.* New York, 1889.

A detailed description of New York City and its people in 1789.

Sparks, Jared, *Life of Washington.* Boston, 1839.

Stone, William L., *The Campaign of Lieut.-Gen. John Burgoyne.* Albany, 1877.

Sullivan, Wm., *Public Men of the Revolution.* Philadelphia, 1847.

Sumner, William Graham. *The Financier and the Finances of the American Revolution.* 2 vols. New York, 1891.

A highly meritorious contribution to history. It is a biography of Robert Morris, but the background consists of a detailed and very readable exposition of the financial operations of the Continental government during the Revolution.

Thacher, James, *Military Journal of the American Revolution.* Hartford, 1862.

Diary of a surgeon who was attached to the Continental army during the Revolution.

Thayer, William Roscoe, *George Washington.* Boston, 1922.

Bibliography

Toner, J. M., *George Washington as an Inventor and Promoter of the Useful Arts.* Washington, 1892.

Trent, W. P., and Wells, B. W., Editors, *Colonial Prose and Poetry.* New York, 1901.

Trevelyan, Rt. Hon. Sir George Otto, *George the Third and Charles James Fox.* 2 vols. New York, 1912.
Excellent for understanding the state of England during the Revolution.

Upton, Emory, *The Military Policy of the United States.* Government Printing Office, Washington, D. C., 1917.

Van Tyne, Charles Halstead, *The Loyalists in the American Revolution.* New York, 1922.
An impartial and informative work. It gives in short compass a clear view of the situation of the loyalists before and during the Revolution.

Waln, Robert, *Life of Lafayette.* Philadelphia, 1827.

Washington, George, *The Diaries of George Washington.* 4 vols. Edited by John C. Fitzpatrick. Boston, 1925.

Washington, George, *The Writings of George Washington.* Edited by Worthington Chauncey Ford. 14 vols., New York, 1889.

Watson, Elkanah, *Men and Times of the Revolution.* New York, 1856.

Weeden, W. B., *Economic and Social History of New England.* Boston, 1890.

Weems, Mason L., *A History of the Life and Death, Virtues and Exploits of General George Washington.* Philadelphia, 1918.

Wertenbaker, Thomas J., *The Planters of Colonial Virginia.* Princeton, 1922.

Wharton, Anne Hollingsworth, *Martha Washington.* New York, 1907.

Bibliography

Wharton, Anne Hollingsworth, *English Ancestral Homes of Noted Americans.* Philadelphia, 1915.
There is a good chapter in this book on Sulgrave.

Willard, Margaret Wheeler, *Letters on the American Revolution, 1774-1776.* Edited by Margaret Wheeler Willard. Boston, 1925.

Williams, Gomer, *History of the Liverpool Privateers, with an Account of the Liverpool Slave Trade.* London, 1897.

Wilson, Woodrow, *George Washington.* New York, 1896.

Winsor, Justin, *The Reader's Handbook of the American Revolution.* Boston, 1879.

Wright, Thomas, *Caricature History of the Georges.* London, n. d.

Wrong, George M., *The Fall of Canada.* London, 1914.

INDEX

INDEX

Index

Index

Index

Index

M

McGachen, Mr., 164
McMaster, 80, 81
Macaulay, 204
Macdougal, 221
MacKaye, Captain, 59
Mackenzie, Captain, 252
Madison, James, 364, 418, 421, 428, 443-444, 452
Manhattan Island, 366
Marbois, Barbé de, 286
Marie Antoinette, 378
Marshall, John, 35
Marye, Rev. Mr., 29
Mason, George, 110, 111, 223, 225, 419, 446
Massachusetts, 414
Massachusetts Circular Letter, 234
Massachusetts Provincial Congress, 259
Young Man's Companion, The, by W. Mather, 25
Matthews, David, 309
Mein, John, 241
Mercantile System, 178, 179, 181, 184
Microcosm, the, 90
Monmouth, 350, 354, 355
Montgomery, General, 120
Moore, Captain Samuel, 168
Morgan, Daniel, 300
Morris, Gouverneur, 267, 419, 424, 427, 428, 440
Morris, Robert, 285, 349, 364
Morse, Jedidiah, 397

N

Napoleon, 319
Navigation Acts, 178, 180, 181
New Jersey, 349, 406, 408, 420
New Molasses Act. *See* Sugar Act
Newport, 121-122, 349, 358, 366, 376, 377, 381
New York, 121, 280, 348, 349, 378, 383, 385, 406, 408
New York Provincial Congress, 265
Niagara, 349
North Carolina, 374, 375

Northwest Ordinance, 425
Notes on Virginia, by Thomas Jefferson, 287

O

Ohio Company, 51, 58, 59, 86
Old Molasses Act, 193, 194
Ollive, Elizabeth, 283
Otis, James, 122, 179, 221, 232

P

Paine, Thomas, 281, 282, 283, 284, 451
Paint, Paper and Glass Act. *See* Townshend Acts
Parkinson, 166.
Parliament, 79, 176, 252, 315, 384
Peace of Paris, 171
Pearce, William, 398, 399, 400
Pendleton, Edmund, 251, 266
Peyton, Col. John L., 67, 68
People's Revolution, 243, 244, 259, 268, 286, 381
Penn, Hon. John, 124
Penn, William, 129, 187
Pennsylvania, 348, 406, 407
Philadelphia, 121, 273, 294, 298, 347, 349, 350, 409, 438
Philipse, Miss Mary, 97
Pickering, Timothy, 336
Pierrepont, Sarah, 146
Pigot, Sir George, 176
Pinckney, Charles, 424
Pitcher, Molly, 327
Pitt, William, 190, 196, 253, 297-298, 347
Pompadour, Madame de, 70
"Poor Richard's Almanac," 147
Poor Soldier, 438
Potomac, Canal. *See* Chesapeake and Ohio Canal
Potts, Isaac, 342, 343
Princeton, 409
Privateers, 359, 360, 361, 367, 369,
Puritans, 137, 138, 139, 140, 141, 142, 144, 145
Putnam, Israel, 259-260, 275

Index

Index

W